The Science Game

An Introduction to Research in the Social Sciences

Sixth Edition

Neil McK. Agnew
Sandra W. Pyke
York University

Prentice Hall
Englewood Cliffs, New Jersey 07632

Library of Congress Cataloging-in-Publication Data

Agnew, Neil McK.
  The science game: an introduction to research in the social
sciences / Neil McK. Agnew, Sandra W. Pyke.—6th ed.
    p.   cm.
  Includes bibliographical references and index.
  ISBN 0-13-098583-X
  1. Social sciences—Research   I. Pyke, Sandra W.   II. Title.
  H62.P96 1994   93-40931
  301'.072—dc20   CIP

DEDICATION

To Donald Campbell
for providing a luxurious supply
of intellectual care packages

Production supervision
  and interior design: Keith Faivre
Acquisitions editor: Pete Janzow
Managing editor: Heidi Freund
Production coordinator: Tricia Kenny
Cover design: Design Source

© 1994, 1991, 1987, 1982, 1978, 1969 by Prentice-Hall, Inc.
A Paramount Communications Company.
Englewood Cliffs, New Jersey 07632

Printed in United States of America
10 9 8 7 6 5 4 3 2 1

ISBN 0-13-098583-X

Prentice-Hall International (UK) Limited, *London*
Prentice-Hall of Australia Pty. Limited, *Sydney*
Prentice-Hall Canada Inc., *Toronto*
Prentice-Hall Hispanoamericana, S.A., *Mexico*
Prentice-Hall of India Private Limited, *New Delhi*
Prentice-Hall of Japan, Inc., *Tokyo*
Simon & Schuster Asia Pte. Ltd., *Singapore*
Editora Prentice-Hall do Brasil, Ltda., *Rio de Janeiro*

Contents

Preface   ix

PART I: FROM COMMON SENSE TO SCIENCE

1. Science Constructs Maps of Reality . . . or Does It?   1

Introduction   1
Where Is Reality Hiding? 1   Wrestling with Rumors 3   Messages from Missing Toes 4   Experts as Fallible but Trusted Editors and Messengers 5   The Messenger Model Helps Us Make Sense When . . . 6 The Happy Chair 7
A Map Is Not "Reality"   8
A Sample of News 10   Consumer's Guide to Science 11
Science as a News Service   10
The Quality of News   12
A Second Look: Personal Experience 12   A Second Look: Beliefs and Expectations 13
Explanation, Speculation, Theory   17
Cause and Effect 18   Antecedents and Consequences 20
The Scientific Method: Five Key Ingredients   20
Compelling Motivation 23   Systematic Observation 24   Systematic Experiments 2   Probabilistic Thinking 28   Intuition and Theory 29
Levels of Observation and Speculation   32
Summary   34
Example   35
Review Quiz   37

2. The Languages of Science   39

Introduction   39
Science Speaks with Three Tongues   40
The Three Languages of Science 43
Summary   67
Example   67
Review Quiz   68

PART II: SIEVES OF SCIENCE

3. After-the-Fact Method   70

Introduction   70
A Case for the Courts   72
The After-the-Fact or Case Method 73
A Case for the Historian   75
A Case for the Physician   76
Reduction of the Risk of Error   77
Summary   79
Example   82
A Case for the Counselor 82
Review Quiz   89

4. Before-and-After Treatment Method   91

Introduction   91
Four Misleading Suspects   93
*Historical (in-the-Gap) Suspects 93 Maturational (Time-Tied)
Suspects 94 Instrument-Decay (Elastic-Ruler) Suspects 95 Testing
(On-Stage) Suspects 95*
Skillful Use of the Before-and-After Sieve   96
*Stable Observations 96 Quick-Acting Suspects 97 Elimination of
Stray Suspects 98*
Summary   99
Example   100
Review Quiz   108

5. Control-Group Method   110

Introduction   110
Rogue Suspects   111
*Historical (In-the-Gap) Suspects 111 Instrument-Decay (Elastic-
Ruler) Suspects 112 Testing (On-Stage) Suspects 112 Maturational
(Time-Tied) Suspects 113*
Now What?   113
Selection of the Control Comparison Group   113
Elaboration of the Control-Group Method   115
*Statistical Regression 119 Differential Mortality 120 Biased
Selections 120*
Limitations of the Control-Group Method   121
Extending the Control-Group Method   122
*The Natural Experiment 122 The Field Experiment 123 Simulation
Research 123*
Unobtrusive Measures   124

Summary   124
Overview of Three Methods   125
Example   126
Review Quiz   128

PART III: EXTENDING THE REACH OF SCIENCE

6. Validity—The Reach of Research   130

Introduction   130
Internal and External Validity   131
Threats to Internal Validity   132
Threats to External Validity   133
Sampling Restrictions   134
Measurement Restrictions   135
   Types of Test Validity 136
Treatment Restrictions   137
Research Context Restrictions   138
Validity and the Three Languages of Science   140
Summary   142
Research Checklist   143
Review Quiz   144

7. Developmental and Longitudinal Studies   146

Introduction   146
Rate of Change   147
Upper Limits of Change   148
Cross-Sectional Studies   149
Retrospective Studies   151
Longitudinal Studies   152
   Interrupted Time Series 153
Evaluation Research   154
   The Hawthorne Effect 159   Regression Toward the Mean 160
Summary   161
Example   161
Review Quiz   164

8. Qualitative Methods: Ethnographic and Archival Research   166

Introduction   166
Quantitative versus Qualitative   167
Characteristics of Qualitative Methodology   168

Ethnographic Research   169
The Setting 171   The Observational Task 172   The Role of the Observer 176   Classification/Interpretation 178   Conclusion 179
Archival Research   180
Content Analysis 181   Spoor Analysis 183   Strengths and Weaknesses 184
Summary   186
Example   186
Review Quiz   189

9. Qualitative Methods: Survey Research   190

Data Collection Instrument   191
Questionnaire 191   Telephone Interview 194   Personal Interview 195   Focus Groups 196   Q Methodology 196
Sample Selection   198
Administration   200
Strengths and Weaknesses   201
Summary   202
Example   203
Review Quiz   207

PART IV: THE NUMBER GAME

10. The Number Game   208

Introduction   208
Black Magic?   209
On Being Number-Numb 210
Measurement Scales and Rules   210
Nominal Rule 211   Ordinal Rule 212   The Interval Rule 213   The Ratio Rule 215   Arbitrary Zero 217
Science and Measurement Go Together   220
What to Look for in Pilot Studies 224
Summary   226
Review Quiz   226

11. Statistical Foundations I: Packaging Information   228

Introduction   228
Central Values 229   Measures of Variability 231   The Normal Curve   233
Correlation   234
What Does a Correlation Tell You? 238   Beware of Correlations 239   Correlation, Regression, and Prediction 239   Correlations and Factor Analysis 240

Summary   241
Review Quiz   242

12. Statistical Foundations II: Prediction   243

Introduction   243
Inferential Statistics   244
   Maps of Chance 245   Sampling Theory 246   Sampling Error Theory 247
Analysis of Variance (ANOVA)   251
   One-Way Analysis of Variance (One Independent Variable) 252   Two-Way Analysis of Variance (Two Independent Variables) 253
Meta-Analysis   254
Chi Square   256
Which Statistical Test?   260
   Type I and Type II Errors 262
N-of-1 Research (Studying One Case)   264
Summary   267
Review Quiz   268

PART V: BEING GOOD AND CLEAR

13. Ethics   269

Relativity of Ethics   270
   Ethics and the Social Scientists 272   Why Have a Code of Ethics? 272
Ethics Quiz   273
Illustrative Case Studies   278
The Animal Controversy   281
From Principle to Practice   283
   Cost-Benefit Ratio 284
Science, Government, and Law   285
Summary   287
Example   288
Review Quiz   290

14. Research Report Writing   291

Language and Style   292
Structure
   Abstract 293   Introduction 294   Method 294   Results 296   Discussion 296   References 296   Appendix 296
Publication Pollution   297
Summary   298
Example   298
Review Quiz   301

PART VI: PATTERNS AND NOISE

15. **Sex and Science**   303

Science and Symbolism   304
Science and Objectivity   305
Women's Role in Science   306
Sex Bias in Science   306
*Historical   Examples 307   Content 308   Subject   Selection 308
Theory   Bias 308   Evaluation 311   Inference   Bias 312   Language
Bias 312   Selection and Distortion of Evidence 313   Statistical Bias
314   Publication Bias 316   Design Sources of Bias 316   Researcher
Bias 317*
Restructuring Science   318
Reform 318   Restructure 319
Summary   320
Example   320
Review Quiz   322

16. **The Truth Spinners**   323

Introduction   323
What Does the World Rest On?   324
The Reach of Human Reasoning   326
Building Defended Islands of Truth 327
Males Have Superior Analytical Capacity   330
Putting Your Core Assumptions in a Safe Place   332
Theory of Science   333
Nonrational Wisdom   334
No Conclusions without Premises   335
Management of Uncertainty   336
*Confidence in Initial Beliefs 337   Confidence as a Keystone Concept
338   Confidence in Hypothesis and Editing Mechanisms 341*
An Overview: The Model and the Sieves of Science   344
Conclusions   347
Review Quiz   350

References and Suggested Readings   351

Answers to True/False Questions   361

Index   363

Preface

Science consists of infinite speculative space,
sparsely sprinkled with observational checkpoints.

Way back in 1967, while we were writing the first edition of this book, a reviewer criticized our tentative title, *The Science Game*, claiming that it "trivializes the scientific enterprise [and] implies that the findings of science are not to be trusted."

But we believed then, as now, that science must be portrayed in a human context—at times heroic, at other times fallible. In attempting to decode nature's puzzles we play a difficult and sometimes dangerous game. The complexity of the multilayered and moving puzzle we call "reality" sorely tests our problem-solving skills. Nevertheless, through trial and error, we create increasingly powerful probes, and we must thank our scientists for that evolution—for improving our odds in understanding the world. Although we have tamed the atom, improved public health, and increased literacy, we have at the same time degraded our environment, failed to solve the cancer and AID's puzzles, and remain baffled by tragic deviations in human behavior. Furthermore, we appear to be helpless in controlling our continued dependence on violence to solve disputes between individuals and nations.

Although we may not always win, science remains "the biggest game in town." In the not-too-distant past, we relied solely on magic and religion to locate the hidden causes for visible events. Increasingly, however, we now rely on science to provide windows into the unknown—to provide, if not answers, at least clues to life's mysteries, ranging from the origins of the universe to the origins of the pain an amputee feels in his nonexistent toes.

In this book we introduce you to progressively powerful methods for solving puzzles in the behavioral and social sciences. As you become familiar with these methods, you will also become a more discriminating consumer of scientific news, you will become a better player in the science game, and you will be better able to distinguish major achievements from the "scientific hype" so prevalent in the popular press that bombards us daily with sensational headlines screaming out: "Scientists say!"

The sixth edition of *The Science Game* contains significant revisions. Each chapter now opens with a brief statement of the chapter goals, and each chapter concludes with a review quiz. The true/false quiz questions enable students to test and review their knowledge of the main ideas of the chapter they have just read. The answers to the questions, and the relevant page numbers on which they appear, are provided at the end of the text to help integrate and "fix" the material.

Additional revisions appear in all chapters designed to provide conceptual and methodological links between them, and to reflect suggestions by users of previous editions. For example, the long statistics chapter has been divided in two, one focusing on descriptive statistics and the other on inferential methods. Furthermore, selected chapters have been modified to reflect recent developments around key issues such as constructivist views of science, qualitative methods, ethics, sex and psychology, and how we manage uncertainty in science.

We gladly express our appreciation to the faculty and students who use our book; to those among them who, through their suggestions, have helped us modify subsequent editions; to Eleanor Ames for sharing her wisdom concerning control groups; to Mary Barr and Zehra Bandhu whose word-processing skills took over when ours failed; to the friendly folks at Prentice Hall—Peter Janzow, Heidi Freund, and Keith Faivre—for their support and expertise in shepherding through to completion yet another edition; and to Ernest Harburg for continuing to let us include in our book his delightful and instructive Island of Research map.

Neil McK. Agnew
Sandra W. Pyke

❦ 1 ❦
Science Constructs Maps of Reality . . . or Does It?

──────── **Chapter Goal** ────────

To provide an overview of science, our most trusted news service. It collects messages from atoms, rats, and people, cobbling them together into "reality."

INTRODUCTION

> *. . . to wonder . . . that is the seed of science.*—Emerson

A worried client seeks help from a psychologist.

> CLIENT: Doctor, I'm not feeling myself.
> PSYCHOLOGIST: You want me to help you find the real you?
> CLIENT: Yes I do . . . but how much will that cost?
> PSYCHOLOGIST: A thousand dollars.
> CLIENT: If this is not the real me why should I pay you all that money? Let's wait till we find the real me and then let him pay you the thousand dollars. Furthermore, how can I ever be sure we've found the real me?
> PSYCHOLOGIST: I'm an expert, I'll know if it's the real you!
> CLIENT: But experts make mistakes. How can I be certain we haven't found another pretend me?
> [*Psychologist starts to say something but client interrupts.*]
> CLIENT: In fact, if he pays you a thousand dollars, I'll be certain he's not the real me.

Where Is Reality Hiding?

In its various versions this old joke pinpoints the challenge facing scientists. Because scientists typically look for the hidden "causes" (e.g., the real you) underlying visible events (your variable behavior), how can scientists ever be sure they've found the right answer? When you marry someone, or hire someone, all you have to go on are bits of surface behav-

1

ior out of which you construct the hidden "someone" who presumably lives "inside" and runs the show. You could be wrong—and according to divorce statistics many of us are very wrong. In all walks of life we construct false pictures of the "real you."

However, just as science has its methods, you have your methods of checking your conclusions. Before marrying, or committing yourself, you ask, "But do you *really* love me?" Does the real somebody inside you truly love me? But most men know that many women put a lot of confidence in that easily uttered phrase, "I love you." So males ranging from con men to young studs to true loves say the words. Furthermore, it may be uttered with ultimate sincerity one steamy night and melt away by dawn. Unfortunately, it's difficult to come up with foolproof "truth tests," for like the bird pretending to have a broken wing to lead you away from its nest, humans lay false trails as well—some wittingly, others unwittingly.

Most cultures have evolved procedures for helping us avoid false leads, for helping us discover the "real" someone living inside. That's why "old-fashioned" parents plead with you to "really" get to know someone before making a major commitment. This way there's a chance for each partner to get some idea of how many different people live hidden away inside and which one seems to run the show most of the time. Then you have to decide whether your inside boss and their inside boss can get along over the long haul. Sadly, the number of failed relationships suggests that our current cultural methods of identifying the "real you" and the "real him or her" don't work so well. But could science do much better? We'll discuss this issue later in the book.

All right, so we've made the point that small samples of surface behavior fail to provide reliable information about the real me or you. But wait a minute. Our best friends often point out that it's not just the message "I love you" from your current heart throb that may be unreliable but also that someone inside you desperately wants to hear the magic words. Your friends remind you that they repeatedly warned that your true love scatters his, "I love yous" around like frisbees, but you (or someone inside) keep ignoring your friends' warnings. Still, from your perspective you didn't feel you had any choice; you were at the mercy of an overpowering someone inside. It is not simple and doesn't make sense—well, doesn't make common sense. Commonsense reasoning relies on simple assumptions like, "seeing is believing," "your senses don't lie," "loved ones don't lie . . . well, not about really important things."

Conversely, scientific reasoning examines the kind of errors people make—like choosing the wrong partner, or walking through a glass door—and comes up with some revised assumptions that cover both common experience and its exceptions. Commonsense reasoning assumes that we have pretty direct access to our world, whereas in contrast, various forms of scientific reasoning assume we don't. Rather, we only have access to our inner and outer world through a long chain of messengers, any one of which transforms or distorts the message.

Wrestling with Rumors

Have you ever played the game "Rumor"? In this game one person whispers a message to another, and then the message is passed down the line of players. When the final message emerges, at the end of the line, and is compared with the original, the differences are astonishing. Each person has unwittingly edited the message. As the message passes in and out of even one individual that individual is playing rumor inside his or her own head. The original message is carried in by a series of messengers, processed by the inside editors, and sent out through a series of messengers. It's a wonder we can communicate at all!

You may not clearly *hear* what the person whispered to you, so one of your inside messengers fills in the gaps, adds a bit or shortens it, and sends the revised version along. Then inside editors change it a bit to fit with past experience and send it out. But on the way out one or more outgoing messengers tidies it up a bit more, so it doesn't quite come out the way you wanted it to (i.e., there's many a slip between the mind and the lip). According to this multiple-messenger view of human behavior, rather than having direct and reliable contact with our world, we must rely mainly on rumors—many, unwittingly, of our own making. Chains of couriers separate us from our world. We rely on endless strings of messengers for information about our inner and outer world; some are more reliable than others, carrying messages into and out from the editors living inside.

It's starting to sound like we're knocking commonsense reasoning. We shouldn't because we use it successfully thousands of times a day. If we tried to apply the notion that "life is a series of rumor games," we'd get so hung up double-checking messages that we'd never get out of bed. Thus, scientific reasoning doesn't replace commonsense reasoning; rather it becomes an alternative way of thinking when commonsense reasoning fails badly. Scientists, like the rest of us, are particularly interested in surprising events. But unlike us they have the time and resources to investigate a few selected puzzles more thoroughly to try to map message routes, to identify the messengers and editors, and to identify how we make sense of ambiguous and conflicting messages. In subsequent chapters you will become familiar with some of the evolved methods scientists use to decode the wonders and the puzzles of human thinking and behavior. These scientific ways of thinking and investigating, although far from infallible, provide us with a level of understanding that goes beyond that provided by commonsense reasoning.

Messages from Missing Toes

Try out your common sense on the following surprising observation. Why do people who have had a leg amputated still get all kinds of signals (e.g., touch and pain from their toes) from toes that are no longer attached to the body? How would you explain this astonishing phenomenon? You may say, well he's only imagining it. Fine, that's a good example of a commonsense solution; it's good enough to satisfy your passing curiosity. But if you thought about it a bit more you would realize that such an explanation explains nothing. It only restates the puzzle by saying "it's in his head, not in his foot." We know that already. But we don't know how it got into his head from his nonexistent toes.

Next try exploring the puzzle using the rumor or messenger model outlined earlier. *Hint*: When you know someone very well (i.e., exchange a lot of messages), he or she can pass a message to you by merely giving you a tiny part of it and yet you "get it" all. With practice you shrink the number of cues you require, which enables you to receive messages faster and faster, messages that others, who are not so familiar with the sender, do not get. But not only does speed of transmission go up, something else goes up as well. Can you guess what it is?

If you guessed, "errors go up as well" you would be right. As you cut down the number of cues as to what the message is, that is, as you reduce the redundancy in the message, you increase the probability of error. As long as one messenger, located anywhere in the familiar chain, sends a message those ahead pass it along in some form. You think you got a message from your toes, but it may have come from a restless messenger in your thigh—a messenger who is an active member of the very familiar chain that used to start at your toes.

You already know partial messages can lead to confusion. When a friend gives you a "dirty look" without explaining why, you can interpret that brief visual message in various ways. First, you can assume she is sending the message that you just did something dumb. Second, you can assume she is sending the message that she's cranky, and so little things make her angry. Third, you can assume that she is teasing or joking, or merely practicing her dirty look. When you say, "Hey, why the dirty look?" you're asking her to send more messages, or messengers, to help you decide which message she is "really" sending. In this case "seeing is not believing" so you're asking for *ear messengers* to supplement the brief eye messages, or maybe touch messengers, to help you decide which of the possibilities is "the real message."

Now back to the unfortunate man with the amputated leg. He gets a very strong, clear message of pain in his toes. Family members in the hospital room are astonished to "hear" him say this, because they can "see" that his leg is amputated. When he looks down he also "sees" that he has no leg. He is receiving two very strong, contradictory messages. Obviously such contradictions lead to high stress, which continues until it is re-solved, until one messenger emerges as more **trusted** than the others. When you're getting strong conflicting messages, you must manufacture a con-clusion, fabricating it out of messages from your most trusted couriers.

When we deal with contradictions about solid visible objects like toes we usually trust our eyes to resolve conflicting messages from other sources. When we *feel* something crawling on our arm we immediately look to *see* what it is. If we see nothing we assume it's just a tingling in the skin, or something behind the skin, that has given us a "false alarm." Similarly, in the case of the amputee who feels pain in his toes, some messenger in the chain has given a false alarm. But notice the signal is false only in the sense that it contradicts the signal; of a more trusted or popular messenger. A messenger is sending a signal, it's just not being sent from the location we expect, a location we can see. From the per-spective of the commonsense model, it's a puzzle. From the perspective of a messenger model of experience, it's not so much of a puzzle, because (1) we expect all kinds of messengers; (2) we expect messengers to modify the messages they deliver; (3) we expect messengers to deliver some fuzzy and conflicting messages; and (4) we expect internal editors to magnify some messages and suppress others.

Experts as Fallible but Trusted Editors and Messengers

Speaking of trusted messengers, what happens when you feel something disturbing in a place you can't see and so unlike the amputee can't check it out by appealing to your most trusted messenger, your eyes? Vitally important parts of your world lie beyond the reach of your eyes. The pain in your chest you take to a physician; uncertainties about the future you take to a career counselor; uncertainties about how you really feel you take to your friends or to a clinical psychologist. We rely heavily on others to help us construct worlds we cannot see. In so doing we must take on faith the "views" or constructions of physicians, teach-ers, druggists, mechanics, family, friends, religious advisers, news media, politicians, and psychologists.

Notice, like us, these experts must also rely on messengers deliver-ing edited and conflicting messages; they too must base their decisions on their most trusted messengers. Consulting a physician involves the patient and the physician exchanging "rumors," exchanging constructions of experience based on small samples of trusted messages. And, of course, the history of science and technology informs us that trusted messages from one period are rarely trusted 50 years later. It's a miracle! How can humans survive in this flood of different and conflicting messages from outside and inside? We not only survive on rumors but thrive on them, going about our daily business with relative ease and confidence. It's a miracle. You're a miracle! Social science studies miracles like you.

The Messenger Model Helps Us Make Sense When . . .

The commonsense view of the world is that, through our sense, we have direct access to our world, or to reliable messages about it. And common sense works a lot of the time. In contrast, the messenger model helps us make sense of our experience when the commonsense model breaks down—when we get conflicting messages, or when what we see, hear, or feel confuses us. Then the messenger model can be helpful, for example, when trying to find the "real" you, or the real him or her, or in helping make sense of the phantom limb puzzle.

Keeping the messenger-editor model, and the phantom limb phenomenon, in mind, how might you explain the following?

- Hallucinations
- Altered states of consciousness brought about by drugs, alcohol, or hypnosis
- Daydreams
- Night dreams
- Imagination
- Illusions
- Walking into a glass door
- Misidentifying people
- Getting lost in a movie
- Falling in love
- Choosing a mate
- Selecting a career
- Virtual reality experiences

All of the preceding examples, like the phantom limb state, consist of situations involving incomplete information, and they can be explained in terms of trusting some signals or messages over others. *The messenger model is based on the premise that there is a degree of ambiguity or uncertainty surrounding all signals, and particularly complex signals over time.* We resolve the ambiguity or uncertainty; we make sense of them or make decisions about them by "trusting" a selected sample of messages over others. In this sense perception of the world is a matter of trust! By doing so we "trick" ourselves into believing we have direct access to "reality" rather than to our own construction of it based on a biased (trusted) sample of messages. These trusted biases help us to make automatic decisions, to ignore ambiguities, and to navigate an uncertain world with relative certainty.

Where do the biases come from, and why are some messages trusted over others? Some functional biases are wired into our nervous system as a result of the trial-and-error winnowing of evolution. The biases that favor some messages over others are not infallible (e.g., we walk into glass doors, misidentify familiar faces in strange cities, etc.), but evolutionary biases have so far proved functional for the human race. Other functional biases are wired into our nervous system by our culture (e.g., wash your hands before eating, get vaccinated, don't drink with strangers, get an education, get a government job, etc.) Such evolutionary and cultural biases lead us to trust some messages over others and help us make decisions that although not infallible are typically not immediately followed by disaster. Identifying evolutionary and cultural biases in message processing leads to understanding and predicting human behavior. Politicians devote their lives to it. So too do artists and scientists. Consider first artists.

Artists know how to "trick" your mind into "seeing" three-dimensional space in a two-dimensional picture by capitalizing on certain visual ambiguities and emphasizing some signals over others, by playing on some of your wired-in biases, which we call the laws of perspective. Most of the time we know it's only a picture, unless a scientist restricts our access to certain signals, for example, by placing us in an unfamiliar situation and having us view the scene through a peephole. Notice, the experimenter has arranged, or programmed, a highly edited set of trusted messages, and if he does it well you will not be sure whether you are viewing, through the peephole, a picture, on the one hand, or viewing a "real" landscape, on the other. Three-dimensional movies and Disneyworld productions are designed to confuse the dividing line between "reality" and "illusion" by magnifying some messages over others, by capitalizing on wired-in biases.

The Happy Chair

What will they think of next? Well, virtual reality experts are now tricking us into experiencing a more and more compelling sense of reality—seeing, feeling, hearing, smelling, and so forth merely by putting on a helmet through which a computer delivers selected signals that we are genetically or socially programmed to trust. These programmed, trusted signals, like all trusted signals, determine what we experience; they help construct our "reality." People who have worn such helmets report an eerie sense of reality, a strong sense of "being part" of the ongoing scene. Such systems, although in their infancy, are being used not only for arcade entertainment, but also to help train pilots, athletes, and surgeons. As the graphics, sound, and timing improve we will experience a heightened sense of reality in these computer-generated worlds.

We appear to be approaching the time when researchers, by programming trusted signals, can construct "artificial" worlds that we cannot distinguish from those we call real. The pros and cons of such "perceptual engineering" are unclear. Sixty years ago Aldous Huxley predicted a future where we would plug ourselves into machines that transported us to simulated worlds of continuous, happy, sensuous experiences—the "feelies." In a few years the current TV couch potato could actually get up and move—not far, just to his or her happy chair—then hook up and turn on to the simulated highs of booze, drugs, sex, sports, food, heroism, calm, or whatever. And all of it so "real" that the "happy chair potato" would become lost, unaware that it was a perceptually engineered illusion. But whether you approve of such developments or not, they indicate that psychologists and computer scientists appear to be gaining an impressive understanding about wired-in perceptual biases, about how humans make sense out of the flow of ambiguous messages and which messages they trust for good or ill.

But let's unplug from our "happy chair" and return to the here and now of the science game. We've stated that individuals rely on a small, trusted sample of messages to resolve uncertainties about the pain in your toes, the real you, or the real her, whether the space ahead is clear, which mate or career to choose, and so forth. But so too must psychologists rely on small trusted samples of messages that flow from you, the subject, through the researcher's message-gathering tools (e.g., questionnaires, interviews, tapes, brain-wave machines, etc.).

Notice, these message-gathering tools magnify some messages, and miss or suppress others. So scientists, like nonscientists, must rely on small samples of biased, trusted messages to help them resolve their uncertainties about your intelligence, anxiety, career potential, sociability, conformity, creativity, sex stereotyping, and so forth. If you keep the "message model" and the phantom limb phenomenon in mind you will better appreciate the challenges facing scientists in their attempts to draw reliable maps of human experience and behavior. Their maps will not be based on all messages available. Like any map they will, out of ignorance or choice, omit some messages. Like any map they will highlight messages of interest to the map maker. Therefore, you can expect different map makers will draw somewhat different maps of the "same territory" of intelligence, anxiety, or sex stereotyping. Nevertheless, because of the methods they use, and because of the critical scrutiny of other researchers, scientific maps, although fallible, remain the most conscientiously constructed we have.

A MAP IS NOT "REALITY"

A menu is a kind of map of the food available. But you don't eat the menu. Furthermore, we know that like other maps menus can be unreliable and out of date. You also know that a road map is not the territory. But we sometimes mistake social science maps for the territory; we reify them. We treat an IQ or anxiety or conformity score as if it was the territory rather than treating it as a map of highly selected messages.

A map is similar to but simpler than the territory it represents. A map, to be useful, must be much *simpler* than the territory. Lewis Carrol tells the story of British map makers who proudly proclaimed that they had made a map of England *scaled at 1 inch to the mile*. German map makers denigrated this accomplishment claiming to have made a much more precise map of Germany *scaled at 1 inch to the inch*, but the farmers would not let them unroll it.

Like map makers, scientists can only make detailed maps of small slices of experience. They select one little part of the territory we call "reality," and, from their particular perspective, create an abstract map or model of that slice. Some scientists work with hard pieces of experience like rocks, iron filings, or warts—things that usually stay put when you turn your back to answer the phone. Other scientists work with less stable bits of experience like liquids, subatomic particles, feelings, and behavior—things that don't stay put when you turn your back or even when you blink! You encounter this problem when you try to predict or "map" mood changes in a temperamental friend, or when you attempt to locate "the real you." The social sciences face the exciting task of attempting to map, or to find patterns in, such dynamic slices of experience.

Although social science deals with moving targets, fortunately some targets move more slowly than others (e.g., beliefs, personality structure, sensory acuity, habits, group norms, aging, etc.). Other slices of experience flash by, like the flow of ideas, moods, food and fashion fads, political preferences, and teenage crushes. In the following chapters we examine the methods social scientists use to look for patterns in the behavior of both slow- and fast-moving targets.

You will better understand the science game if you keep in mind the fable of the four blind people examining (i.e., mapping) the elephant. First, you appreciate that most interesting targets are too large to get the "whole picture" (e.g., to get to know the "real you"), so we end up with edited maps or fragments of the whole picture.

Second, you know that even a simple stimulus or message from the outside is modified as it travels through the chain of messengers and editors inside a given observer; so two different observers examining an elephant's trunk will come away with different "maps" of the trunk, with different output messages, or stories, about that fragment of the elephant. Thus, the partial picture or map we do get always reflects the viewpoint of the observer (e.g., the prisoner in the dock as viewed by his mother, the prosecuting attorney, a psychoanalytic therapist, a neuropsychologist, or two different clinical psychologists).

Third, in the case of moving targets, you usually end up with a snapshot of part of the target, from a particular perspective, at a given time, in a given place (e.g., your personality test score at 9:15 A.M. on the morning of January 15 after getting caught in a traffic jam because of a freak snowstorm).

Fourth, most of the targets we want to study are not as solid as an elephant, so we must use detectors that, it is hoped, don't push the target out of shape (e.g., a person's mood can be pushed out of shape by the way you attempt to map it; some interviewers, or questionnaires, can make you angry just by the way they attempt to probe your feelings).

If you keep these four points in the back of your mind you will understand why the Science Game is the biggest game in town. You will also appreciate the ingenuity built into various methods researchers use to locate reliable patterns in our internal and external world. In subsequent chapters you will become familiar with some of the evolved methods social scientists use to map reliable patterns in the flow of message fragments that humans miraculously use to make sense of their experience.

We next consider Science as a news service. Keep the rumor game, and the messenger model of perception, in mind as you consider the reporters and editors as messengers providing highly selected and transformed samples of news.

SCIENCE AS A NEWS SERVICE

In this section we shall view science as a news service, enabling you to bring to bear on scientific news the critical wisdom you periodically use to evaluate or interpret daily news that captures your attention. Thus, as your curiosity is aroused, you take second and third looks, and have second or third thoughts, about an item of news—an observation or explanation—and in so doing you enter into the spirit of science. You can think of carefully applied common-sense methods as overlapping with some of the simpler scientific methods.

A Sample of News

1. The average person has 8 sexual fantasies a day, and 16 laughs.
2. Pepsi must sell 875,000,000 cans of pop to recoup the cost of its Michael Jackson commercial.
3. 10 percent of the Japanese have IQs above 130.
4. 2 percent of Americans have IQs above 130.
5. There was a 400 percent increase in government seizures of LSD "tabs" in 1982–83.
6. The average length of sexual intercourse for humans is 2 minutes; for chimpanzees, 7 seconds.
7. There has been a 300 percent increase in teenage suicides since 1953.
8. 60,000,000 Americans read below the ninth-grade level.
9. 95 percent of Americans break their New Year's resolutions within a week of making them.

10. Approximately 15,000 scientific and technical articles are published each day.
11. Each year about 2,000,000 husbands beat their wives.

Where do these numbers or messages come from? Are they true? What do they mean?[1]

If you read these observations and numbers in a Sunday newspaper you would probably have less confidence in them than if you saw them in a scientific journal. Why?

Both publications provide a message service. What are the similarities and differences between the popular press on the one hand and scientific coverage on the other? Both rely on observers—reporters in the first instance and researchers in the other. And both also rely on commentators or explainers—the newspaper editors and columnists in the one case, and scientific journal editors and theorists in the other.

Consumer's Guide to Science

You don't believe everything you read in the papers—on the news pages, the sports pages, the entertainment pages, or in the editorials—because you know that some reporters are lazy or rushed, and some editors blatantly biased. On reflection, you also know that there are several "layers" to most stories—surface news and deep news, casual as opposed to probing observation, crude categories as opposed to multiple, refined ones.

You recognize a big difference between the reporter who simply takes his or her story as a handout from the political press secretary, compared to the investigative reporter who digs into the story from different angles. From Watergate, and life, we learn that there is always more to any story than meets the eye, that news comes in endless layers. Furthermore, you understand that any news—surface, middle, or deep—has several explanations and that usually something can be said for each of them.

Similarly, scientific news has endless layers, many more than meet even the scientific eye, or the scientific imagination. If you take your accumulated wisdom about news services in general and apply it to scientific news and commentary, you will take one more step toward becoming a more critical and appreciative consumer of scientific information and speculation.

Now take your accumulated wisdom and a critical perspective and reconsider the "Sample of News." Notice first that these are all news stories rather than editorials or commentary—they are the products of reporters or researchers.

---

[1]Items 1, 3, and 4 are from *Harpers Magazine*, May, 1984, p. 9. Item 6 is from *Harpers Magazine*, February, 1985, p. 13. Item 11 is from Matlin (1992).

Read through them quickly and pick out which observations and numbers you consider to be "hard" news and which ones you judge to be only surface, soft, or fuzzy news.

First-year students usually list all the observations as hard news with the exception of the following:

8 sexual fantasies

Only 2 percent of the Americans have IQs above 130.

The average length of sexual intercourse for humans is 2 minutes.

These three items the students categorize as "fuzzy" or questionable messages.

How do their choices compare with your selection of hard and soft news items from the list? What might a second look, a little digging, a little investigative reporting, or research, uncover?

THE QUALITY OF NEWS

Most news, scientific or otherwise, we simply ignore, or skim uncritically as you probably did on first reading the items on page 10. This is just as well, as otherwise reflective and critical reading of a newspaper would take days. As we said earlier, we only have so much mental energy and attention, and therefore, it must be rationed.

A Second Look: Personal Experience

But when our attention becomes focused on a message through personal interest we take a second, and maybe even a third and fourth look. In bringing to bear your curiosity and your critical faculties on an observation, you are being a personal scientist (Kelly, 1955). You are deciding whether it "makes sense" on the basis of your experience, on the basis of your observations, beliefs, and expectations. If from a second look the message makes sense to you, your curiosity drops it, becoming available for other things. If not, it takes more looks until you are either satisfied, exhausted, or bored.

For example, take a second look at the observation that: "The average person has 8 sexual fantasies a day." How on earth would you go about getting that number?

If you were a reporter, or a researcher, how could you obtain reliable messages about sexual fantasies? Interview people? Send them a questionnaire? How well do you remember your sexual fantasies? Do you keep a tally? When does a romantic daydream become a sexual fantasy? The boundaries are frequently vague or fuzzy. How would you respond in an interview, or fill out a questionnaire? Would you report "high" (to create a macho image) or report low (because of guilt)? Or would you have trouble even figuring out what "high" means, perhaps discussing it with a trusted friend, together inventing a "reasonable" number? So what does it mean when a researcher reports that: "The average person has 8 sexual fantasies a day"? Among other things it means there is a large margin of error, perhaps as large as when you try to count ghosts, where you learn more about the person making the observation than about the ghost population.

So by taking a second or third look at a news item, or a "scientific" message, you discover that what first appear to be "facts" turn out to be fuzzy. We can use our personal experience, just as scientists use their research experience, to examine critically the validity and the plausibility of other people's observations and numbers.

So in science, as well as in daily news, we must learn to question observations that "count fuzzies"—that tie numbers to events that, on second thought, we know from personal experience don't come packaged in hard, easily counted containers—experiences like fantasies, passing thoughts, suicides, or the IQs of 250 million people.

A Second Look: Beliefs and Expectations

On closer examination, why might you question the news item that only 2 percent of Americans have IQs above 130?

When asked, the main reason first-year students gave was that they didn't like that message; they just didn't like having the Japanese scoring higher. So if consumers don't like some particular "news" they typically become more careful critics. First-year students asked various critical questions, such as:

"Where did they get the Americans (in the civil service) and where did they get the Japanese (in the universities)?"

"I read that group IQ tests aren't all that accurate, so how can they be sure?"

"How many Americans did they measure?"

"Who scored the Japanese tests—the Japanese I'll bet."

So we become more critical and perhaps more sophisticated consumers not only when personal experience and a second look tell us the information is hard to get (for example, fantasies), but also when we encounter observations or numbers we don't like or believe (such as numbers that put us or our beliefs in a bad light).

Personal and professional scientists alike concentrate their curiosity and critical faculties around *unexpected* or surprising messages. Why might you question the unexpected news that the average length of sexual intercourse for humans is 2 minutes? One first-year student summed up the response of many when he said: "Maybe two minutes in the laboratory, but not in the bedroom." Another asked: "When did they start timing?" A third student said: "If that's true a lot of my friends are liars."

So this "observation" was questioned both on the basis of personal experience and on the basis of reports and beliefs concerning the experience of others.

A fourth student commented: "Where do they get all the 'average people' for these stories?" Where do average people, and average time, come from? Do they ask 10 people, then add the scores and divide by 10 and generalize to the whole population? Who do they choose? Where do they get them? As Bill Cosby said, "How come those people in the ads never choose Coke? Who buys all the stuff?"

So when you take second, third, or more looks at a given observation, or message, you as a personal scientist are behaving in the *spirit* of the scientific tradition, which recognizes that all observations contain regions of uncertainty that are exposed by asking such questions as:

1. Where did they get those numbers, or observations?
2. Who was the messenger or researcher (casual; rushed; probing; Republican; Democrat; pro-life; pro-choice; creationist; evolutionist; male; female; and so forth)?
3. At what level (surface; middle; deep) were those observations made? Even if you had excellent reporters and researchers would this news, these numbers, be tough or almost impossible to get? If so, the news is probably a fragment of surface news supported by counting or measuring fuzzies (the observers reported seeing an average of 3.73 ghosts, having an average of 8.52 sexual fantasies per day, while drinking an average of 4965.1329 beers a year!).
4. What "paper" does he/she work for? What "side" of the news are they looking for? Reporters' and researchers' messages or stories are screened by the news editor, who decides whether they go on the front page, the back page, or in the garbage. Did you know that the majority of articles submitted by researchers are rejected by scientific-journal editors?

But even if you don't know anything about the competence of the researcher, or the editorial policy of the source of the news story, you can be certain that most observations, scientific or otherwise, include enough uncertainty surrounding them, and embedded in them, to warrant further critical examination. Furthermore, you can be certain that such critical examination will expose many more questions than the original message or explanation can handle. In this sense, then, all scientific observations and explanations are *temporary* and *tentative*.

Think of any observation as being surrounded by a region of doubt, or uncertainty, and of containing an area of uncertainty. We recognize these fuzzy regions in everyday language when we say: "We had a few beers, *more or less.*" We recognize these regions of uncertainty in scientific language when we say: "Life originated 2 billion years ago, plus or minus 500 million years;" or "The average person has 8 sexual fantasies a day, plus or minus 7;" or that "Teenage suicide is up 300 percent, *more or less.*"

Teenage suicides up 300 percent? Give that a second look and a bit of reflection. Would you guess that number was high or low? Is there bias operating against accurate reporting of suicides: a family bias (hiding suicide notes), a medical bias (protecting the family), a religious bias (it's a sin), an economic bias (loss of insurance), and so forth? All these factors acting in concert would affect the statistics. So a more accurate statement might be that: "*Reported* teenage suicides are up 300 percent." Perhaps an even more accurate statement would be that "Reported teenage suicides are up by at least 300 percent, but actual suicides are probably up by much more."

On the other hand, with computer linkages we are probably getting more of the *reported* suicides into the national data bases, so better bookkeeping rather than more suicides might account for most of the increase. As we said, "Teenage suicide is up 300 percent . . . more or less!" There's more to most observations than meets the eye, more uncertainty than can be solved with only a second, or third, look.

Stop and think how much of our experience consists of messages that contain a "more or less" rider attached to them, implicitly if not explicitly. Some contain large regions of uncertainty, such as the origins of life, fantasies, the potential duration of a marriage, or the number of suicides. Others possess relatively smaller regions of uncertainty, such as your weight, skunk odors, precise time of death, and the labels on Coke, Pepsi, and Tylenol. For the last three, the region of uncertainty is not on the surface; it's on the inside. Is there any real difference between Coke and Pepsi? Advertisers would have us believe so. Is there only Tylenol inside the bottle?

So-called *objective observations* involve small regions of uncertainty, in the sense that different observers agree (for example, assign the same numbers) even without peeking at each other's notes. For instance, both Republican and Democratic reporters can agree that the President spoke for 17 minutes, plus or minus a few seconds, but strongly disagree about what he "really" said or what it meant (large regions of uncertainty or subjectivity).

Similarly, different observers can agree that one can is *labeled* Pepsi and the other Coke (small region of uncertainty), but disagree over which tastes better (large region of uncertainty or subjectivity). Notice what happens when you cover the labels and ask people to identify, by taste alone, their favorite—you will probably find that over a series of trials most "observers" can't tell the difference when they can't see the labels.

Thus, we have several ways of making decisions or choices when operating in high-uncertainty regions. We can rely on external surfaces or labels; we prejudge the hidden layers on the basis of the surface appearance or labels, whether judging soft drinks or people. Although "you can't judge a book by its cover," most of the time we do; we can't spare the time to perform blindfolded taste trials and "get to know" everyone.

Our confidence in surface observations accounts for most of the choices we make every day.

When we lack subjective confidence, or time, or energy, we rely on others to guide us—"trusted" others, or "experts" like family, friends, priests, professionals, technicians, and of course scientists. Society provides science with the time and technology to explore beneath the surface, to conduct our blindfold trials for us, gradually to shrink given regions of uncertainty, and pass its "more or less" findings down the imperfect communication channels to the professionals (for example, doctors) and technicians (for instance, electronic experts) who, in turn, pass them on down to us.

But we have only discussed one side of a news service—the observational side (reporting and research). There was no editorial or explanatory material attached to these stories; they only covered observations—fuzzy, surface, limited, or otherwise.

Commentary and theory focus on explaining the news, on speculating about what factors produced the news, and what the consequences might be. Through commentary and theory, we make connections between a given piece of news and other events—earlier, current, or future events. In this way, we place news items in a larger frame of reference—larger temporal, experiential, or conceptual frameworks, for instance.

Consider the following news item, which lists the top seven discipline problems in public schools in 1940 and the top 17 in 1982:

1940	1982	1993
1. Talking	1. Rape	1. ?
2. Chewing gum	2. Robbery	2. ?
3. Making noise	3. Assault	3. ?
4. Running in the halls	4. Burglary	
5. Getting out of turn in line	5. Arson	
6. Wearing improper clothing	6. Bombings	
7. Not putting paper in wastebaskets	7. Murder	
	8. Suicide	
	9. Absenteeism	
	10. Vandalism	
	11. Extortion	
	12. Drug abuse	
	13. Alcohol abuse	
	14. Gang warfare	
	15. Pregnancy	
	16. Abortion	
	17. Venereal disease	

Where do they get these "observations"? Who counted the rapes? the suicides? the extortions? the pregnancies? the abortions? the venereal disease?

Notice, no editorial comment is included, but with the two lists placed side by side, and given the dates, most readers spontaneously generate commentary and explanations. What comments come readily to your mind?

Make a guess as to where this "news" item was published?

1. A Harvard University research institute journal?
2. A school board newsletter?
3. An evangelical church publication during the presidential election?
4. A police circular?

If you guessed item 3 you are correct.[2]

What "observations" would you add under the 1993 column? Then ask a friend to do the same and compare your "observations."

To appreciate the powerful role different points of view or vested interests can play in interpreting an event, refer to the news clipping at the end of this chapter. It describes the radically different frames of reference used by the prosecuting and defense attorneys in a trial involving the bombing of three abortion clinics.

EXPLANATION, SPECULATION, THEORY

Observations—facts or fuzzies—piled on a table or merely listed page after page cry out for organization. Whether scientist or citizen we seek linkages.

Which current events are tied together?

What events in the past caused them?

What events will they cause or lead to in the future?

Once again, scan the "sample of news" listed earlier. Which ones seem linked together in some way?

The mind's eyes of first-year students reported the following possible linkages:

1. The linkage (contrast) between the American and Japanese IQ figures.
2. The possible causal linkage between increased LSD use and teenage suicide.

[2]From *Harpers Magazine*, March, 1985, p. 25.

3. The possible causal linkage between 60,000,000 Americans reading below the ninth-grade level and American IQ levels below the Japanese.

Cause and Effect

Our mind's eye provides linkages and organization for our flow of observations—facts, fantasies, or fuzzies. The mind's eye naturally seeks cause-and-effect connections. Our outer eye focuses on "What?" questions, whereas our mind's eye seeks out "Why?".

Some linkages are so obvious and so close in time and space that the real eye can detect them without much help from the mind's eye:

Question: What caused the broken window?

Answer: This baseball that just came through it.

Some linkages are pretty obvious, with the real eye providing most of the answer and the mind's eye (speculation and memory) adding some supporting arguments.

Question: What led to the touchdown?

Answer 1: The intercepted pass.

Answer 2: Yes, but that was caused by poor blocking.

Answer 3: Yes, and don't forget about the intended receiver being out of position.

Answer 4: Yes, and don't forget that the coach threw that new quarterback in without having prepared him for such an emergency by giving him some previous big-game experience.

So ... what really "caused" the touchdown?

In this puzzle we have the real eye and the inner or mind's eye working together on direct and indirect, or additional, causes or linkages. We see an expanding list, even a flood, of proposed causes or explanations.

Some linkages are hard to see or trace, and the mind's eye must do most of the work, with selected supporting arguments provided by the real eye.

Question: What caused the death diagrammed in Figure 1-1?

Answer 1: A gunshot wound to the head.

Answer 2 He was in with a fast crowd.

Answer 3: I heard he was on drugs.

Answer 4 No, it was an accident; he was cleaning a gun.

Answer 5: I heard he had cancer or maybe it was just the flu.

Answer 6: He was down in the dumps about his girlfriend.

Answer 7: Depression runs in his family. . . .

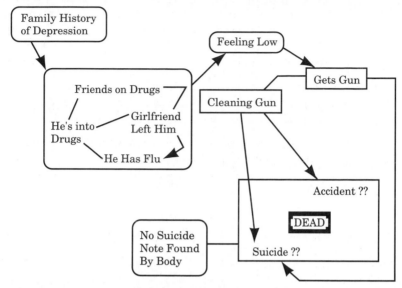

FIGURE 1–1   A Network of "Causes"

So, . . . what "caused" the death or suicide?

Notice that the only "hard" messages are probably the gunshot wound and presumably the death. All the rest are the work of the mind's eye puzzling away inside different heads.

What caused the death? The simplest answer is: A gunshot wound to the head (more or less, until an autopsy is performed). But what caused the gunshot wound? Obviously a gun, probably the one found beside his body (more or less, until ballistic tests reduce that region of uncertainty). But surely it was an accident. Maybe, but he knew how to handle guns, more or less. Probably suicide then, but he left no suicide note, more or less (at least the person who found him reported no note was found). Still, he was feeling low, more or less; and he and his friends were on drugs, more or less; and his girlfriend had walked out on him, more or less; and he had the flu, more or less; and depression ran in the family, more or less.

Of all these "causes," which were relevant? How much did each one contribute? Was his mother right: "He must have sneezed because of his flu and the gun went off accidentally"?

We see, from this example, that talking about "what caused what" can become very complicated with hidden, imaginary, or invisible linkages going off in all directions further and further back in time. So although the term *cause* is still widely used in daily conversation and in common-sense explanations, most scientists avoid the word. They avoid it because it only designates the last explanation you have—the one you are holding when you stop asking questions, or when, owing to confusion, fatigue, or boredom, the mind turns its eye away from that particular puzzle.

Antecedents and Consequences

Instead of talking about cause and effect, scientists talk about *antecedents and consequences*. Notice, they don't talk about *the* antecedent, but about antecedents (plural), which is a way of acknowledging that there are usually many antecedents—usually more than the mind's eye can perceive, more than the real eye can see even when the mind's eye gives it hints about where to look. Moreover, each antecedent has an endless network of ancestors stretching back in time.

The best that investigators can hope for in their search for explanations is to attempt to trace a few of many possible antecedents part of the way back in time, whether they are attempting to explain the origins of life; of subatomic particles; of depression; of touchdowns; or of an accidental death or suicide.

Most interesting questions facing citizens, or scientists, come surrounded with more antecedents than the outer eye can see, or the inner eye can manage or imagine.

Both citizens and scientists must constantly deal with uncertainty. However, there is a fundamental difference in how science and common sense approach uncertainty. Science deals with the unknown, and attempts to push back the endless horizons of uncertainty by employing what we popularly think of as *the scientific method.*

THE SCIENTIFIC METHOD: FIVE KEY INGREDIENTS

Since antecedents and consequences frequently contain large regions of uncertainty, and since interesting questions come surrounded with more antecedents than we can see or imagine, we require more than casual curiosity and casual observation to solve them.

Common-sense problem solving, on the one hand, typically involves having the external eye take a second or third look at one or two antecedents, and having the mind's eye take a second or third look at how they might be linked to each other (the flu to a sneeze to an accidental gun shot), and how these in turn might be linked to the consequence in question (the death . . . the accidental death?). Scientific problem solving, on the other hand, typically involves having *many* external eyes—plus their technical extensions and magnifiers—take repeated looks at various antecedents in an effort to reduce their regions of uncertainty, and having *many* mind's eyes take repeated looks and run repeated tests on possible linkages. This process, known as the *scientific method,* draws its power from a variety of sources that will be discussed throughout the book. But let us begin with five key ingredients, and then consider two others.

The first and most important ingredient is *driving motivation*; otherwise we have no questions or observations or solutions or explanations other than those generated by casual or temporary curiosity—those generated by the short reach of commonsense problem solving.

A second ingredient is *systematic observation*—involving repeated, magnified examinations—aimed at reducing the regions of uncertainty surrounding selected antecedents and their linkages.

A third ingredient is *systematic experimentation*, which involves testing different antecedents to see which one, or which combination, produces a given consequence.

A fourth ingredient is *probabilistic thinking*, which recognizes that a given antecedent does not always produce a given consequence, and so talks about probability rather than certainty.

A fifth ingredient is *theoretical thinking*, which involves systematically organizing observations (messages) from a particular viewpoint, or within a given theoretical framework.

So one way of comparing the scientific method with commonsense methods of problem solving is in terms of the relative emphasis each one places on these key ingredients. Figure 1-2 illustrates the differences between these two methods in the case of the first three ingredients.

As indicated on the left-hand side of Figure 1-2, *commonsense* solutions mainly arise from a combination of casual or temporary observation and experimentation. This combination of casual or temporary problem-solving activity typically yields a grab bag of conflicting solutions: The death was accidental. . . . No, it was suicide. . . . It was due to drugs. . . . It was due to bad genes. . . .

On the other hand, *scientific problem solving* relies on a combination of factors—driving motivation; systematic observation; systematic experimentation—a combination likely to generate more reliable solutions.

As noted on the right-hand side of Figure 1-2, by combining persistent motivation with systematic observations we generate the *observational sciences* in which researchers become increasingly accurate in describing, predicting, and explaining a host of phenomena ranging from the heavenly movements of stellar bodies to the earthly movements of political opinion and voting patterns.

When the third ingredient—systematic experimentation—is combined with driving curiosity and systematic observation, we generate the *experimental sciences*. This combination represents our most powerful puzzle-solving strategy, which allows us not only to predict and explain phenomena, but also to shape and control them.

In the experimental sciences, researchers not only track public opinion, but also manipulate it; they not only observe and predict human

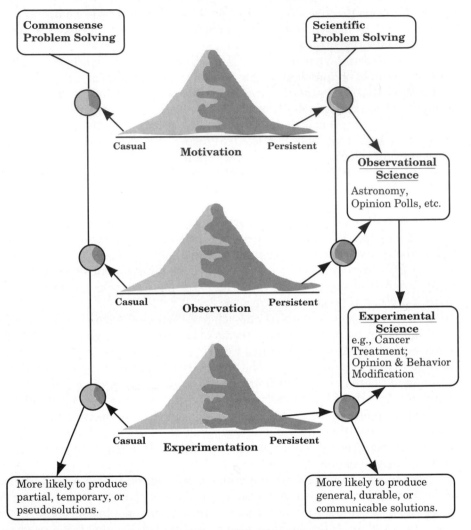

FIGURE 1–2   How Science Differs from Common Sense

behavior, but they shape it—with information, drugs, advertising, indoctrination, rewards, training, and so forth.

But remember, scientific predictions, manipulations, controls, and explanations operate within different margins of error—some small, some large, some unknown. This is true not only because all researchers are "casual" commonsense problem-solvers some of the time (and a few are casual most of the time), but also because certain dimensions of the physical world and of human nature continue to surprise and confound science and its most dedicated researchers using its most powerful probes and magnifiers. Thus, even science cannot penetrate some regions of uncertainty.

Next we will examine these five vital components of the scientific method: compelling curiosity, systematic observation, systematic experimentation, probabilistic thinking, and theoretical thinking.

Compelling Motivation

A colleague named Grayson is hooked (and has been for the past five years) on exploring human thinking, feeling, and acting in relation to making *resolutions* about all kinds of behavior: smoking, eating, drinking, worrying, daydreaming, sleeping, speaking out, test anxiety, procrastinating, cramming, and so forth.

Whereas you or I temporarily focus our attention on a particular puzzle (a resolution to stop cramming, or to cease smoking), Grayson focuses his on a general puzzle (many people's resolutions about *many* types of behavior) and his attention remains locked on it; his career revolves around it.

He looks forward to New Year's just as a child looks forward to Christmas. He avidly collects resolutions and tracks their limited spans. He publishes papers in learned journals that describe the few success stories he discovers. He presents alternative explanations why these few smokers, or boozers, or crammers succeeded in changing their behavior, whereas thousands of others failed.

At cocktail or dinner parties he corners unsuspecting guests, interrogating them about their resolutions, collecting treasured specimens for his growing collection. His wife pleads with him to stop badgering friends and acquaintances, to limit his lectures to the classroom and his research to his laboratory at the university. She even got him to make a New Year's resolution that he would, but she doubts he'll keep it . . . "Doctor, heal thyself!"

Compelling curiosity is the engine of science. Whether the goal is prediction, control, or understanding, it requires a combination of persistence and fascination to map and untangle the complex and shifting network of antecedents and consequences.

But although such curiosity is a necessary tool of the researcher and the theorist, it alone does not distinguish scientists from the rest of us. Each of us gets hooked on something: our careers, our children, our lover, music, football, the stock market, fashion, foods. Furthermore, each of us knows that "getting hooked" rarely follows a tidy, predictable path; trial and error seems to play a larger role than planning in establishing our "addictions" or our fascinations.

Similarly, a scientist's compelling curiosity usually hooks on to a problem or a puzzle by trial-and-error gambits rather than by rationally picking a "good one" off the scientific shelf. Like some people, not all scientists get hooked, so they end up going through the motions.

As with some people, some scientists get hooked on "bad" or insoluble puzzles. While walking one spring day with a colleague and his three-year-old daughter, Leslie, we commenced to climb the river bank. After a few unsuccessful attempts Leslie sat down and lisped: "That hill is too big for my shoes!" Her father, a cancer researcher, looked down, smiled, and replied gently: "Leslie, that hill is like daddy's work. Sometimes it's too big for his mind, maybe too big for all our minds . . . time will tell."

However, like many people, some scientists hook on to compelling engagements, and their driving curiosity sustains them through the unpredictable ups and downs that arise in any complex relationship—whether engaging a person, a career, or one of human nature's knotty puzzles.

But while compelling curiosity is a necessary ingredient of science, it is not sufficient. It must be combined with at least one other ingredient: systematic observation.

Systematic Observation

Solid research requires driving curiosity generating and focusing the power to build a foundation of reliable observations.

Our colleague Grayson's foundation of observations includes the fate of thousands of New Year's resolutions. Each December, through student questionnaires, interviews with faculty, television appearances, and newspaper ads, he collects hundreds of resolutions. Then starting in January he and his research assistants, using questionnaires or interviews, follow the fate of each fragile resolve.

Grayson's observations indicate that over 90 percent of the resolutions have dissolved or self-destructed by the end of January. Approximately another 5 percent have actually been broken but reported as still in force through "white lies," wishful thinking, or poor memory. Grayson and his sleuths conduct investigations on a sample of "successful" resolutions by such methods as checking ashtrays, interviews with family and friends, weight checks. . . . They even go as far as to smell the fingers of "ex-smokers."

Like tenacious investigative reporters, these researchers don't necessarily believe everything they're told. They learned early that data come in all shapes and sizes, and some data on close scrutiny turn out to be garbage. GIGO (garbage in/garbage out) is a favorite acronym of computer scientists to highlight the point that if you start with bad data no amount of fancy analysis will transform it into "the truth." All researchers live with the vague awareness that today's data may be tomorrow's garbage. Well, all jobs involve some risk—even scientific jobs; all solutions are "more or less" solutions.

The hope of society is that when scientists are afforded the time and money to search for solutions to important puzzles, they will arrive at more accurate predictions than could be achieved through casual commonsense methods.

In his research on resolution making and breaking, not only does Grayson make general predictions covering large numbers of observations, but notice he also couches his predictions in terms of probabilities—the odds are 9 to 1 against keeping a New Year's resolution. Like race track touts and professional gamblers, researchers understand that unknown antecedents always play a role, that chance sits in on every game and plays its cards. If we're lucky, chance plays from a weak hand; if not, it confounds our arrogant predictions and exposes our fragile understanding.

By assigning different probabilities, or odds, to their observations, scientists attempt to estimate the size of the regions of uncertainty surrounding and embedded in their observations and to acknowledge the potentially powerful influence hidden or unknown antecedents can exert.

Furthermore, experienced researchers know they can't believe everything they see or hear. Some of their sources talk a good game but can't play one, or even if you actually "see" them play one it may be a flash in the pan—maybe it was luck playing its cards in their favor. Therefore, experienced researchers invariably seek several lines of evidence. That is why Grayson and his sleuths probe below the surface of the few "success" stories they encounter, finding that over half of those claiming success were talking a better game than they played. That is why Grayson tenaciously follows up those who start out playing a better game, to determine whether the change is fragile and temporary.

Therefore, when driven by persistent curiosity, scientists, via systematic observation and repeated examinations of a puzzle, aim to reduce the regions of uncertainty in which all antecedents and their linkages reside. Otherwise we settle for temporary or unreliable solutions that arise from casual first and second looks and the simple cause–effect logic of commonsense explanations—fuzzy antecedents fuzzily linked to each other and to fuzzy consequences.

For example, observe the commonsense problem solving of a student who crams for exams (if you happen to know one): procrastination, plus or minus; leads to cramming, plus or minus; leads to anxiety, low grades, self-disgust, plus or minus; leads to resolutions to start studying earlier, plus or minus; leads to drawing up a study schedule and a few days studying, plus or minus; leads back to procrastination and repetition of the cramming cycle.

This familiar recycling of ineffective commonsense solutions suggests that casual or temporary curiosity combined with casual observation frequently fails to identify clearly important antecedents and critical linkages or leverage points and so produces pseudo-solutions.

Without systematic observations we end up linking one vague observation to another, like glibly tying "teenage suicide" to "a history of depression in the ancestors." And yet simply reducing the size of the more-or-less regions of uncertainty surrounding the incidence of one antecedent (family history) and one consequence (teen suicide) remains a formidable challenge to systematic observation before we can even address the question of whether they are tied together in some way—weakly, moderately, or strongly.

In brief, without compelling curiosity we don't have the engine to drive systematic observations, and without systematic observations we end up with fuzzy explanations of fuzzy networks of antecedents and consequences. We end up with New Year's resolutions, and with "right wing" and "left wing" explanations of any fuzzy puzzle you can name.

All science, whether observational or experimental, whether aimed only at description and prediction, or also aimed at control, is at the mercy of the regions of uncertainty surrounding and embedded in its observations. The goal of systematic observation is to reduce continuously that uncertainty—to shrink the size of the "more-or-less" rider attached to all our measurements, our counts, our "solutions."

Systematic Experiments

By necessity or preference, some scientists, like astronomers and pollsters and New Year's resolution trackers, limit themselves to making increasingly accurate descriptions or predictions of accessible portions of a given network of antecedents and consequences. They can't or don't try to manipulate or control the network under observation—the astronomers can't manipulate the orbits or position of the planets, and pollsters presumably don't try to influence the vote.

In contrast, the popular view of science highlights gaining control over physical and social networks through experimentation.

Experimentation is not the exclusive domain of scientists. All of us experiment. But our "experiments" are typically casual, trial-and-error affairs that involve manipulating one fuzzy antecedent (a New Year's resolution) and casually observing what happens to a fuzzy consequence (studying). If that doesn't seem to work, we usually throw a bunch of fuzzy antecedents into a bag (drawing up a study schedule; asking your boyfriend not to ask you out weeknights; putting a "do not disturb" sign on your door; turning off the TV and so forth) and see what happens.

What happens? Not much more or less, but it's hard to say because you didn't make systematic observations. Looking back, your memory is a bit vague, but as you recall your boyfriend had hurt his knee playing football so needed extra time and attention. And somebody stole your "do not disturb" sign, and there were some important educational programs on TV you "had" to watch.

But what about your studying? "Well ... I think it improved ... more or less!" How did you keep track? Did you keep a record of minutes studied per day? Or pages read and underlined? Or pages summarized? "Well, no, none of those, but my general impression is that it improved, more or less, and I've drawn up a new schedule so. . . . "

Yes, we all experiment, but the process is complicated for many reasons: you have to (1) decide which antecedents are important; (2) then try to put them in place; (3) then try to keep them in place; (4) all the while keeping accurate records of all that, plus what's happening to your studying the consequences.

Experimental scientists face the same problems, for they must:

1. Decide which antecedents and consequences in the network to focus on.
2. Reduce the regions of uncertainty enough so that they can keep track of them.
3. Decide which antecedents they're going to manipulate and which ones they're going to control (eliminate or hold steady).
4. Figure how to do that, then do it.
5. Systematically observe what's happening:
   —Is the antecedent they're manipulating behaving itself?
   —Are the antecedents they're controlling staying controlled?
   —Are the consequences changing in the direction and by the amount their hunch or theory predicted they would?
6. Wonder why it didn't work.
7. Repeat the above using a more precise measure of consequences.
8. Wonder why it still didn't work.
9. Try bigger dose of the pet or favorite antecedent.
10. Wonder why it still didn't work.
11. Try more precise control of other antecedents.
12. Aha, finally get some changes in one of the consequences.
13. Repeat the experiment again, as the change might have been due to chance, or some hidden, unobservable antecedent.

Yes, there's a difference between commonsense and casual "experimentation" and the systematic experiments that researchers employ. And not only do they have to be systematic but they have to be lucky enough to pick relevant antecedents—to pick one, or a combination, that is really linked to an important consequence. Otherwise that careful one-by-one testing, while keeping all the other antecedents quiet (controlled), can take a lifetime or more, and frequently does. Think how complicated it is to try to untangle the relative influence on human behavior of such complex antecedents as heredity on the one hand and environment on the other. What is their relative contribution to depression, for example?

To help us untangle these two powerful yet complex types of antecedents we can sometimes capitalize on *natural experiments*—for example, studying identical twins who have been separated at birth and raised in different environments. If one twin subsequently suffers from depression, what is the probability of the other showing similar symptoms?

If the probability turns out to be high for a number of such pairs, then because their hereditary antecedents are identical and their environmental antecedents are different, it suggests that their hereditary antecedents are playing a significant role—more or less. Since we can't "experiment" with people's heredity, identical twins raised apart offer social scientists a rare opportunity to *more or less* untangle the relative contribution of hereditary and environmental antecedents as they relate to everything from intelligence to abnormal behavior. As you will find in subsequent chapters, our current explanations contain large regions of uncertainty and generate heated debates.

Although we can't systematically experiment with human heredity as it relates, for example, to depression, we can do so with various treatments for depression. When you or I feel low we unsystematically experiment with a bagful of "treatments" and usually give credit to the last one we tried before we got better, completely forgetting that feeling low usually lasts a week, more or less, no matter what we do about it. That's commonsense problem solving, and no harm done.

Systematic experimentation, on the other hand, would involve a group of depressed patients divided into two "matched" groups, with one getting the traditional treatment, or a placebo (sugar pill), and the other group getting the new treatment. The researcher would then systematically observe any changes in symptoms, while controlling other antecedents like diet, time on treatment, ward environment, ward staff, number of visitors, and so forth.

Future chapters will examine the increasingly powerful methods of observation and experimentation scientists use to reduce the regions of uncertainty surrounding their observations and their solutions. We shall also discuss how they attempt to extend the reach of science in exploring the shifting network of human experience. But let us return to our consideration of the other vital ingredients.

Probabilistic Thinking

We have already discussed a *fourth dimension* that characterizes scientific problem solving and helps distinguish it from commonsense approaches—namely the way scientists think about a problem in terms of antecedents and consequences, rather than in terms of simple cause and effect. To acknowledge the regions of uncertainty that always surround their observations and explanations, scientists attempt to assign odds to the reliability of those observations, or estimate the probability that a particular antecedent, or combination of antecedents, is really tied to a given consequence.

When lacking experience or strong beliefs, nonscientists can also think in terms of odds—what are the *chances* the letter will arrive; the horse will place; that the other person will agree; that the dice are loaded? You carry around crude maps of chance in your head and start getting nervous when a seven comes up "too often" or the coin lands heads "too often." But whereas you may rely on intuition to compute crude odds, many scientists rely on highly sophisticated mathematical and statistical models to help them estimate the degree of certainty they can afford to have in their observations, predictions, and conclusions. We discuss some of these statistical models—or maps of chance—in later chapters.

If only chance is operating, a coin has a 50–50 probability of coming up heads, otherwise more than chance is influencing the toss. But there's another antecedent in addition to chance—a bias of some kind. Similarly, if only chance is operating, certain patients have a 50–50 chance of getting better. If, however, more than 50 percent improve following treatment on a new drug, maybe there's a bias operating, a positive treatment influence over and above chance. But given the fact that you can get a run of heads even from a true (unbiased) coin by chance, how far do your results have to deviate from 50–50 before you decide that something more than lady luck is playing in your game?

Scientists go to great lengths to estimate how much their findings are merely due to lady luck on a roll and how much to the antecedents they're manipulating, or the treatment they are administering. Most scientists acknowledge the significant role chance or unknown antecedents play in their findings. So a fourth dimension characterizing science is a probabilistic way of thinking about reality as composed of complex networks of antecedents, consequences, and chance, in contrast to the simple cause-and-effect way of thinking that is typically employed in commonsense problem solving.

We must also acknowledge a frequently neglected fifth dimension of science—the vitally important role played by hunch, intuition, and theory in guiding scientific discovery.

Intuition and Theory

A fifth dimension of science is its reliance on theory. Theory involves the systematic organization of observations from a given point of view.

Although there are thousands of systematic researchers conducting careful, one-by-one screenings of thousands of potential antecedents, the famous scientists are the few who, by good luck or brilliant hunch, guide the rest of us to selected regions in the infinite network where we can find surprisingly powerful antecedents.

How complicated and time-consuming it is to test even three or four antecedents one by one; then in different quantities or durations; then in different combinations; in different quantities; for different durations; then in terms of different consequences. Consider an experiment involving two different drugs, in three different quantities, for three different durations, on patients with three levels of severity of illness, of different ages, married and unmarried, receiving two different levels of nursing care—already up to hundreds of experiments could be involved to solve this one relatively simple network puzzle.

Such brute force science is not enough. It needs help. To help narrow its focus to relevant regions of the network and then to powerful though hidden antecedents, science needs guidance and help from brilliant hunches and from inspired theory. And while, during their university training, we can identify *potential* scientists—those with compelling curiosity, which drives systematic observation and careful experimentation—we can't reliably separate those with "crazy" hunches from those with brilliant ones; or determine without years of work which theorist will lead hundreds of researchers either on a wild goose chase or to surprisingly powerful antecedents, such as the potential forces locked inside the atom; the chromosomes; the hormones; the unconscious; conditioned responses; partial reinforcement; parent-child bonding; peer pressure; cultural mores; and so forth.

You can perhaps gain a crude feel for the vital role intuition and theory play in science by using the analogy of the scientist as safecracker.

Scientist as Safecracker   As any safecracker knows, you don't gain access to major vaults by one or many casual twirls of the dial; the safe's combination contains several numbers for which both the sequence and timing count, and only one combination out of potentially thousands will work. Similarly, any good scientist knows you don't gain access to nature's major vaults by casually manipulating several antecedents.

Even when you decode the combination you may discover that

1. The door opens to disclose only a little secret, or
2. There is yet another vault requiring another combination. Good puzzles keep expanding, keep a jump ahead of the mind and technology of the researcher. (Remember, "That hill is too big for my shoes") or
3. The combination may change. Just when you seem to have captured a stable truth the trusted combination doesn't work anymore. Remember, *chance* reserves a seat in every game. She decides when she'll play the aces up her sleeve or even change the rules of the game.
4. Sometimes the big secret you seek doesn't even reside in the vault you're working on; often it lies in another bank entirely . . . but which one?

Recall the drunk down on his hands and knees under a streetlight looking for his car key. When asked when he last remembered seeing it he replies: "I just dropped it a few minutes ago when I was trying to get into my car on the other side of the street."

When asked why he wasn't looking for it where he dropped it, he says, "Don't be silly. How could I find it over there? There's no light."

Sometimes researchers also look in the wrong place—for instance, in laboratories because there's more light and their familiar search tools are anchored there. In other words, when looking for solutions to puzzles some researchers work on vaults that fit in the lab, which may or may not contain significant secrets or solutions.

5. Researchers may be in the right vault but working on the wrong safety deposit box, or they may be in the wrong bank altogether. Sometimes the solution's not even locked away in vaults but rather it's lying right out in the open but can only be perceived from a hilltop when walking with a child ... or sitting under an apple tree when an apple falls. ...

6. Of course, sometimes researchers wouldn't recognize an answer if it landed in their hands.

Recall researchers trying to figure out what causes swamp fever and malaria while busy swatting those pesky mosquitoes. Or doctors blaming "humors in the air" for killing so many young mothers with childbed fever, when all along it was due to live, invisible dirt on the doctor's hands.

So the answer to the puzzle of malaria and the puzzle of childbed fever literally lay in the palm of their hands, but because they were expecting a different kind of solution they were "blind." The idea of germs hadn't been planted in the scientific mind—*the mind was blind.* Later, after the idea of germs was planted, we had to wait for the invention of the microscope so the actual eye could see what the mind's eye imagined.

So, if the mind's eye is looking in the wrong direction, the real eye may see everything ... except the solution.

If you keep in the back of your mind the analogy of the scientist as a safecracker seeking the right combination to the right vault, and the right key to the right safety deposit box, you have a crude but useful model of science. The analogy highlights not only the need for systematic experimentation to solve the combination but also highlights the overriding importance of selecting, by luck, hunch, or theory, the right vault—the right region of the network.

We know much more about working on combinations, about systematic experimentation, than we know about choosing the right vault—

about pointing the mind's eye in the direction where powerful antecedents and solutions are likely to lie.

Consider then the cast of players involved at various levels in the scientific enterprise.

Great scientists combine a wizard's mind with a safecracker's touch.

Great theorists possess a wizard's mind; they point to richly stocked vaults, to regions where powerful antecedents can likely be found by skilled researchers.

Great researchers possess "great hands" that make them master safecrackers, that enable them to expose the validity or error of the theorist's predictions.

As you can well imagine, a popular theorist can keep an army of researchers and technicians occupied for years, as did Einstein, Darwin, Freud, and Skinner, for example.

Technicians help design and build equipment to aid researchers in their magnification of the very far, the very fuzzy, and the very small, and they also take the discoveries of theorists and researchers and turn them to practical use, or keep them "tuned" (for example, engineers of all kinds, electricians, computer specialists).

Professionals borrow some of this technology and combine it with professional custom and common sense, and apply the mixture to our daily problems (doctors, dentists, clinical psychologists, social workers, and others are examples of these professionals).

LEVELS OF OBSERVATION AND SPECULATION

Psychology, whether considered as a science, a technology, or a professional practice, has successfully broadened its scope to the extent that psychologists have come to understand that a human event, like any other event in nature, is determined by the simultaneous action of many factors. The major point made about the newer, realist view of science is that it opened up, in a logical way, the study of psychological phenomena at a number of different levels. (Crawford, 1985, p. 421)

Where do we look for the origins of human behavior—for the really powerful antecedents? There are just too many potential antecedents to be tested; even those within our reach are beyond counting, let alone testing via systematic observation or experimentation. Where in the network should we search and test? Which of the millions of vaults should we work on?

As we noted earlier, we rely on favorite theorists to guide us, and we select search spaces—our vaults—according to our theoretical preference. Some theorists and researchers look inside the individual for the major antecedents—in their genes, their hormones, their brains, or their minds—while others look outside—at their parents, their institutional ties, their cultures.

So we see theorists and researchers specializing at different levels of speculation, observation, and experimentation, as portrayed in Figure 1-3.

When you ask questions about depression, the answer you get—the powerful antecedents proposed—will depend on which levels, or vaults, the theorist or researcher is working. If at the level of the gene, you will

Levels of Observation and Speculation

"To produce an individual put genes and culture in a bag and shake just right"

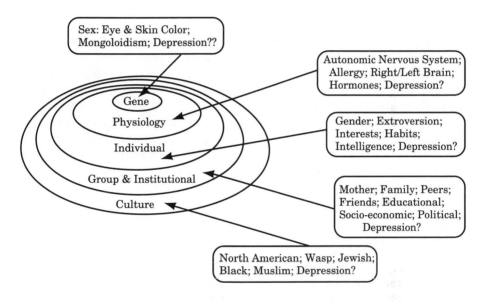

Specialization

Different social sciences tend to focus their observations, speculations, and theories at certain levels; for example:

Gene/Physiological Level: Physiological/Experimental Psychologists.

Individual Level: Developmental/Clinical/Personality Psychologists.

Group/Institutional Level: Social Psychologists; Sociologists; Economists, etc.

Cultural Level: Anthropologists; Sociologists.

Note: Increasingly scientists are crossing traditional boundaries and creating new interesting and controversial fields like sociobiology.

FIGURE 1–3   Where to Look for the Answer

get the results of genetic observations (remember the identical twins raised apart) and experiments tied together by genetic theories or editorials. If at the level of the culture, you will get the results of cultural observations tied together by sociological or anthropological theories (depression is concentrated among poor, single mothers, and other lower socioeconomic classes).

Also, within each layer will be subspecialists—theorists and researchers working perhaps on the twenty-first chromosome safety deposit box. Within these subgroups will be cautious theorists and researchers not straying too far from what is known, exploring a limited, close-to-home region of the more-or-less uncertainty space. But there will also be the risk takers, speculating and probing in highly uncertain, improbable regions—working on "way out" vaults but within the same bank, or same level.

And then there will be theorists who, to the dismay of some of their colleagues, will pogo-stick around within and across layers, picking up an antecedent here and there and tying them together into a provocative theory that attracts young or bored or disenchanted researchers who then excitedly hammer away at vaults all over the place, to the delight of the press and to the disgust of "real" specialists. Examples of such multilevel explorations are those conducted by sociobiologists linking genetic and social behavior, and by the solid state chemist linking "ghosts" to the echoes of history recorded in the memory of stones.

Just like everyone else, theorists and researchers differ in temperaments ranging from the cautious and conservative to the grand speculators and gamblers. So at what levels they choose to work is not merely a matter of theoretical preference, but also of personal style. But regardless of level and style, luck, hunch, and theory play powerful roles in determining what vaults they work on and what they find inside.

What's found is always a composite picture compiled by both the outer and inner eye. As two researchers peer into a newly opened vault, one "sees" only a mosquito; the other "sees" the answer to malaria; one "sees" a fuzzy pattern on a microscopic slide; the other "sees" the antecedent of mongolism; one "hears" a funny story; the other "detects" the structure of prejudice. From this perspective, the categories in which we store our knowledge are constructed by the mind's eye interacting with the world in which we live; in this sense, there is no such thing as purely objective knowledge.

SUMMARY

We don't believe everything we read in the newspaper, nor should we believe everything that scientists tell us. For in each case news comes in layers—surface, middle, deep—and also in each instance it comes nested in a region of uncertainty.

Nevertheless, we understand that scientific problem solving is more powerful than commonsense problem solving. We rely on science to explore regions of uncertainty we can't reach, even though the reach of science itself is limited, and even though each scientific probe reveals new and often larger puzzles.

Commonsense and scientific problem solving can be distinguished by the relative emphasis they place on five ingredients: (1) casual versus persistent curiosity; (2) casual versus systematic observation; (3) casual versus systematic experimentation; (4) simple cause-effect versus probabilistic antecedents-consequences thinking; (5) atheoretical versus theoretical thinking.

Beginning in Chapter 3 we will commence discussing the increasingly powerful methods scientists and researchers use to reduce the regions of uncertainty located in certain regions of "reality"—in certain networks where antecedents generate consequences, of course, with help from the fickle hand of chance, more or less.

But in order to get into the mind-set of scientists and researchers it will be helpful to become a bit more familiar with their way of thinking and talking—they speak with three tongues—as discussed in Chapter 2. You use these languages on occasion, too, so you won't find them foreign.

EXAMPLE

A "seeing is believing" theory works pretty well with simple, here-and-now events. But when you encounter multilayered events, stretching into the past, or future, you must rely increasingly on a different kind of theory, a "believing is seeing" point of view. The news story to follow illustrates how different people "construct" radically different images of what is "really true."

Reality in the Mind's Eye of the Beholder

ABORTION BOMBERS LIKE 'KNIGHTS' NOT TERRORISTS, LAWYERS TELL TRIAL

By Tim Harper, Toronto Star
Pensacola, Fla.

Four young people who embrace religion, old-fashioned family ethics and have "an abiding sense of American values" went on trial yesterday charged with bombing three Florida abortion clinics last Christmas Day.

The four were described by a defense lawyer as "knights in shining armor," not terrorists.

"The government has brought charges against innocents, as [in] the trial of Jesus and the trial of Socrates," lawyer T. Patrick Monaghan said in his opening statement as he outlined plans for an insanity defense.

The trial of the four anti-abortion youngsters has put the spotlight on what can happen when the ongoing, increasingly violent abortion debate in the United States gets out of hand.

Lawyers defending the four youngsters are attempting to turn the trial into a referendum on the abortion issue.

The prosecution wants to keep the focus on the charges of bombing the three clinics and conspiracy to build weapons.

Strange Blend

In opening statements at a U.S. courthouse in the middle of the Gulf Coast, dubbed the Redneck Riviera, the defense introduced a strange blend of ol' time religion, Bible quotations and American apple pie in its address to the jury of six men and six women.

The abortion debate careened out of control when three blasts within 20 minutes rocked this town near the Alabama border in the foggy predawn of last Christmas Day.

Charged are Matthew Goldsby, 21; his fiance, 18-year-old Kaye Wiggins; James Simmons, 21; and his 18-year-old wife of eight months, Kathren.

"Matthew Goldsby is not a terrorist," said Monaghan, a Kentucky lawyer who is chief spokesman for the defense.

"James Simmons is not a terrorist and Kathren Simmons and Kaye Wiggins are not terrorists . . . just two young girls very much in love with their knights in shining armor."

Monaghan said abortion is not an issue in this case.

"But we'll see how the controversy hits on young people individually and particularly these young people," he continued.

"We'll see how abortion is okay—it's in the Yellow Pages—and how it conflicts with the story of Luke these kids were taught."

Abortion has been legal in the United States since a 1973 Supreme Court ruling.

But Monaghan also alluded to recent anti-abortion remarks made by U.S. President Ronald Reagan as fuelling the defendants' confusion.

Monaghan said the defendants were getting conflicting signals from authority figures. Their religious training and even Reagan, whom he called a national "father figure," led them to believe abortion is evil while the Supreme Court says it is legal.

"They saw unborn children being killed at three abortion clinics and what they saw were people being taken there to be killed," Monaghan said.

He called the defendants "four outstanding young people."

"They don't smoke. They don't drink. They don't engage in drugs. And they believe sex is properly a part of marriage.

"They have a deep and abiding sense of God, America and American values. They identify with the American way of helping the underdog."

Monaghan said it was their virtues, not their vices, which brought them to the courtroom.

"These are four of our own kids. Try to understand what in American youth—their beauty, their idealism, their zaniness or their craziness— compelled them to do this."

Pensacola lawyer Paul Shimek, who earlier had backed down on his attempt to represent all four, went further in his remarks in defense of Wiggins.

"They are horses in a race," he said, "and God is their jockey. They are winners."

"They obey God's law, not man's law. Take it or leave it. There are absolutes."

Prosecutor Susan Novotny said there was nothing symbolic about the Christmas bombings. She said Goldsby told agents he chose that morning because there would be fewer police officers on duty.

Escape Detection

The four went to great lengths to prepare the bombs, plan the bombings and escape detection, she said.

She also said she would introduce evidence to show the four bought powder in one- to two-kilogram installments until they had enough for their bombs.

The four are all devoutly religious. None had ever had a criminal conviction before and they are the epitome of clean-cut, good-looking, pure-living southern young achievers, Shimek said.

Goldsby was arrested after attending church.

There have been 29 bombings of abortion clinics in the United States since 1982. Last year, federal authorities reported 24 acts of vandalism, including bombings, on U.S. abortion clinics.

Reprinted with permission of the *Toronto Star*, Wednesday, April 17, 1985, A25.

The following True/False questions enable you to review your knowledge of the major ideas of this chapter. Also, you will find the answers at the end of the text, as well as the relevant page numbers on which they appear. Try answering the questions within 24 hours of studying the chapter because your memory fades fast. A timely review helps "fix" the material in your mind and makes future studying much easier.

REVIEW QUIZ

True or False?

1. The messenger model is based on the premise that the human senses and nervous system are reliable and accurate perceivers and conveyors of reality messages.

2. A map is similar to but simpler than the territory it represents.

3. Science is similar to a news service.

4. Each year about 2 million husbands beat their wives.

5. The first test applied to a piece of news is the goodness of fit with personal experience.

6. Unlike scientific observations, facts in the daily news often turn out to be fuzzy.

7. Another test applied to a piece of news is its goodness of fit with personal beliefs and expectations.

8. Most observations, including those made by scientists, carry with them regions of doubt or uncertainty.

9. Most articles submitted by researchers to scientific journals are published.

10. Some observations are objective in the sense that different observers agree on what is observed.

11. Scientists avoid the word, "cause," and instead of talking about cause and effect, they talk about antecedents and consequences.

12. The key ingredients of the scientific method are common sense, systematic observation, systematic experimentation, probabilistic thinking, and theory generation.

13. GIGO, a favorite acronym of computer scientists, means "get in/go on."

14. Observational science provides prediction and control, whereas experimental science is aimed at description.

15. One strategy for untangling hereditary and environmental antecedents is to study identical twins separated at birth and reared apart.

16. Scientists rely on mathematical and statistical models to help them estimate the degree of certainty or confidence they can afford to have in their observations, predictions, and conclusions.

17. Theorists provide researchers with speculations about the potentially important and powerful antecedents, and in so doing guide or steer research.

18. The discipline affiliations of scientists focusing on cultural level antecedents and consequences include experimental psychology and biology.

☙ 2 ☙

The Languages of Science

———————— **Chapter Goal** ————————

*To introduce you to the three languages of
science that researchers use to describe
different layers of experience or analysis,
ranging from observational to speculative.*

INTRODUCTION

> *He is coming . . . I know by my heart . . .
> by my ears . . . by my eyes.*

An anthropology professor told of an Indian tribe that "labeled" the sources of their information, or in other words tried to identify the "messengers" on whose information they based their conclusions. Thus, one Indian might decide that a loved one was returning, and in doing so rely on messages from their heart. Furthermore, they might trust that message for weeks without corroborating messages from their ears or eyes, or from the eyes of others. Similarly, families of Vietnam veterans missing in action for years trusted messages from the heart.

Science too must rely on messages from many messengers. Fuzzy messages arrive from hidden sources, and so we must try to pick up their echoes, or tracks, or shadows. We seek messages from the very tiny and the very distant by attempting to decode the ghostly tracks on the screens of microscopes and telescopes. We seek messages from deep inside individuals by attempting to decode the pattern of ticks they place on questionnaires or rating scales, or by attempting to decode the meaning of changes in the tonality and rhythm of their speech as they flow across video screens. Because science relies on different messengers, delivering messages—ranging from very clear to very fuzzy—science, like the Indian tribe, needs to reflect in its language the source and quality of the messages it uses to construct maps of ghostly worlds that lay hidden within the atom or inside your mind.

SCIENCE SPEAKS WITH THREE TONGUES

If you think of reality as multilayered—some layers visible to the outer eye, and others only perceived, or imagined, by the mind's eye—you gain a clearer understanding of science. Scientific language acknowledges these distinctions between observation, speculation, and formal theory.

Similarly, our everyday language acknowledges a multilayered reality and identifies surface as well as hidden layers:

Laughing on the outside, crying on the inside.

Which layer is true—the visible laughing layer or the invisible crying layer? Both are true—in their way.

The visible laughing layer is *publicly* true; the message is clear. The words "laughing on the outside" are tied to *objective* behavior. It is a public fact that you are laughing. This statement, with supporting evidence (direct observation or a photograph) would stand up in a court of law, or in a court of science.

Fine. But how can we determine the "facts" or the quality of the message about the invisible layers? How do we determine the truth about the part of the statement that describes "crying on the inside"—on what message or messenger does it rely?

We have at least three obvious options in deciding the accuracy of statements describing the invisible layers of nature and experience.

First, we can conclude that such a statement as "crying on the inside" cannot either be proved *or* disproved because it isn't tied to anything objective—to anything available for public inspection—the message is too fuzzy. Furthermore, we can continue to adopt such an "open-minded" stance until someone figures out how to make "inside crying" objective—until someone figures out how to "part the curtains" that cover that hidden event so we can measure it, see it, photograph it, or weigh it.

Our second alternative in deciding the accuracy of statements is to agree that the statement is *subjectively* true, even though its public truth remains indeterminant. In this second option the truth or falsity of the statement becomes a matter of personal opinions or convictions anchored to internal images and feelings—to what is called *phenomenology*.

Or third, we can agree that both kinds of information—objective and subjective—help us explore and map nature's many layers. This third position anchors confidence in objective evidence but recognizes that we must make many critical decisions in the absence of adequate objective evidence (choosing a mate, prescribing a new treatment for depression, evaluating the risk of nuclear waste). Therefore we must learn to get by with a few concrete observations, bolstered by a network of subjective, invisible, or indirect evidence—we must rely on "guesstimates," on what we feel, or sense, or hypothesize lies below the surface or behind the curtains of the future.

This third alternative reflects the view of science as a news service that not only relies on objective observations (facts) but also relies heavily on speculative frameworks concerning: (1) what lies beneath the surface facts; (2) what lies beyond current facts; and (3) hypotheses about hidden relationships, or mechanisms, that tie available facts together. Each of us maps our world using messages that we trust. To the extent different people trust different messages they draw radically different maps and so experience different "realities." We anchor our beliefs on different, highly trusted messages; we cannot afford to question too many of our beliefs at any given time or our world falls apart. On what solid foundations does your world rest?

> "What you have told us is rubbish. The world is really a flat plate supported on the back of a great tortoise." The scientist gave a superior smile before replying, "What is the tortoise standing on?" "You're very clever, young man, very clever," said the old lady. "But it's turtles all the way down." (Hawking, 1988, p. 1)

By means of objective and speculative descriptions, or maps, science reduces our sense of uncertainty in selected regions of that infinite antecedents-consequences-chance network we call reality.

Science = Observations + Speculations
Science draws maps of reality based on perceptual messages and trusted speculations.

Sophisticated consumers of science appreciate that "facts" represent the tip of the scientific iceberg—appreciate that the underlying superstructure of science consists of logical and speculative frameworks that support and link the surface facts together.

The simple local bit of news that "She's laughing on the outside but crying on the inside" contains the basic ingredients of complex scientific puzzles. It includes *observations* and *speculations*.

Observation 1:
   "She's laughing."—*All* observers agree!
Observation 2:
   "The laughing seems forced."—*Some* observers agree.

Speculation 1:
"She's happy. She's really happy! Simple as that."—*Some* observers make this speculation.

Speculation 2:
"She's happy, but a bit nervous in a new situation."—*Some* observers make this speculation; perceptual messages plus editorial speculation.

Speculation 3:
"She's really sad, but putting up a good front."—*Some* observers make this speculation; strong editorial speculation, perhaps based on prior personal experience.

Like scientific news, the analysis of this statement includes some observations about which all reporters agree, some observations about which only some reporters agree, and alternative conflicting explanations or speculations about possible but "invisible" connections or relationships between the surface layers and the hidden layers, or regions of uncertainty.

Many times each day you spontaneously make such differentiations; distinctions between "hard" news (he spoke for 45 minutes) and "soft" news and speculation (he's a closet Democrat, not a real Republican); or his *reported* IQ score is 103 (hard news), but he's much brighter than that; his academic potential is very high (soft news or speculation).

Furthermore, we recognize that what is perceived to be hard news by some (he definitely has high academic ability) may only be confident speculation masquerading as fact. On the other hand, such "observers" may be the early detectors of "emerging hard news" that will eventually become publicly available—everybody laughed at poor Ignaz Semmelweis and his crazy belief that invisible bugs cause disease until emerging germ *theory*, the invention of the microscope (*technology*), and a host of systematic observations and experiments (*research*) brought the ghostly bugs into public view and scientific respectability.

Just as you now distinguish between hard and soft, or fuzzy observations, and between casual and disciplined speculations in attempting to make sense of local news, you will learn to make sense of scientific news with the aid of the same distinctions. And you would be wise to do so because each day "you bet your life" on scientific observations and speculations and their subsequent technical spin-offs, and professional and "expert" interpretations of messages. Each layer in the communication chain inherits and contributes regions of uncertainty—more or less— to the air you breathe; the water you drink; the brake pedal you push; the aircraft you recline in; the nuclear power station down the road; the health advice and treatment you take; the counseling and "expert" advice you receive on everything from diets to dying.

Science and its technological and professional satellites constitute "strong stuff"—for good or ill—and so are worthy of both appreciative and critical attention. If you learn to listen, most scientists and many technicians and professionals will freely disclose the degrees of confidence they have in the different messages underlying their observations, predictions, and speculations or theories. In our search for peace of mind and certainty we often filter out the qualifiers scientists build into their language.

Each individual scientist, and each scientific specialty, must work not only with the "facts," but also with the logic, and the hunches of their era. Our purpose in this book is to discuss how scientists evaluate alternative guesses about reality and how you, as a consumer of science, can evaluate scientific guesses by fine-tuning skills you already possess. As you improve these skills you will better learn to distinguish robust scientific observations from flimsy ones and to distinguish casual and sloppy scientific speculations from disciplined ones.

This view of science as an evolving speculative map with observational checkpoints not only helps protect you from pseudoscience but also can yield an enriched understanding of your world. Such a perspective might even lead you into a scientific career, where you join others exploring and mapping the fascinating and shifting surfaces of human experience.

Consumers of science, like its practitioners, will understand and appreciate its products as well as its arguments to the degree they understand the three types of language that scientists use to describe nature's many layers.

Each of the three languages focuses on different levels of description. The first, *observational language*, focuses on the exposed, currently accessible, or "factual" layers of nature. The second, *speculative language*, focuses on the hidden, speculative, or subjective layers of nature. The third, *formal language*, focuses on the logical, mathematical structures or models that scientists use to build formal frameworks, or symbol systems, to help link together their observations and speculations, and to help them predict new observations. A famous example of such a formal framework or symbol system is Einstein's formal speculation that $E = MC^2$.

The Three Languages of Science

In considering the three languages of science, remember that all language consists of symbols (spoken or written) and rules for their use. Keeping this in mind, pay particular attention to the different rules employed in observational language, as opposed to speculative language, as opposed to formal language.

Observational language (semantics)   Observational or "objective" or semantic language deals with realms of high certainty, as discussed in Chapter 1. Such language refers to clear observations and connections between antecedents and consequences. Even traditional opponents, such as Republicans and Democrats, feminists and male chauvinists, Arabs and Jews, could agree about the main boundaries of such observations, could agree that the observations are surrounded by a very small region of uncertainty (e.g., 198 pounds plus or minus 1).

Remember all language consists of symbols (spoken or written) and rules for their use. Observational language (semantics) employs

1. Symbols or labels
2. Rules for linking them to concrete objects or events

The key rule in using objective language states: "Different observers, familiar with the symbols and the events in question, can *independently* and *consistently* tie a particular label to a particular object or event."

The following examples will help clarify this rule as well as indicating how it is both practiced and broken regularly in everyday language.

1. *"That man weighs 198 pounds."* In this example you are familiar with the symbols (the language); you can identify the key object as it (the man) has been *pointed* out to you; and you are familiar with the rules for tying them together—that is, with the procedures for weighing the man. You know how to assign weight numbers to him—you can do it independently (alone) and consistently (repeatedly) and within a reasonable time period assign more or less the same numbers.

Here we have a clear instance of objective language: we know the symbol system; the key objects (the man and the scales) are publicly available; the procedure for combining them (weighing) is common knowledge; the procedure for labeling the result (assigning a weight number to the man) is agreed upon. So we end up with a solid observation that can be made independently and consistently by most adult members of the culture.

2. *"Tuo mies painaa yhdeksankymmenta kiloa."* Since you probably don't understand this particular symbol system, you cannot judge the objectivity of the statement—not until you learn the language or have someone translate it for you. If you did, it would translate from Finnish as "That man weighs 90 kilograms"—which is about 198 pounds.

But for all you know, it might have said, "198 angels can dance on the head of a pin." So to judge whether a statement meets the rules of objective language you must know the language, or system of labels; the object or events in question; and the rules for labeling them. Just because numbers are used doesn't mean that the statement is objective.

3. *"That woman is highly intelligent."* Here you are familiar with the symbols (the language), and you can identify the woman objectively (she's being pointed at). But how do you decide *objectively* whether the label "highly intelligent" can be tied to her? Although the woman is publicly visible, her intelligence is not.

Unlike her weight, you don't know how to measure her intelligence. After watching her and asking her questions, the same observers who could agree about her weight cannot agree about her intelligence—some label her as being of average intelligence, some label her as highly intelligent, and a few label her as stupid.

One way to handle such problems is to delegate them to an expert, in this case to a psychologist to "test" the woman and "label" her. The psychologist reports back that the woman's IQ (intelligence quotient) is 132, and since, by custom, all people with IQs over 125 are labeled "highly intelligent," she is so labeled.

As a consumer of science, are you satisfied? You may know nothing about I.Q. testing; however, you need to know little to decide whether you're dealing with objective language. First, you know that numbers may mean nothing. Next, you know that to be classed as objective language, labels must be assigned independently *and* consistently by different observers, or, if delegated, by different experts. Since only one expert has tested the lady and tested her only once, the argument can't be settled, not until at least two independent experts each test her twice. Let's say this is done and the first expert reports scores of 132 and 129, while a second reports scores of 125 and 128.

So, the different consumers of science may now agree that the woman has a high IQ—125 or higher. But they will probably continue arguing about whether or not she is "highly intelligent"—some observers saying, "If she's so smart how come she can only get high marks in math and not history, and how come she's so stupid socially, and so dumb with her money?"

In brief, wise consumers of science learn to distinguish objective language—independent and consistent labeling—from speculative language—from subjective language, and special interest group labeling. They learn as well to recognize that similar labels can differ greatly in their degree of objectivity—as do the labels "intelligence quotient" and "intelligence." Finally, informed consumers learn to see science as an expanding system of guesses, an evolving landscape with outcroppings of high-certainty observations. Starting from these outcroppings, scientists explore different lines of speculation that extend beneath the surface and beyond the horizon. Each new observation creates vantage points for disappointment or excitement, for radically revised or more confident speculations, and for starting points for new explorations.

When using observational language—which identifies these objective outcroppings, or hard news surface layers—we will enclose the object or event under discussion in a heavy bordered circle

or in a heavy bordered circle nested in a narrow, dotted, surrounding circle to indicate a small region of uncertainty:

When a scientist or any expert makes a statement, a consumer has every right to inquire (1) what parts of the proposition describe an observed outcropping, (2) what parts represent speculation—disciplined or casual, and (3) whether the statement is a stewpot of observational and speculative language. We now turn our attention to speculation and to stewpot labels—to speculative language.

Speculative language (pragmatics) Speculative language involves tying symbols to unobservables, like mental images, hopes, fears, ghosts, the past, the future, the hidden (like guilt or innocence in some trials). How do we tie the label guilty to people? We certainly don't do it by having each member of the jury go into a separate room and decide whether to label the suspect innocent or guilty. Why? Because each of us experiences a different chain of trusted messages, and we would not get agreement or consistency, as demanded by the rules of objective language. Rather, when an event is surrounded by a large region of uncertainty which, by definition, unobservables are bound to be, we rely on group pressure, negotiation, fatigue, and cultural or peer group norms to bring about more or less consistent labeling to force a decision regardless of the different message chains experienced by different jurists.

> **The key rule in using speculative language is that labels are assigned to reflect cultural and group modeling, instruction, and pressure.**

We can readily cast our mind's eye into regions of "pure specula-tion." What images do you have of "heaven," or "hell," or "life on another planet," or the "edge of the universe," or of your old age? Such specula-tions are "pure" in the sense that they are currently devoid of objective outcroppings. Therefore, observational language is inappropriate except when used in an obviously metaphorical or analogical sense: "I imagine heaven to be like Miami Beach on a big expense account with me con-trolling who comes and goes." Or "I imagine life from outer space would look like. . . ." Through history, professional "healers" have speculated about and prescribed treatments on the basis of demons, humors in the air, invisible bugs, nerves, and so forth.

Similarly, theorists explore realms of uncertainty, devising possi-ble networks, relationships, connections, hypotheses, and theories. They may be searching for a cure for the common cold or for cancer, studying the structure and dynamics of personality, exploring the possible mech-anisms of forgetting, or inventing different models of intelligence.

When using speculative language, which identifies high-uncertainty regions, we will enclose the contents in dotted or hatched circles, as shown in Figure 2–1, or show spreading—concentric—regions of uncertainty, with small, heavily bordered circles nested within them to indicate that they contain some isolated or linked objective outcroppings—crude empir-ical reference points, as depicted in Figure 2–2.

Objective outcroppings or discoveries, represented by observational language, are the bench marks of science. Scientific explorations begin from such "observational checkpoints." Scientists use them to find their bearings and to avoid becoming lost in speculative space. It is a new ob-jective landfall they seek to discover or uncover in their explorations and experiments. Although these objective checkpoints represent the naviga-tional aids of science, the bulk of scientists spend their time drawing and exploring speculative maps between or beyond observational check-points—some staying close to the observational outcroppings, some ranging "far out" in speculative space into high-uncertainty regions of the network, where antecedents, consequences, and chance play unfa-miliar—sometimes weird—games.

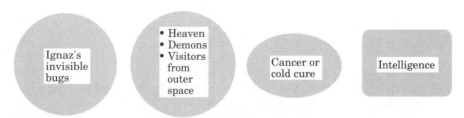

FIGURE 2–1   Most Words Have Fuzzy Meanings

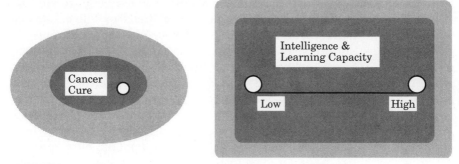

FIGURE 2–2   Regions of Uncertainty Surround Words

What are the tools for exploring speculative space? According to a Nobel prize winner, they are simple:

> In theoretical physics we use simple tools: pencil, paper, eraser, chair, and table. More important than these is the wastebasket. Almost any idea that occurs to a physicist is wrong. (Murray Gell-Mann, 1985, p. 94)

As you can appreciate, every observational checkpoint (like an intelligence quotient) can spawn a host of messages or speculations (about its genetic or environmental origins, about its importance in shaping your personal and professional future). Therefore the large speculative maps of science are relatively sparsely spotted with observations and will remain so, for each new observational checkpoint generates a cornucopia of speculative maps—some focusing their guesses closely around the observational outcropping, some linking the observation to other close or distant outcroppings, some linking it to safe, and some to radical guesses.

This view of science, as perhaps one part observation and many parts speculation, is what led Einstein to refer to science as "a system of guesses" (Einstein & Infeld, 1966, p. 30).

This multilayered view of reality is also reflected in the following quotation by Einstein:

> Physical concepts are free creations of the human mind, and are not, however it may seem, uniquely determined by the external world. In our endeavour to understand reality we are somewhat like a man trying to understand the mechanisms of a closed watch. He sees the face and the moving hands, even hears it ticking, but he has no way of opening the case. If he is ingenious he may form some picture of a mechanism which *could* be responsible for all the things he observes; he may never be quite sure his picture is the only one which could explain his observations. He will never be able to compare his picture with the real mechanism and he cannot even imagine the possibility or the meaning of such a comparison. But he certainly *believes* that, as his knowledge increases, his picture of reality will become simpler and simpler and will explain a wider and wider range of his

sensuous impressions. He may also believe in the existence of the ideal limit of knowledge and that it is approached by the human mind. He may call this ideal limit the objective truth. (Einstein & Infeld, 1966, p. 31)

In this view of science as a system of guesses and imperfect observations based on fuzzy messages, we must become skilled at recognizing disciplined, as opposed to casual or sloppy, speculations. We need to develop a sense of how such systems evolve.

For example, consider how a series of observational checkpoints and speculations helped us zigzag our way to a more powerful system of guesses and treatments of illness, including "fever deaths."

LANGUAGE TYPE	OBJECTS AND EVENTS COVERED
1. Objective checkpoint (observational language)	Some people get recurring fever and die.
2. Popular speculation (speculative language—invisible layer or cause)	Fevers caused by "demons" occupying person's soul or body.
3. Observational checkpoint	Poor Harold Winch who died of fever was cursed by old Nell Blackstock at tavern last Michaelmas.
4. Enlightened speculation (invisible humors)	Illness not caused by demons, but by humors in air—by bad air. Keep windows closed.
5. Observational checkpoint	People who live in swampy areas get the fever.
6. Speculation	Fever caused by swamp "gas"—fits bad-air speculation theory.
7. Observational checkpoint	People who live on high ground or move from swamp areas don't get fever (further support for bad-air speculation).
8. Observational checkpoint	Some people who live in swampy areas don't get fever, and some people who live on high ground do.
9. Speculation	Supporters of demon speculation see this as support for their theory—demons travel everywhere.
10. Alternative speculation	Supporters of bad-air theory generate patch-up speculations—some bad air drifted to high ground, some swamp dwellers live on second floor so don't get so much bad air.
11. Emerging speculation	Maybe illness not caused by demons or bad air, but by invisible bugs (beginning of germ theory).
12. Observational checkpoint	Many mosquitos in low swampy areas.
13. New speculation	Maybe mosquitos carry fever—maybe they inject invisible bugs when they bite.

With the aid of further speculation and the discovery of the microscope, the "malaria" carried by mosquitos was identified.

Notice the leapfrogging from observations to speculation to observations—with observations providing a focal point around which speculations gravitate and fan out. Some speculations stimulate the search for and discovery of additional observational checkpoints, some of which fit the given speculation, some of which don't, thus generating patchwork speculations. Here we get a sense of the rhythm of science as it wends its zigzag way through nature's veils, very much a joint venture of the outer and inner eyes, very much a complex mix of observational and speculative language, which to the untrained ear sounds "observational."

The malaria example provides a view of multilayered reality; an *objective surface layer* including fever, death, and concentration of fever in certain areas. We see too the selective linking of *observations*: death by fever is linked to encounters with old women or death by fever is linked to living in swamp areas. We see as well *speculations* about invisible or vague layers or causes: demons, humors in the air, invisible bugs.

Notice the mosquitos were "invisible" in a sense, as were hundreds of other "swampy" objects or events until a chance observation or speculation made them suspect. Certainly germs were invisible and remained so until a mutually reinforcing combination of speculation (Ignaz Semmelweis's medically unpopular invisible bug theory) and improved technology (the microscope) moved germs from the level of crude guesses to a sophisticated framework of speculation linking hundreds of internationally tested observational checkpoints.

Of course, speculation continues. Speculation, and science, gravitate around differences, around exceptions. For example, not all people who get fever have been publicly cursed by an old woman (a witch). So "believers" speculate that witches could curse you secretly from a distance—a patchwork, but effective, speculation for those who believe in witchcraft.

Not all people who encounter germs get the disease. Why? Well, maybe they have "something" inside—a stronger disease-fighting system. Here we go again! Some scientists focus their speculation and research on outside sources of disease—cigarettes, liquor, bad air (pollution), new invisible bugs (viruses)—while others focus their speculation and research on inside sources of explanations like the body's immunological system—much of which is still vague and invisible.

So then how do we decide which speculations to believe—to publish, to give research funds to, to teach, to try out? We can't rely only on the objective rules because they illuminate only a tiny fraction of our vital questions. While scientists can usually agree that the patient died or got better—an observational checkpoint—there are always several schools of thought (schools of speculation) as to why the patient died or got better. Some speculators bet that it's due to a new virus; others that it has something to do with the immunological system, or God's will, or the patient's "will to live."

Since we don't get *independent* and *consistent* agreement among the observers about the answers to many important questions, we have to resort to other decision rules for deciding which speculations to accept. The decision rules or methods we use to judge speculative language are the rules of majority vote, expert *judgment*, group pressure, force, and argument. The guesses, or maps, of science are judged by rules similar to those used in the courts of justice.

The court of speculation   Proponents of a given theory or speculation each present their stewpot of objective evidence and speculative linkages, and then the jury of scientific "peers" or a group of scientific "judges" chooses the "strongest" case, which prevails until a theory with a stronger case evolves.

The courts of justice represent our most familiar public means of labeling stewpots of objective and speculative evidence. They give up all pretense of aiming for independent labeling—relying instead on coaching and group pressure to achieve agreement. In the courts, observers are coached first by lawyers of the prosecution and then by defense lawyers concerning which parts of the stewpot of evidence to "see" as hard objective evidence and which parts as soft; they are coached and cajoled concerning what should be seen as a reasonable speculation and what as weak conjecture. Even then each jury member is not permitted to retire to a private place to *independently* reach his/her decision. No, they are locked together in order to let group pressure, argument, and fatigue generate agreement on what labels to apply to the regions of uncertainty—to the fuzzy and conflicting flow of messages.

Although foregoing the rule of observer independence, courts still provide opportunities to test the consistency of labeling through the appeal process. While costly, retrials and review boards provide tests for the consistency of judicial labeling—tests of the consistency with which the important labels "innocent" or "guilty" are applied.

In some "courts" we use a judge rather than a jury. Here we still provide for argument and coaching, but delegate the labeling of innocent or guilty not to a jury of peers but to one "expert," who does not pretend to be completely objective but rather aims to choose and label the "stronger" case. Once again (recognizing that even for experts guilt or innocence lies partly, perhaps significantly, in the eye of the beholder) opportunities for appeal and retrial are provided.

In the case of the Supreme Court, we have several judges (a panel of experts) hear the arguments and then vote—relying ultimately on a majority rule to assign the label of guilt or innocence.[1]

In science as well as the courts, majority vote by peers and by senior judges (journal editors, research grant committees) plays a pow-

[1]For one fascinating "picture" of how the U.S. Supreme Court labels its stewpots of evidence, see Woodward and Armstrong (1981).

erful role in deciding which mix of observational evidence and speculation receives grant funds, is published, or is awarded Nobel prizes. In science as well as the courts, such judgments are influenced by which judges preside—whether, as is usual, a preponderance are "establishment" scientists or whether, by accident or sloth, a majority of "radical" speculators or a block of "reactionaries" have gained control—of a journal, a research funding agency, or an award-giving institution.

Nevertheless, "cases" are continuously under review in science, through its journals and conferences. Granted, certain cases receive more press and more sympathetic judgments than others, but the popularity of given observational checkpoints and related speculations shift with time.

Thus to what extent the scientific "bench" is loaded by "demonologists," "pollutionists," "germ sleuths," or "immunologists" strongly influences the flow of scientific funds, information, and awards.

As a consumer of science you need not, and cannot, be informed about the intricacies of the judging process, but you would be wise to keep informed about which "school" of scientists presides on the major courts of science—in the main they will probably be "establishment" scientists with a sprinkling of scientific reactionaries and radicals raising "unreasonable" speculations and arguments. Gradually, as was the case with fever, the reactionaries (the demonologists) will be displaced by the current establishment members (the germ hunters), who in turn will be displaced by one of the new radical schools (immunology), who then become the establishment school, *for a while*. Then of course new "radicals," or scouts, will vie for positions on the leading edge of the discipline.

And so science evolves, with each passing theory or speculation giving way to a more powerful successor after having played a significant role, in its time. A scientific theory is a highly edited set of messages providing stepping stones on a zigzagging exploration of multilayered "reality." A given theory reflects the scientific beliefs and technology of the times; as the beliefs and technology change so too do scientific theories.

Formal language (syntactics)   Not only do scientists rely on objective language to provide observational checkpoints and on speculative language to help map the endless uncharted regions between and beyond observational checkpoints, but science relies too on formal language to provide powerful simplifications and models of nature's Chinese puzzle boxes.

Symbol relationships

Formal language, or syntactics, involves tying symbols not to natural outcroppings, nor to unobservable images, but to other symbols. The rules of the symbol game are determined by group agreement among peers, among mathematicians and logicians.

The accepted practitioners of formal language share certain assumptions, or axioms and rules, and explore the symbol space so contained, just as we were all instructed to explore the symbol space of plane geometry—the shortest distance between two symbol points is a straight line . . . on a plane, but not on a curved surface . . . ah yes!

Formal language, or syntactics, like grammar, deals with abstractions, with relations between symbols.

$$1d + 2d = 3d$$

These abstract relations are powerful shapers of our thought patterns. They carry with them (or suggest) observational chunks and speculative packages that restrict or channel our thinking into habitual modes, along habitual tracks. Deviation from these modes is jarring.

$$1d + 2d = 1d$$

"That's not right! What are you talking about?"

1 drop + 2 drops = 1 big drop

"Oh, well, I thought you were talking about solid things—you didn't say that *plus* meant *pouring* and that *d* meant wishy-washy things like drops."

That's right; we didn't. But in playing such a trick, we make the point that when you describe relations in abstract, or observational, or speculative language, keep an eye on the underlying and surrounding assumptions. When you're not sure what the symbols mean, enclose them in a dashed/hatched circle: e.g., $\left(\dotplus\right)$ $\left(\dot{d}\right)$.

Some important abstract relations that provide habitual tracks for scientific minds to run along include the following:

1. *Equivalence relations*

   $A = B$

   Which can mean:
   a. There are one or more ways in which $A = B$ even though there are lots of ways in which they differ. For example, they're both male, or both psychologists, or both depressed, or both possess triangles, even though they may differ in other ways.

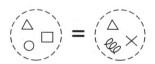

   b. *A* and *B* are identical on *all* dimensions. All dimensions? Well, that certainly doesn't apply to people, even identical twins, so that particular kind of equivalence relationship will have limited application in the behavioral sciences.

2. *Order relations*

> A is greater than B, and B is greater than C, therefore A is greater than C.
>
> $A > B$, and $B > C$, therefore $A > C$
>
> Which can mean that if A is taller than B, and B is taller than C, then A is taller than C.

This kind of abstract relation can provide a valuable track for the mind to carry *physical* information like height and weight and interestingly enough helps the mind make predictions about some physical observations that it has not yet made. But notice that this track is not so useful for carrying more complex information or making complex predictions. For example, just because the Dallas Cowboys can beat the Pittsburgh Steelers and the Steelers can beat the Houston Oilers doesn't mean that the Cowboys can beat the Oilers:

> $A > B$, and $B > C$, but A may not be $> C$

So, abstract statements that fascinate logicians and mathematicians and furthermore that can help describe and predict certain observations (stable physical observations) may be quite inappropriate for describing and predicting other kinds of complex and unstable observations.

In dealing with less stable phenomena which combine in dynamic ways, we rely on other abstract relations or complex mental pathways. For example, when we want to say that a given phenomenon A is tied in vague ways to many other phenomena we may say:

> $A = f, B, - C, D \ldots T \ldots e$

which may mean that the consequence A is a function of (is somehow tied to) the antecedents $B, - C, D, T,$ and e.

Now here is the kind of abstract relation, or mental track, that may be useful to help describe relationships (observations and speculations) of interest to social scientists and their consumers—the kind of mental track that can do justice to multilayered, shifting reality.

Notice when we ask how someone will behave, the answer, whether from a scientist or a friend, will include a statement equivalent to "It all depends." This is like saying A's behavior depends on (is a function of) a lot of antecedents: $B, - C, D \ldots T \ldots e$.

For example, it might depend on B (on what his best friend does) *and* depend on $- C$ (which means the opposite of what his parents advise) *and* depend on D (on what his girlfriend wants), *and* it might depend on T (on the time of day or the time of the week), *and* it will depend to a certain extent on e (on irreducible errors of prediction, on *chance* factors, on the fact that even scientists and best friends get surprised). Here we see that in certain areas the minds of scientists and knowledgeable laypeople run along similar paths of complex relations. Usually, however, when we're busy, or ignorant, or new to a field, or in a crisis, we ignore the fact that many antecedents influence human behavior, and instead practice a form of mental economy that allows our minds to run along simple tracks like:

$$A = f(B + e)$$

which means behavior A can be explained almost wholly by antecedent B, with a little unpredictability left over in e.

Such simple mental tracks reduce intellectual effort, allowing one so-called expert to conclude that personality (A) depends on genetics (B) or, just as simplemindedly, on environment (BI).

Similarly, as a result of being a novice or a bigot, other simple tracks let our brains compact complex information into oversimplified mind-sized packages:

A	=	f	B	e
Behavior	depends on		Sex	?
			or skin color	?
			or intelligence	?
			or political affiliation	?
			or area of experience	?
			or genetics	?
			or etc.	?

Although it can be argued that our brains perform magnificent feats of storing and processing information, nevertheless our capacity for short-term memory is very limited. We normally can handle only one short train of thought at a time.[2] Therefore, most of our mental traffic involves messages about simple relationships. However, when we focus on something repeatedly, our minds develop more sophisticated paths to do justice to the multilayered and shifting relationships—like those we explore in science, or in friendship, or in a special hobby.

The scientific answer to a question generally takes the following form:

In any network a given consequence *depends upon* a variety of antecedents, acting independently and in various combinations— and don't forget the tricks those two rogues time and chance can play.

This is the kind of answer that a multilayered, changing universe deserves. Proper formal language doesn't talk about "real things," like

[2]Did you ever try to remember a new phone number as you walked through a noisy room?

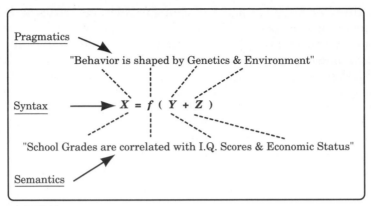

FIGURE 2–3

pigs, porcupines, or people. It only talks about abstractions as designated by symbols like: A's, B's, X's, +'s, and so forth.

In science we frequently link the three languages together and
make translations from one to the other. As indicated in Figure 2-3 we
might start out with the pragmatic statement: "Behavior is shaped by
genetics and environment." We could then translate that into a syntactic
statement: $X = f(Y + Z)$, which in abstract terms says there is one variable X that is a function (depends on, or is influenced by) two other variables Y and Z. Furthermore, we could translate this into semantics by
saying: School grades are correlated with IQ scores and economic status.

Linking formal and observational languages   Although formal
language focuses on abstract relations, such as addition, subtraction,
and multiplication in mathematics and "and," "or," and "not," in logic,
we frequently use abstract statements to provide shorthand descriptions
of parts of the observational world.

1 doctor + 2 doctors = 3 doctors

When we use formal language as a shorthand way to describe concrete objects and events, we will use special symbols in order to indicate
that we are talking about established observational checkpoints—ones
that can pass the test of independent and consistent labeling—and we
will enclose the symbol in a *solid* circle:

$$\textcircled{1d} \ + \ \textcircled{2d} \ = \ \textcircled{3d}$$

Such solidly enclosed symbols represent the solid outcroppings of
observational or semantic space, and so are reserved for objects and
events which have pretty clear boundaries—that is, things that strongly
excite our senses: our sight, like the sun does; and our smell, like a

skunk does; and our hearing, like a child's shriek of pain does; and our touch, like a needle does.

However, in science we don't rely only on our unaided senses; we augment our senses and their power in order to detect additional boundaries by extending our nervous system with technical probes and instruments.

Such extended sensory probes enable us to map multiple boundaries of nature—tiny boundaries like those of the virus; fragile boundaries like those of a single cell; distant boundaries like those of Venus and Mars—and not only their spatial boundaries but their temperature and weight boundaries as well.

In the behavioral and social sciences we extend our casual observations by designing more sensitive probes and recording devices, ranging from carefully structured interviews to intelligence tests and questionnaires. These methods and devices include careful case histories; systematic study of historical documents and records; one-way observation rooms; and Skinner boxes. They also include automatic computer-assisted systems that deliver a preset program of antecedents and record a variety of responses or consequences, all precisely timed and with careful attempts to keep stray or chance elements out of the "network."

The "reality" you locate depends on the probes and detectors you use; the surfaces or boundaries you identify, or invent, depend on what you bring with you to the network; for example, your world is much emptier of smells and sounds than the rich variety a dog detects in the same "location"—the same space/time network. Similarly, while you can't locate snowflakes in a darkened room by throwing a baseball—baseballs don't bounce back after striking snowflakes—you can, however, readily locate them by throwing photons at them (by using a flashlight) because light waves or particles do bounce off snowflakes. And sometimes when we're strongly "set" to see or hear or catch a given signal, our mind's eye or ear can manufacture it out of the noise that emanates from every network. The experience we capture, the categories we use, the reality we construct depends both upon the organism doing the exploring (be it bat or human, Democrat or Republican) and upon the environment being explored (be it auditory or visual, tactile or gustatory).

Some of our social science probes are so "heavy" they demolish the event we seek—probes like clumsy interviews and questionnaires—while others are so "light" they don't penetrate below the surface of white lies, or contrived responses, and so we record and count lies and fuzzies—like the notion that the average person typically has 8 sexual fantasies a day, as "reported" in the first chapter.

Does this kind of thinking make you stop and wonder how many boundaries or layers of reality remain to be explored and how many "teeming" regions of a network appear empty only because the "inhabitants" are demolished by our social science baseballs. Or, if they do respond, how often we fail to see, hear, feel, smell, or catch the "bounce back?"

As a notational aid, in the remainder of the book we use solid circles (◯) to indicate those parts of experience where our senses or probes "locate" clear or firm boundaries. We use hatched circles (⬚) to indicate regions where our senses or probes encounter uncertain or fuzzy boundaries. Quite simply, solid circles (◯) represent categories with clear boundaries where it's easy to tell whether something belongs inside or outside. Hatched circles (⬚) represent categories with fuzzy boundaries where it's difficult to tell whether something is in or out, or on the border.

Much of science and daily experience deals with vague and shifting boundaries and speculations about their relations—speculations about vague subatomic particles, viruses, genes, ailments, talents, personal relations, futures, heavens, or hells. For such fuzzy objects and events we need special symbols to indicate when we are talking about uncertain or imaginary boundaries.

$$1 \text{ demon} + 2 \text{ demons} = 3 \text{ demons}$$

$$\overset{\frown}{1d} \quad + \quad \overset{\frown}{2d} \quad = \quad \overset{\frown}{3d}$$

$$1 \left(\cdot \right) \quad + 2 \left(\cdot \right) \quad = 3 \left(\cdot \right)$$

For most observers the term "demon" is empirically fuzzy or empty. Therefore, it can by symbolized by a fuzzy, hatched circle. We put a point in the middle. This point occupies no space, but it reserves a place just in case a speculative concept later captures some empirical content—just in case we invent a new probe (e.g., a more powerful theory or microscope) that helps us locate a stable boundary. Note the important role "points" play in geometry, namely a location that occupies no space—an excellent example of an empirically empty but highly functional symbol.

In addition to highly speculative terms like demons, undiscovered viruses, and distant futures that are currently empirically empty, a myriad of important terms possess some empirical or observational content surrounded by an area of doubt or speculation—terms, like genes, that have captured some observational content about which independent observers can agree but surrounding which there remain significant regions of disagreement or vagueness.

We are not here referring to concepts like your weight of 162 pounds, plus or minus a small region of speculation due to measurement errors, variations in the scales used, or angle of vision of the person reading the scales. Such concepts represent observational checkpoints and can be symbolized as a solid circle (◯) or, for accuracy's sake, a solid circle surrounded by a very narrow band of uncertainty or speculation (⬚).

Between such empirically full concepts as weight and height on the one hand and such empirically empty concepts as demons or imaginary subatomic particles on the other lie a host of concepts with varying degrees of observational content. Here we refer to important empirically anchored phenomena like intelligence, cancer, health, love, habits, genetics, learning, or marijuana. While surrounded by a fluctuating region of speculation, all these terms contain some reliable observational checkpoints about which independent observers can usually agree. We symbolize such empirically anchored, but not empirically full, concepts by enclosing one or more solid circles inside a dotted or fuzzy circle:

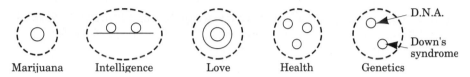

Marijuana   Intelligence   Love   Health   Genetics

For example, concerning genetics, while experts speculate and argue about the genetic contribution to most behavioral characteristics, they can agree specifically that Down's syndrome (mongolism) is strongly anchored to an observable abnormality on the 21st chromosome. Furthermore, different specialists can agree that a variety of observations indicate that IQ and certain forms of mental illness have genetic components. While they argue about how strong the genetic contribution is, they all assign it some empirical space.

Concerning intelligence, for example, specialists from very different schools would probably endorse the following general formula:

Intelligence $= f$(Genetics $+$ Environment $+ e$)

$$\text{⬭} = f\left(\text{⬭}_G + \text{⬭}_E + \text{⬭}_e\right)$$

Some specialists argue for a large genetic contribution and a small environmental one; they "see" a large genetic contribution:

$$\text{⬭} = f\left(\text{⬭}_G + \text{⬭}_\circ + \text{⬭}_\circ\right)$$

while other specialists argue just as strongly for the reverse weighting of environmental influences, "seeing" a large environmental component:

$$\text{⬭} = f\left(\text{⬭}_\circ + \text{⬭}_E + \text{⬭}_\circ\right)$$

Not only should the key terms in these statements be surrounded by circles of uncertainty but so should the linking symbols (=, *f*, +). In social science we probably assign these relating or linking symbols more precision than they deserve because of our experience with them in mathematics and physical science.

For example, anyone with a little high school math can determine the value of *X* given the value of *Y*, *Z*, and *e* in the following formula:

$$X = f(Y^2 + Z + e)$$

So if *Y* = 2 and *Z* = 3 and *e* = 1, then it can be readily determined that *X* = 8. Anyone who knows the language of algebra can make such calculations independently and consistently.

Furthermore, we all understand what it means to add together things with solid boundaries:

1 doctor + 2 doctors = 3 doctors

Here the plus sign means placing the objects physically together in one place, or in one bag, or in one room:

$$\textcircled{d} + \textcircled{d\ d} = \textcircled{d\ d\ d}$$

However, what does adding or a plus sign mean when you're trying to combine things that don't have clear boundaries?

1 demon + 2 demons = 3 demons

$$\textcircled{d} + \textcircled{d}\,\textcircled{d} = \textcircled{d}\,\textcircled{d}\,\textcircled{d}$$

Most of our students accept this equation, but a few question it. One says, "No! Demons combine not like blocks, but like drops of water." Therefore:

1 demon + 2 demons = 1 big demon

$$\textcircled{d} + \textcircled{d}\,\textcircled{d} = \textcircled{D}$$

Another student says, "Nonsense. When demons come together they instantly multiply, faster than rabbits, as fast as the speed of light." So:

1 demon + 2 demons = millions of demons

$$\textcircled{d} + \textcircled{d}\,\textcircled{d} = \frac{\textcircled{d}}{\textcircled{d}}\text{etc., etc.}$$

Without belaboring the point further, remember that our mathematical and logical ways of thinking are usually based on the big assumption that we are combining or subtracting relatively stable things with clear boundaries.

Now, keeping this point in mind, what does it mean to say:

$$X = f(Y^2 + Z + e)$$

here X = Intelligence ⟨o⟩

      Y^2 = Genetics ⟨o²⟩

      Z = Environment ⟨o⟩

      e = error and chance factors ⟨o⟩

In this formula all the key terms have vague boundaries, and furthermore we don't know whether the plus signs mean:

1. To add together like balls of wool or sticky marshmallows
2. To pour like water on Alka-Seltzer or like hot chocolate on ice cream; or to insert like seeds in soil, or a host of other alternatives

Although very vague, the formula is not empty. First it is not speculatively or theoretically empty. It advises us where to look in multilayered reality for connections—in genes and in the environment. Furthermore, it instructs us not to expect to find all the answers in either or in both of these layers combined. This is so because errors of measurement and chance factors play tricks with intelligence.

Second, the formula is not empirically empty; it includes some observational checkpoints. For example, while we may argue about who is the smartest student in a high school history class, we have no difficulty differentiating between the class members' intellectual abilities, individually or as a group, and those of students with Down's syndrome. In other words, we can independently and consistently label such obvious and extreme differences in intellectual ability.

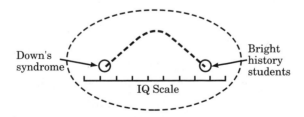

Furthermore, chromosome studies and studies of identical twins provide crude observational checkpoints for estimating genetic influences on all kinds of physical and psychological characteristics—some of which may or may not be linked to intelligence. Therefore, although our methods of studying genetic effects are still crude, we do possess some methods, such as microscopic studies of chromosomes and twin studies, that are starting to provide some observational checkpoints in the field.

In addition, reliable observational checkpoints have been mapped within the broad concept of *environmental* influences. Various specialists have mapped *extreme* differences in nutritional and social environments—for example, differences in nutritional deprivation and disease (e.g., measles) in pregnant females—and have also reliably mapped some of the extreme differences in the amount of parental "cuddling" given different infants. Therefore independent observers can consistently detect extreme differences on these dimensions, thus providing some observational checkpoints that may or may not be tied to intelligence.

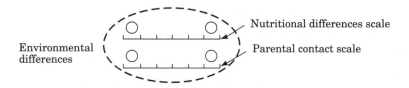

Once having mapped some of these extreme differences in intellectual abilities, in genetics, and in environment, we can then start to determine whether extreme differences in one appear to be linked to extreme differences in the other. Indeed, we discover that some linkages exist—strong linkages, for example, between some chromosomal abnormalities and intellectual deficit. We also find evidence, some of it controversial, showing that identical twins (genetically identical) score very much alike on IQ tests, even when raised apart.

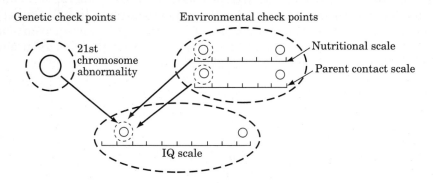

Thus we get some observational evidence supporting the speculation linking intelligence to genetics, but only crude evidence, limited usually to extreme cases. Similarly we have evidence linking extreme nutritional and social deprivation to low intelligence.

Now having some evidence supporting our overall speculation link-ing intelligence both to genetic and environmental factors, how do we put the genetic *and* environmental influences together—how do we com-bine them? What does the first plus sign in the following formula mean?

$$\left(\underset{IQ}{\circ\!\!-\!\!-\!\!\circ}\right) = f\left(\left(\circ\right) + \left(+\right) + \left(\circ\!\!-\!\!\circ\right) + \left(\circ\right)\right)$$

Genetics   Environment   Chance

Does it mean that they're to be added together in the traditional sense: 2 units of genetics + 2 units of environment = 4 units of intelligence? Not likely!

Some people think of "adding" in the sense of putting a seed in the soil—a seed represents the genetic contribution, and the soil represents the environmental contribution. As you can see, such a metaphor for "addition" suggests many questions about the relative contribution of the seed and the soil on a host of human characteristics.

Another popular way of defining how genetic and environmental influences combine, or add, involves using a rubber band analogy—with the band representing genetics and the stretching force representing the environmental factors. Notice that this analogy provides for very large environmental influences and so reflects a particular theoretical bias. Similarly, using the seed and soil analogy to represent the addition sign represents a theoretical bias as well—a genetic bias. These widely differ-ing analogies indicate that we are a long way from any precise knowledge of how genetics and environment combine. Therefore we should write our formula without plus signs or multiplication signs, merely saying that intelligence is "some" function of genetic factors, environmental factors, and chance factors, combined in complex, yet-to-be determined manners:

$$\left(\underset{IQ}{\circ\!\!-\!\!-\!\!\circ}\right) = \left(f\right)\left(\left(\begin{smallmatrix}\circ & \circ \\ \circ\end{smallmatrix}\right) \left(\begin{smallmatrix}\circ & \circ \\ \circ & \circ\end{smallmatrix}\right) \left(\circ\right)\right)$$

Genetics   Environment   Chance

The preceding formula involves large speculations dotted with observational checkpoints and linked together in complex and mysteri-ous ways.

The life expectancy of a scientific concept   When first appearing on the scientific scene, new concepts and linkages possess little empirical content—possess few observational checkpoints. No one knows how durable or expandable are these observational checkpoints. For example, do the new diseases (AIDS) and new treatments (interferon) represent recently discovered stable layers of reality, unreliable speculations, or passing tricks of chance? Will they grow into durable observational checkpoints:

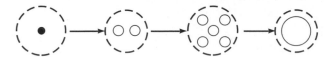

or will they melt away under the heat of close scrutiny? Or will they perhaps, for a time, reach a high level of respectability—like bloodletting—only to retreat to occupy a small or large space on the shelf of the history of failed speculations and chance observations—part of the wreck heap of discarded hypotheses on the Island of Research.

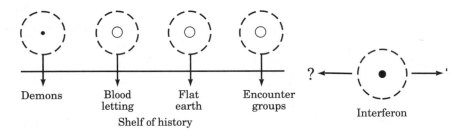

Demons   Blood   Flat   Encounter   Interferon
          letting   earth   groups
          Shelf of history

We have no Scientific Insurance Company to insure the life of a young scientific concept or speculation. For some people a concept may die in infancy; for others it may live on even after an official scientific burial. Demonology still lives in some cultures, for you can still kill a person with words or cast a spell and call it hypnosis. For many, mysterious humors in the air prevail, and we call them "pollution."

Perhaps we should use a verb rather than a noun to describe our explanations—call them "sciencing" rather than science. In this way we build an image of endless explorations through nature's infinite veils, of perpetual attempts to unveil and map the invisibles in the air, in the ground, in the organism, in the past, in the future, and map as well how they are all linked together.

Using formal language to decode scientific news   When examining a piece of scientific news, or an argument favoring a particular speculation or theory, you can better distinguish the observational from the speculative language by translating the story into formal language. Consider two examples, one dealing with drugs and the other, a bit more controversial, dealing with doctors.

Example 1: Consider the newspaper headline "VALIUM MAY BE LINKED TO CANCER." Translated into formal language we have:

Valium   linked to   cancer

Consider the *quantity* and *quality* of the observational checkpoints in the key terms "Valium," "cancer," and "linked to." The reporter, however, is sloppy, focusing on the millions of people who may be "eating cancer pills," rather than providing details concerning how many cases were involved in this study and how much Valium they were taking for how long. Nor does the reporter even mention alternative speculations. In science there are always *legitimate* alternative speculations. So we are left to do our own speculations concerning what the news release might mean. Certainly the statement remains essentially meaningless until the key term "linked to" is given some observational anchors. The following are examples of what the term "linked to" might mean in observational terms:

1. "I noticed my last four cancer patients were heavy and prolonged Valium users." (What a tiny observational checkpoint that is!)

2. "We found 60 percent of 4000 cancer patients used Valium regularly for three or more years." (Now here we have a larger observational checkpoint, but where is the evidence for using the words "linked to"? What about the other 40 percent, and what about the hundreds of thousands of people who have used Valium for three or more years with no evidence of cancer?)

3. "We find that many cancer patients are Valium users *but* that most started receiving Valium only after they learned they had cancer." (So . . . Valium may be more a symptom of cancer than a cause.)

4. "Valium users are frequently heavy smokers and drinkers, so it may be alcohol and nicotine that link Valium users to cancer—if indeed there is a linkage." (So again Valium may be found near cancer cases but as an innocent bystander or merely as a neighbor of the real villains, nicotine and alcohol.)

In brief, translating the statements of experts into formal language can frequently expose the claims to be loose rather than disciplined speculations, and can help protect the consumer of science from "scientific noise." Appended to this chapter is an example not only of good press coverage of the Valium-cancer controversy, but also of the risks a scientist runs by challenging the establishment.

As indicated in the preceding examples concerning Valium and cancer, consumers must learn to distinguish between the sloppy and the disciplined use of connecting terms like "caused by," "tied to," and "linked to," and to spot qualifiers like "*may* cause," "*reportedly* linked to," and "*suspected* tie between." Sure, creatures in outer space "may cause" your headaches, but on the basis of current observational checkpoints, it isn't ruddy likely. Now consider another unlikely example; or is it?

Example 2: "Doctors cause illness." We have a tendency to assume that, because two things or events appear frequently together they are somehow *intimately* tied together or that one "causes" the other. Often that's a useful assumption, but it can also be misleading or result in gross oversimplification. For example, because they appear together frequently or "hang around" together, someone might actually assume that:

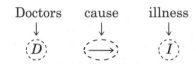

However, you "know" that's silly, and so you rewrite the statement as follows:

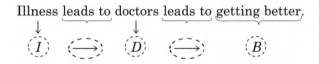

But wait. According to my doctor it's not quite that simple. He says, "Never go near a doctor unless you're really sick," because:

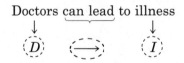

He writes the following formula covering doctors and illnesses:

Self-correcting illnesses	can lead to	doctors	can lead to	treatments + side effects + germ-filled waiting room	can lead to	big illness
↓	↓	↓	↓	↓	↓	↓
I	$\rightarrow$	D	$\rightarrow$	$T\!\!+$	$\rightarrow$	BI

So my doctor argues that because most illnesses are self-correcting, you should stay away from doctors. Furthermore, he observes that because all treatments carry some risk (side effects, addictions) and because germs gravitate to, and hang around, doctors, you could really get sick going for treatment. Now you see what a powerful tool formal coding can be. Or is this an example of irresponsible speculation?

SUMMARY

As both beneficiaries and victims of science, consumers require a clearer understanding of this most awesome human enterprise.

To understand science better, consumers must become more familiar with its three tongues. *Objective* language provides observational checkpoints on the surfaces of multilayered reality. *Speculative* language describes guesses about the unmapped regions lying between or beyond observational checkpoints. *Formal* language helps scientists describe in a shorthand, abstract manner the alternative ways in which observations and ideas may be linked together.

In the remainder of the book we examine various methods scientists use to establish observational checkpoints and to test speculations—in brief, to explore multilayered, moving reality. In the next section we commence with familiar and popular methods of tying speculations to observations. The "after-the-fact" and "before-and-after" methods are popular with everyone because they require little mental effort. However, as you may suspect, they are very prone to error. We discuss their weaknesses and strengths, and then introduce the premier method of experimental science, namely the control-group method. Although control groups help eliminate many of the weaknesses of the after-the-fact and before-and-after methods, we will discover that they, too, have their limitations.

EXAMPLE

Consumers Worry While Experts Disagree

SCIENTIST FIRED IN PILL CONTROVERSY[3]

The Valium controversy springs from a David-and-Goliath conflict involving an outspoken Montreal researcher, cautious international scientists, and a wealthy multinational drug company.

Dr. David Horrobin, 41, who sounded the alarm that there could be a link between Valium-like tranquilizers and cancer, lost his $40,000-a-year job at a Quebec research centre for his efforts.

[3]By Ellie Tesher, reprinted with permission of the *Toronto Star*, Monday, April 16, 1981, A2.

Hoffmann La Roche, the Swiss-owned company with $3 billion in total world revenue last year, responded to Horrobin's claims by citing sparse details of an unpublished private study and by relying on a hired consultant who refuted Horrobin and said no further studies were needed.

Now a significant number of leading scientists agree that tests to date are inadequate to assure that Valium is safe for public use, though it's been on the market for nearly two decades.

Won't Speak Out

The scientists say they've been reluctant to speak out on Horrobin's behalf because of traditional avoidance of publicity outside the academic community, and because of increasing financial restraints on new research.

Dr. Emmanuel Farber, of the University of Toronto, said emphatically, "In the case of a drug that millions of people are taking, somebody should be doing studies. There are many different ways available for studying tumor promotion. It's not mysterious."

Horrobin, widely considered to be a brilliant if unorthodox scientist, is a medical doctor and neurophysiologist trained at Oxford University. He discovered, in 1977, that when he fed diazepam [Valium] to rats with implanted breast tumors, the tumors grew to three times the size of those in rats without the drug.

Roche executives also claim that the Huntingdon study can be interpreted to prove that Valium doesn't enhance tumor growth, and that specific tests for tumor promotion aren't possible.

But Dr. Ian Henderson, of Ottawa's health protection branch, says he has yet to see the full data of the British study. So far he's only received a summary.

Henderson said it was "odd" that the study only used rats when conventional tests for cancer call for experiments with three animal species.

Dr. Donald Zarowny, 41-year-old medical director for Roche's Canadian operations, speaks with conviction.

"We feel that there is excellent data that totally absolves diazepam and Valium from causing or increasing the growth of tumors."

REVIEW QUIZ

True or False?

1. Phenomenology deals with subjective feelings and states.
2. The underlying superstructure of science consists of logical and speculative frameworks that support and link the surface facts together.
3. The qualifiers or caveats scientists employ in their language reflect the degrees of confidence they have in different observations, predictions and theories.
4. Scientists use four types of language to describe nature's many layers.
5. Formal language focuses on the exposed currently accessible or factual layers of nature.

6. Einstein's formula, $E = MC^2$ is an example of speculative language.

7. All language consists of symbols (spoken or written) and rules for their use.

8. A key rule in using objective language is that different observers, familiar with the symbols and the events in question can independently and consistently tie a particular label to a particular object or event.

9. The statement, "That woman is 5 feet, 9 inches tall" is an example of semantic language.

10. Whenever numbers are used in a statement, we are dealing with objective language.

11. Pragmatic language involves tying symbols to unobservables.

12. In observational language, a key rule is that labels are assigned to reflect cultural and group modeling, instruction, or pressure.

13. Which of many competing scientific theories or speculations receives support is determined by processes or criteria similar to those employed in the courts or justice system.

14. Syntactical language involves tying symbols to other symbols.

15. Established abstract relations are powerful shapers of thought patterns.

16. Equivalence relations and order relations are examples of observational language.

17. Assume A, B, and C represent observations of some kind; if A is greater than B and B is greater than C, then C must always be less than A.

18. The reality science describes is contingent on the probes and detectors that are used.

19. Many empirically anchored concepts, such as genetics or health, are surrounded by an area of ambiguity or uncertainty.

20. In science there are almost always legitimate alternative speculations to any given explanation.

꒰ 3 ꒱
After-the-Fact Method

―――――― **Chapter Goal** ――――――

*To introduce you to a flawed but nevertheless
most popular method for sorting fact from
fancy. You use it; doctors use it; the courts
use it; and scientists use it.*

INTRODUCTION

We believe what we want to believe.—Demosthenes

JOYCE: Willie, why did you punch the bus. That's really dumb.
WILLIE: That stupid bus driver must have seen us running. He did it on
purpose; and now I'll miss my psych quiz and I have a cold. Anyway everybody in my family has bad tempers, and you were late and. . . .

Is Willie searching for something he wants to believe, or is he being
an amateur scientist crudely tying speculations to an observation, trying
to make sense (after-the-fact) of why he punched the bus?

Embarrassed and holding his bruised hand, Willie looks inside his
mind and asks, "Why did I punch the dumb—and very solid—bus?" In
reply he receives several messages—several messengers respond from
deep in his cranium. One says, "Simple, you punched it *because* you
were going to be late for your psych exam." Another internal messenger
says, "No, all kinds of people miss buses and get frustrated, but they
don't punch buses! You did it *because* you come from a temperamental
family with cranky genes." Still another messenger chirps in, "Don't listen to that gene garbage. Your family is fine, and your genes are normal. You punched the bus *because* your head cold made you ornery!"
Finally, the last messenger, a real troublemaker, zips in and whispers,
"It's not your fault; it's Joyce's. She's always late and does it to show
she's the boss. Then naturally you get mad, and she calls *you* dumb. Get
rid of her *because* she's nothing but trouble!"

70

Poor Willie, which messenger should he believe? Each one champions a different reason, cause, or speculation of why he did that dumb thing. Which messenger should he believe or trust? Unlike the amputee with pains in his toes, who resolves his dilemma by trusting his external eyes, Willie's messages come from internal eyes or ears, and he's not sure at this time which one(s) to trust.

Scientific theories and methods attempt to identify the most trustworthy messengers and messages. Freud, the theorist, advised us to look at our animal ancestry (e.g., Willie's aggressive genes) for the most reliable messages or speculations about human behavior. According to Freud despite our pretty clothes and dainty table manners, underneath this thin veneer of civilization we remain mean, sexy beasts, and so, violent, sexy messages control our behavior. In a contrasting theory, the behaviorists tell us to ignore Freud's obsolete advice and instead look for environmental cues that trigger and reward different behaviors; perhaps Willie has learned that when he loses his temper the messengers he wants come running, that is, he gets attention or sympathy—except from Joyce. Hence, she triggers the messenger who whispers "get rid of her!" Notice then that different theories provide different advice about which type of speculations or messengers to trust.

In this chapter we consider the most popular and error-prone method of all for tying speculations to observations. When something unexpected happens and we want to know how or why it happened, we go back in time and attempt to reconstruct the past—or at least those aspects of the past that *appear* to be connected with the unexpected event. (This method differs from naturalistic observation, which focuses upon presently occurring events.) We face a variety of after-the-fact questions: Who or what led to the punching of the bus; the stomachache; the car breakdown; President Bush's defeat; the fall of Rome; the murder; or the nervous breakdown. Or, for that matter, what led to the development and acceptance of psychoanalysis? Subsequently, what led to its decline, and to the development and decay of behaviorism? Which of the many different or conflicting speculations or messengers should we believe and which messengers should we ignore? Recall that ancient kings knew how to deal with messengers bringing unwelcome news— they killed them. Being more civilized, we usually just *discredit the messenger.* Loyal Bush, or Clinton, supporters discredit negative messages about their man, and remember and repeat negative messages about the opponent. But the uncommitted voters who heard a run of negative messages about the economy tied them to Bush; he was no longer a trusted messenger.

How do we sort fact from fancy, messages to be trusted from those not to be trusted? We must do it every day using this crude after-the-fact method.

This popular method is used to study an individual (as in counseling or the courts), a family (as in social work or sociology), small groups (as in social psychology or sociology), and organizations and institutions (as in history or anthropology).

A CASE FOR THE COURTS

Our courts attempt to sift fact from fancy, to sift durable evidence from perishable evidence. An event occurs, and we trace back in time to find a likely suspect. For example, a crime is committed—a murder—and the investigators look out over the city, faced with an apparent impossible task—"Who did it?" Of all the thousands or perhaps millions of people out there, which person or mob played the key part in the crime? The prosecution must go back in time and attempt to tie the crime to a few selected people.

First, they must sort suspects from nonsuspects and then gradually separate the most likely suspects from the least likely. They continue screening until a group of neutral people, the jury, can decide beyond a reasonable doubt whether the crime can be tied to a given suspect. The jury must decide how closely the crime and the suspect are tied together. Is the suspect, for example, a lone plotter and executioner and therefore strongly tied to the crime? Or is he an unwitting accomplice and therefore only tied to the crime by a thin line?

The problem facing the court is a stewpot of observations and speculations collected after the event has occurred—or, as we call it, *after the fact*. After-the-fact situations face us daily, whether in the courtroom, the history class, the doctor's office, at an afternoon tea, a pub, or a garage. The problem is to select from a variety of suspects the one most strongly tied to, or leading to, the event of interest—whether it be a murder, a war, a pain in the stomach, an elopement, a lost football game, a car that won't start, or the causes of lung cancer.

The most common approach used in sifting suspects in these after-the-fact situations is sometimes known as the *case method*. It is a sieve with relatively big holes, one that permits a large amount of fancy to slip through with the facts. Nevertheless, this kind of sieve can be a powerful aid in narrowing down the number of suspects or alternatives, particularly when the person using it is aware of its limitations. We must be aware of the limitations of the particular method used in selecting the suspect; otherwise it is impossible to decide how much confidence the selection of a particular suspect warrants.

Consider the following methods of selecting suspects in a murder case:

Method 1:   fortune teller using crystal ball ("A tall dark stranger is the guilty one.")

Method 2: opinion of murdered man's wife ("The business partner is the guilty one.")

Method 3: pretrial judgment of the district attorney ("A hired gun from the West Coast is the guilty one.")

Method 4: decision of jury ("The jealous mistress is the guilty one.")

Method 5: retrial decision of jury ("Yes, the jealous mistress is the guilty one.")

It is apparent that these five different methods of deciding between suspects deserve different degrees of confidence.

In science, too, different methods of selecting suspects warrant different degrees of confidence. While the case method, for example, warrants more confidence than does casual opinion, it usually warrants less confidence than does the controlled experiment. Since the case method, however, is used in many fields in which other methods are difficult or impossible to employ, we must examine its strengths and weaknesses carefully.

The After-the-Fact or Case Method

This model is simple. An observation (O) is made. A murdered man is found, or a patient is diagnosed as depressed, or Diana slaps Charles. Next we attempt to decide what previous event (X) led up to O, or what previous events were necessary in order for O to happen. In the language of common sense we are asking what caused O. In the language of science we are asking what key antecedent(s) (X's) were linked to the selected consequence (O). There are usually several possible X's; that is, several antecedents (independent variables) that could lead to a given consequence (dependent variable) and the problem is to select the most probable one or ones: X_1? X_2? X_3? . . . , X_n? When our murder victim is first discovered, there are a large number of X's or suspects.

Possible
suspects

Harvey found
shot to death

How do we narrow down the number? What aids do we use to sort the most likely suspects from the least likely ones? Our decision aid is *time*. When the time of death is determined to within two hours, all suspects who have reasonable alibis for the shooting time (1:00 A.M. to 3:00 A.M.) are separated from those who do not. Notice we say "reasonable alibi" because we can't be dead certain in each case; hence an area of uncertainty remains.

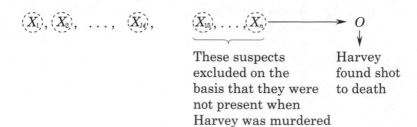

These suspects
excluded on the
basis that they were
not present when
Harvey was murdered

Harvey
found shot
to death

Thus perhaps all but 14 of the original suspects go free.

Let us narrow the list of suspects still further, this time using the decision aid of *motive*; 12 others are now eliminated because they have no obvious motive. Notice we say no "obvious" motive; again, circles of uncertainty always remain. That is one reason hired guns are used—they have no obvious connection with the victim.

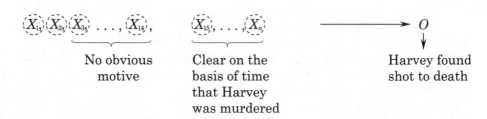

No obvious
motive

Clear on the
basis of time
that Harvey
was murdered

Harvey found
shot to death

Of the suspects who still remain after the "time" and "motive" screening, Suspect 1 is focused on when it is found that the murder weapon is his. This, plus the fact that he had a motive and has no alibi, links him to the death with three lines of evidence. Nevertheless, Suspect 1 is quickly replaced by Suspect 2 when the latter's fingerprints are found on the murder weapon. As well as being the suspect most closely tied to the murder weapon, he has a motive and no alibi.

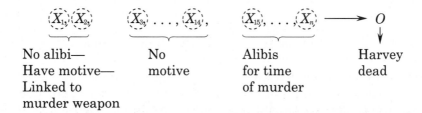

No alibi—
Have motive—
Linked to
murder weapon

No
motive

Alibis
for time
of murder

Harvey
dead

So gradually, with the aid of the time and motive sieves, we have eliminated some X's and tied others to the crime in question—some with only one fine thread of evidence (motive) and others with several lines of evidence (motive, no alibi, murder weapon).

The case method consists of eliminating certain suspects and then attempting to determine which of the remaining ones are most heavily tied to the observation or event being studied. *Its main strength lies in helping rule out certain suspects rather than in guaranteeing the selection of the best suspect from among those who remain.* It is not a foolproof procedure, as wrongly condemned men will hasten to tell you (at least those who still have use of their vocal cords).[1] Nevertheless, it has great advantages over the crystal ball or the casual opinion or the widow's bias or the D.A.'s hunch.

A CASE FOR THE HISTORIAN

This same after-the-fact method is used by historians to explain what led to what in the past. Whereas the problem for the courts is to determine what preceding events and people are tied to a given crime, the problem for the historian is to determine what preceding events and people are tied to a given historical observation. What key events (X's) led to or were tied to the circumstances that provoked the beginning of World War II (O)? Were the key events economic, growing out of Germany's need for raw materials and markets? Were they psychological, growing out of the personality structure of the German people, coupled with the resentment over their defeat in World War I? Was the single key event the mistake of allowing a clever madman to gain control during troubled times? Or did the war result from a combination of all these, and if so, what relative importance should we assign to each?

$$\underbrace{X_1, X_2, \ldots, X_n}_{\text{Economic}} \quad \underbrace{1X_1, 1X_2 \ldots, 1X_{n'}}_{\text{Psychological}} \quad \underbrace{2X_1, 2X_2 \ldots, 2X_{n'}}_{\text{Political}} \longrightarrow O$$

Economic   Psychological   Political   Beginning of World War II

This is the task of the historian, to make a case for his or her particular selection of suspects—a challenging task because there are so many. This fact leads many to conclude that history is an art rather than a science. Thus any one interpretation of history must leave many suspects unnoticed or unaccounted for; the risk of error is so high that the historian may be seen as an artist rather than as a scientist. Accordingly, historians faced with a formidable number of suspects develop a

[1]We noted that, although none of the methods is perfect, all are designed to reduce the risk of error—the risk of certain types of error. Our courts are presumably set up to reduce the risk of condemning an innocent person on the principle that it is better to let a hundred guilty persons go free than to condemn one innocent individual.

point of view to help them in their task; otherwise they would literally be driven to distraction.

Many historians look for economic suspects as explanations for historical events; as a result they miss, ignore, or minimize other types of explanation. Nowadays, many historians look for sociological or psychological suspects as well as economic ones. But if the kinds of suspects on the historical hit parade change, how are we to tell a good historian from a bad one? The good historian is one who can sell other historians on using his or her theory or point of view in selecting suspects. In addition, good historians carefully document the suspects that they have the time, inclination, and techniques to consider.[2]

Notice that when faced with an overwhelming number of suspects, many of them fuzzy, historians require a theory, a bias, or a point of view in order to focus their limited resources on one or two main suspects— economic, psychological, or religious. *In brief, anyone using the after-the-fact method requires a theoretical viewpoint, or bias, to reduce the problem to mind size.*

A CASE FOR THE PHYSICIAN

Consider another situation in which the after-the-fact or case method is employed. You have a stomachache, and you present your case to the physician. The doctor is faced with the same problem as the court and the historian—that of narrowing down the list of suspects and then attempting to deal with the many that remain. Just as historians are governed in their approach by current theories or points of view about history, so doctors are influenced by current medical theory, which leads them to bet on one suspect or group of suspects over others. Thus a mixture of experience, current medical theory, and personal biases determines what types of sorting devices your doctor uses and therefore what kinds of suspects he or she will select from the many available.

For example, what happens when you present your physician with a history of a stomachache that comes and goes?

$$X_1, X_2, X_3, X_4, X_5, X_6, \ldots, X_n \longrightarrow O$$
$$\downarrow$$
$$\text{Stomachache}$$

Various alternative suspects come to mind. Some are remembered from classes at medical school, some have been encountered often in practice, and others are remembered from reading recent articles—if your doctor

---

[2]In an impressive effort to make their work more objective and quantitative, an increasing number of historians are adopting some of the methods of the social and behavioral sciences.

has had time to read and digest them. What are some of the suspects that might be considered: appendicitis, ulcer, mild food poisoning? Your physician does not concern him/herself with *all* of the alternatives but initially focuses on one at a time. The doctor examines the stomach and attempts to localize the site of discomfort. He or she tries to determine the time of onset and the kind and degree of pain. These bits of information are applied to each of the possible common suspects. Perhaps none of the common suspects gets much support, and so all are discarded. To limit the number of suspects, your doctor had initially focused on recent events; now he or she must look further back in your history—the doctor extends his or her time frame, asking about similar illnesses in parents and grandparents. If nothing is found there, the physician will likely consider rarer causes, seeking information from lab tests, X-rays, or specialists. Thus facing this stewpot of evidence, the doctor, with the aid of theory, observations, and hunches, gradually reduces the large number of possible suspects, eventually choosing one that emerges within the scope of his or her medical vision.

REDUCTION OF THE RISK OF ERROR

In the foregoing discussion we considered examples from the fields of law, history, and medicine in which a large-hole sieve—the after-the-fact method—is employed. The same method is employed in economics, political science, anthropology, sociology, and business administration. We use the after-the-fact method when it is impossible, or too difficult, or unethical, or too late to experiment.

You will have noticed that any time we can reduce the number of suspects we increase our chances of picking the correct one. The same principle holds in a raffle drawing for a car. Which would you prefer: to have our ticket in a drum with 1000 other tickets, with 100 other tickets, or with 10 other tickets? Any method that helps reduce the number of suspects appeals to the scientist as much as any method of reducing the number of tickets in the drum appeals to the ticket holder. Notice then the two main ways we use to reduce the number of suspects in the after-the-fact method: the time frame and the theory frame.

Whenever you draw a *time frame* around the event or observation under study, you include some suspects and exclude others. Recall how the knowledge of the time of death of poor Harvey helped rule out a large number of suspects and so helped shrink the scope of the investigation. A time frame helps us exclude certain suspects, whether the problem faces the court, the historian, the physician, or the counselor, thus enabling them to focus their limited investigative resources on a few suspects—it is hoped the right ones.

Another method of cutting a problem down to investigative size is to place it inside not only a time frame but also inside a *theory frame* as well. A theory frame reduces your decision burden or search space by focusing your attention on certain kinds of cues: motive cues, economic cues, psychological cues, feminist cues. Notice in the instance of Harvey's death that we first drew a time frame around those suspects that had no alibi and then reduced that group still further by applying a theory frame, by focusing only on those with a motive.

The application of time frames and theory frames doesn't guarantee that you'll find the right suspect—the after-the-fact method, no matter how skillfully applied, offers no guarantees—but by shrinking the investigative space, time frames and theory frames protect juries, historians, physicians, and citizens from drowning in an ocean of speculative-observational evidence.

Consider the case of Elvis, a tall, blond, good-looking young man of 20 who is referred to a psychiatrist. Elvis has difficulty sleeping, is tense and anxious, and seems to spend a lot of time worrying about his courses at the university, his looks, and his dates. We start then with Anxious Elvis as our observation (O), as our dependent variable.

The psychiatrist has the job of attempting to see what led to O. How many suspects are there? The number of suspected reasons or events contributing to Elvis's unhappy state is infinite. Everything that has happened from the moment of his conception is a potential suspect, and thus a potential independent variable.

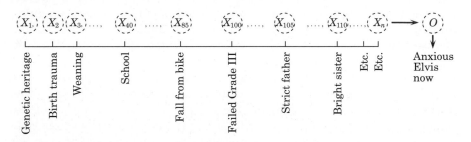

Elvis's problem, then, may be due to a lot of things: a genetic factor (bad genes—"his grandfather was the same way"); a mother who did not want him, handled him roughly, and weaned him too early; a witch of a

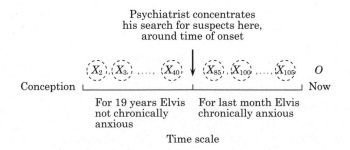

first-grade teacher who terrorized the boy; a bang on the head received from a fall off a bike at the age of eight; a stern father who was always smiling but never satisfied, no matter how hard Elvis tried to please; or any one of a thousand things or combination of things. Like historians, psychiatrists must have some biases or theories about what events lead to anxious people; otherwise the avalanche of possible suspects could drive them . . . well, to see a psychiatrist. Thus some psychiatrists look to your genes and your biochemistry (using genetic or biological sieves), others to your weaning and toilet training (usually early experience sieves), others to your attitude toward authority. If Elvis has been anxious for years, the doctor needs a theory frame to help reduce his or her medical search space down to a size where the doctor can sift through a certain class of suspects—biochemical, genetic, or psychological.

Notice how using a time sieve can reduce the overwhelming search space facing the psychiatrist. If Elvis has only been anxious for a month, think how this time frame drastically reduces the number of suspects. Now the psychiatrist has a better chance to home in on some contributing suspects by examining events just preceding the onset of anxiety. This is not to say that events during the first 19 years are irrelevant, but at least they were not sufficient alone to lead to an anxiety state. The psychiatrist can use a time frame (the last month), a theory frame (a biochemical frame—allergies), or a psychological stress frame (fight with his girlfriend). The doctor now has at least a chance of reaching a reasoned conclusion—right or wrong.

SUMMARY

Before proceeding to a useful extension of this method, let's summarize. Even though highly fallible, the after-the-fact method remains the most popular tool humans use for tying speculations to observations. If it's so fallible why is it so popular? It's popular for several reasons: (1) Because it lets us make decisions on the run; (2) because we don't realize how error prone it is; and (3) because even when we make errors—that is trust the wrong messenger—the negative results often don't come home to haunt us for years (e.g., choosing the wrong mate or career). Without immediate negative feedback we don't learn how to identify where exactly we went wrong, so it's difficult to pinpoint the after-the-fact method as the culprit or as the error-prone method that led to our subsequent trouble.

Using this method we attempt to go back in time after an event has occurred to find the most probable cause or suspect. However, two major problems plague us: (1) there are usually a great number of possible causes or suspects, and (2) it is often extremely difficult to get reliable information about past events or symptoms (possible causes or suspects). For example, the courts must rely heavily on the memory of the witnesses, and such memories prove time and again to be unreliable. Also much of the evidence becomes unavailable as eyewitnesses melt in the crowd or fail to volunteer evidence for fear of getting involved in lengthy or unpleasant court proceedings. Your doctor, too, relies heavily on the fragmentary bits of information you provide—bits you select from the large file of fact and fancy you call your memory, that wonderful data swamp. The historian also deals in fragments of the past, documents written perhaps from the fallible recollections of someone who knew someone who knew someone who saw "it" happen. We rarely know how time has taken an event and shaped and reshaped it to fit the minds and tongues through which it passes. Remember playing the party game "Rumor," in which a message is passed from person to person in the same room, and recall how quickly the message became unwittingly distorted and reshaped by each person in the chain.

Thus the case method with its large numbers of suspects—some lost to view, some distorted by time—presents a great challenge to those who would sort fact from fancy. With an awareness of the difficulties, however, and in the knowledge that no more practical method is readily available, dedicated men and women in law, medicine, and history have demonstrated that useful and durable packages of information can be produced. Others in the same fields, less dedicated or less aware of the limitations of the method, have posed and have been accepted as authorities, only to be unmasked later as pushers of perishable goods. Some people are a double threat: a threat to themselves, in that they assume they know and so are less open to other evidence, and a threat to those who rely on their advice. Perhaps the best safeguard exists when both the experts and the public are aware of the strengths and weaknesses of the various methods used to sift fact from fancy.

Despite its limitations, do not reject this after-the-fact or case method simply because it is error prone, or because it requires you to use arbitrary time frames, or the blinders of bias, to cut the search space down to manageable size. Its main strength is that it is simple to use. Recall that we have limited memory and analytic capacity, so we must rely on simple methods for most of our information processing for the sake of mental economy. In many (most?) situations, it's the only method we can afford, and it is useful, at least, in narrowing down the number of suspects so that we can at least make some decision—probably a more functional one than that derived from the rules of evidence of the armchair, the pub, or the afternoon tea party.

We must make decisions every hour of every day on the basis of incomplete and unreliable information. But the point is, we must make hundreds of decisions. We must make them right or wrong, so any method that helps us do so with minimal mental effort is valuable—the after-the-fact method works in this regard. Finally, in much of our decision making, we don't have to be right, so we can afford an error-prone method. Scientists and citizens can be wrong, as judged by hindsight, and still get paid and promoted, have their work published, and raise reasonably healthy, happy kids. We live much of our lives in benign environments where the yardsticks are vague, or where our mistakes don't come home to roost for years and years. So, the after-the-fact or case method is very functional, whether or not it locates valid antecedents and whether the resulting decisions are judged right or wrong in the long, long run.

Because we live in a relatively "rich" environment like North America, we can afford to be wrong about a lot of things, to trust the wrong messenger, and still get by. Furthermore, we never know before the fact how it would have turned out for us if we'd trusted a different messenger—Bush instead of Clinton, Joyce instead of Willie, or the guidance counselor instead of the football coach.

In brief, in many benign environments you don't have to be right, but you do need an affordable way of deciding which messengers to believe. The after-the-fact method is affordable. Rather than requiring careful, time-consuming analysis, this method relies on gut feelings and hunches to sort through the messengers automatically and select the one(s) to trust, for the time being. If we lack strong gut feelings we typically delegate the job to a loved one, or an expert, and they become our trusted messengers telling us what to believe in that situation.

Finally, though seldom acknowledged, the after-the-fact method plays a vital role in science. It is typically the method that great theorists and researchers use to choose their hypotheses, to evaluate the literature, and to speculate and theorize about their findings. For example, thousands trusted Freud, the psychoanalytic messenger, other thousands trusted Skinner, the behaviorist messenger. Although their theories were in conflict they nevertheless tutored legions of disciples, teachers, and researchers, guiding them to look for and trust this speculation rather than that one. But now we trust new messengers—the cognitive theorists; no doubt they too "will pass," and we will assign many of their once-treasured messages into the dust bin of history. But because it is the nature of the beast, the after-the-fact method presents us with an overwhelming number of suspects, so we must narrow them down to mind size; our popular theorists help us do so. Although our great theorists fade away, each in his or her way leaves a growing legacy of winnowed wisdom, slowly adding to our store of trusted speculations.

In the next chapter we examine another simple method of tying speculations to observations, the "before-and-after" method. If used properly, it is less error prone than the after-the-fact method because it usually involves a reduced time frame, and so, a reduced number of suspects. Also, we will introduce you to the "four rogues," suspects that frequently sabotage our efforts to tie sound speculations to observations.

EXAMPLE

Before proceeding to the next chapter, we present a "case for the counselor." Here we provide an example of how a clinician sorted through a client's messages, trusting some messages over others and organizing the trusted messages (suspects) into a pattern or template.

A Case for the Counselor

This fourth example of the after-the-fact method in action derives from the experiences of a client in counseling who reported concerns related to the initiation, development, and maintenance of interpersonal relations with women—the observation (*O*) to be explained. In seeking to understand the nature of the client's problem with forming rewarding relationships with females, the counselor explores the personal history of the client and endeavors to enhance the client's insight through the use of a cognitive templating technique (Pyke, 1979). Essentially, this technique is a mechanism to identify key suspects and their interrelations. Readers wishing to try their hand at after-the-fact researching should read through the history below and attempt to isolate suspects, subsequently comparing those selected with those identified by the counselor.

The Client's Chronicle

Michael, at 38, is in the second year of a Ph.D. program in political science. He is the eldest and favorite son of upper-class conservative parents. His father, a devout and moralistic Christian, was an extremely successful businessman whose work frequently required that the family live for extended periods in foreign locales. About his father, Michael says, "He was always serious, uptight, sometimes petulant, a chronic worrier, but always just and fair and I was proud of his success and status. He's extremely sensitive to criticism and nonemotional, self-possessed."

Although well educated, Michael's mother had never supported herself but assumed the demanding role of charming and capable social hostess for her spouse's many business associates, in addition to assuming most child care responsibilities. Recurring bouts of serious depression resulted in repeated suicide attempts, but her children had no knowledge of these acts until long after they had left home. Michael noted that he valued some of his mother's qualities—her sensitivity and interpersonal skills, in particular.

Family interactions were not characterized either by overt displays of affection or acrimonious, angry scenes. Maintaining a calm, civilized, and cultured demeanor was stressed. Rational and intelligent behavior, reflecting good self-control, was expected. Academic achievement was especially rewarded.

At the age of 14, Michael was enrolled in a private boys' school, which he described as a brutal authoritarian environment. "I tried to avoid situations where my ignorance about sexual matters would be apparent, with the result that there was relatively little diminution in the depth of my naiveté. Physical violence was commonplace. For my own protection I developed a relationship with one of the enforcers; I helped him with his assignments and he, in turn, kept the other kids off my back. I felt like a coward and still do. I reacted in a cowardly way, responding by withdrawal rather than confronting. I always want to win without risk. That's a pattern in my life."

At 16, Michael entered a university, majoring in philosophy. "I saw myself as a failure in male–female relationships—felt emasculated and upset. I was also preoccupied about having my inexperience exposed." Divergence from the family values crystallized during this period. "I became an atheist, adopted a Marxist political orientation, and was extremely active in a campus radical group. We were superintellectual, strongly idealistic, and totally alienated from the university academic structure, which to us appeared antithetical to learning and challenge. I was incredibly arrogant and so openly disrespectful to some of my professors that I was thrown out of several classes. I didn't date during the four years I was there—much too busy with the political and philosophical issues. Again, it's the same pattern, more withdrawal. So, I was still a virgin at 20."

After a year working with the peace movement, he enrolled in a graduate school in California. Once again, Michael joined a group of activists and was soon recognized as part of the upper echelon of organizers in the group. An 18-year-old fellow activist, Laura, initiated contact with Michael and they began cohabiting in a commune setting. "I had more status so I probably looked attractive to her. I mentioned that because I'm a bit paranoid about attraction and success. It was a good relationship, both emotionally and physically, but we were intellectually competitive. Being older, I had the edge."

Michael's disenchantment with academic environments continued unabated and he was debarred after participation in a series of rather dramatic protest activities, the last of which culminated in his arrest for civil disobedience. Coinciding with the escalation of Michael's difficulties with the university and the police was a deterioration of the relationship with Laura. "It was a bad period politically. I didn't know what I wanted and that showed. I felt held back by any kind of monogamous relationship and was openly engaging in extracurricular sex with other women."

Now denied access to the university, Michael and some comrades founded a New Left Marxist group off campus. Headquarters for the group was a large, old, private home in which 15 to 30 core organizers lived and worked communally for about four years. Soon after the establishment of this new movement, which included nonstudent radicals, Michael developed a friendship with Sharon, "a very gutsy, beautiful, sexy, and sexually active woman." Michael reports, "She initiated sexual contact and I was delighted. It was a status symbol to relate to her in sexual terms—it was a real conquest. And, as for her part, I was becoming an increasingly important figure in the movement and was receiving a fair amount of public recognition."

In a short time Michael became the designated leader of the group and his responsibilities included the organization of protest marches, public rallies, speaking engagements, writing for the newspaper, and maintenance of security (from police infiltration). Sharon wanted a child and although Michael was initially opposed, believing the revolution to be more important, Sharon persuaded him.

Concurrently, the tension on the political scene was mounting. "Violence was in the air—from the right, from the police, and even from within our own ranks. I was extremely ill at ease under conditions of violence. I felt responsible for my people and worried about sending them out into the streets. Our activities received a lot of media coverage and since I was the spokesperson it was my face on the TV and my words in the paper. I received a certain number of threats and hate literature and was picked up by the police several times, even shot at. Once she became pregnant, Sharon seemed to be becoming more and more dependent on me and that was an added strain.

"Then there was a challenge to my leadership. Both Sharon and I were accused of being undercover cops and I was removed from the leadership pending an investigation by the Security Committee. When this happened, Sharon decided to get an abortion. I was very upset. I helped set it up and paid for it but with tears in my eyes. I felt threatened by what I saw as her withdrawal of solid love and affection, and I became defensive, not only because of the abortion but also because she decided to work in a nightclub as an erotic dancer. She asked me if I would come with her if she left the movement and I said no, and maybe that was the end. The relationship finally terminated a month or so later when she took up with a fellow on the Security Committee—one of my detractors. Sharon's abortion was a watershed. I haven't had a satisfactory relationship with a woman since then. When I'm rejected I withdraw, retreat, deploy resources, and go someplace else."

Michael was exonerated from the "police informer" allegation, but devastated by these experiences in his personal and political life he moved to the East Coast and joined a Marxist-Leninist group oriented more toward working-class politics. Michael also obtained a teaching position and essentially held two full-time jobs, working 80 to 85 hours a week. Michael spent seven years with this organization. Increasing recognition of the inadequacy of the theoretical philosophical model underlying the movement led ultimately to its demise.

"The feminist critique of the Marxist model of social change was particularly telling. At a mass self-analysis meeting of all members and hangers-on, it became apparent that the criticisms of the feminists couldn't be handled within the model and since the organization had no better alternatives to propose, the group decided to disband," Michael explained.

"Part of what was wrong with the movement was the denial, the absence of common-sense selfishness. After the collapse of the New Left movement, I had to rethink some basic assumptions. Concern with myself and my own happiness is legitimate, not selfish. Twenty years of my life have been devoted to being a professional activist. I sacrificed my career for the sake of the movement, but I can't say that I regret the activity nor do I see it as over. My experiences in these groups were overwhelmingly positive and opened up all sorts of choices. I still have libertarian views but no longer want to give voice to them within a framework of Puritan self-denial. I am no longer prepared to give up everything for the movement."

Concerning his problem, Michael commented, "I've never seen it as legitimate to ask someone out: It's a shame thing or a Christian thing. I don't like to admit an interest in someone in front of anyone else. If I get rejected and other people know I was interested, I'll look bad. Maybe sexuality is associated in my unconscious mind with something evil or dirty or it could be the competitive thing—fear about revealing any weakness at all. Perhaps I've narrowed myself down to activities I know I'll succeed in. I'm relatively cautious, prudent, or conservative, I guess."

About his general sense of himself, Michael observed, "I have a positive self-concept when my self is object but not when it's subject. I seem to be preoccupied with my presentation of self—how I'm coming across to others. My sense of ideal self is so strong that I'm driven by my sense of what should ideally be the case. What I want is so much greater than what is. Do I have hidden desires to exploit others? Is this why I feel guilty? I have difficulty stating baldly that these are my needs, maybe because of my Christian training. When I say I want X, it comes out cynically—my moralistic attitude poisons it.

"I don't feel inferior to others; my basic self-concept is positive yet I have a strong sense of not being worthy. My failure to establish intimate relations with women threatens my sense of myself. My self-concept is fragile, though. I seem to have a need to hit back if someone doesn't recognize and respect me. I'm too easily insulted."

On another occasion Michael confessed, "I seem to be worried that people will see through me but I'm not sure what I'm hiding. When I'm with others I seem to be play-acting. I'm truthful in that I show both the positive and negative aspects of myself, but somehow I maintain control in how it comes across. Because I anticipate criticism I use a variety of strategies to allay it—humor, taking on the role of the clown; invective; even self-criticism. My principal concern when I'm involved with a woman is how other men will see me with that woman. The woman herself is incidental. I'm playing for the audience. It's not nice to say it, but I see a woman as a commodity, as a potential contributor to status. The woman is not even part of the audience; she's a prop. The audience isn't necessarily real. I'm still playing to the jocks in the club. I want to look good to others; to put on a good face. I have to battle with myself to bring up negative things and I spend a lot of time justifying myself."

"I'm judgmental (but am afraid of being judged) and have a strong sense of what's right. I've always had to be better than everyone else—more revolutionary, more feminist—then I'm invulnerable to reproach. But no matter how well I do, I feel it's not good enough. I can't handle praise because although I want it and appreciate it, I tend to analyze the motives of the person giving me praise. What's their status? Are they manipulating me? I have high expectations for others and always see their strengths before their weakness. I find it hard to believe they will be base. To avoid being taken in or gulled I superanalyze everything so I won't make a false move. It's a strategy to help handle my naiveté and innocence."

With respect to his future, Michael reflected, "I'm playing makeup now, racing against time. I'm impatient because I'm in the second half of my life and in some sense I'm just starting. But I don't really like the idea of achieving adult status. I really enjoy being young and don't want to surrender my youth."

Summing up his difficulties in the area of developing intimate relationships with women, Michael said, "I have a great capacity for forming superficial relationships. It was a habit not to get too deeply committed as a kid because I knew we would likely move soon. But I've always been well liked even by my political adversaries. I like social situations and thrive in them. It's unusual for me to be this withdrawn from people. I'm preoccupied with not blowing my academic work. My problem is one of timidity or shyness in situations where there is a possibility of loss, especially in the area of initiating relationships with women. I'm just not bonding well with women. That's the crux of my feelings of inferiority. It threatens my sense of my own masculinity. I don't feel normal vis-à-vis other males. What blocks me from taking emotional risks?"

Cognitive Template

Faced with the *myriad potential suspects* embedded in Michael's narrative, how does the counselor sort key suspects from less influential factors? Helpful clues available to the counselor include: (1) the number of different times Michael mentions a feeling or incident; (2) the total amount of time Michael spends describing an issue; (3) the intensity of the affect or emotion associated with the experience; (4) Michael's own assessment of the importance of a particular event or feeling; (5) any obvious reluctance on Michael's part to explore a particular issue; (6) the counselor's *theoretical orientation*, which will lead to a focus on suspects related to behavioral habits, or feelings experienced in the "here and now," or illogical thought processes, or sex and gender-role socialization, or on the resolution of the oedipal complex.

Figure 3–1 represents the counselor's attempt to depict the personal history variables (key suspects) relevant to the presenting problem. From the client's chronicle, the key suspects are identified and tied to the client's cognitions (his descriptions) of his life experiences and of himself. Figure 3–2 presents abstracted themes representing clusters of key events that seem interrelated and, additionally, the connections among themes.

The feminist orientation of the counselor is clearly apparent in the analysis below. This theoretical orientation focuses on the importance of sex roles, and on the belief that they are learned early—how the twig is bent so grows the tree! Accordingly, the counselor's main category or "net" for fishing out preferred suspects is the "Family" net. Counselors of other theoretical persuasions (and readers) would no doubt select out a different category of suspects, perhaps using a net of peer group influence, or a genetic net to do so. The ultimate test of who is right lies in the utility of the approach, and the ultimate judge of that is the client— the consumer.

Interpretation

Michael's sense of his own *specialness* derived in no small measure from his father's success in achieving a prestigious position of extraordinarily high status and respect. The benefits of travel (familiarity with other cultures, facility in several languages) contributed to this specialness. As horrendous as the private school was for Michael, attending the school added to his differentness. Adoption of an unpopular political

Family	Other
x 1. Mother—failure/weak x 2. Father—success x 3. Achievement (task-oriented) emphasis x 4. Intellectual emphasis x 5. Emotionality discouraged (cool, objective, calm, rational) x 6. Parental relationship (lack of intimacy) x 7. Christian/Puritan/conservative tradition x 8. High status & class x 9. Masking/disguise	x 10. Travel (instability, isolation, special) x 11. Private school—no females, new x 12. Private school milieu—negative emotionality x 13. Cultural influences—sex stereotypes x 14. Experiences with female friends & lovers x 15. Political ideology—priorities & communal intimacy x 16. Political experiences

FIGURE 3–1   Key Suspects Leading to Michael's Problems

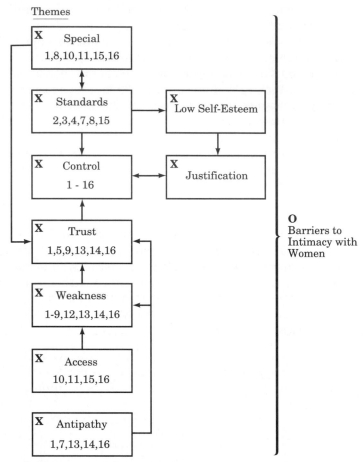

Themes

FIGURE 3–2   Clusters of Key Suspects

position combined with atypical experiences (getting arrested) further enhanced Michael's sense of his own uniqueness.

Related to the specialness was Michael's development of high *standards* and expectations for both self and others. Again, several family variables were instrumental in this development as well as in the idealism and self-sacrifice expectation inherent in the political ideology embraced by Michael. One by-product of the high standards was *low self-esteem*; Michael could never measure up to his own expectations and hence had developed a number of strategies for dealing with constant failure (withdrawal; intellectualization and rationalizations to *justify* his own performance). Another by-product was that Michael was frequently disappointed in the behavior of others because they, too, failed to meet his standards.

Attempting to live up to high standards required that Michael maintain iron *control* and self-discipline. This theme of control seemed central to Michael's cognitive style and was certainly reinforced in the family environment where emotional expression was regarded as inappropriate or immature or sloppy while a dispassionate, objective, and cool style commanded respect. Coping with fears of looking foolish, inept, or ignorant, coupled with the need to put on a good face, necessitated the maintenance of a high degree of control.

Michael grew up in a family where surface serenity was highly valued—not surprising given that the family was on frequent public display. Family conflicts or personal problems were kept under wraps. Even the enormity of the mother's suicide attempts could not penetrate the wall of respectability, the facade of the well-adjusted family. Such an environment, with its emphasis on masking and disguise, is not conducive to the development of *trust* or to learning how to establish trust in an interpersonal relationship. More specifically, with respect to relationships with women, Michael's mother's erratic behavior indicated she couldn't be relied upon (trusted), and exposure to the general cultural stereotypes would suggest that women in general can't be trusted. With few exceptions, subsequent personal experiences with women only reinforced this bias. Michael's involvement in a revolutionary political movement also reinforced a pre-existing bias. The constant concern about police infiltration, informers, police entrapment, and the like inspired constant suspicion. And Michael's specialness also contributed to the general lack of trust. "People like me not for who I am but rather what I am."

This lack of trust fosters the tendency to maintain control, as does Michael's abhorrence of *weakness*. It would never do to let anyone perceive a vulnerability, a chink in the armor. A self-declared weakness exists in the area of relations with women, which derived in part from the limited *access* or opportunity to forge and maintain relationships with females. Perceiving women as weak and not to be trusted is part of a general *antipathy* toward women. This antipathy stems from several factors: the unsatisfactory female model provided by Michael's mother; his exposure to the Christian view of women; his social conditioning into the traditional masculine role; his personal unfulfilling relationships with women. The death knell might well have been the role women played in the destruction of a political movement near and dear to his heart.

REVIEW QUIZ

True or False?

1. The after-the-fact method can be used to study individuals, families, small groups, organizations, and institutions.
2. The essence of the after-the-fact method is to select from a variety of suspects the one(s) most strongly tied to, or leading to, the event of interest.

3.   The case method is a highly precise scientific technique comparable with a controlled scientific experiment.

4.   The main strength of the case method lies in eliminating suspects rather than in guaranteeing the selection of the best suspect from those that remain.

5.   The after-the-fact method has few advantages over casual opinion.

6.   A theoretical viewpoint or bias is a considerable asset in using the after-the-fact method.

7.   A time frame is of considerable help in applications of the after-the-fact method.

8.   The after-the-fact method is typically used by everyone to help them sort fact from fancy.

9.   The after-the-fact method is used when it would be too difficult, impossible, or unethical to use one of the other methods of science.

10. One of the problems with the after-the-fact method is the unreliability or unavailability of information about past events.

11. A clear weakness of the after-the-fact method is its complexity.

12. In our everyday lives, we must make decisions, but we can afford to be wrong, so the after-the-fact method has great functional utility in this context.

❦ 4 ❦

Before-and-After
Treatment Method

─────── **Chapter Goal** ───────

*To introduce you to the "four rogues" who
trick you into false conclusions when you try
to separate fact from fancy.*

INTRODUCTION

With treatment a depression only lasts 90 days.

When you're depressed, messengers with disheartening signals flood in: "You're going to fail. You're dumb. You've never really succeeded at anything."

First, you try to ignore these denigrating signals. In an effort to help, your friends bombard you with positive messages: "Don't be silly. Remember how well you did on the first psych quiz? You play the guitar so well. I wish I had your hair." But the messengers with the bad news elbow aside the ones carrying good news and finally you seek treatment.

The preceding chain of events typifies the three stages of the before-and-after method: (1) In the "before part" you focus on a state of affairs you want to change (e.g., feeling depressed, smoking, math grades, etc.); (2) in the "treatment part" you try to do something about it (e.g., consult an expert); and (3) in the "after part" you determine whether the state of affairs has changed for the better.

In the previous chapter we observed that the after-the-fact method involves speculating about antecedents (suspects) in a huge search space which stretches back in time. We also observed that one important way of reducing the search space was to focus in on a limited time period. The before-and-after study capitalizes on this idea and, although still error prone, it is a more powerful method than the after-the-fact method.

The before-and-after method applies to the kinds of questions that start out with a statement such as "I wonder what will happen if . . . ." That is, you start with O_1—for example, the onset of Susan's rash—and then introduce X, a new skin lotion—Hornet Honey. After the prescribed three-month treatment, you make another observation (O_2) and report "complexion improved." But did the Hornet Honey help—or was it one or more of the many other X's in the stream of events taking place between O_1 and O_2 that did the trick? Was it one or more of a host of other independent variables?

Researchers refer to X's as independent variables and to O's as dependent variables; changes in O depend on changes in X.

Can you think of some other suspects? In that given period many other suspected reasons could account for the rash's clearing up: Susan may have finished exams, started holidays, gotten a new boyfriend, washed her face with water treated in the family's new water softener, stopped eating so much junk between meals, finished some biochemical growing up, been exposed to more sunshine, or gotten used to the rash so that even a small improvement looked great. But Hornet Honey would be only too happy to take credit for the improvement, and probably in such a situation, most of us would be quite content to give the salve a testimonial, even though, as we have just indicated, it is only one of many suspects. Many medical treatments parade as cures, but are likewise one of many suspects. It requires a comprehensive series of experiments of the kind to be discussed shortly to obtain durable information about the adequacy of the supposed treatment.

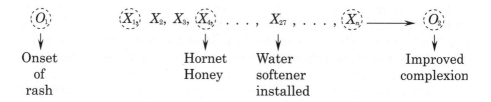

This before-and-after method pretends to be scientific but would not be regarded so by most scientists because too many suspects always remain, even after we have ruled out many others. Suspects always remain, so whether a method passes as scientific is a relative question. Four main types of suspects, or rogues, challenge us in our attempts to sort fact from fancy, in our attempts to locate or manufacture stable packages of information (Campbell & Stanley, 1966).

The following medical example helps us identify these four troublemakers. After exposing them we will consider various tactics we can use to minimize the mischief they do.

FOUR MISLEADING SUSPECTS

A psychiatrist has been given the job of evaluating a new drug for treating depressed patients in a hospital. He examines the patients before the treatment (O_1) and after the treatment (O_2). The treatment (X_d) consists of a six-week period during which two of the new pills are taken three times a day. After the treatment period the doctor decides that most of the patients have improved.

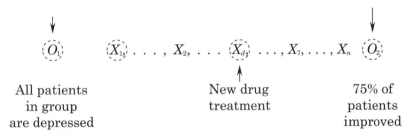

$$O_1 \qquad X_1, \ldots, X_2, \ldots X_d \ldots, X_7, \ldots, X_n \quad O_2$$

| All patients in group are depressed | New drug treatment | 75% of patients improved |

The psychiatrist is very pleased and writes an article for a medical journal. A scientist reads the article and irately writes a letter to the journal editor complaining that the psychiatrist's so-called research is badly flawed. The scientist points to four alternative explanations of why the patients improved, adding that the drug is probably useless. He then lists four suspects that usually distort the results of before-and-after studies but that are typically ignored, as they were by the well-meaning doctor.

For example, when, at the end of the study, the psychiatrist asks himself, "Why did these patients improve?" The message comes back to him loudly and clearly: "Look at me," yells the drug, "I did it!" Because the drug is the psychiatrist's favorite suspect, like the teacher's pet, it gets the attention, whereas other suspects or messengers go unnoticed. What four powerful, but ignored, suspects could account for the patient "improvement" between O_1 and O_2? The four suspects are outlined in Table 4–1.

Historical (In-the-Gap) Suspects

In the case of the depressed patients what other changes, besides the drug, occurred between the time they were diagnosed as depressed and the time they were judged to have improved? Notice that any other change in the routine of their lives is a legitimate suspect and could account for their improvement.

"Were there any changes in ward routine or any ward staff introduced during the treatment period that may have contributed to patient welfare?" A new cook or a new ward supervisor may have been more

TABLE 4–1   Common Suspect Types

Type		Examples
Historical (in-the-gap)	(X)	Exam
		Stock market crash
		Catching cold
		Death of mother
		Hangover
Maturational (time-tied)	(X_t)	Hungry
		Tired
		Older
		Rested
		Menstruating
		Male midlife crisis
Instrument-decay (elastic-ruler)	(O_2)	Boredom, fatigue, or mood of researcher
		Instrument wear or breakdown
		Bias of researcher, practice
Testing (on-stage)	(O_2)	Recall
		Putting best foot forward
		Lying

influential than the drug in bringing about patient improvement. Remember that, after careful study, many wonder drugs turn out to be duds. Since the physician was looking at the drug and not at other possibilities, the drug got credit, and other possible suspects went unnoticed.

In other words, the history of the period between O_1 and O_2 is filled with suspects in addition to the drug. *Thus, anything that occurs between O_1 and O_2 is an in-the-gap suspect or rogue, and may influence O_2.* We typically focus attention on our "pet" suspect—the drug—which like a noisy child cries "look at me," whereas other important messengers remain unheard because they are at the back, or out of sight, and, more important, "out of mind." That's one of the reasons why the speculations we make and the conclusions we draw using the before-and-after method are prone to error.

Maturational (Time-Tied) Suspects

The researcher asks another question. "Would 50 percent of the patients have improved in a six-week period even without treatment?" Given time alone, some illnesses cure themselves—that is, there are variables, such as natural recovery time in the case we just mentioned, or maturity in the case of Susan's complexion changes during adolescence. In many instances of the simple before-and-after design, time alone, rather than the pet treatment of a given investigator, deserves the credit for the improvement. *Thus, if time alone can produce changes* *in O_2 without any specific "treatment," we are dealing with a matura-tional or time-tied suspect or rogue.* Because we tend to focus on our prize or "treatment" suspect, we tend to forget that time alone may account for changes in O_2. So this is a second reason why conclusions drawn using the before-and-after method are error-prone.

Instrument-Decay (Elastic-Ruler) Suspects

The researcher mentions a third explanation apart from the drug—namely, the doctor's ability to measure depression may have changed. We cannot measure depression with a precise ruler; rather we measure it with a person's judgment, which, as we all know, fluctuates from time to time like an elastic ruler. For example, doctors want drugs to work, and this could affect their judgments so that they actually imagine improve-ment, whereas an unbiased observer would not. *Thus, measuring instru-ments, human or otherwise, can change or deteriorate between O_1 and O_2: when that happens, we are dealing with elastic-ruler suspects or rogues.* Because we focus our limited attention and analytic capacity on our prize or "treatment" suspect, we tend to forget that the change in O_2 may be attributable to a change in the yardstick or judge. This is a third reason why decisions based on the before-and-after method are prone to error. In other words, the elasticity of O_2 warrants particular attention in the before-and-after design.

Testing (On-Stage) Suspects

Finally, the researcher suggests yet another factor (other than the drug) that could explain the patients' improvement. The very act of interviewing the patients at the beginning to see how sick they were may have influenced them, particularly if they knew what was happen-ing. Some people respond for a while to almost any new treatment. On the second interview they might well want to appear better so as to be able to go home or to help the nice young doctor. *Thus, some organisms (including humans) change between O_1 and O_2 merely because they are "on display" or being studied; when this happens we are dealing with on-stage suspects or rogues.* Because such suspects typically remain outside our realm of attention, we tend to ignore them, and may erroneously give credit for the change to the "treatment." This, then, becomes a fourth reason for questioning speculations or conclusions based on the before-and-after method.

In brief, the psychiatrist can draw no conclusions with confidence about the effects of his new pill on depressed patients. First, and fore-most, he doesn't know what percentage would have "improved" in 3 months with no treatment; it may well be 75 percent because most depressions are temporary. So it may well have been a maturational or time-tied suspect, not the drug, that deserves credit for the change. Second, removing the patients from the stresses at home or at work, and placing them on hospital ward may have done wonders—a change is as good as a rest. Thus, the real "treatment" may have been the changed environment, an in-the-gap suspect, not the drug. Finally, in such research, onstage and elastic-ruler suspects typically influence the results, with the patients wanting to appear better, so they could go home, and the psychiatrist unwittingly wanting them to look better, so he could publish his positive findings.

No, the psychiatrist erred badly in choosing the before-and-after treatment method for his research. He should have chosen the control-group method described in the next chapter. But don't reject the after-the-fact method out of hand; under some conditions, as we shall now see, it can be very useful.

SKILLFUL USE OF THE BEFORE-AND-AFTER SIEVE

The before-and-after model, such as in the case of Susan's rash, can be used to advantage when (1) the observation under study has remained stable, or inelastic, for a period of time; (2) a quick-acting remedy is being tested; (3) the number of suspects pouring into the gap between O_1 and O_2 can be carefully controlled; (4) the remedy works on a second and third trial; and (5) research participants are unaware they are being studied.

Stable Observations

Consider the first instance, the one in which the observation remains the same for an appreciable period of time. This can be portrayed as follows:

$$\text{Hornet Honey} \downarrow$$

$$1X_1, (1X_2), \ldots 1X_n \downarrow \quad 2X_1, (2X_2), \ldots 2X_n \downarrow \quad 3X_1, \ldots 3X_2, \ldots (3X_n)$$

$$(O_1) \quad = \quad (O_2) \quad = \quad (O_3) \quad \neq \quad (O_4)$$

$$\downarrow \qquad\qquad \downarrow \qquad\qquad \downarrow \qquad\qquad \downarrow$$

$$\text{Rash} \qquad \text{Rash} \qquad \text{Rash} \qquad \textit{No } \text{Rash}$$

In this instance O_1 equals O_2 equals O_3. Then after the third observation, we try the new treatment, the Hornet Honey, and find a marked improvement in the rash—that is, O_3 does not equal O_4. Now we probably have more justification in getting excited about Hornet

Honey because the rash has been exposed to a wide variety of other suspects between O_1 and O_3 with no obvious change. Similarly, the other main suspects (in-the-gap, time-tied, and on-stage effects) have had considerable opportunity to work prior to O_4 without any evidence that they are potent agents in this instance. The possibility still remains that there would have been a change in O_4 even if Hornet Honey had not been used—that is, that the natural course of the rash of pimples could have run out (a long time-tied suspect at work) and that the improvement could represent a spontaneous recovery that happened to coincide with or follow the administration of the Hornet Honey.

However, let us suppose that, following O_4, we stop the treatment with the Hornet Honey, and that by O_5, the pimples return again. Now we reintroduce Hornet Honey, and at O_6 the pimples disappear. At this point confidence increases that the change is "somehow" connected to treatment with Hornet Honey. It may well be that the person's anxiety has been reduced, so that had she taken anything in which she had confidence, the same results would be obtained; or it may be directly related to some chemical in the honey. Nevertheless, we have confidence that some part of our treatment ritual is useful. You can probably figure out how to continue the study in order to increase confidence that the improvement depends specifically on Hornet Honey.

Quick-Acting Suspects

The before-and-after method also has considerable power when we feed a quick-acting and powerful suspect, or X, into the gap between O_1 and O_2. For example, it is much easier to detect the effect of a cure for depression that takes one day to work than one that takes three months because there are fewer alternative suspects to pour into the 24-hour gap than into the 3-month gap (n is much smaller than n^1). There is also less time for time-tied and elastic-ruler factors to operate.

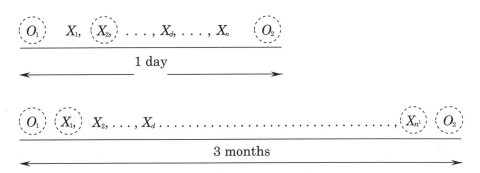

Penicillin is an example of a quick-acting independent variable, the effects of which are relatively easy to detect—that is, with the administration of such an antibiotic, the temperature quickly returns to normal, or the infection soon shows obvious signs of abating. However, some of the unpleasant side effects, which appear more slowly, may take longer to tie to the antibiotic. Again, the longer the time interval between X and its effect, the more difficult the research problem. Think, for example, how long it must have taken primitive people to understand the relationship between the birth of a child and the act of procreation.

Slow-acting X's, whether diseases or treatments, confound us. In using the before-and-after method in such instances, we must be prepared for relatively slow progress and a period of trial-and-error treatment with favorite, but often fictional, cures.

Elimination of Stray Suspects

Obviously if we can greatly reduce the number of stray suspects pouring into the gap between O_1 and O_2, we simplify our task. However, controlling the flow of stray suspects into the gap is difficult in economics, political science, sociology, medicine, and psychology. The method gains in power, however, in those investigations in which you can carefully shield the gap between O_1 and O_2 from almost all suspects except the one you wish to study. Furthermore, if you can control for elastic-ruler effects, on-stage effects, and time-tied effects, you have a very powerful investigative method.

Certain observations in physics and chemistry meet these conditions. Let's examine a hypothetical example. A physicist may wish to test the effects of heating a compound on its radioactivity.[1] The physicist places a Geiger counter near the compound, takes the reading, then heats the compound to the desired temperature, takes another reading, and notices that the radiation has decreased.

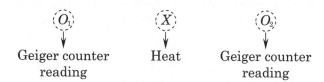

O_1	X	O_2
Geiger counter reading	Heat	Geiger counter reading

Now you ask the physicist how he or she knows it was the heat and not a reduction in stray sources of radiation (as from the sun, a wristwatch dial, or dust from bomb-testing fallout) that resulted in the reduced readings, since the Geiger counter was exposed to all of these, as well as to the compound under test. Or you suggest that the change in reading is due to an elastic-ruler effect—the batteries in the Geiger counter

---

[1]Actually, heat has very little effect on the radioactivity of a compound, so it requires a carefully controlled experiment to measure such small effects.

wearing out between O_1 and O_2.

If the physicist is a careful researcher, he or she would say that the compound and the counter were placed in a shielded box so that only the rays from the compound being tested could operate on the counter. The physicist would have tested the sensitivity of the counter before and after the study and found no change, thus indicating there had been no instrument-decay or elastic-ruler effect of any consequence. Also, there is little concern over time-tied suspects because the natural reduction in radiation of the compound under study is very slow, with appreciable changes taking years, not minutes. Finally, there is no evidence that on-stage effects are operating—that is, that the measuring process itself would affect the compound in any way—it would not radiate less at the end of the study just to please the nice young physicist! A critic might suggest that the effect was not due to a physical change, but to a chemical change—the heat led to the giving off of radioactive gas, which escaped from the chamber in which the counting was done. However, the scientist can test this by redesigning the chamber.

While it is true that many studies in the physical sciences require extensive and precise equipment, relatively simple research methods (such as the before-and-after method) are adequate for two reasons, even though this method is more difficult to use in the behavioral sciences. First, as we noted, it is usually easier to control the relevant rogue suspects in physical science. Second, the rogue suspects are usually fewer and better known. Nevertheless, as the physical sciences deal increasingly with less stable materials, researchers must use more complex research methods and statistical procedures.

Alternatively, some behavioral scientists attempt to add precision to their work by restricting their studies to more or less stable materials, like white rats, maintained under laboratory conditions where factors such as diet, weight, love life, and the cost of living can either be controlled or assumed to be irrelevant to the rat. In behavioral science situations where the rogue suspects cannot be directly controlled or assumed to be irrelevant, we often require more complex designs, such as the control-group method to be discussed in the next chapter.

SUMMARY

The before-and-after method typically makes the mistake of focusing on one pet suspect, or messenger, occupying the time gap between two observations. But, as we now know, four rogue suspects plague every before-and-after study. Two of the rogues (elastic-ruler and on-stage) typically distort O_2 in favor of the treatment. The two other rogues (in-the-gap and maturational) occur in addition to the treatment. Therefore we can't untangle the influence of these suspects from those of the treatment suspect. If the patients improved we don't know which suspect, or combination of suspects, to thank. For example, it may be that the pill is useless, but the rest in the hospital helped. Or, on the contrary, that the pill improved the patient two points, but the anxiety over being away from the children set him or her back 4 points, for a net loss of 2 points.

As typically used, the before-and-after study is seriously flawed. However, we saw that under certain stable or sheltered conditions it becomes a powerful research method. But the control-group method, to be discussed in the next chapter, is required to manage the rogues effectively.

Prior to discussing this important method, however, we present a detailed example of applying the before-and-after method taken from a student research project. The example deals with one student's attempt to increase classroom participation. In reading this study you will be able to detect possible influences of the four rogues and become more aware of their confounding impact on your decision making, for you use this before-and-after method regularly in your own life.

EXAMPLE: STUDENT SELF-CHANGE PROJECT

PROJECT INSTRUCTIONS

Using as a guide Watson and Tharp's (1977) book *Self-directed Behavior: Self-modification for Personal Adjustment,* conduct a study of your own behavior based on a before-and-after design.

pretreatment observa-   treatment   posttreatment
tions or baseline   observation

You will recall that the before-and-after design is weak unles you have a stable pretreatment baseline and also a reasonable posttreatment follow-up, making the improved design look like this:

pretreatment baseline of two   posttreatment observations and
to three weeks' observation   recording of four to six
and recording   weeks

STUDENT REPORT

Step 1. Sources of Dissatisfaction or Desired Change

These include wasting a lot of time; skipping classes; smoking heavily; not getting as much out of university as hoped, either academically, recreationally, or socially; not feeling relaxed or acting naturally on most dates—seeming to act a part; wanting to get more out of classes and personal relationships.

Step 2. Target Behaviors and Situations in Which They Occur

I have chosen the three following target behaviors from the preceding list:

A. *Behavior.* Chain-smoking or smoking at an increased rate. Smoking even though I don't enjoy most of the cigarettes—it's automatic and I regret it next day.
   Situations: The situations in which this chain-smoking occurs include bull sessions, beer sessions, dates, tutorials.
B. *Behavior.* Not paying attention and not asking questions or stating opinions in class.
   Situations. I rarely, if ever, ask questions in any class—small or large. In some tutorials I think of questions and ideas but rarely speak. In large classes I sit at the back where it's easy to daydream or read. In tutorials it's hard to do that.
C. *Behavior.* Feeling tense and acting unnatural on dates. I seem to be acting a part, and it's a part I don't know very well, so I suspect neither of us is happy with the performance. I end up talking as if I know everything and also being very critical—not of the girl so much as of everything else. The behavior I would like to increase is talking about things that I know something about and am interested in, and the behavior I would like to decrease is acting like a phony big-time operator.
   Situations: The situations include those where I am on a date and alone with my date. When I'm with a small group, I feel much more relaxed and behave more naturally.

Step 3. Principles of Learning as They Relate to One of the Target Behaviors

Not participating in class, for example, can be accounted for by several principles of learning.

A. *Lack of reinforcement.* I can't remember being reinforced or rewarded for past attempts at participation in high school, so I probably never did build up skills or habits of this kind. At the university very few professors clearly reinforce students who ask questions, so it is unlikely that such responses will be developed at this stage in my education. Therefore the principle that withholding reinforcers will weaken behavior is relevant to my lack of early development of class-room skills.

B. *Punishment.* My impression is that not only was I not reinforced for participating in class (either asking questions or stating my ideas or opinions), but rather I was usually ignored, punished, or ridiculed. (Some of this may have been imagination on my part, but whether it was or not, it would probably serve as punishment.) Thus the second learning principle appears to be relevant—namely, behavior that is punished will occur less often.

C. *Avoidance behavior.* A third principle of behavior that appears to be relevant to my lack of class participation is the principle that behavior that is punished not only occurs less often but that punishment leads to escape or avoidance behavior as well. This might account for the fact that not only do I not participate actively but that I also skip classes or "avoid" becoming attentive when I do go to class. Apparently avoidance behavior, once started, is difficult to correct, so that if this principle is operating in my case, I may encounter difficulty in changing my behavior toward more active classroom participation. In one sense I get rewarded by skipping classes and by not asking questions. My reward is that I feel less tense for a while. Then, of course, I feel very tense when exams arrive and I have no lecture notes. Obviously immediate rewards are stronger (reduced tension immediately) than are future punishments (feeling tense at exam time).

The professor suggested identifying the stimuli (things, events, people) that trigger my avoidance of studying or going to class or asking questions. These triggers are powerful antecedents that control my behavior. So if I can control them (rapid heart beat) or avoid them (beer-drinking buddies in the afternoon), I should be able to attain some positive changes in my behavior.

Step 4. Selecting Target Behavior and the Situation in Which It Occurs

I decided to select classroom behavior as the behavior to focus on for several reasons: it is important; it is easy to measure changes; I can test out my plan immediately; I can get enough data to meet the course deadline and complete all the steps.

It is difficult to reduce to concrete terms the many ideas, feelings, and behaviors I have developed around classroom situations. In brief, it appears to consist of a general withdrawal of attention, interest, and activity; when I anticipate overtures or pressure to participate, my heart beats rapidly, and my palms sweat. I realize that for the purpose of this project, I must describe a particular target behavior that I wish to increase and also specify the situation or situations in which it is supposed to occur. The target behavior I plan to increase is that of asking questions in class, and there are two situations I will focus on. The first is the small classroom situation or tutorial. If I am successful there, I will then attempt to ask questions in large classes.

Originally I decided to increase the time I paid attention in class as the target behavior. However, it is difficult to keep track of such behavior, since attention ebbs and flows almost imperceptibly, whereas the number of questions I ask is easily counted, and presumably if I am asking questions I am also paying attention, to some degree at least. In brief, my target behavior is asking questions, and the specific situation during which the target behavior is to occur is whenever I am in a classroom.

Step 5. Collecting Baseline Data

Once the target behavior and the target situation are clearly defined, and before working out a method to improve things, the next step is to determine my current level of performance—that is, to see how frequently I now ask questions so that I have a baseline against which to measure any improvement that might take place following the introduction of a behavioral modification strategy.

In order to keep my record(s) simple and also to make sure I didn't lose them, I simply put a check mark in the upper right-hand corner of my course notebook whenever I asked a question in that particular class. I kept a record for one typical week, so all classes were covered—except one I skipped, which was also typical. Interestingly I asked a question in my first class of the baseline week, which turned out to be the first and last question I did ask that week. So merely collecting baseline data served to get me to ask one question, but that's all. My heart thumped, my palms were sweaty, and my voice broke. All of which suggests that I don't ask questions for pretty obvious reasons—not asking questions lets me avoid all that thumping, dripping, and squeaking.

I think the one-week baseline gave a fair picture of how frequently my target behavior (asking questions in class) typically occurs. In fact, it overestimates my base rate by one—I don't remember having asked even one question in my first eight weeks at the university, the ninth week being my baseline week.

Step 6. Reinforcers

According to behavior theory the most effective way to increase the frequency of any behavior is to have it followed as soon as possible by a strong reinforcer or reward.

Surprisingly at first I found it difficult to list what were reinforcers for me. While I won't cover my whole list here, it includes reading mysteries and science fiction; going to rock concerts; horsing around on my guitar; listening to records; beer-bull sessions; necking, etc.; watching football and hockey on TV, or better still, going to the games; having a sauna; going swimming; eating Turtles (the chocolate kind).

Concerning the Premack principle—that is, things I do habitually to which I can tie in a new behavior—I shower every morning, eat three meals a day, and listen to records and read before going to sleep almost every night. I guess one idea might be to use the Premack principle in the following way: I would only listen to records and read if I had asked a question in class that day. However, this seems like punishment, which I gather isn't a good idea to use in attempting to change behavior. Also, since I already do read and listen to records, it couldn't serve as a reinforcer unless I did more of it when I had asked a question. However, as it is, I usually read and listen to records until I fall asleep, so I don't see how I could do more of it. I guess I'm still not too clear on how to use the Premack principle.

Step 7. Drawing Up a Behavior Contract

I had more trouble than I expected drawing up a contract that was clear and that I thought would work. My final contract was as follows:

> On this 17th day of November, 1994, I, John Doe, make the following commitment to myself—namely, that I will attempt to ask at least one question in each small class I attend and that for each question I ask I will immediately reinforce myself with one Turtle and also with a token which is worth 1/2 hour at the regular afternoon beer-bull session. When I have achieved this goal, I will apply the same contract in large classes.
>
> Signed: _____
>
> John Doe

I feel a little silly about the Turtle reward; it seems childish, but it meets conditions of an immediate reinforcer I can afford and one that represents an overall gain because I don't normally eat them all that often. But I am a little concerned that I may cheat—that is, if I have the candy with me I'll eat it whether or not I ask a question.

Also, I usually go to the regular afternoon beer-bull session, but my contract calls for withholding a strong reinforcer if I fail to carry out the target behavior of asking questions. Therefore granting myself only one half-hour at the beer session per question asked turned out to be rough on the days I only asked one question. Once I get there I *stay*. So if I had only earned one token for a half-hour, I tried to go to the session late. As tokens I used beer session "tickets" I manufactured immediately after I asked a question. I would scribble on a scrap of paper something different each time, for example: "Admit this great question asker to 30 minutes of Golden Happiness—Molson's Golden, of course." Creating my "tickets" captured some attention that might have better gone to listening to the lecturer. However, I gather that in the beginning of a behavior modification project, one should be grateful for even a very small improvement.

Incidentally, the guys at the beer-bull sessions found out about my project and would demand my "ticket" when I appeared. It would be passed around, and occasionally I would be told my 30 minutes were up and that I had to leave or produce another ticket. This supportive behavior of my friends helped a lot. If they had all got on my back, the way one of them started to do, I would have had to use another reinforcer.

Step 8. Antecedents

Learning theory states that much of my behavior is under the control of immediately preceding events or signals called *antecedent stimuli*.

For example, if I happen to run into one of my drinking buddies (antecedent stimulus) between classes, we will likely go for a beer. One beer becomes the antecedent, or triggering, signal for another beer and for a bull session, which becomes the triggering signal for another beer and a wasted afternoon and also, usually, an unproductive evening. Therefore my drinking buddy and I are antecedent signals for each other that start a chain reaction of antecedent, or triggering, signals that control or strongly influence our joint behavior.

Incidentally, running into a drinking buddy is also an antecedent condition for skipping classes that afternoon and also the following morning, because I tend to sleep late due to a combination of fatigue, disgust, and (sometimes) hangover.

The antecdent conditions that affect my not asking questions in class appear also to constitute a chain reaction, for if a question pops into my head there is a brief period of interest, which triggers nervousness, which triggers a suppression of any question-asking tendency, which, in turn, triggers withdrawal of attention.

It is difficult to list antecedent conditions that favor asking questions, since I don't ask any. However, asking questions should be increased through any reduction in nervousness, plus the "awareness" that I will get something I badly want if I do ask a question. That awareness is an antecedent signal, I guess, if it is conscious. In summary, if my plan to ask questions in class is going to work, I must somehow avoid, or reduce, the potency of certain antecedent triggering conditions by:

1. Steering clear of drinking buddies in the early afternoon, or learning to replace a "yes" with a "no" response. Come to think of it, sometimes it's me who suggests we go for an early beer, so I am often not under any great pressure from others to go.
2. Reducing the nervousness surrounding the idea of asking a question by practicing relaxation.
3. Increasing my awareness during class of the benefits of asking questions, both in terms of short-term reinforcements (candy and bull-session tokens or tickets) and long-term payoffs (learning something).

Relaxation. As noted, I get nervous at the thought of asking a question, which serves to suppress question asking. Learning theory suggests that you can replace one response with another through practice. I practiced replacing my "nervous" response with a "relaxed" response. I practiced relaxing by:

1. Getting comfortable and loosening any tight clothing, and cutting out as many distractions as possible.
2. Taking three very deep and very slow breaths, exhaling very slowly and completely on each breath.
3. Starting with my feet, tensing and relaxing each set of muscles in my body, coordinating the relaxation with exhaling. This way I learned to recognize when and where I was tense and worked up from the feet to the legs, to the thighs, to the stomach, chest, arms, shoulders, neck, face, and scalp. My neck and shoulders are frequently very tense. I now notice this and can relax them at will.

I practiced for a couple of weeks just before getting up in the morning. Then when I was lying there relaxed, I would imagine asking simple questions in small classes. Also, I then practiced relaxing in class, particularly the neck and shoulders.

It's easy to forget, so I kept a record in my notebook of when I practiced relaxation in class. It's easy to forget to keep a record, so I wrote another contract in which I rewarded myself by ordering a big pizza on Saturday or Sunday when my record-keeping system was complete for that week.

Step 9. Behavioral Change Plan Goes Into Operation

It is difficult to decide precisely when my behavior modification plan was put into operation. I guess in one way it started the day I commenced to plan it. In another way it started when the period of gathering baseline data was over and I started to record progress. In any case, Table 4–2 summarizes my intervention plan.

TABLE 4–2   Intervention Plan

Goal:	To increase the frequency with which I ask questions in small and in large classes.
Plan:	1. Draw up a contract specifying target behavior and the situation, and also reinforcements (candy and beer session tokens) to be gained for each behavior unit performed.
	2. Select critical antecedent conditions to be modified in order to increase the likelihood of producing the target behavior. The antecedents to be modified include:
	a. Beer-buddies: not accepting or proposing early afternoon beer sessions
	b. Nervousness: to be reduced through relaxation training
	3. Record results, including a baseline period.

I believe my behavior modification commenced the first day I started to work on this assignment. Nevertheless, for the purposes of this section of my report, I will say it started when I put my contract into operation, after the collection of baseline data. Table 4–2 presents an inadequate summary of my intervention plan.

The key elements of the plan from my point of view are avoiding certain antecedents, reducing the potency of others through relaxation, and using strong reinforcers right after performing the target behavior. Also, it helped to think of it as a kind of game—a game I was committed to play, but one that included a lot of human interest and humor.

Step 10. Results

I have summarized the results of my project in Figure 4-1.

It can be seen from an examination of this figure that, during the baseline period, I only asked one question, so this behavior is very improbable under ordinary conditions.

For the next three weeks I focused on small classes. I recorded each class day and indicated how many questions I asked. I started off the first week of the intervention plan with two questions on Monday, followed by two on Tuesday, then dropped down to zero toward the end of the week. At the commencement of the second week, I was up to four questions early in the week, dropping to zero at the end of the week. However, by the third week, I seemed to have more or less stabilized, asking questions in small classes at around three or four questions per day. It is interesting to note how the behavior fell off at the end of weeks 1 and 2. This is not surprising, since Thursdays and Fridays are typically down days, almost as if one were warming up for the weekend.

Commencing the fourth week, I continued to ask questions in small classes but also attempted to start asking questions in large classes. From Figure 4–1 it can be seen that the small-class behavior change appears to be stabilized, and there is some evidence that I am learning to ask questions in large classes. However, I don't expect the frequency to reach the same level in large classes as in small classes, since question asking in large classes should not be done frivolously, since you are taking an awful lot of other people's time.

Generally speaking, I am happy with my progress. I am certainly getting more out of my small classes. The questions I ask in large classes are still pretty simple, and I am still not completely relaxed about it.

I plan to continue the same procedure for another two weeks, and if my small-class performance continues as it is, I will let it fly on its own and focus on large classes.

I am still not completely happy about my reinforcements. I have replaced candy with "girl watching," except in one tutorial where I don't

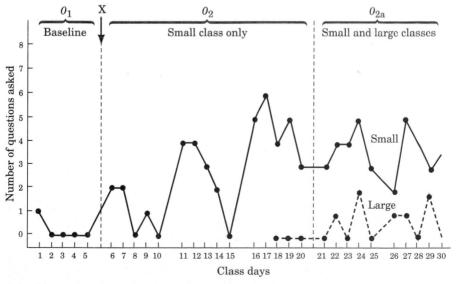

FIGURE 4–1   Mapping Behavior Change

seem to need any artificial reinforcements. Also, I use my tokens to buy new records rather than for the beer-bull sessions, which are a mixed blessing. The relaxation training is working relatively well, I feel, except for the odd morning when I sleep late and so don't have time. Sometimes it works too well, and I relax myself right back to sleep. My roommate has agreed to wake me, provided I'm not too cranky.

I am in the process of drawing up a plan and a contract to tackle another one of my dissatisfactions that I listed in Step 1 of this project to see if the system will work again.

In evaluating this before-and-after design, I appreciate the difficulties of deciding just what factors did contribute to my change of behavior. I am satisfied that it was not an elastic-ruler effect. I did ask more questions; even my professor noted that. But trying to sort out what aspects of my intervention plan—what suspects or combination of suspects—were responsible is very difficult.

For example, I believe the on-stage or testing effects were probably more powerful influences than were the reinforcers. If this had not been a class project and also if my buddies had not become supportive, I don't believe the supposed primary treatment (the contract and the reinforcers) would have had much effect. Time-tied or maturation variables might also contribute—that is, becoming more familiar with my class and the university setting. I don't think so, however, since I have a long history of not asking questions, even in high school.

I can't think of any in-the-gap suspects other than that toward the end of the study when my professor congratulated me. But since I had already started asking questions, that is not a prime suspect, although a reinforcing one.

In summary, I think the prime suspects or influences in this study were "testing" (on-stage effects) and examining my own behavior—particularly collecting the baseline data. In other words I think collecting the O_1 data motivated me to change more than did the so-called reinforcers—Turtles and girl watching. But with this before-and-after design, who knows?

REVIEW QUIZ

True or False?

1. The before-and-after method capitalizes on the effective use of a limited time frame.

2. The before-and-after method is a less powerful method than the case study approach.

3. The before-and-after method pretends to be scientific but would not be regarded so by most scientists.

4. If time alone can produce changes in O_2 without any specific treatment, then we are dealing with a historical suspect.

5. Some organisms (including humans) may change their behavior merely because they are "on display" or being studied.

6. Four classes or types of suspects (or variables) plague every before-and-after study.

7. The before-and-after method can be used to advantage when a quick-acting remedy (or treatment) is being tested.

8. One problem with the before-and-after method is that measuring instruments can change or deteriorate between O_1 and O_2.

9. If an observation (O_1) has remained the same or stable for an appreciable period, then the before-and-after method should not be used.

10. Reducing the number of stray suspects pouring into the interval between O_1 and O_2 strengthens the power of the before-and-after-method.

11. Relatively simple research methods such as the before-and-after method are typically quite inadequate for studies in the physical sciences.

12. Collecting baseline data is a necessary first step to testing the effectiveness of any technique to change individual behavior.

☙ 5 ❧

Control-Group Method

──────── **Chapter Goal** ────────

*To introduce you to a "classical" research
design, one that helps control the four rogues
that caused so much trouble in the
last chapter.*

INTRODUCTION

*With treatment a depression only lasts 90 days,
whereas without treatment it lasts 3 months.*

The before-and-after method, discussed in the previous chapter, helped us write the first part of the preceding line and gave us false hope. The control-group method allowed us to write both parts of the preceding sentence, suggesting that the psychiatrist's magic pill might as well have been filled with sugar for all the difference it made. Given the opening statement in this chapter, which of the four rogues would you bet is playing a strong role in shaping the results? What about the time-tied one (maturational), suggesting that the "natural course" of some depressions is about 3 months.

We have learned that determining "what causes what" is no simple matter regardless of what method we use. When introducing a particular "treatment" (independent variable) in the before-and-after method, it's difficult to tell whether a difference between O_1 and O_2 (the dependent variable) results from the treatment or from something else. In the previous chapter we indicated that the control-group method represents a major breakthrough in helping deal with the four rogues: in-the-gap, time-tied, elastic-ruler, and on-stage. Therefore one of the first questions a consumer of science should ask is whether a control group or groups were used in helping select prime suspects. As we will see, control groups don't guarantee that we will come up with the correct suspect, but they do reduce the risk of error considerably.

Consider what happens if we use two groups of patients instead of one when evaluating a new drug treatment. We split the group of depressed patients in half. One group gets the new wonder pill, and the other group gets a *placebo*, a pill that looks exactly the same as the wonder pill but contains only sugar. Some people feel better if they take a pill—any pill. We divide the patients so there is little chance of getting more of the healthier patients in one group than in the other. Ideally, the groups should start out identical in as many respects as possible. To protect yourself from bias in assigning people to groups, pick the names out of a hat; the first name goes to Group 1, the second name to Group 2, the third to Group 1, and so on. Unless you use some such method, you end up with a special collection of patients in one group (for example, as a result of staff members attempting to get their patients or relatives into the group that gets the wonder pill).

Having established two comparable groups, we treat them exactly the same way with one exception: One group gets the wonder pill, while the other group gets the sugar pill or placebo.[1]

The procedure now becomes:

Group 1 (O_1) (X_{1}) (X_{2}) . . . , (X_{d}) . . . . , (X_n) (O_2)
New Drug

Group 2 (O_{1a}) (X_{1}) (X_{2}) . . . , (X_{p}) . . . . , (X_n) (O_{2a})
Sugar Pill

Thus the two groups start out supposedly with the same amount of depression—that is $O_1 = O_{1a}$—or in other words, one group does not have more seriously depressed patients than the other does. Following treatment we see whether O_2 is less than O_{2a}—whether the level of depression is now less for Group 1 than for Group 2.

ROGUE SUSPECTS

Historical (In-the-Gap) Suspects

The main point is to try to run the experiment so that the individuals in the two groups are treated exactly the same, except for one suspect—the drug X_d. Thus we attempt to make sure that the same X's

---

[1]In some studies instead of giving a sugar pill, the researcher uses the treatment pill in common use. Thus the researcher can see whether more people improve in the new pill group than in the group receiving the usual treatment.

pour into the gap between O_1 and O_2 as between O_{1a} and O_{2a}. To ensure that the nursing staff does not spend more time with the patients in one group than with the patients in the other, the patients in the two groups are mixed up or made indistinguishable as far as anyone who can influence the experiment is concerned. The nurses and other doctors are not told which patients are getting the new wonder drug (X_d) and which are getting the sugar pill (X_p). All patients receive pills that look identical.

By not letting either the doctors and nurses, or the patients know who is receiving the drug and who the sugar pill, you are keeping both groups "blind" as to the design of the study. Such studies in which both ward staff and patients remain ignorant of who is in the treatment and who is in the control group are called "double-blind" studies. Such studies help control elastic-ruler, in-the-gap, and on-stage effects.

If both groups are to be open to influence by the same historical or time-tied suspects, then both groups must occupy the same space and time frame—for example, they must occupy the same hospital ward at the same time for the same duration. That is, you don't run the treatment group and then the control group. If you did run your study that way the groups would not only differ in terms of the treatment but in other ways as well. For example, they might have different nursing staff, cooks, or weather, leading to different in-the-gap suspects. Furthermore, the people doing the evaluation of patients may be getting bored with the study leading to elastic-ruler effects.

Instrument-Decay (Elastic-Ruler) Suspects

If the experiment is run properly, the doctor who measures the depression at the beginning and at the end does not know which patients received X_d and which received X_p, so the physician's biases, or elastic-ruler effects, cannot systematically influence the doctor's assessment of one group over the other, either during the study or when deciding which patients have improved and which have not. This *double-blind* procedure, where neither the patients nor the treatment evaluator knows who got what pill, helps protect against elastic-ruler and on-stage effects. Only the researcher knows the code, which is not disclosed until O_2 and O_{2a} are completed.

Testing (On-Stage) Suspects

The on-stage effects of having been interviewed would influence patients in both groups. There will be patients in both groups who want to impress the doctor that they are well enough to go home, as well as some who merely want to "help the nice young doctor." Thus we hope that the resulting influence on O_2 and O_{2a} will be about the same—that is, that both groups will probably show about the same amount of on-stage improvement apart from any effect of the new drug.

Maturational (Time-Tied) Suspects

Furthermore, spontaneous recovery should be about the same for both groups, since the time between O_1 and O_2 is the same as between O_{1a} and O_{2a}. Thus time-tied or natural-recovery suspects should affect each group the same way.

NOW WHAT?

Notice that the control-group method does not eliminate the individual or combined influences of the four rogues; rather, *the control-group design provides the rogues with* equal *access to both groups.* Thus O_2 reflects the influence of the four rogues combined with the drug, while O_{2a} reflects the influence of the rogues combined with the sugar pill.

We should not be surprised, therefore, if both groups show some improvement: O_2 shows an improvement over O_1, and O_{2a} shows an improvement over O_{1a}. These changes reflect the effects of such suspects as spontaneous recovery (time-tied), a biased doctor (elastic-ruler), a nice ward supervisor (in-the-gap), and a desire to go home (on-stage). If, in addition, X_d has had an effect greater than X_p, we should have O_2 showing a greater shift than O_{2a}. If the two groups were the same to begin with, the difference between O_2 and O_{2a} provides us with a measure of the effect of X_d over X_p. This is in contrast with the simple before-and-after model where we have X_d effects all mixed up with the effects of the other suspects without being able to untangle them. It was this kind of tangle that led some wit to wisely observe that a good doctor keeps the patient occupied while nature works the cure. It is easier to wait for a natural change when under the illusion that some potion is bringing it about.

When we divide a group in two to make the two sections as identical as possible and then give them the same treatment except for one X, we are using a *control-group* method—a much more precise sieve than the after-the-fact, and before-and-after sieves discussed so far. Representing a remarkable leap forward in helping us produce packages of durable information, in one stroke the control-group method permits researchers to assess the effects of their treatment over and above the effects of the four rogues alone. Of course, this applies only if the groups are equivalent to begin with, and this is a big "if."

SELECTION OF THE CONTROL
COMPARISON GROUP

Unless Groups 1 and 2 are "more or less" equivalent at O_1 and O_{1a}, our efforts to rule out alternative suspects are thwarted. Random assignment to each group is a commonly employed technique that allows us to assume that all relevant or influential suspects are probably equally represented or distributed across the two groups because it is the luck of the draw which determines whether any individual patient will be in the treatment group or the control (placebo) group. However, random assignment does not necessarily produce a balanced outcome, at least in the short run or with a finite sample as examination of any table of random numbers will reveal.

It is possible to test the assumption of equivalence, on relevant variables, of the treatment and control groups by comparing the two groups before the introduction of the treatment of placebo, that is, does $O_1 = O_{1a}$? Are the patients in the two groups roughly the same age? Have they been hospitalized for about the same amount of time? Even if the patients in each group are equally depressed, differences on other dimensions may affect observations at O_2 and O_{2a}.

Another strategy for creating a control group is to pair each individual in your treatment group with a "matched" partner in the control group—matched in the sense of being similar to the person in the treatment group on all relevant dimensions. This is easier said than done because we may not know in advance what all the relevant variables are, and we may not have access to a sufficiently large or appropriate pool of potential research participants.

The following example, abstracted from an actual research study (Ames, 1992), vividly captures the difficult decisions and tradeoffs surrounding selection of the "best" control group when operating outside narrow laboratory conditions.

The purpose of the research conducted by Ames and her colleagues was to determine the effects of institutionalization on the subsequent development of Romanian children who had been adopted into a North American family. Before adoption, these children had been institutionalized in Romanian orphanages under conditions of appalling deprivation (e.g., toddlers confined to cribs for 20 hours a day). Many children were severely undernourished and suffering from various illnesses, and most were developmentally delayed (e.g., the average 2½ year old could neither walk nor talk).

What is the appropriate comparison (control) group for these Romanian adoptees, ask the researchers? To separate the effects of the institutionalization from those of adoption, we would need to find a matched group of adopted children who had not previously been institutionalized but who were adopted at the same ages as the Romanian sample (i.e., from 9 to 68 months). Such a comparison group does not exist because only rarely does a 1 to 4 year old move directly from the birth home to the adoptive home. More typically adopted children of this age have either spent some time in an institution or have been through a series of foster homes.

"Alternatively," comments Dr. Ames, "one could conceive of a sample of children institutionalized but not adopted. This would tell us how much better off our children are than those left behind in Romania (but that is probably pretty obvious anyway), and such a study would not tell us anything about how our children compare with children reared at home."

What about a comparison group that was both institutionalized and adopted, but whose institutional experience was vastly different from that of the Romanian children—perhaps children adopted from Peruvian or Mexican orphanages? To locate such a sample would be extremely difficult (e.g., finding a 37-month-old boy who had been adopted from a non-Romanian orphanage at the age of the 2 years 1 month and repeating this type of search for all 38 of the other children). Even then we might well have a confounding variable of darker skin color leading to biased responses.

Dr. Ames observes: "Finally, we might wait for the children adopted as newborns from Romanian hospitals—i.e., children who would have gone to orphanages had they not been adopted—to grow to the ages at which our orphanage children were adopted. This would be the best group to help control for background variables."

The conclusion that may be drawn from this analysis is that different types of control or comparison groups answer different kinds of questions and some good control groups are simply not available or feasible. In Ames' research, the comparison group ultimately selected was a group of never institutionalized, nonadopted children living with their biological parents. These children we matched with a Romanian child on the basis of sex; age; parents' educations, occupations and ages; family income; and number of children in the family. Subsequent statistical testing of the differences between the two samples revealed no significant differences on the matching variables.

In brief, if you recall the problems created by the four rogues you will appreciate that a control group that controls for even one of the rogues is better than no control group at all.

ELABORATION OF THE CONTROL-GROUP METHOD

Suppose that in the example just discussed all depressed patients had been given a stimulant pill each day as part of the regular hospital routine. At the time of the study, Group 1 individuals were given both the new wonder drug as well as their regular pep-me-up pill. Group 2 patients, however, were administered the stimulant drug only.

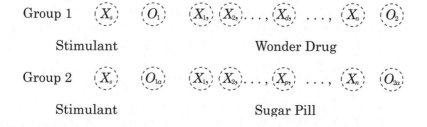

Group 1	X_s	O_1	$X_1,$ $X_2,$ $\ldots,$ $X_d,$ $\ldots,$ X_n	O_2
	Stimulant		Wonder Drug	
Group 2	X_s	O_{1a}	$X_1,$ $X_2,$ $\ldots,$ $X_p,$ $\ldots,$ X_n	O_{2a}
	Stimulant		Sugar Pill	

Can we conclude that if O_2 is different from O_{2a} the difference is due to the wonder drug? One is tempted to answer yes and to argue that, since both groups were given the stimulant, any difference between the groups must be due to the difference between X_d and X_p. It is possible, however, that it was the *combination* or interaction of the stimulant and the wonder drug that led to improvement and that the wonder drug alone may be ineffective. In this instance repeating the study with two other groups of patients while omitting the stimulant pills would inform us what improvement results from the wonder drug alone. Similarly, the effect of making the first observation (O_1) may get mixed or combined with the treatment, and so we may want to know the effect of observing or measuring alone, the effects of treatment alone, and the interaction of the two.[2]

Consider another example. Assume we are interested in determining whether providing children with training in physical coordination will improve their intellectual ability, so we design a control-group study to test it. In order to ensure that our two groups are equal in intellectual ability to begin with, we administer an intelligence test to all the children and divide them into two groups with similar numbers of bright, average, and dull children in each group. Group 1 is then given two weeks of training and subsequently both groups are retested.

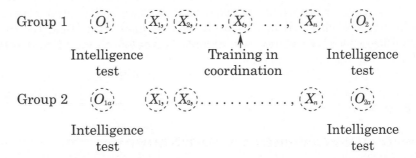

If the difference between O_2 and O_1 is greater than the difference between O_{2a} and O_{1a}, we may conclude that training in coordination improves intelligence test scores. But a sophisticated critic argues, "You may have controlled for the four rogues, but you still don't know whether the improvement is due to a combination or interaction of the pretest (O_1) and the training (X_1). Maybe the children in the first group were just more familiar with the experimental setting. The relaxation that comes with familiarity, plus the extra attention during training, may have produced the difference between O_2 and O_{2a}."

[2]The distinction between O and X can become somewhat vague or arbitrary. In essence an O may be considered as a suspect, or X, when the first O has effects on subsequent observations.

How can we answer this critic? One way is to randomly select two extra groups of children from the same classroom. Neither group is given the first intelligence test; but we assume, since they were picked at random from the same classroom, that they would have the same average I.Q. scores as the other groups. In addition, we give training to one of the groups but not the other. The model thus becomes:

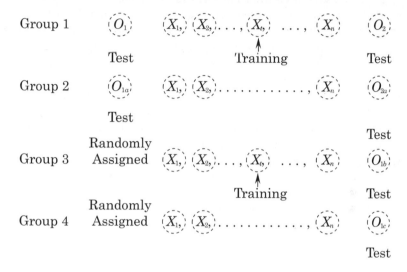

Assume that we obtain the following results:

$O_1 = 60$ $O_2 = 110$ $O_{1b} = 85$

$O_{1a} = 60$ $O_{2a} = 80$ $O_{1c} = 60$

If we compare O_2 and O_{2a}, we have a measure of the effectiveness of training combined with a pretest—30 units difference. A comparison of O_{1b} with O_{1a} gives an indication of the effect of the treatment alone—25 units difference. The difference between O_{1c} and O_{2a} gives a measure of the pretest effect—20 units difference.

We now conclude that training plus test practice accounted for the greatest improvement. Testing alone and training alone were not as effective as the two combined. Knowing the size of the test effect alone and the training effect alone would not lead to the correct prediction regarding the size of the two effects "interacting" together.

When there is a strong possibility of an interaction between X and O, it is advisable to test the effects of each separately.

By using the control-group design and by assigning subjects randomly to groups, we try to reduce the risk of the four rogues or of chance factors influencing one group more than another. Nevertheless, even under such circumstances, the hand of chance may play a hidden part—by dealing more quick-healing subjects into the experimental group and letting the new wonder drug receive unwarranted credit; by unpredictable shifts in the sensitivity or bias of the measuring instrument that happens to favor the treatment group; or by mistakes in transcribing or calculating the results.

The best defense against such chance factors leading to faulty conclusions is to consider the conclusions tentative until the study has been repeated and similar results obtained. Chance, being a fickle customer, shouldn't play the same tricks twice in a row. Another defense against chance factors making the independent variable (treatment) look unwarrantedly good is a so-called crossover design. In this design each group serves as a treatment *and* as a control group—that is, each group is tested under the influence of the independent variable and also tested without its influence, with the order of testing being counterbalanced. For example, to test the effects of threat of shock on errors of addition, we would use the following design:

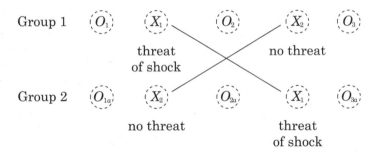

If the performance of *both* is impaired under threat of shock, you have increased confidence that your independent variable is having a predictable influence. It is a form of replication of the study.

The crossover design is particularly appropriate when studying processes that can readily be reversed. For example, a multiple crossover design (Agnew, Pyke, & Pylyshyn, 1966) employed to investigate the effects of tension on absolute judgment of distance, used heart rate as an index of tension. Figure 5–1 provides reassuring evidence that we were not dealing with mere chance fluctuations in heart rate, but rather that our independent variable (brief induced muscle tension) was having a systematic and replicable effect on heart rate. This design is, of course, not viable for the research described earlier with Romanian adoptees.

In addition to the four rogues already discussed, three more difficulties plague researchers' attempts to untangle the influence of the experimental treatment from that of the rogues, acting singly, or in combination: statistical regression, differential mortality, and biased selection.

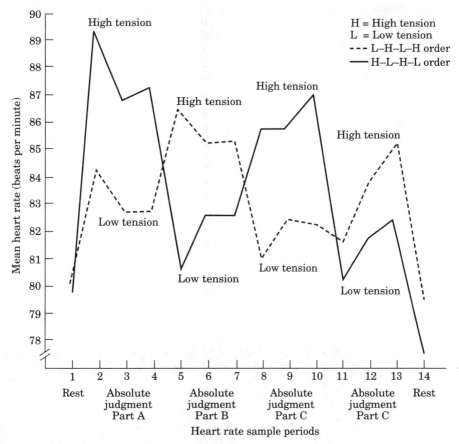

FIGURE 5–1   **Heart Rate (Beats per Minute) Under Strong and Mild Tension and Rest Conditions**

Statistical Regression

Statistical regression (*drift toward the average*) reflects the fact that, even without treatment, people with extreme scores subsequently score closer to the group average. That is, high scorers, on retest, tend to score relatively lower, and low scorers, on retest, tend to score relatively higher.

Many students find this regression effect difficult to understand. Intuitively, however, you encounter this phenomenon when you do exceptionally well on an exam, when *everything* has worked in your favor— you studied all the right material, didn't have a cold, had a good night's sleep, wrote the exam midmorning (your best time), etc. In other words, the invisible hand of chance arranged everything in your favor. Thus, the high mark you obtained doesn't necessarily provide a reliable or fair estimate of your ability; rather, it provides an inflated estimate. Therefore, under less ideal conditions, your mark would have been relatively lower, would have been a more typical reflection of your ability, and would have been closer to the class average.

Similarly, when you do exceptionally badly on a test, this usually reflects not only that you were poorly prepared academically but also that chance arranged everything against you—by chance you missed a crucial lecture, you had a cold, didn't sleep well, and the bus broke down, making you late for the exam, which was held first thing in the morning (your "dumbest" period of the day).

Therefore, statistical regression refers to the fact that extreme scores typically reflect an unusual constellation of forces, unlikely to be repeated on retest. On retest the scores will reflect a more typical constellation of factors, and so produce a less extreme score.

Statistical regression reflects the trend of things to return to "normal" even without treatment. For example, when you're feeling low, or when you've "bottomed out," there's only one direction to go—up. But when you're low, or when things are bad, is also when you're most likely to take "treatment." Thus corrective measures frequently occur when a natural, or spontaneous, return to normal is most likely—and, of course, the treatment gets the credit. This can be seen as a special case of a time-tied suspect (maturation), but also, as a case of statistical regression, in which extreme measurements reflect a floor effect or a ceiling effect, and then move or regress toward the mean, or the average. Thus whenever dealing with extreme values, whether they concern *low* moods, or *high* temperatures, you need a control group to estimate the contribution of statistical regression effects alone.

Differential Mortality

Differential mortality (*biased dropout*) occurs when, during an experiment, you lose subjects from your experimental or control group. For example, the subjects you lose from your experimental group (subject attrition) may be, unknown to you, the sickest subjects. Therefore your treatment group improves more than your control group, not because the treatment worked, but because it happened by chance that the sickest patients dropped out. Differential or biased mortality is difficult to control. Some safeguards include: (1) attempting to use matched pairs of subjects in the experimental and control groups, so if one drops out the other member of the pair is also excluded from the analysis; (2) carefully reporting the number, and characteristics, of dropouts when you publish your results; and (3) viewing your results as tentative until the experiment has been repeated.

Biased Selections

Just as the experimental and control groups may end up different because of biased dropouts, so too they can start out different. No guaranteed method exists for matching the control and experimental groups on all relevant connections—some of which remain unknown. Nevertheless, four safeguards against biased selection include: matching subjects on obvious dimensions; assigning individuals at random to the two groups; using large groups; and having the experiment replicated by an independent investigator.

Finally, while we include *experimenter bias* as a form of elastic ruler, or instrument decay, others assign it a separate category. So if you prefer you can reserve the concept of instrument decay to describe changes in sensitivity of measurement equipment, which can be controlled by the use of the standard control-group design. Experimenter bias, on the other hand, is more difficult to control. You can use "blind" procedures so that the experimenter doesn't know which subjects are in the experimental and which in the control group. However, when blind controls are not possible, the main protection against experimenter bias is having the experiment repeated by an "independent" investigator.

Summarizing, then, we can say that (1) science has no perfect methods for collecting and packaging knowledge or information; (2) scientists use a variety of methods, which differ in precision and cost; (3) a sieve or a scientific method is useful to the extent that it assists a scientist to make decisions by reducing the number of suspects involved; and (4) it is not always possible to use a fine sieve on a problem—a coarse sieve often becomes acceptable if it reduces ignorance even a little bit.

Consumers of science need to be told or to determine for themselves which sieve or sieves of science were used in naming prime suspects; otherwise it is impossible to decide how much confidence to place in the pronouncements of "experts."

LIMITATIONS OF THE CONTROL-GROUP METHOD

Replacing after-the-fact with control group methods yields increasing confidence in our results—for example, even taking into account the influence of the rogues, we find that the new drug did indeed help reduce depression under our particular experimental conditions.

Under our particular experimental conditions? Aye, there's the rub. Although we have high confidence that the drug works with that particular group of patients, on that particular ward, with that particular ward's staff, diet, routines, support therapies, and so forth, we don't know to what extent the drug will work on a different group of depressed patients, chosen by a different doctor, housed on another ward, in another hospital, in another country. As you well know, one person's meat may be another person's poison, and you also know another cook using the same recipe can spoil the broth.

We face a dilemma. In order to be increasingly confident that it was our treatment that did the trick, we try to "control" the possible influence of other factors such as diet, age, sex, duration of illness, physical health, ward atmosphere, and other treatments. We usually control such factors by narrowing them—for example, by limiting the patients who can get into the study to females under 40 with no previous history of depression, with no major physical disability, all living on the same ward with the same nursing and medical staff. In doing so we limit the number of *external* factors that might affect the results. We test the drug under internal "hothouse" conditions.

If we get a difference between our experimental and control groups under such protected hothouse conditions, we can be relatively certain that it was due to our drug and not to chance influences like variations in diet between the two groups. But we buy such confidence at a price, for while busy eliminating external influences to establish the internal hothouse effectiveness, or validity, of our drug, we at the same time narrow the claims we can make about its validity *beyond* the hothouse conditions. Each control we use reduces the generalizations we can make about the drug's effectiveness—reduces our external validity.

EXTENDING THE CONTROL-GROUP METHOD

There are at least three experimental paradigms, based on the control-group model, which help overcome some of the limits of traditional laboratory research: the natural experiment, the field experiment, and simulation research. Each of these approaches to scientific investigation maintains the manipulative feature of laboratory work but allows for the intrusion of a great many external factors.

The Natural Experiment

Campbell (1969) provides us with an elegant example of the use of the natural experimental design. In 1956 Senator Ribicoff of Connecticut instituted a crackdown on speeding as a result of a very high traffic fatality rate the previous year. Was his program effective? Forty fewer deaths occurred in 1956 than in 1955, but if 1956 was an exceptionally dry year, we would expect fewer accidents due to lack of rain or snow. Or perhaps the price of snow tires dropped dramatically, and hundreds of drivers availed themselves of the opportunity to purchase safety at a bargain. Or perhaps the state had invested in a mammoth highway improvement program. These in-the-gap variables confound our interpretation of the simple pre-versus-post model. Public knowledge of the high fatality rate might have produced the reduction in 1956 (on-stage effect), or the accuracy or techniques of recording accidents may have changed concurrently with the crackdown (instrument decay). Traffic fatalities fluctuate yearly, and perhaps the drop after the crackdown merely reflects this normal up-and-down fluctuation. Plotting the number of traffic fatalities for the five-year period preceding, and subsequent to, the crackdown helps to rule out some of the rogue suspects. A control group, consisting of the traffic fatality rates in neighboring states where there was no crackdown, further reduces the number of competing suspects and helps confirm that the crackdown did indeed have a beneficial effect.

The Field Experiment

Experiments are sometimes conducted in natural (nonlaboratory) settings and are superior to laboratory control-group experiments in that they reduce the confounding effects of on-stage suspects and enhance external validity. These advantages are of course counterbalanced by the minimal control that the investigator has over many components of the experimental situation (a reduction of internal validity). Nevertheless, the method has great utility for the study of certain phenomena which are not suitable for laboratory investigation.

One such experiment was reported by Milgram, Bickman, and Berkowitz (1969). These researchers arranged for small groups of research confederates to stop in the middle of the sidewalk of a busy thoroughfare and gaze upward at a building across the street. The size of the group of confederates, ranging from one to 15 people, was the treatment (or independent variable)—the manipulation.[3] To what extent would passersby also stop and glance up, and would a larger group of confederates be more influential in terms of inducing others to stop and stare? Many more passersby looked up than stopped, and even one research confederate gazing upward was enough to produce imitative behavior in 40 percent of the passersby. A similar percent of passersby were induced to stop when the group of confederates numbered 15.

Simulation Research

Zimbardo and his colleagues have produced perhaps the most dramatic example of simulation research (Haney, Banks & Zimbardo, 1973). In a very realistic mock-up of a prison, university students role-played either prisoners or guards. In a matter of days the guards developed and utilized oppressive and domineering tactics on the prisoners, while the latter degenerated into passive, dependent, pathetic creatures. The experiment was terminated prematurely because of the pathological reactions of both groups.

---

[3]This experiment is analogous to the different treatment approach of the doctor who compares the new wonder drug, not with a placebo (or nontreated control) group, but rather with the "old" treatment.

Again this type of experimental paradigm may be employed to investigate under systematic, controlled conditions events which are otherwise outside the realm of scientific study (for example, international negotiations). Subject awareness, however, has unknown effects on the results obtained, and thus conclusions derived from research of this type are only suggestive.

UNOBTRUSIVE MEASURES

Extensions of the control-group model enhance external validity and so does the use of unobtrusive measures. Such measures may be employed in many types of research paradigms—most common in field studies, they may also be utilized in laboratory experiments.

When we eavesdrop on the conversation of the diners at the next table, watch the stewardess handle the drunken, amorous passenger, or admire the Adonis on the subway, we may well be making unobtrusive observations. A minimum of deception, or feigned indifference, or our studied air of passionate absorption in a newspaper provides us with abundant opportunities to observe how people behave when they don't know they are being watched.

For example, one student, curious about what police officers talked about while cruising, adopted an unobtrusive measure by hiding in the back seat of a cruiser. In so doing he obtained a radically different picture of the content and style of police officer conversations than he had obtained through questionnaires, interviews, and archival research. However, when the officers stopped for coffee and our researcher tried to leave the cruiser as unobtrusively as he had entered, he learned to his dismay that, in the back seat of police cruisers, there are no handles on the doors. He was therefore apprehended, and only after careful examination of his person and his credentials and after repeated assurances that it was only a college prank was our trembling novice researcher sent on his humble way. While laboratory studies protect you from many facets of the question under study, unobtrusive probes, if discovered, can teach you more than you bargained for.

The Watergate goof remains a classic example of a politically motivated unobtrusive probe that not only failed, but shook a nation in the process. The ethical implications of applying unobtrusive measures are serious and complex, and any student would be well advised to consult several faculty advisors before launching into this important—but sometimes risky—extension of research methodology. Notice, however, that archival sources provide a rich, ethical, and safe source of unobtrusive data.

SUMMARY

The control-group method adds great power to the research repertoire, permitting us to assess the "impact" of the independent or treatment variable over and above the impact of the four rogues. In skilled hands, this classic research method helps untangle scientific knots.

However, just as the behavior of bodies in a vacuum is different from their behavior under "uncontrolled" conditions of pressure, temperature, wind, dirt, and so on, so, too, will behavior in the controlled atmosphere of a psychological laboratory likely differ from that displayed in the hustle and bustle of "real" environments. The concept of external validity refers to the degree to which results garnered under controlled laboratory conditions can be generalized or exported to the uncontrolled world in which we live. We must always ask how robust are our laboratory findings, how similar are they to hothouse plants that wither outside their protected environment? To answer this question we rely on extensions to the control-group method. We rely on research strategies, such as natural and field experiments, simulations, and unobtrusive measures. In addition to providing opportunities for investigating questions not amenable to controlled laboratory study, these strategies also inject a few (or many) impurities into the scientific stew and so extend the external validity of the findings.

OVERVIEW OF THREE METHODS

In the last three chapters we discussed three different methods of tying speculations to observations, of trying to decide "what causes what." Before we continue, let's take a moment to compare them.

I.   After-the-Fact Method and Archival Research

$$X_1, \; X_2, \ldots\ldots\ldots\ldots\ldots\ldots\ldots, \; X_n \quad O_1$$

Number of possible suspects large and often difficult to identify or locate—poor memory, data loss, or decay.

II.   Before-and-After Method

$$O_1 \ldots \quad 1X_1, \; 1X_2, \ldots, \; X_t, \; \ldots, 1X_n \quad O_2$$

Reduces number of suspects but still can't untangle in-the-gap, time-tied, elastic-ruler, and on-stage suspects from treatment or X_1 under study.

III.   Control-Group Method

Group 1 $O_1 \; \ldots \; 1X_1, \; 1X_2, \; \ldots, X_t, \ldots, \; 1X_n \ldots \; O_2$

Group 2 $O_{1a} \; \ldots \; 1X_1, \; 1X_2, \ldots\ldots\ldots\ldots, \; 1X_n \ldots \; O_{2a}$

Reduced number of suspects. Major effects of the four rogue suspects should influence Groups 1 and 2 about the same. So if groups start out the same and end up different, we assume the difference is due to X_1 or X_1 in combination with the rogues.

The following is a student's example of applying, or misapplying, the control-group method to smoking.

EXAMPLE

CASE (STUDENT PROJECT)

Premack (1970) lists increased heart rate from nicotine as one of the intrinsic rewards or consequences of smoking. Therefore one of the reasons why smoking is difficult to give up may be that each time inhalers have a cigarette they give themselves a small "high" from the nicotine and feel refreshed from the increased blood flow.

Not only can smoking pick you up if you feel tired, but it can also calm you down if you're tense. Strange as it may seem, this may also be caused by the nicotine. A stimulant like nicotine can calm you if you're tense by what is called a *paradoxical effect*. Overactive and overtense children are sometimes given stimulants that for some unknown reason calm them down (Black, 1977). Nicotine can work the same way on tense adults; even though it is a stimulant, it may have a calming effect.

Anyway the purpose of our research is to use the control-group method to see if smoking does raise heart rate.

Procedure

Through naturalistic observation we selected 10 heavy smokers from the smoking section of a large introductory psychology class to participate in our study. Two said they were too busy, so we selected two more. We told them that we were studying memory, so they didn't know we were really studying smoking.

We divided them into two groups by drawing their names out of a hat. All subjects were tested individually. The general procedure was as follows:

After they arrived at our laboratory, which was a spare office in the psychology building, they were asked to sit down and were told this was a study to test the effects of relaxation on memory. They read a short passage, were tested for recall, relaxed and had a smoke, then read another passage and were tested for recall again. Group 2 subjects followed the same procedure, but they were not allowed to smoke.

To see how well they were relaxing, a pulse meter (San-Ei Pulse-meter, Medical Systems Corp., Great Neck, N.Y.) was used. The pulse meter dial reads out heart beats per minute. The pulse meter is about the size of a pocket calculator. A metal finger sleeve serves as a single slip-on electrode. We used the middle finger of the nonwriting hand, cleaning it first vigorously with alcohol.

After the subjects were hooked up to the pulse meter, they read from the procedure section of a mirror-drawing experiment for three minutes. Meanwhile, one of the experimenters recorded pulse rates every 30 seconds. Following the three-minute reading, subjects were asked to answer a number of standard questions about the passage they had just read. Then members of the experimental group were told to have a smoke and relax for 10 minutes. The members of the control group were told to relax for 10 minutes but were not allowed to smoke. During the 10-minute period, pulse rate was recorded every 60 seconds.

We were supposed to observe to see if the smokers were deep inhalers but forgot to do it for two of them; from memory we concluded that they were, so all members of the experimental group were inhalers.

At the end of 10 minutes, each subject read for three minutes from another standard passage and was questioned, during which time pulse rate was recorded every 30 seconds. The subjects were not told the real purpose of the experiment at this time for fear they would blow our cover; rather they were informed of the real purpose of our study when we reported our results back to their class.

Results

We calculated the average pulse rate for each group at each recording point, but we did not do statistical tests because we had so few subjects.

From the graph in Figure 5-2, you can see that the groups started out approximately the same in the beginning and at the commencement of the 10-minute rest. While both groups showed a decline in pulse rate, the smokers did less so, suggesting some support for the hypothesis that smoking increases heart rate. Also the smokers' pulse rate continued to be somewhat higher during the second reading passage, indicating that the nicotine was still working.

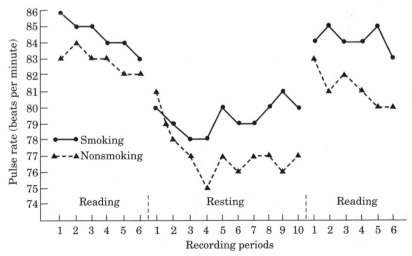

Figure 5–2   Heart Rate Changes as a Function of Smoking

Discussion

Our results support the hypothesis that smoking produces increased heart rate.

However, we should not get too confident of these results for several reasons. We had only five students in each group, so our samples were pretty small.

Also we made a big mistake and tested all the experimental subjects before the control group. Therefore our design looked like this:

Group 1 (O_1) $(O_2 X_1)$ (O_3)

           Reading   Resting   Reading
                   and
                 Smoking

Group 2 (O_{1a}) (O_{2a}) (O_{3a})

                               Reading Resting Reading

This means that in-the-gap and elastic-ruler suspects could be different for the two groups. For example, a possible in-the-gap suspect operating differently on the two groups could have been experimenter relaxation. By the time we tested the control group, we knew what we were doing and so were more relaxed ourselves, and this may have had a relaxing effect on them as well.

There is also an obvious elastic-ruler and instrument-decay suspect, for the pulse meter is battery-operated and it could have been losing some of its charge toward the end of the study and so giving lower pulse rate readings for the control group. The graph shows that while they were not a lot lower to start with, they were a bit. Whether this was due merely to chance or to the pulse meter's losing some of its juice, we don't know.

Anyway it was stupid not to test each experimental and control-group subject alternately, for by not doing this we really blew our experiment and failed to take advantage of the strength of the control-group method. Correcting this mistake and having bigger groups would have improved this study a lot. Also we could have used a standardized test for memory and seen whether smoking really did affect memory as well as heart rate.

References

Black, W. (1977), Personal communication, November.

Premack, D. (1970). Mechanisms of self-control. In W. Hunt (Ed.). Learning mechanisms in smoking. Hawthorne, N.Y.: Aldine.

REVIEW QUIZ

True or False?

1. An independent variable refers to the response of the research participant.

2. The difference between O_1 and O_2 is referred to as the dependent variable.

3. Use of a control group ensures that the researcher will come up with the correct suspect.

4. A placebo is intended to enhance the cooperativeness of the research participants.

5. To help ensure that bias isn't operating in the placement of research participants in specific experimental conditions, the researcher assigns individuals randomly to groups (i.e., treatment group and control group).

6. Use of a double-blind procedure means that neither the research participants nor the researcher is aware of the experimental condition to which each participant has been assigned.

7. Spontaneous recovery is an example of the operation of an elastic-ruler suspect.

8. A control-group design eliminates the individual and combined influences of the four types of rogue suspects.

9. The control-group method permits researchers to assess the effects of their treatment over and above the effects of the four rogues alone.

10. Choice of an appropriate comparison group depends on the kind of question the researcher is asking.

11. To address the possibility that it is the combination of a pretest with the treatment that is responsible for the effect, researchers may expand their design to include two additional groups that are not given a pretest.

12. In a crossover design, each individual participates in both the experimental group and the control group.

13. People who score high on a measure tend, on retest, to score relatively lower, and low scorers tend to score relatively higher on retest.

14. The effects of differential mortality (the biased dropout of subjects) can be minimized through the use of matched pairs of subjects in the experimental and control groups.

15. Field experiments and simulation research overcome to some extent the limits of the traditional laboratory model.

☙ 6 ❧
Validity—The Reach of Research

─────── **Chapter Goal** ───────

To introduce you to the notion that some "truths" are fragile and can only survive in a greenhouse, whereas others are robust enough to thrive in the rough and tumble of the outside world.

INTRODUCTION

Such a beautiful flower, but will it survive outside the hothouse?

Just as we seek new flowers that can thrive in the rough world outside the greenhouse, so too we seek new treatments that will work out in the large world, out beyond sheltered laboratory-like conditions. For example, suppose our psychiatrist (the one we first met in Chapter 3) with his "magic" pill for depression did test it under control-group conditions and found that it worked on his ward. Great!

But when other psychiatrists tried the new treatment on their patients, on their wards, with their nurses, cooks, cleaners, and so on, they found no difference between the magic pill group and the sugar pill group. What do we say? Well, we can say that although the treatment appears to be "valid" (i.e., it works), it only works "locally." The treatment appears to have only "local validity." The treatment, in its current form, doesn't travel well. Its "reach" is limited only to those patients who can be treated by the one particular psychiatrist, on his ward, with his staff. Although we appreciate treatments with "local" validity, we seek treatments, or research findings that have widespread validity, that travel well, that have a long reach.

Scientists, like the rest of us, face a conundrum. To look for key antecedents in large search spaces involves using economical but error-prone strategies, like the before-and-after and after-the-fact methods. To reduce the risk of error, you can shrink the search space down to fit the control-group methods, but you have to shrink the size of the questions you ask as well. So, scientists, like the rest of us, realize its easier to be certain about the answers to little questions than the answers to big ones. In the next three chapters we will discuss some of the methods researchers use to explore large questions. In this chapter we want to talk about the reach of science, about the *validity* of the maps scientists draw in exploring both little and large questions in multilayered reality. We discuss two kinds of validity: internal and external.

INTERNAL AND EXTERNAL VALIDITY

Campbell and Stanley (1966) provided the key concepts of *internal* and *external* validity which we, like a host of other writers, use to analyze research validity.

When you do obtain a significant difference between pretreatment and posttreatment observations or between experimental and control groups, you must still decide whether or not that difference was due to your favorite suspect—that is, to your "treatment." Or was the difference due to the four rogues (history, maturation, testing, instrument decay) acting singly or in combination; to data "mortality" (selective data loss) or to data "drift" (technically called *regression toward the mean*); to fraud; to data error (mistakes in data recording or calculation); or to bias. Of course, we make it sound simpler than it is because all of the foregoing suspects can combine in various ways, and one multiply the effect of one or more of the others, producing what are called *interaction effects*. These questions all concern internal validity—internal in the sense that they can all influence the results *within* the time-space frame of your specific hothouse or laboratory.

The following are some of the ways these internal validity threats can be reduced: by using control and experimental groups to which subjects have been assigned at random; by using reverse treatment designs; by obtaining stable baseline and long-term follow-up observations; by plotting our data; by using statistical tests; by using nonreactive measures; and, most importantly, by *independent* replication of the experiment.

By skillful use of these methods we confront questions of internal validity—we help assure ourselves and skeptical others that our *specific* treatment, conducted by specific experimenters, or observers, does indeed lead to significant differences between our specific samples of subjects, on our specific measures, in our specific experimental context, at that specific time, using that specific statistical test. No mean accomplishment, but . . . surely not the prime purpose of research.

The purpose of using a specific sample of subjects is to *represent* a larger parent population. The purpose of using a specific treatment was to represent a class of treatments; the purpose of using a specific researcher was to represent a class of researchers; and so on. To what degree the specific subjects, treatments, measures, or researchers are representative of their parent populations determines the extent of their *external validity*—determines how far our results, obtained inside the experimental space-time frame (*internally valid* results), reach beyond, or generalize, to a larger space-time frame—that is, how well a specific drug treatment in a given setting generalizes to similar drugs, administered by other trained researchers, in other settings.

In brief, whether or not a specific mix of the treatment procedure worked on the specific subjects inside the particular experimental context involves questions of internal validity. Whether the specific treatment mix will generalize to a useful class of treatments, a larger class of subjects, a larger class of experimenters, or a larger class of measures outside, or external to, a specific experimental context involves questions of external validity.

Issues of internal validity refer to *observed* subjects, to observed treatment procedures, and to observed experimental contexts. Questions of external validity refer to the generalization of these observations to classes of subjects, classes of treatments, and classes of experimental contexts not yet observed but of which the sample of specific observations is representative!

The following sections summarize the rogue sources of variance that can threaten internal and external validity.

THREATS TO INTERNAL VALIDITY

1. History—in-the-gap suspects
2. Maturation—time-tied suspects
3. Testing—on-stage suspects
4. Instrument decay—elastic-ruler suspects
5. Statistical regression—extreme data points drift toward the mean
6. Subject selection—pretreatment differences between experimental and control samples
7. Mortality or data loss—a biased "drop out" of subjects or data from either the experimental or control group
8. Interactions—any of the above may combine with the treatment (that is, prime it, magnify it, depress it)
9. Fraud
10. Error

THREATS TO EXTERNAL VALIDITY

1. *Sample restrictions.* The people studied, or observed, are not a representative sample of the target population—of the people you really want to study.

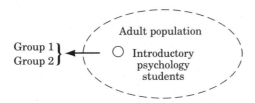

Do you think introductory psychology students fairly "represent" our adult population (e.g., in terms of age, education, values, work experience, etc.)? What about our psychiatrist's depressed patients? How representative were they of depressed patients in general? Or, how representative were the Romanian adopted children of all the institutionalized children in Romanian orphanages?

2. *Measurement restrictions.* The specific observations you make are not a representative sample of the target behavior—of the behavior you really want to study and understand.

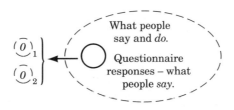

Do you think questionnaire or interview responses provide reliable predictions of how people actually behave? Do you think the interview responses depressed patients gave the nice, young psychiatrist provide reliable predictions?

3. *Treatment restrictions.* The specific treatment you apply is not a representative sample of the target treatment—the type of treatment you really want to study and evaluate.

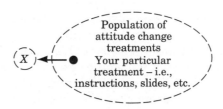

Do you think colored slides of starving Ethiopians have as much impact on attitudes as TV pictures, or as actually being there and witnessing the starvation? Do you think the psychiatrist's "magic pill" was a good representative of drug treatments or of that form of chemical substance?

4. *Research context restrictions.* Your specific research context is not a representative sample of target contexts—your "hothouse" conditions place restrictions on how far you can generalize to field conditions.

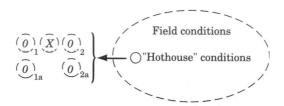

Do you think how you behave in a laboratory experiment on cheating is a fair indicator of how honest you are outside the laboratory? Do you think that the psychiatrists ward, staff, and so forth in a university hospital are a fair representative of the kinds of ward, staff and so forth that treat most depressed patients?

SAMPLING RESTRICTIONS

In considering threats to external validity, remember that researchers may not be able, or willing, to select a representative sample of subjects from their target populations; they may end up, for convenience, studying attitude change in undergraduate psychology students (accessible population). No problem—if you recognize the resulting sampling restriction, if you recognize the limitations this restricted sampling places on the generalizations you subsequently make.

Your results obviously cannot be generalized to adult Americans, but only to introductory psychology students. To all introductory psychology students? No, only to those who have a chance of getting into your sample—the ones on a given campus. Yes, if you put the names of all first-year psychology students on that campus into a hat and then draw your sample at random. But that is rarely done. More commonly, researchers use students from Professor X's introductory class because it's readily accessible (that is, he's interested in your research topic, or he's happy to give up an hour's lecture time). You can now generalize to all introductory psychology students in Professor X's class. Or can you? You can if you put all the names in a hat and draw your sample at random—or include the whole class in your study. But you may have had to settle for volunteers. So you put their names in a hat and select your experimental and control group samples—now you can generalize to volunteer introductory psychology students in Professor X's first semester 1994 psychology class.[1]

This represents a drastic shrinkage from the adult American target population—a drastic shrinkage even from the general population of introductory psychology students. As a practitioner or a consumer of science, you can see how important it is that you identify the actual population the experimental sample represents—it includes only the people who had an equal chance of getting their names into the hat. If they were a random sample of volunteers from Professor X's psychology class, then you can generalize the results you obtained from the sample of volunteers to the hatful of volunteers from which you drew that sample.

But surely that's being unduly cautious. Why not generalize to Professor X's whole class? In fact why not generalize to psychology students on that campus or to all introductory psychology students?

Such generalizations are unwarranted for a variety of reasons: because volunteers frequently respond differently from nonvolunteers; because Professor X lectures long and loud on the evils of prejudice and so has probably primed his students; because this particular university has very high entrance standards and so the students are not intellectually or academically representative of psychology students on many other campuses. In brief, sampling restrictions usually place strong limitations on the external validity, or generalizabiity, of social science research. Researchers frequently generate sample-biased research by studying only males, but presenting their findings as a study of the general population. For example, the respected Swiss child psychologist Jean Piaget, who developed a widely accepted theory of cognitive development, did almost all of his research with boys.

MEASUREMENT RESTRICTIONS

Just as the samples you select may underrepresent the people you wish to study, so too the measure or dependent variable you select may be a limited measure of the behavior you wish to study. Just as the limited sample of people you select restricts the generalizations you can make about people, so also the specific measuring scales you select and apply further restrict your generalizations to the behavior accessible through that measuring scale or that method of observation.

Therefore if we select a questionnaire to study attitude change and use only volunteers from Professor X's class, our generalizations are doubly restricted. First, we can only generalize to the hatful of volunteers from which we drew our research sample; second, we can only generalize to changes in *questionnaire* behavior. We may legitimately claim that, fol-

---

[1]If you had been measuring height or weight, would you be less cautious about generalizing? No? Maybe volunteers are oral gratifiers and eat more.

lowing treatment, our subjects can indeed "talk" a better game, but we can't claim that they can play a better game—not unless we also employ unobtrusive follow-up observations in our sample of dependent measures.

How far you can generalize from what people *say* they will do to what they *actually* do concerns a growing number of social scientists. While the details of the debate lie beyond this discussion, consumers of science should be aware that the strong relationship assumed to exist between attitudes and behavior appears to be much more flimsy than we once supposed (Ajzen & Fishbein, 1980). Yes, wise consumers of science will be cautious about generalizing too far from observations obtained by questionnaires, ratings, and interviews because people appear to talk a better game than they play—whether the target behavior is bridge, tennis, or tolerance for minorities.

Before considering the validity of tests and questionnaires, recall that measuring scales should be reliable as well as valid. A clock is reliable if it keeps *consistent* time. The clock is valid if it keeps the *correct* time. If your clock is consistently two hours behind the official time, it is nevertheless a reliable clock—it measures time consistently, but it is not a valid measure of the time in your zone. Therefore you can have a measure that is reliable but invalid; however, to be valid, a measure must also be reasonably reliable.

Since so much social science and educational research employs tests and questionnaires, the validity of such instruments deserves special mention.

Types of Test Validity

When you complete a test or questionnaire you usually want to know (1) what your score is and (2) what that score means. There are at least four related kinds of larger meaning or validity associated with a test: (1) content validity, (2) predictive validity, (3) concurrent validity, and (4) construct validity.

If we critically examine the items on a test—say a mathematical aptitude test—and determine that they include a representative sample of simple, average, and difficult questions drawn from each of the domains of arithmetic, algebra, trigonometry, and calculus, we conclude that the test has reasonable *content validity*—that is, it represents well the population of mathematical questions.[2]

Next, to the degree your score on one test helps estimate your current score on a different test, then the first test shows *concurrent validity* with the second. For example, if by knowing you scored two standard deviations above the mean in a mathematical ability test, we can then

---

[2]Whether the scoring is objective (e.g., multiple choice) or subjective (e.g., essay-type answer) will help determine all forms of test validity. To the degree different markers assign different scores to the same answer we lose confidence in the test.

accurately estimate your *current* score on a mechanical aptitude test to be one to two standard deviations above the mean—we have evidence of concurrent validity.[3]

Furthermore, if, on the basis of your high score in mathematical ability, we can make a better-than-chance prediction that in two years you will graduate in the top half of your class in electrical engineering, we have evidence of *predictive validity*—predictive validity involves a significant interval of time between the two measurements or observations.

Now we come to *construct validity* which, while important, is also difficult to explain. A construct is a complex speculative dimension (for instance, anxiety, intelligence, sociability) that represents a network of relationships. No single test or study defines a construct. In fact, a given test may be related to several constructs—for example, observed performance on a mathematical test may help infer (1) mathematical ability, (2) intelligence level, (3) anxiety level, (4) vocational interest.

Estimating the validity of a construct—intelligence, for example— is an ongoing research activity and involves exploring the emerging network of concurrent and predictive relationships through which "intelligence" appears to run.

The value of a construct lies not only in helping you organize and simplify a network of current knowledge but also in enabling you to make valid and surprising predictions.

While these four types of validity typically apply to tests and questionnaires, the principles on which they are based apply to almost all forms of measurement—a measure lacks generalizability to the extent that it lacks content, concurrent, predictive, and construct validity.

TREATMENT RESTRICTIONS

Just as the specific sample of people and the specific measures you select may both underrepresent your target populations, so too may your specific treatment underrepresent the general treatments (or treatment construct) you wish to study.

For example, your hypothesis may be that attitudes change toward minority group members following an emotionally involving experience in which the experimental group members witness a majority group member helping a minority group member out of a crisis. It's your belief that the experience of witnessing the rescue scene should be as realistic as possible. Since such scenes are difficult to engineer, you settle for a movie scene—you restrict your population of treatments to film simulations. In order to get your experimental subjects emotionally involved (to identify with the "hero" and the "victim"), you want them to watch the whole movie. However, you can only have 50 minutes of Professor

[3]For a discussion of "standard deviation" see Chapter 11.

X's class time for everything: pretest $(O)_1$ film (treatment (X)), and posttest $(O)_2$. Therefore you have to settle for a film clip—further restricting your treatment population to accessible film clips.

As if that weren't bad enough, the sound on the film clip is poor at times, and you're not sure whether it "broke the mood" of those who were emotionally involved.

Thus you drastically and successively reduce the size of the population of treatments you started with. Nevertheless, you did get a shift in questionnaire responses in the predicted direction. What kind of generalizations can you make? Well, you can make them only to Professor X's volunteers, tested on that questionnaire, before and after that film clip.

Next time, you decide you'll prescreen a series of appropriate film clips and draw one at random—then you can generalize to all the treatments (all the film clips) you've chosen, as well as to all the students who volunteered. If you draw your questionnaire at random from a hatful of appropriate questionnaires, you can generalize to those as well—keeping in mind the tricks that chance plays with small samples.

RESEARCH CONTEXT RESTRICTIONS

Just as the specific sample of people, *and* the particular measures, *and* the specific treatment all underrepresent your target populations of people, measures, and treatments, so too does the specific experimental context in which you do your study underrepresent the population of contexts you'd like to study and generalize to.

A host of features of the research context come to mind: the room was hot; the study was conducted between four and five in the afternoon; Professor X made a long introduction, not only making you rush your testing, but also actually hinting at the purpose of the study.

So research context includes rogues that idiosyncratically can shape your results so as to reduce the generalizations you can make and, in turn, reduce your external validity. Major rogues to be watched for include (1) in-the-gap suspects combining with your treatment (hot room, darkness, sleepy); (2) time-tied suspects combining with a treatment (late in day, tired, cranky); (3) pretest or posttest priming (Professor X's hints at the purpose of the study); (4) temporary effects (easy to change your prejudice for half an hour or so); and (5) experimenter effects. Oh yes, we forgot to mention the experimenter in the study was black—maybe the subjects changed their "attitudes" (questionnaire responses) because they sympathized with him, not with the "victim" in the film. What if a white experimenter were to replicate this study? Any guesses about the results? Some experimental results may be difficult to interpret because the results may be attributable—in whole or in part—

to characteristics of the research context, like the color of the experimenter, and not to the specific manipulation of the independent variable or "treatment." Such results are called *demand characteristics* because such cues seem to elicit or "demand" certain types of responses from the research subjects.

Surely we're not now going to suggest that to increase generalizability a researcher should describe various and relevant research contexts, place them in a hat, draw one at random, and then use that one to guide a particular piece of research. Theoretically not a bad idea, this approach is not so practically farfetched as it seems.

In a curious way science practices what we've been preaching—in a haphazard, semirandom way, different researchers dip into these various hats, drawing out this sample of subjects, that dependent variable, this independent variable, that research context. Taken one study at a time the external validity of any given study remains highly circumscribed, drastically restricted. But taken together the many researchers add up to . . . to what? To just one hat dipper after another? No, to a host of loosely coordinated explorers, driven by curiosity, probing accessible nooks and crannys of multilayered reality.

Loosely coordinated explorers? What forces coordinate them? The scientific culture coordinates them: The language and logic of science help coordinate them; the currently popular dependent and independent variables help coordinate them. For example, psychologists draw samples of introductory psychology students from a subject pool hat and subject them to an array of measures—O's—drawn from dependent variable hats, before and after subjecting them to an array of treatments—X's—drawn from independent variable hats, conducting their studies in an array of classroom and laboratory contexts drawn from the research context hat.

But couldn't all this be done in a more coordinated manner? Yes, but to the extent that you coordinate, you also control the size and content of the hats; you place restrictions on the explorations of multilayered nature. The creative scientist is one who draws from a larger or different hat, or who draws out a powerful new construct, or who builds a new dependent or independent variable. Creative scientists frequently work on the fringes of their discipline—too much coordination shrinks their work space, crowds them—crowds out some error but also crowds out precious creativity.

Nevertheless, one creative person or promising idea can provide an opportunity for coordinated explorations by many others. Coordinated or programmatic research leads to a systematic investigation of a given population (for instance, autistic children) using a sample of measures representing a given dependent variable (social interaction) or a sample of treatments representing a given independent variable (reinforcement) within a sample of research contexts (schools, hospitals, and private homes.)

Such studies represent one small segment of a much larger series of studies focusing on *reinforcement* as an important independent variable —as *the* most important independent variable, according to B. F. Skinner.[4] Thus an independent variable can become the focus for coordinating the research of thousands of researchers. These researchers draw samples from many population hats, draw sample measures from many dependent variable hats, draw a variety of treatments from many reinforcement hats, and conduct their studies in a variety of research contexts. Surely then we now have a reasonable example of external validity as applied to reinforcement. Yes, this is so, except the follow-up time of many conditioning studies on humans has been nonexistent or brief. Thus we are restricted in the generalizations we can make concerning the durability of many of the changes brought about through selective reinforcement—is it in some instances a Hawthorne effect, lasting no longer than a New Year's resolution? Time will tell!

Notice that external validity issues are never settled; external validity refers to the expanding reach of research in the exploration of multilayered shifting nature. External validity, like the future, always lies around the corner.

VALIDITY AND THE THREE LANGUAGES OF SCIENCE

You can think of science as ongoing exploration of open spaces bounded only by our three languages: speculative (pragmatics), observational (semantics), and symbol space (syntactic).

Research and applied science focuses on semantic space, sprinkling it with observational check points. For tiny semantic spaces—like how much you weigh on a given day—we can sprinkle that 24-hour one-person observational space with one observational checkpoint by weighing you once. Or we can weigh you every 10 minutes and sprinkle it with 144 checkpoints in the form of a line graph. Or we could place you on scales hooked to a computer and take readings of your weight every 10 seconds and sprinkle the space with 8640 observational checkpoints in the form of a graph or table.

Now, after exploring this 24-hour one-person observational space, how much do you weigh? Well, when we only make one observation the answer is easy. You have only one checkpoint so you use it: 155 pounds.

---

[4]B.F. Skinner, a famous psychologist, challenged many popular assumptions. His speculations and experiments led him to conclude that behavior, far from being free, is shaped and controlled by reinforcements and rewards.

But when we have multiple checkpoints, which one(s) should we use? We find that over that particular 24-hour period your weight fluctuates between 154.173 and 157.291 pounds.

So, mapping even a small semantic space for something as simple as one person's weight takes a lot of work. So we typically rely on one or two small samples and let them "represent" that space, and hope they do more or less. And for something as stable as weight this small sample of observational space works.

But notice what happens when we shift to less stable variables than weight. When we shift to less stable variables like voting preference our small samples fail to serve as valid representatives, and so we get election day surprises. That is why pollsters now attempt to take observational checkpoints right around the voting time, taking polls as people enter and leave the polling place. However, the closer the poll is to the vote, the less significant is its predictive value; wait ten minutes and get the "real" results.

Now we can better appreciate the problem facing a clinical psychologist trying to get valid observational checkpoint on people's mood. Mood varies much more than weight, and furthermore we don't have simple, reliable mood scales like weight scales. How might you map an individual's degree of depression over a 24-hour period, a week, or 3 months? *Hint*: Mapping semantic space requires that we make some explicit, and implicit, assumptions about the stability of whatever behavior we are studying.

Recall, from Chapter 3, that the psychiatrist treating depressed patients with his magic pill used only two observational check points, one at the beginning and one at the end. He was obviously assuming that the patient's level of depression was highly stable—that one observational checkpoint at the beginning, before treatment, and one at the end, after treatment, was all that was necessary to was map valid results. And he was probably correct over days or even weeks. But he forgot that degree of depression might change significantly in 3 months, even without treatment.

In brief, the best we can usually do is to sprinkle a few observational checkpoints in semantic space. In most cases we can't afford the time, trouble, and cost of high-density mapping of even brief semantic spaces concerning weight or mood. So we conclude that most semantic space remains essentially unexplored; if you're interested in social science, opportunities abound.

But semantic space is minuscule when compared with speculative space, which is bounded only by our imagination. So although semantic space shows only a light sprinkling of checkpoints, speculative space remains wide open for those with a theoretical turn of mind. So too does syntactical space for those of you with a mathematical or logical mindset. Thus the external validity of a theory (speculation and syntax) and its supporting observations (semantics) can be small, as it is when speaking of one person's behavior in a given situation, or can be very large when speaking of human behavior across cultures and time. We discuss the exploration of these three language spaces further in the final chapter.

SUMMARY

In this chapter we discussed validity, how far research results generalize, and how far they reach beyond a particular study.

1. Threats to *internal validity* include rogue suspects (uncontrolled or chance variables), other than the treatment (independent variable), operating within the particular research context; these may account for the differences you observe between your pretest and posttest observations or between your experimental and control group.

2. Threats to *external validity* include a series of restrictions on generalizations you can make beyond your particular research setting:

    a. Sampling restrictions

    b. Measurement (dependent variable) restrictions

    c. Treatment (independent variable) restrictions

    d. Research context restrictions

While the degree of generalization or the degree of external validity of a particular research study may be severely restricted, researchers investigating a given topic usually (1) sample from a variety of populations and so extend the sampling validity; (2) employ different variations of popular dependent variables and so extend measurement validity; (3) experiment with different versions and amounts of popular independent variables and so extend treatment validity; and (4) conduct their studies in a variety of research settings and so extend the context validity.

Most researchers, while having an eye on external validity, probably focus their energies on establishing the internal validity of their study. Other researchers, engaged in programmatic research, are balancing their attention between ensuring internal validity as best they can, while at the same time systematically designing and conducting a series of studies so as to extend the external validity of their findings. But it is perhaps the theorist reviewing a wide array of individual research studies who focuses most on the issues of external validity.

The expanding production of individual research studies and the endless extension of the external validity of such studies consumes the scientific enterprise in its compulsive exploration of our expanding multilayered experience. In the next three chapters, we discuss methods of extending your observations and speculations beyond the space/time constraints imposed by many laboratory situations; we also present studies focusing on internal validity.

RESEARCH CHECKLIST

The following checklist may help you decide how much confidence to place in a given research finding:

1. Does the investigator demonstrate that he or she has made a careful attempt to control the four rogue suspects? Yes _____ No _____ For example, would you have more confidence if a control-group design had been used than if a before-and-after design had been used?

2. If two or more groups were used, was there a reasonable attempt made to ensure that they were equal to begin with (randomization)? Yes _____ No _____

3. Did the investigator use enough people in each group to make you feel that the samples adequately represented the target population the investigator wanted to end up talking about (kids of different ages and from different socioeconomic backgrounds)? Yes _____ No _____

4. Does that particular dependent variable represent a reliable and valid means of measuring the target behavior under study? Yes _____ No _____

5. What prior evidence is presented to justify the selection of the particular treatment, to assume it is strong enough to influence the target behavior significantly?

6. How representative is the research context of target research or treatment settings?

7. Did the investigator publish or make available raw data so you could check the investigator's calculations or data packaging procedures? Yes _____ No _____

8. Did the investigator repeat the study and get similar results? Yes _____ No _____

9. Is the investigator an established one whose work has usually proved to be durable in the past? Yes_____ No _____

10. Has another investigator repeated this study and published similar findings? Yes _____ No _____

11. If so, was the second investigator independent of the first investigator (not his or her graduate student or employee)? Yes _____ No _____

12.   Do the findings make sense in terms of other durable findings in the same field? Yes _____ No _____ [5]

In summary, all that statistical procedures do is identify any trend in the data that the investigator chooses to include in his or her analysis. This trend may be there because of Treatment X or because of how the investigator, wittingly or otherwise, built it into the data. It is only through an examination of the research methods employed that you can decide how much confidence you have that the data pattern or trend is related to Treatment X.

REVIEW QUIZ

True or False?

1.   Internal validity refers to factors that can influence the results of an experiment within the time-space frame of the project.
2.   Internal validity may be enhanced by using an after-the-fact design.
3.   Internal validity may be enhanced through random assignment of research participants to the treatment and control groups.
4.   The degree to which specific subjects, treatments, measures, or researchers are representative of their parent populations determines external validity.
5.   Good internal validity allows the researcher to generalize the results of her or his experiment to the real world.
6.   Questions of external validity refer to the generalization of observations from a specific study to classes of subjects, treatments, and experimental contexts not yet observed but of which the sample of specific observations is representative.
7.   Fraud and error constitute threats to both internal and external validity.
8.   Results of studies employing introductory psychology students as research participants may not be generalized to adult Americans but may be generalized to all introductory psychology students.
9.   What people say they will do in a given situation is a very good indicator of how they will actually behave in that situation; hence, it is quite legitimate to generalize from questionnaire and interview responses to real behavior.
10.   It is possible for a measure to be unreliable but valid.
11.   Questions about what a test score means involve issues about the validity of the test.

---

[5]Too much reliance on item 12 will reduce the possibility of introducing new and startling information into the literature. Therefore if most of the other questions are answered positively, item 12 should not be used as a basis either for denying the investigator his or her right to publish or for denying those who are speculative their right to explore new ideas.

12. Concurrent validity refers to the extent to which the items on a test are representative of the population of questions relevant to the factor the test is designed to measure.

13. The demand characteristics of an experiment relate to features of the research context that seem to elicit certain types of responses from the research participants.

14. External validity is enhanced through the haphazard, semirandom behavior of a set of loosely coordinated independent researchers exploring various aspects of a research question using different subjects, measures, and research contexts.

ꕽ 7 ꕽ

Developmental and Longitudinal Studies

———————— **Chapter Goals** ————————

*To underline the importance of studying
behavior over time and to be able to view the
rhythms of human behavior. Typical studies
take only snapshots of bits of behavior that
need to be supplemented by longitudinal
perspectives.*

INTRODUCTION

*How the twig is bent so grows the tree.
The best bet is that people who lose
weight will put it back on again.
Depressions tend to recur.*

Some depressions recur each year. Therefore an effective treatment, one
with strong external validity, should not only reduce the length of a particular depressive episode but should also prevent, or reduce the severity of, a recurrence. Consequently, our psychiatrist with the magic pill
should follow the progress of his patients not just for 3 months but for
several years to see if the treatment has long-term effects and validity.

One way to extend the reach of science and to increase external validity is to look for patterns over time. Such patterns enable you to generalize your findings and to make predictions.

In this section, we consider a kind of "time-lapse" research method
involving snapshots over time (time series studies). The only thing you
can be sure about is that things will change: babies grow up, and then
grow old; organizations move in fits and starts; some memories fade fast,
some slowly.

In this chapter we review some ways of mapping change in individuals and organizations. If we plan to map change, whether individual or
organizational, we must have some idea ahead of time about what routes
that change might take. We can't cover all possible routes; we can afford

to stake out only a few. What then are some of the popular routes that change can follow?

Notice that these simple up-and-down maps of change (see Figure 7–1) can differ in several respects: They can differ in the rate of growth and decline, in the level they reach, and in the duration of such plateaus, and whether they recur. Therefore for comparative purposes we need to elaborate the basic up-and-down curve so that we can focus on *rates*, *levels*, and *cycles* of change.

FIGURE 7–1   Up-and-Down Curve

RATE OF CHANGE

Individuals or organizations frequently differ in how slowly or rapidly they change, and how rapidly they reach a certain state or level of performance (see Figure 7–2).

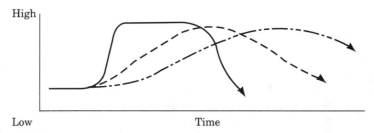

FIGURE 7–2   Level and Rates of Change

All children learn a variety of skills but at different rates of acquisition: toilet training, walking, talking. Similarly, adults lose their capacities but at different rates of decline—some losing their memory, eyesight, or coordination much faster than others do. Organizations also differ in the rate that they reach certain organizational states: the rate at which they reach a certain size, degree of specialization, rate of return on investment, or market penetration. Moreover, there can also be regular cycles of change in hormonal secretions, in alertness, in mood, in market activity, and so on.

Important developmental and longitudinal research questions focus on such rates of growth and decline and on possible factors that may hasten or retard them—genetic, nutritional, maturational, technological, political, or market factors.

UPPER LIMITS OF CHANGE

Not only do individuals and organizations differ in their rates of change on selected measures but they differ also in the levels they reach (see Figure 7–3).

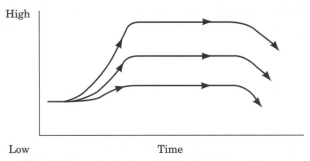

FIGURE 7–3   Levels of Change

For example, children differ not only in the rate of growth, but they differ also in the maximum height they reach. Why is that? What combination of genetic, nutritional, and maturational factors help establish such *ceiling* effects? We observe such apparent ceilings, or limits, in individual measures of intelligence and in organizational measures such as span of control—the number of people or operations that an executive can manage.

Thus we see change taking many routes: the common up-and-down route can vary in terms of rate of growth or decline, the ceiling or limits it reaches, and the duration of such limits or plateaus.

In some cases one relatively simple up-and-down curve can describe the growth and decline of certain individual or organizational characteristics. Usually, however, we string a series of such curves together to describe the repeated and uneven up-and-down route that change follows (see Figure 7–4).

Such a *time series* may describe the health of an individual or the productivity of an organization. The overall growth and decline of such a curve may, in the case of the individual, reflect the growth and aging

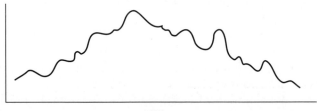

FIGURE 7-4   Time Series

process, or, in the case of an organization, reflect an increasing then decreasing share of the market.

The smaller up-and-down blips may, in the case of the individual, represent hormonal changes (puberty), stress (failure at school), or chance (financial inheritance). In the case of organizations, such blips may reflect the influence of temporary shifts in the market, temporary increases in productivity attributable to the new incentive system, new competition, or government write-offs.

Thus the up-and-down map of change, while descriptive of many familiar processes, may follow a given course for a combination of reasons—which makes researching the nature of changes a complicated, but challenging process.

Now that we have seen how change may take various routes at variable rates to different levels, we need to examine how we can stake out and at least partially map the zigzag courses of change. We rely mainly on three research strategies to provide observational checkpoints: (1) cross-sectional studies, (2) retrospective (after-the-fact) studies; and (3) longitudinal studies.

CROSS-SECTIONAL STUDIES

This method provides most of the observational checkpoints in developmental psychology—with this method we map, from birth to death, the growth rates, ceiling effects, and declines in physical and psychological characteristics.

Called *cross-sectional* because it takes age slices, this method enables a researcher to measure a given characteristic—say, height—in samples of people of different ages at the same time (for example, July 1994), compute an average for each age, and then draw a curve or map of how average height changes with age (see Figure 7–5).

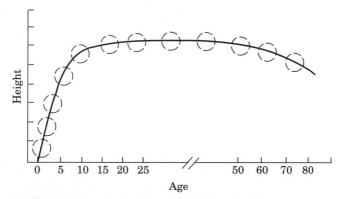

FIGURE 7–5   Cross-Sectional Research

The cross-sectional method allows you to map such curves without taking 70 or 80 years to follow *one* large sample from birth to death. It is a relatively quick method to get average trends—that is the advantage of it. For curves that are strongly determined by age alone, the method is adequate.

Where age is only one of several strong factors influencing the rate of change, the cross-sectional method can be misleading. If some samples used to represent the height of a certain age group have benefited or been hampered by other strong factors, then that sample is not typical and so should not be compared with other points on the curve.

For example, it is assumed that height, which reaches its ceiling or limit in early adulthood, starts to decline when people reach their fifties or sixties, but there is some evidence that this "decline" may be an arti-fact of cross-sectional data because our current 20 year olds are taller than their fathers and grandfathers. Thus is may not be that fathers are shrinking; rather their sons, who are large, produce sons who are even larger, thus providing an inappropriately taller baseline against which the fathers are compared (Damon, 1965).

Briefly, the cross-sectional method provides an average curve for age-related characteristics, but given points on the curve may be pushed up or down by other strong factors not related to age, but rather to nu-trition or social factors. Such atypical points on the curve, supposedly comparable to all other points, are not actually comparable and so distort the age curve. Therefore when using the cross-sectional method, you must be cautious and must repeatedly ask yourself the question, "In what other important ways, beside age, do my samples differ?" It is a safe bet the samples do differ in various ways, and so, rather than using a fine line curve, you would do well to at least visualize a curve surrounded by a region of uncertainty (see Figure 7–6).

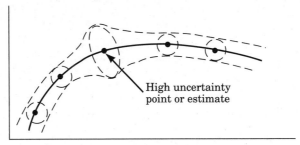

High uncertainty point or estimate

FIGURE 7–6   Uncertainty Band

Visualizing it in this way is clear acknowledgement that cross-sec-tional curves represent crude estimates that may deviate significantly from a curve that is based on following and measuring the *same* individual through time (longitudinal method). Maps of change based on cross-sec-tional studies should be updated frequently and compared with earlier cross-sectional curves for evidence of atypical bulges or dips so that particular points of uncertainty are highlighted and used with caution.

The obvious way to increase the comparability of points on the curve is to avoid cross-sectional studies, to go to longitudinal investigations where you study the same people over time rather than a cross-section of people at the same time. Alternatively, we can obtain cheap and crude estimates using retrospective studies.

RETROSPECTIVE STUDIES

Rather than trying to determine whether 60 or 70 year olds are shrinking by comparing them with 20 year olds (cross-sectional studies), we can compare their current height with a *recalled* height at age 20 or in early adulthood. This solves one problem—you are now comparing a person against him/herself rather than against a 20-year-old stand-in. However, you run smack into another problem—namely, the unreliability of recalled data—the problem of the fallibility of human memory.

When recalled data are compared with data recorded at the time of the event, we find ample evidence of distortions in memory, not just random distortions, but also on-stage, rose-colored distortions.

For example, mothers are unreliable sources of recalled information concerning the length of labor, their health during pregnancy, or their baby's weight and health; mothers may also provide "favorable" distortions concerning the age at which their child's toilet training and weaning occurred.

There may be instances when only a retrospective approach is viable. Consider an investigation of the developmental aspects of supervisory relationships for graduate students. How does the supervisory relationship change as one moves from B.A. honors to M.A. to Ph.D. years, and within the Ph.D. years how does it change? It would be preferable to collect these data as the student progresses through the system—while the information is still fresh in their minds and less distorted by forgetting. However, many students will be understandably reluctant to criticize their supervisors until they are safely out from under the supervisor's influence, until they have the diploma securely in their hand. In such situations a retrospective approach, although not ideal, may be the only feasible method.

In brief, beware of recalled data as a means of charting age curves for any characteristics, unless you are using it only in a supplementary manner: (1) to help check cross-sectional data, (2) with some archival data to back it up,[1] or (3) to fill in gaps in a longitudinal study.

---

[1] When you have adequate archival data (see Chapter 8), retrospective research deserves increased confidence.

In any case, enclose such recalled estimates within a large uncertainty circle.

LONGITUDINAL STUDIES

In order to avoid the unreliability of recall that affects many retrospective studies and to avoid confounding facts that the different samples used in cross-sectional studies differ in more ways than age, we should, whenever possible, use a proper longitudinal study to map the curves of change.

The longitudinal study differs from the cross-sectional study in that the *same* subjects are observed repeatedly during the period under investigation; it differs from the retrospective in that current observations rather than recalled or archival data are involved. Furthermore, longitudinal studies provide a way of mapping, not only general group trends in the growth and decline of various physical and psychological characteristics (that is, boys versus girls, identical twins versus fraternal twins). but also information about individual differences in rate of change, level achieved, duration of plateau, and onset and rate of decline.

Although the longitudinal method represents a major improvement over the cross-sectional and retrospective designs, it, too, poses problems, including the following: (1) sample shrinkage—subjects disappear because of change in residence, illness, boredom, death; (2) testing effects —repeatedly measuring the same people with the same yardsticks can lead to instrument decay (see Chapter 4), boredom and loss of motivation—that is, to systematic on-stage effects; (3) external validity limits— the societal conditions under which this sample grew up (nutritional, social, educational) may shift so that this sample's developmental curve no longer provides a valid picture, or map, of the curve that would emerge with a new sample of people under current environmental conditions.

Hence, longitudinal studies require large samples to counteract the effects of sample shrinkage; such studies also require nonreactive, or alternate form, measures to help counteract the effects of boredom and practice; finally, these studies must be periodically updated by contemporary longitudinal studies using new samples to reflect the influence of shifting environmental conditions on developmental curves.

Nevertheless, in spite of these reservations, the longitudinal study represents an important research tool, not only in psychology, education, and organizational behavior, but also in anthropology and sociology (historical method) and in economics (time series). Because of its many applications we now examine some of its variations.

In considering the following research designs, remember that, like any designs, they can't tell the whole story of "what leads to what"—the best that any research method can do is to help reduce the number of suspects. Furthermore, because longitudinal studies are usually conducted outside the laboratory, large numbers of uncontrolled influences can affect the results and raise serious questions about their internal validity. Donald Campbell (1969) and Cook and Campbell (1979) have provided models of a variety of "quasi-experimental" longitudinal designs.

Interrupted Time Series

This design involves a series of observations or measurements before and after the particular "treatment" or event occurs (see Fig. 7–7). The term *interrupted time series* comes from the fact that the "treatment" interrupts the time series.

Which of the seven time series mapped in Figure 7–7 would you choose as good bets for demonstrating a treatment effect—an effect over and above that of the various rogues? Time Series 1 and 2 look like reasonable bets, Series 3 and 4 are possible bets, whereas Series 5, 6, and 7 warrant no bets at all. Series 6 deserves particular attention because it presents the typical course of change of many of life's important processes: health, mood, energy level, productivity. Because of the zigzag pre-

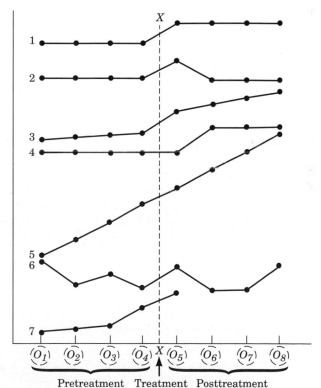

FIGURE 7–7   Interrupted Time Series

treatment and posttreatment course of this series, we can usually have little confidence in any study of such a time series unless we have major shifts in behavior, or unless a control group is employed.

Notice that the time series is a variation of the before-and-after design discussed in Chapter 4 and is subject to the same limitations. It gains in power to the degree that the pretreatment observations are stable and precise so that posttreatment changes stand out. It also gains in power to the degree that the treatment is potent and quick acting; otherwise historical and maturational suspects can produce changes in the treatment group that are wrongly attributed to the treatment.

This design is also at the mercy of instrument-decay effects, as is any repeat measurement design. It is particularly vulnerable to experimenter bias, to the degree that the observations are unreliable or subjective—that is, to the extent that the observations are surrounded by large areas of uncertainty.

A repeated interrupted time series, where feasible, provides increased confidence in the treatment—that is, when the introduction of the treatment leads to a significant shift from pretreatment baseline, and then a withdrawal of the treatment results in a return to pretreatment baseline.

EVALUATION RESEARCH

As an example of a question that lends itself to longitudinal research of the time series variety, consider the introduction of a management training program into an organization—how are such programs typically evaluated?

The desired map of change probably will look like that in Figure 7–8: This curve, presenting management skills, portrays a multitude of characteristics: delegation of responsibility, clarity of communication, effective use of time, morale building—in brief, a multifaceted curve.

Typically in most management training a pretreatment baseline is rarely measured; if at all, it is estimated by retrospective methods—that is, by supervisors or trainees *recalling* how they performed before treat-

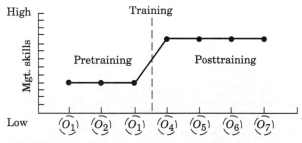

FIGURE 7–8   Desired Curve of Change

ment. We recognize this as a notoriously unreliable method of establishing observational checkpoints, so we should enclose the pretreatment curve within a large band of uncertainty.

Now we come to the treatment which is usually a stew of treatments (audiovisual displays, lectures, handouts, discussion groups, workshops, individual assignments, parties). Probably neither the people paying for the training program nor the people providing it have any precise idea about rate or levels of change beyond the crude picture in Figure 7–8.

However, from an outsider's viewpoint it would be reasonable to assume that if the training program has any effect at all there will be individual differences in rate, level, and dimension of change. On any given dimension (for instance, more efficient use of work time), we might have at least the following curves reflecting individual differences in rate and level of change (see Figure 7–9).

In Figure 7–9, trainee A shows a rapid rate and a high level of stable or durable change, whereas Trainee B demonstrates a lower rate, a lower level, and less stable change, and Trainee C exhibits little change at all. On the basis of a posttraining questionnaire (O_4), we find most trainees reporting a Type A curve—that is, they're using a *recalled* pretreatment baseline and *reporting*, after training, a rapid rate and significant level of improvement.

So, using a self-report measure, we obtain a rosy picture of rate and level of change. The personnel department that sponsored the training program is happy, the president is happy, and consultants who put on the program are happy with their extended contract to train more managers. But what kind of questions might you raise about the results?

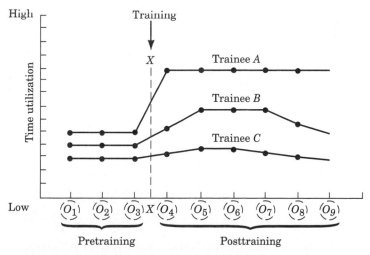

FIGURE 7–9   Individual Rates of Change

Appropriate questions might be based on the following: (1) a recalled pretreatment baseline is probably highly unreliable; (2) on-stage and instrument-decay effects strongly influence how individuals respond to ratings and questionnaires (for instance, the training seminars sure beat working; can you really admit you learned little or nothing; you had a good time and would like to go next year); (3) you've only got a soft measure to estimate rate, level, and duration of change, and that's a self-report measure, notoriously open to bias.

Now a new president takes over the firm and is concerned about the costs (time away from work, consultant fees) of all this training. Furthermore, the president is not convinced that it does all that much good, in spite of the posttraining questionnaire results. The president hires you to help evaluate the "real" effects of training. What might you do? The following are examples of how you might improve the evaluation procedure:

1. Increase the reliability and duration of the pretraining and post-training observations—that is, have trainees keep pretraining and post-training diaries of how they utilize their time. Furthermore, supplement these estimates with unobtrusive pretraining and posttraining observations in order to provide a check on diary-training accuracy.

2. Delay training for half of the subjects selected randomly and use them as a no-training control—that is, a *multiple interrupted time series control-group design* such as that in Figure 7–10.

The inclusion of this "equivalent" control group permits you to estimate the effect of keeping a diary on time utilization and also allows other historical and maturational suspects to influence the control group as they would the experimental group.

Now you return to the president with the following results (see Figure 7–11).

On the basis of these results, you report that

1. Diary reports of efficient time utilization show marked increases *before* training for both experimental and control groups; here we have evidence of a testing or on-stage effect—that is, merely keeping track of how you spend your time leads to "reporting" more efficient time utilization.

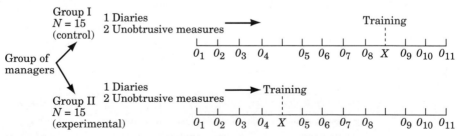

FIGURE 7–10   Interrupted Time Series Control Group Design

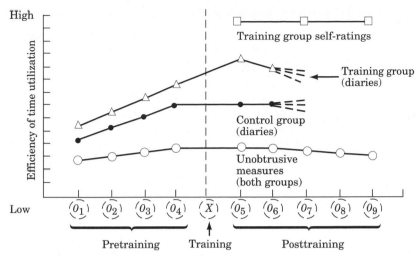

FIGURE 7–11   **Efficiency Time Utilization**

2. Unobtrusive time-sampling surveillance of a random sample of both experimental and control-group members before training reflects only very small increases in efficiency of time utilization.

3. Following training the experimental-group diary reports continue to claim increased time utilization efficiency; however marked individual differences soon start to appear, and quality and number of diary reports diminishes markedly—sample shrinkage and data mortality.

4. The no-training, control-group diary reports do not show the posttraining "booster" effect shown by the experimental group—but soon show similar sample shrinkage and data loss.

5. The unobtrusive measure has settled back to the pretreatment, pretesting baseline for both experimental and control groups, except for one member *in each group* who continues to maintain pretreatment gains —that is, subject by treatment interaction. (For instance, while most subjects fail to show significant or stable unobtrusive measure gains resulting from diary keeping or training, one manager from each group, *for unknown reasons*, did show such gains. Further study of these two may provide productive hypotheses for further research.)

6. Questionnaire ratings of the overall value of training by trainees remain high for 3, 6, and 12 months following training.

Summarizing, if we base our conclusions on unobtrusive measure data, we conclude that diary keeping alone or in combination with training has little enduring effect on efficient time utilization. If we rely on diary reports, we conclude that diary keeping and training increase *reported*, but not necessarily actual, efficiency of time utilization before training and for a short time after training. If we rely on general self-report rating by trainees following training, we conclude the training leads to rapid and significant improvements on a variety of dimensions.

While acknowledging that you are measuring only one dimension of managerial skill (time utilization), the new president places most confidence in the unobtrusive measure and decides such workshops may build morale but probably are an ineffective means of training—at least concerning the dimension of more efficient time utilization.

Notice that even if an equivalent control group, as was used in this study, is impossible, a *nonequivalent* control group can be useful in obtaining estimates of the role of testing or time in shaping the curve of change. For example, you could have probably obtained a fair estimate of the effect of keeping diaries even if the control group had been run at a different time from the experimental group or in a different plant. Certainly it's not as powerful a control, but it's better than no control. Notice in this study the greatest increase in *reported* time efficiency and unobtrusive estimates of time efficiency occurred *before* the training.

Also observe that if you want to map precisely the rate of increase or decline of a characteristic, you require multiple measures over the relevant time period. The diaries recorded time utilization for every 15-minute period during the working day for four weeks before the training and supposedly for three months following. Thus the diary method is designed to provide a fine-grained measure of change—15-minute units over a 16-week time span. The fact that these 15-minute units were filled with rose-colored data indicates that you can also end up with fine-grained *distortions* of the rate of change. How might the time taken to complete the diaries affect the dependent variable (time utilization)? Is this an instance where your measurement methods influence or confound the thing being measured?

The unobtrusive measure likewise sampled 15-minute units, but only one per morning and one per afternoon for each subject, taken more or less at random, and then compared with the same time period in diary reports. As noted, the unobtrusive measure data not only differ markedly from diary data but also reflect a much deflated rate and level of change for comparable time periods. Unobtrusive measures also picked up interesting, "casual" comments: "I'm three days behind in my diary; I've got to get caught up by Friday" (thus the diaries in some cases reflected *recalled* data); "What kind of things are they looking for in these damned diaries anyway?" (This person seems to be asking what kind of on-stage performance one should give); "We better get together on our diaries; we don't want to turn in conflicting information."

Not only do these comments raise important questions regarding the reliability of the diary reports, but they also place grave ethical responsibilities on the researchers—people's jobs and careers could be placed in jeopardy as a result of identifying their source. Research ethics are discussed in Chapter 12.

We've indicated the importance of having relatively fine-grained and objective estimates to map rates of change. The same requirements apply in order to map the duration of change. Failure to conduct fine-grained, objective, posttreatment follow-ups probably constitutes the most single glaring weakness in studies of change; consider, for example, the famous Hawthorne effect.

The Hawthorne Effect

The basic up-and-down curve of change is a powerful model for describing many time-related phenomena including charting the course of problem-solving intelligence from birth to old age, mapping the "melt rate" of New Year's resolutions from December 27 to January 27, or plotting the course of management skills from before training to a few weeks after (see Figure 7–12).

Among the most famous investigations of organizational change are the Hawthorne studies (Roethlisberger & Dickson, 1948). From this research has emerged a phenomenon known as the *Hawthorne effect*, which describes temporary changes that are due mainly to on-stage or testing effects or to the effects of novelty. For example, in the Hawthorne studies it was found that when illumination levels were raised, production in the factory increased temporarily: But it was also found that when illumination levels were lowered, production also increased briefly. The important point to note is that *novelty*, like New Year's resolutions, can produce change, but not necessarily enduring change.

In evaluating longitudinal studies, consumers of science must ask one critical question: "How do I decide how much of the ups and downs of human or organizational behavior to assign to chance (that is, to the rogues) and how much to specific 'treatments'?"

In brief, you decide by obtaining some estimate of the range of variation in the behavior without the influence of some selected treatment or intervention. Then you add your "treatment" and determine whether

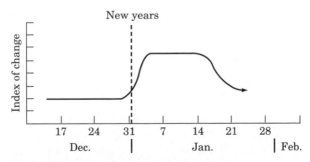

**FIGURE 7–12   New Year's Resolution
Meltdown—A Classic
Hawthorne Effect**

the behavior (1) obviously shifts to a new range—higher or lower, (2) maintains the new range (longer than a New Year's resolution), and (3) is maintained when using observations that are not readily open to on-stage and elastic-ruler effects. Science is in the business of mapping heavyweight changes in behavior over significant periods.

You can analyze shifts in behavior by plotting the maps of change and making eyeball assessments of whether there has been an "impressive" shift. If a neutral observer agrees with you, then your conclusions warrant increased confidence. If a hostile observer agrees with you—one who doesn't believe in your treatment—your discovery is astonishing.

With the advent of computers and complicated statistical models, science relies less on eyeball analysis; rather, we compare statistical estimates of day-to-day variability and statistical estimates of whether the shift is larger following an experimental intervention that can "reasonably" be expected by chance, larger than the four rogues usually manage on their own. The four rogues, singly and in combination, can engineer some remarkable shifts in the ranges of human behavior. Therefore it is wise to use a control group, equivalent or otherwise, whenever possible, or lacking a control group, to use extended baseline and follow-up observations involving nonreactive measures and treatment reversal designs.

Regression Toward The Mean

In discussing the value of the control method in Chapter 5, we briefly referred to statistical regression. This effect pervades many longitudinal studies and warrants further discussion here. When you do unusually well on an exam, or unusually poorly, what will likely happen on the next exam? Before you answer, think of all the reasons you can about why you did better than usual, or worse than usual. Then answer the question: How will you likely do on the next one?

The answer is that you probably won't do as well, or as poorly, on the next test. That's because we usually perform better, or worse, than usual because of an *unusual combination of circumstances*—a combination of positive, or negative, events that is unlikely to occur again. So a person who performs worse than usual can take heart that their grade will likely rise, and the person who performs better than usual can prepare for a lower grade next time. In other words, unusually high or low scores tend to gravitate toward the average or mean score, hence, referred to as "regression toward the mean."

The example at the end of this chapter discusses three kinds of time series, all of which demonstrate random variations around a mean score or trend.

Unusual combinations of circumstances influence your behavior, moving it up above, or down below, the usual level. Therefore, anytime you see a score describing human performance—like a test score—you should see it as the end result of a combination of two influences: (1) the person's ability or skill, and (2) chance factors associated with that particular testing session that push the score up or down. Because a different combination of chance factors will likely be at work on the next testing occasion they will have a different influence on the score. Therefore, even if ability or skill remain relatively constant, performance scores will change up or down as a result of different chance factors operating on different testing occasions.

SUMMARY

In conducting longitudinal studies, keep the following recommendations in mind:

1. Cross-sectional studies and retrospective studies provide very crude maps of the curves of change.
2. Interrupted time series gain in power:
   a. when control groups—equivalent or nonequivalent—are used or when treatment reversals are feasible.
   b. when at least some of the observations or measures are robust—are relatively resistant to on-stage and elastic-ruler effects.
   c. when such robust measures are continued long enough to determine whether you have a change over and above a New Year's resolution meltdown or a Hawthorne effect.

Longitudinal investigations help us extend the reach of science by exploring an extended time frame. In the next two chapters, we discuss additional methods that help us look for patterns in space/time frames beyond the confines of the laboratory or the control-group method. But before concluding this chapter, we provide an example of a student's exploration of time series models.

EXAMPLE

The following is adapted from a student project on testimonials in relation to interrupted time series.

THE TESTIMONIAL

Introduction

Testimonials arise from something the subject consumed or did which they claim improved their condition. However, since such claims are typically based on after-the-fact or uncontrolled time series observations, testimonials remain highly suspect.

Testimonials usually arise from informal time series "studies" conducted by the subject on themselves. Besides the fact that recalled data is very open to bias, these people fail to take into account the usual ups and downs of whatever symptoms or behavior they're looking at, even when it is not treated at all.

In class we discussed three types of time series: (1) unstable, (2) reactive, and (3) process. These three types are graphed in Figure 7–13.

The main thing to notice about these time series is that while they show different overall trends, they all contain temporary ups and downs in addition to their different trends. The *unstable* time series shows large variability without any overall up-or-down trend. The *reactive* time series shows variability but also shows a stable baseline to start with, a drop for a while, then a return to baseline level. The *process* time series shows variability plus an overall downward trend; an upward trend could also be called a process series.

The point to remember is that without adequate controls (control groups, treatment reversal designs etc.), the average person will place credit, or blame for any natural up-or-down trend on a favorite suspect.

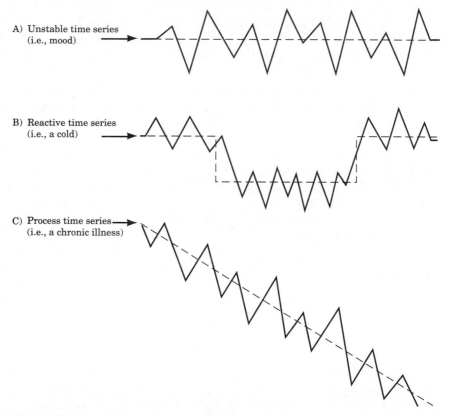

A) Unstable time series
(i.e., mood)

B) Reactive time series
(i.e., a cold)

C) Process time series
(i.e., a chronic illness)

FIGURE 7–13   Three Types of Time Series

The average person fails to appreciate that the rogues can manufacture all kinds of variability and even shifts in trend.

To obtain a rough estimate of which suspects receive testimonials, I conducted an in formal survey of eight of my fellow students in residence. I asked them: "What things have you recently taken, or done, that helped you feel better or that you heard helped someone feel better?" The following is a list of some of the more popular responses:

honey	more sex
distilled water	less sex
no liquor	positive thinking
liquor	additive-free foods
got part time job	moved
dropped a course	yogurt
jogging	skim milk yogurt
no jogging	yogurt, plus yoga, plus jogging
tranquilizer	interferon
stimulant	bee stings
herbal tea	prayer
hard work	smoking pot
less work	stopped smoking pot
Gestalt therapy	olive oil, honey, and ginseng root
stopped Gestalt therapy	seeing a counselor
broke up with boyfriend or girlfriend	stopped seeing a counselor
got new boyfriend or girlfriend	stopped drinking milk

My purpose is not to knock any of the preceding "cures" but to give a sample of the kinds of things receiving testimonials. I also want to suggest that probably *any* nonlethal "treatment," no matter what it contained or required you to do, would receive some testimonials. Because of the hidden work of the rogues, any entrepreneur, peddling almost any treatment, will accumulate some satisfied, if naive customers who, in turn, by word of mouth, will further advertise the innocuous product.

Why should this be so?

Fact 1: Any human characteristic goes up and down—mood, health, energy, aches and pains, weight—even without any specific treatment or planned intervention.

Fact 2: Most of us are bound to try some "treatment" when we're feeling low.

Fact 3: Even without treatment, in the vast majority of cases, you would eventually feel better. You will credit any improvement to the treatment you took. You won't credit it to chance factors; you won't credit it to one or more of the rogues (for example regression toward the mean).

Fact 4: You tend to take treatments when a characteristic has reached its high point (e.g., fever) or at a low point (e.g., mood). At these points the characteristic has probably already reached the ceiling, or floor, level and so usually has only one direction to go—toward improvement. Therefore any treatment, even completely ineffective ones, will appear to have had an early beneficial effect.

Fact 5: If the treatment does not have an *immediate* effect, it can be claimed to be a delayed-action treatment and so still gets credit when your inevitable return to normal occurs (for instance, in a reactive time series).

Fact 6: Even in down-trend *process* time series, dud treatments will get credit for periodic upturns giving false hope to terminally ill patients and also providing "quack" cures.

Fact 7: Innocuous cures, with any kind of advertising, will invariably make money since they capitalize on (1) the natural variability in human characteristics and (2) the failure to recognize the potency of the rogues working singly or in combination.

My general conclusion is that testimonials will flow to ineffective treatments while nature (maturational factors and statistical regression) effects a cure. As doctors like to say: "Without treatment a cold lasts two weeks; with treatment it only lasts fourteen days."

REVIEW QUIZ

True of False?

1. Cross-sectional, retrospective and longitudinal studies are popular research methods for mapping change.

2. Changes differ in (a) their rates of growth or decline, (b) the ceiling or limits to a change, and (c) the duration of such limits or plateaus.

3. A time series design is synonymous with the after-the-fact method.

4. The longitudinal method is a relatively quick method to get average trends; it provides an average curve for age-related characteristics.

5. The decline in the height of people in their 50s and 60s may be an artifact of cross-sectional data.

6. When recalled data are compared with data recorded at the time of the event, we find ample evidence of distortions in memory.

7. The cross-sectional method involves observing the same subjects repeatedly over the period under investigation.

8. Of the three methods, cross-sectional, retrospective, and longitudinal, the cross-sectional approach is to be preferred.

9. Problems with the longitudinal method include sample attrition and testing effects.

10. With an interrupted time series design, the treatment interrupts the time series pattern.

11. Evaluation research often makes use of a longitudinal design of the time series variety.

12. There is no such thing as a multiple interrupted time series control-group design.

13. Participant self-reports (in evaluation research) typically support a conclusion that training leads to rapid and significant improvements on a variety of dimensions.

14. Failure to conduct fine-grained, objective, posttreatment follow-ups probably constitutes the single most glaring weakness in studies of change.

15. The Hawthorne effect derives from studies of organizational change, and refers to permanent and enduring changes that are due mainly to on-stage or testing effects, or to the effects of novelty.

❦ 8 ❦
Qualitative Methods: Ethnographic and Archival Research

─────── **Chapter Goal** ───────

To introduce you to qualitative research, first by distinguishing it from quantitative research and, second, by providing examples of two forms of qualitative research: ethnographic and archival.

INTRODUCTION

In previous chapters, you journeyed across the relatively uncharted jungles of the case method and through the rural outposts of the before-and-after method, arriving safely at the sophisticated control-group metropolis with its sprawling suburbs. But, even in the big city, despite high levels of internal regulation and standardization, dangers abound. Tricksters, con artists, and chance events may still confound your efforts to sift fact from fiction. And you may also wonder about the stultifying effects of all the controls in the police state. The inhabitants behave like automatons; what would they be like if left more to their own devices, when big brother researcher isn't manipulating them?

A recurring dilemma for researchers in the social sciences is how to represent individual reality while at the same time deriving meaningful generalizations. Relatively "objective" quantitative research methods, which aggregate the objects, events, or persons under study, best serve the generalization aim. Such techniques impose an *a priori* structure on the research participants, confining their behavior to dimensions identified by the investigator as relevant. What reality would be revealed in the absence of such structural constraints? Additionally, many phenomena prove recalcitrant to investigation via the methods described thus far—either because our technology is too primitive or because the subject matter itself is not amenable to manipulation or experimentation for ethical or other reasons. *Qualitative research methods* extend the reach of science into these realms.

Some scientific purists decry the use of qualitative approaches (except where no other option exists) because of their alleged sensitivity to subjective influence and their limited utility in yielding general laws. However, as discussed elsewhere in this book, the objective methods do not guarantee immunity to subjectivity, and they may produce results with limited applicability in the uncontrolled real world.

The qualitative methods discussed in this chapter include the field study and its primary research tool—naturalistic observation—and the use of archival material in research. The next chapter focuses on survey research with its typical data collection techniques—interviews and questionnaires.[1] With careful application, the durability of the data packages produced by these sieves of science, their ability to sift charming fancy from beautiful fact, can be substantive. And, they bring the researcher much closer to the real world, out of the hothouse environment of the laboratory. However, before discussing these approaches, it may be useful to explore the general nature of qualitative research and how it differs from that of other methods.

QUANTITATIVE VERSUS QUALITATIVE

From a layperson's perspective, the concept of "science" connotes certainty—the provision of clear-cut answers, the facts. One expects the science world to be crisp, with clear boundaries, divisions, and distinctions, no "ifs, ands, or buts" about it. Unfortunately, this is not the case, and discussion of the nature and role of qualitative methods in the scientific enterprise exemplifies the murky or blurred demarcations, the shades of grey, among the methods of science.

At the most superficial level, it might be assumed that the distinction between qualitative and quantitative techniques reflects the reliance of the latter on numerical analysis. However, many qualitative methods permit at least some form of statistical application. Nor is the difference discipline-based, as examples of research representing either class can be found in most social sciences. To some extent, the difference is problem- or issue-driven. For example, the ethnography of an abortion clinic, the motivations of Hitler, the economy of the Naskapi Indians of Labrador, and Shakespearean conceptions of sex roles all resist investigation via the control-group method and its extensions.

Perhaps the aims, purposes, or goals of the research dictate selection of a qualitative rather than a quantitative approach. If the purpose of the research is to describe or understand, rather than to predict and control (and if the statistical procedures are hence descriptive rather than inferential), qualitative methods may be most appropriate. At a more

[1]Note that the case study or after-the-fact method (Chapter 3), which we presented as a pre-experimental technique, is also typically regarded as a qualitative method.

abstract level, some authors have suggested that the epistemological stance of the investigator determines the choice of research method. Phenomenology, symbolic interactionism, and humanism constitute the philosophical underpinnings of qualitative methodology, whereas quantitative methods flow from a positivist approach to social phenomena with an attendant focus on causality, replicability, objectivity, and operational definitions. Although this distinction has merit, in any individual case, an investigator may employ both types of research strategies. Clearly, then, these epistemological positions seem not to be mutually exclusive, at least at the level of their reflection in research methodology.

Finally, there may be a difference in the scientific merits of these two categories of research tools. Several writers assume a superiority of quantitative methods over qualitative ones in the sense that they yield more accurate or definitive data. The more holistic qualitative approaches are tolerated because they generate a rich, diverse, complex informational fountain from which a host of valuable speculations may emanate, some of which may be amenable to subsequent investigation using quantitative methods. Those on the other side of the debate extol the virtues of qualitative approaches, pointing to the enhanced external validity achieved with these methods. In the middle, we find those who regard utilization of both types of strategies appropriate, who argue that a triangulation of methods produces the best data mix.

As the foregoing illustrates, no hard and fast distinction between qualitative and quantitative methods seems feasible. Nevertheless, it is possible to identify some defining characteristics or points of emphases. Ruckdeschel (1985) has isolated five core elements reflecting the essence of the qualitative perspective.

CHARACTERISTICS OF QUALITATIVE METHODOLOGY

Qualitative methods are based on the assumption that humans do not so much respond to direct stimuli as they do to their interpretations of the information impinging on them. Thus, we are constantly involved in an interaction process with environmental elements that we symbolically transform. These symbolic translations or meanings that humans attach to events must be studied if we are to understand the subsequent behavior. For example, two boys in a class, both of whom experience academic failure, may construe this event very differently—for one, it may be a mark of distinction, ensuring acceptance by the Black Panthers gang, whereas for the other, it may represent loss of privileges imposed by parents. It is the subjective reality of the actor (the person involved), rather than the outsider's (researcher's) view of "objective" reality, that best explains the actor's actions. Thus, a second premise is that reality is multilayered and has many perspectives. Although commonalities in subjective realities may be discerned, differences and, indeed, conflicting perspectives are to be expected, as is illustrated schematically below.

Individual A—   —Symbolic $— O1a$

     Environmental   Transformation XA
     Context X

Individual B—   —Symbolic $O1b$

                                            Transformation XB

Given this assumption, it follows that the background and contextual situation in which the phenomena occur or are studied are regarded as important influences on the nature of the data obtained. A surly, cranky interviewer who is unable to achieve rapport with the interviewee will probably elicit very different responses than one who displays empathy, patience, and a generally pleasant demeanor. Similarly, a subject's political affiliations, socioeconomic status, sex, ethnic heritage, and other shibboleths are not irrelevant, but clearly affect the person's subjective reality or world view and must, therefore, be taken into account.

Qualitative methodologists assume that, to fully understand the issue under investigation, they must participate at some level in the meaning world of their research participants. Indeed, the efforts of quantitative researchers to maintain objectivity by distancing the experimenter from the objects, events, or persons studied (in an attempt to rule out the investigator as a source of influence) are perceived by qualitative researchers as contrived and futile, and as an impediment to full understanding.

Use of multiple data sources and multiple research methods is recommended by qualitative researchers. They believe that, because different methods reveal different aspects of the multifaceted reality of the phenomenon under investigation, only a multiple-method approach will yield maximal understanding. Additionally, a triangulation strategy, assuming some overlap in the results, is seen as enhancing validity and hence confidence in the researcher's findings and her or his construction of reality.

ETHNOGRAPHIC RESEARCH

If you want to know the rituals practiced by the pygmies in their worship of the forest god Ituri, or what people do when they win at the roulette table, or whether bees exhibit social behavior, or how apes communicate, or whether teachers encourage creative thinking in their pupils, the most obvious recourse is to "go and see." In some scientific circles the technique of crude observation of events without technical apparatus is known as the *eyeball technique*, and this is the core of ethnographic research or the field-study method.

The essence of this science sieve is the observation, description, and interpretation of events as they occur in nature or naturally (a stew of observational and speculative language). This method requires no manipulation, no controlled experimentation, but rather the careful observation of episodes as they take place in their usual surroundings. It is perhaps the earliest (and, in some ways, crudest) of science's methods. The "primitive" strategies of careful, methodical observation and classification predate the use of complex experimental designs and elaborate apparatus. However, even with the more advanced methods, observational skills are essential, and increasing awareness of the limitations of laboratory technologies has prompted a revival of interest in the field study and its principal technique—naturalistic observation.

Darwin's (1936) picture of evolution provides an excellent example of this method. By his own admission Darwin devoted five years to the careful, detailed "field" observation of thousands of plants and animals, both domestic and wild. These observations were meticulously (even compulsively) recorded in prose and picture form and subsequently grouped into categories which in turn led to a grand speculation—*the theory of evolution*. If we were to represent this process schematically, we would start with a series of O's (observations) and then impose some grouping scheme on our O's so that they were combined according to certain rules.[2]

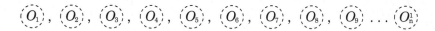

$$O_1 , \quad O_2 , \quad O_3 , \quad O_4 , \quad O_5 , \quad O_6 , \quad O_7 , \quad O_8 , \quad O_9 \ldots O_n^1$$

We would then combine the observational and formal language systems as follows:

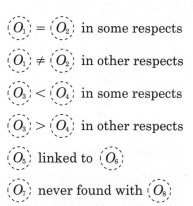

$$O_1 = O_2 \text{ in some respects}$$

$$O_1 \neq O_2 \text{ in other respects}$$

$$O_3 < O_4 \text{ in some respects}$$

$$O_3 > O_4 \text{ in other respects}$$

$$O_5 \text{ linked to } O_6$$

$$O_7 \text{ never found with } O_8$$

[2]Each O stands for a different observation. If there were 19 observations, then n would be 19, and O_n would represent the nineteenth observation.

Finally, the groups would be integrated into a higher classification at the speculative level of language—*survival of the fittest!*

There are four key components to the field-study strategy: (1) the setting, (2) the observational task, (3) the role of the observer, and (4) the classification of observations. In the discussion to follow, we examine each of these in turn. In actual practice, however, these facets of the method do not necessarily operate sequentially or independently.

The Setting

Field studies obviously belong in field settings—that is, in nonlaboratory environments—but research in the field implies a lack of control, implies unpredictability. Although investigators have hunches about how their observations are causally linked, cause-and-effect relationships cannot be established via this method of research; it is descriptive rather than inferential. If other science sieves promise more precision, why use a field approach? As we gain precision and control, we lose *validity.* Would people in a laboratory who passively obey an experimenter's instruction to shock an innocent victim display this same blind obedience in a real-life setting? Perhaps not. There is good reason to assume that people behave differently in natural settings than they do in the lab where they may be on their "best," most compliant behavior. Also, some areas of interest (for example, the reaction to natural catastrophes) cannot be duplicated *realistically* in a laboratory environment.[3] For these important reasons the field study is an essential arrow in the scientific quiver.

Once investigators decide what they want to know, the next decision involves selecting the setting(s). Choosing the setting depends on various factors: the question to be answered, the feasibility and cost of the appropriate setting, which depends on how broadly or narrowly the researchers wish to apply their findings. Suppose our budding scientists are interested in the characteristics of people who burglarize and vandalize abandoned vehicles. They live in New York so they observe an abandoned car in the Bronx. Within the first ten minutes they see a white family of three (father, mother, and young son) remove the battery and the contents of the trunk and glove compartment. By the end of the day, adult vandals have extracted every removable part from the automobile. In succeeding days acts of random destruction occur (breaking windows, denting the hood) mostly perpetrated by well-dressed adult whites. Aha, conclude (speculate) our researchers, vandalism is primarily an adult activity which will occur in any urban center. But is it legitimate to draw this conclusion?

Zimbardo (1970), who actually conducted this study, reports not only that a car similarly abandoned in Palo Alto, Calif., was not vandal-

---

[3]One respected book on decision making excludes data from "contrived" situations because of the questionable validity of such studies (Janis & Man, 1977).

ized, but also that a passerby thoughtfully lowered the hood of the car when it was raining so the engine wouldn't get wet. Zimbardo's speculation is that high population density creates conditions of anonymity and loss of identity. Such conditions, he argues, foster a reduction in one's sense of responsibility and social consciousness. Hence the individual performs acts which appear reprehensible. Certainly Zimbardo's analysis is supported by much of the available data, but it is worth noting that the two settings employed (New York and Palo Alto) differ in many respects, not just population density (Milgram, 1970), and some of these other factors may be just as relevant.

A number of questions must be addressed by researchers in choosing an appropriate setting: (1) Is this a setting in which the event(s) of interest are likely to occur? (2) Is this a representative setting in terms of most settings in which the event(s) of interest are likely to occur, or is it unique in all the world? If the latter, then as consumers of science, we have less confidence that this particular research project provides us with "the big picture."

The Observational Task

Contemporary ethnographic research often combines a potpourri of methods including archival analysis and personal interviews as additional data collection tools or in lieu of naturalistic observation. This multimethod approach enhances the validity of the findings. Issues related to naturalistic observation are presented below, whereas the other techniques are discussed at a later point.

Harry's old Chevy died, much to his disgust, five blocks from the "greasy spoon" where he works as a short-order cook. He decides to walk and call the tow truck from the cafe. As he trudges crankily past the school playground, he glances idly at the children playing. Two future National Hockey League stars are high-sticking each other on the ice, another boy is inscribing a particularly nasty piece of graffiti on the school wall, a big girl is washing a small boy's face with snow, and one little imp, noticing Harry's interest, hurls a snowball with deadly accuracy, hitting him on the temple. Harry angrily shakes his fist and speculates, "Bloody juvenile delinquents—damn kids could sure use a kick in the ass."

Harry has observed a number of events in their natural surroundings, has integrated or grouped them, and has generated some speculations. However, Harry's observational procedure is casual, and so we should question both the validity of his observations and his conclusion. For example, Harry didn't notice that the feisty hockey players were really just trying to disentangle their sticks which were caught in skate blades. Ineptitude, rather than aggression, accounted for their behavior ($\stackrel{\frown}{O}$). Harry also failed to observe the dancing pair of figure skaters at the other end of the rink. Harry was gone when the big girl picked up the little boy, hugged him, dusted off the snow on him, and carefully retied the laces of his boot. And how could Harry know that the miniature Nolan Ryan had actually been aiming for the fence post (Ö)?

Defining what to look for in any observational task becomes the most crucial aspect of the field-study method. As consumers of science we must focus on the quality of the data base or observational checkpoints that researchers use in generating their speculations.

Distortion   Personal experience in observing an event is obviously not a guarantee of truth. Since human senses are fallible, what we think we see isn't always what has occurred. Our observations are not pure—that is, we do not perceive only forms, contours, and certain wavelengths of light or sound; rather we perform symbolic transformations of these stimuli. One might say with some justification that we do not in fact see light waves of 75 microns; we see red. Similarly, we do not hear a sound of 80 decibels; rather we hear a pneumatic drill. Thus any event that is observed is not experienced "in the raw," so to speak, but is altered by our past learning or, as in Harry's case, our mood. Sometimes our interpretations (organization) of what we see can be quite misleading. For example, psychologists have constructed rooms built on a slant in which an individual standing at one side of the room looks like a midget. Viewers, instead of perceiving the room as distorted, distort the size of the individual in the room (Weiner, 1956). If we press this argument further, it will be seen that our opinions, beliefs, and attitudes can also alter our observations since they form part of our past learning. When we are observing the movement of planets, the pelvic bone structure of the apes, the strength of a magnetic field, or the electrical conducting properties of copper, you might argue that political affiliation, religious denomination, skin color, or nationality would not affect our observations. Is this in fact the case? Religious beliefs supporting the theory that the earth was flat prevented many people from making the simple observation that the mast of a ship appeared on the horizon before the rest of the ship. If the area under study involves human behavior, how much more will we distort our observations to fit our beliefs, hopes, or fears? (See Chapter 15—Sex and Science.)

Scientists using the field-study method and the techniques of naturalistic observation strive to be as objective as possible; they consciously try to observe without evaluating. They try not to make value judgements like good or bad, wrong or right, beautiful or ugly. In other words they attempt to prevent their own biases, opinions, values, and beliefs from coloring their observations. They try to keep observations as pure as possible. Although scientists have set an impossible task for themselves, at least knowing how beliefs can distort observations makes them more careful, more cautious about accepting observations, their own or others', at face value. Also scientific training and the use of certain instruments, like hidden cameras, can help in obtaining a more objective picture to increase the size of the empirical chunk relative to its surrounding speculative space: this (O) rather than this (o).

Selection   We know that biases play a role in the selection of information. In other words, we see or notice those things we want to see and screen out information that doesn't fit in with our particular point of view. For example, the biased observer, convinced that civilization corrupts and believing that people living in so-called primitive societies are happier, may fail to notice many negative aspects of the "simpler" life. The poverty, the suffering due to lack of medical attention, the grueling hard work with improvised tools—these things escape attention. The scientist, being aware of this pitfall, attempts to make *detailed, value-free observations*.

Selection operates not only on our observations but also on our recording and report writing. We don't see everything that happens nor do we record everything we see. We can't record all our observations (even if we wanted to) because we forget things, and we forget selectively. We tend to forget those things that don't fit well with our established biases and preferences and to remember those things that do. We have no trouble remembering an appointment to go out for dinner and to the theater, but dental appointments easily slip the mind. In addition, time can distort the memory of observation. Since our memories are both leaky and creative, it is essential to make accurate notes when making observations, a practice most good researchers have developed. Alternatively, in order to avoid relying on our imperfect and creative memories, we may use tape recordings, films, sketches, graphs, or counters. There is still the danger that valuable data may be lost, but such recorded observations are not as subject to distortion, decay, or growth as are the ones we deposit in memory. A further advantage accrues because the data may be perused in all its rich detail at some later date and may be examined again and again, by us or by others.

Even if our memories did not erase some observations from our minds, we still can't record everything that we observe. Secretaries know that exact reproduction of even a short conversation leads to a copious report. Minutes of meetings represent highly condensed and abbreviated versions of what actually occurred; much of the discussion must be omitted. Similarly, researchers must select from what they remember of the events observed. They must decide what to record and what to omit, ignoring material that is not relevant to the thesis being developed. Notice that while not trying to discard observations that contradict their views, they still must discard those observations that add nothing to the point of the research. Such observations are tangential to the topic under study. If one wishes to describe in detail the puberty rites of the Hopi Indians, it is perhaps irrelevant to record that homes of the Indians are constructed of thatched straw and adobe.

Researchers' biases or points of view help them select what is worth recording. Such biases may prevent them from considering alternatives but are vital in terms of providing guidelines for selection from the flood of data surrounding them.

An example   If Harry is really serious about studying the aggressive behavior of little girls and boys on the playground, he must first decide (1) what constitutes aggression, (2) which children he will watch (he can't observe all of them), (3) at what time of the day, (4) for how long, (5) who will do the observing and recording, (6) how many observers he will need, and (7) how the observations will be recorded and checked for accuracy.

To illustrate the complexity of the observational task, consider the following excerpt from a laboratory experiment conducted by Bem (1975). Bem investigated the extent to which a person's playfulness (with a kitten) was related to the individual's sex and sex-role orientation. Although not a field study, the observational strategies employed were similar to those that might be adopted in a field setting. Notice particularly how the experimenter established reliable observational checkpoints.

> During the period of forced and spontaneous play, the subject's interaction with the kitten was time sampled every 10 seconds by one of four female coders, all of whom were blind with respect to the subject's sex role and all of whom observed an approximately equal number of masculine, androgynous, and feminine subjects of each sex. For each subject, the coder made 30 2-second observations during forced play and 60 2-second observations during spontaneous play. Ten behaviors were coded as present or absent: Was the subject looking at the kitten? Speaking to the kitten? Petting the kitten? Nuzzling the kitten? Was the subject playing with the kitten? If so, was he holding it in his hand, on his lap, on his chest, or face-to-face?
>
> In order to establish the reliability of these various measures, two of the four coders simultaneously observed 12 subjects. These double coding sessions were scheduled so that all possible pairs of coders were together twice and so that 2 subjects from every sex role received double coding. The reliability of a given behavior was determined by combining forced and spontaneous play for a total of 90 observations per subject and then by calculating the percentage of observations on which the two coders agreed perfectly. The results indicated very high reliability (over 95% perfect agreement) for all 10 behaviors. (Bem, 1975, P. 640)

Do you have any questions about the independence of observers? Do we know from this description whether they peeked at each other's notes during the session? How might independence have been assured? Would it have been better to use male and female coders? Why?

The Role of the Observer

Knowledge that one is the object of study, a subject in a research investigation, or simply being watched, has an enormous impact on behavior (the on-stage rogue). In naturally occurring settings, this knowledge, of course, derives from the subject's awareness of the researcher's presence. To the extent that the researcher can minimize this awareness or its salience, the subject's behavior will more closely approximate its typical form—that is, what the behavior is when the researcher isn't there, isn't watching. Various strategies have been adopted by field-study researchers to minimize this on-stage effect. However, even when such efforts are successful, researchers still do not rule themselves out of the picture, for they know that their own symbolic transformations of what they see continue to shape and edit the picture. Nonetheless, some of the strategies designed to reduce the impact of the on-stage rogue do double duty in helping to attenuate the magnitude of "researcher variance."

Invisible observers   In an effort to eliminate themselves as one of the suspects (X's) influencing the phenomenon under investigation, researchers employ twentieth century equivalents to the Romulan cloaking device (Star Trek fans will recognize this reference); they hide in blinds or replace themselves with cameras, microphones, electronic tracking signals, and the like. These are the strategies of naturalists studying birds, bats, and beasts. Laboratory researchers may approximate this strategy through use of the one-way mirror (as did Bem, 1975).

Covert observers   Field experimenters (Chapter 5) are covert observers. Participants in these staged research projects don't know they are involved in an experiment; hence, subject reactivity suspects are eliminated. Similarly, researchers employing the field-study method may disguise their data collection aims, blending in with the surroundings, like well-trained, unobtrusive spies. Field studies conducted to examine such issues as courtroom behaviors, what draws people to accidents and fires, scalper strategies at ball games, the return of shopping carts to supermarkets, and the popularity of tourist attractions (e.g., noting the out-of-state license plates) may be amenable to a covert observer strategy.

Covert observers must be alert to the possibility that their cover has been "blown." Data gathered when there is reason to believe anonymity has been penetrated should be discarded. Another problem with covert observation is that it may run us afoul of ethical considerations. In fact, strict adherence to ethical principles (Chapter 12) requires that subjects be aware of the nature of their participation (principle of informed consent).

Nonparticipant observers   Anthropologists, such as Margaret Mead, who study so-called primitive or preliterate societies, rely heavily on the field-study method. Invisibility or covert operations are not options for these researchers, whose purpose is to describe and understand the complexities of entire cultures or some significant aspect of them. Although the presence of the observer cannot be disguised, the researcher adopts or is assigned an outsider's role; he or she is visibly present, but not an active participant or legitimate group member.

Although the observer influences the group to an unknown degree, he or she nevertheless endeavors to minimize this impact by staying on the sidelines, by maintaining passivity, by eschewing active participation, except when required to maintain acceptance or enhance understanding. One procedure commonly used by field researchers to counteract this on-stage effect involves observing the group (being present in the group) for some time before beginning the formal data collection process. This gives the group members a chance to acclimatize themselves to the outsider. Eventually the researcher more or less fades into the woodwork.

Trice (1970) argues persuasively in favor of the outsider's role, noting that disinterested (uninvolved) outsiders may be the recipients of privileged information—private information that would not be shared with other members of the clan or the club or the company. Attempts to ingratiate oneself, to be integrated or accepted as just "one of the gang" may be viewed with suspicion and distrust, as Trice discovered in his study of hospitalized alcoholics and members of Alcoholics Anonymous. In such cases, the researcher may fall into the outsider's role by default.

Participant observers   Another creative strategy for overcoming the reactivity problem is to employ undercover confederates who infiltrate and become active participant members of the society, organization, or group. Alternatively, the researcher or her/his confederate may already have membership in the group or organization under study. Since qualitative researchers strive to uncover and understand the meanings of behaviors to the actors, rather than simply describing the acts themselves, they argue that some degree of researcher involvement is a *sine qua non* of the research.

Many of the complexities of this form of field-study research are detailed by Sullivan, Queen, and Patrick (1970), who describe their experiences in the investigation of an Air Force training program using a participant observer. Other fascinating studies of this ilk include Festinger's (1964) analysis of the reaction of members of an occult group to a failed prophesy, Whyte's (1943) classic study of street corner gangs, and Goffman's (1962) investigation of a mental institution.

Participant observers walk a tightrope between detachment and involvement. They run the risk of "going native," of being absorbed by the culture of the group or organization under study. Alternatively, care must be taken to ensure that a confederate does not shape or mold the group to perform in a manner dictated by the investigator's expectations or pet theory. Participant observation also raises some thorny ethical issues.

An alternative approach was adopted by Barker and Schoggen (1973) in their comparison study of life in two small towns—one in the U.S. Midwest and the other in England. The researchers and their families established residences in the towns and fully explained the purpose of the study to the local inhabitants. They attempted to participate normally in community affairs, following their own interests but avoided initiating new activities.

Multiple observers—multiple observations   Making several observations and having several observers make repeated observations of the same event (the strategies Bem, 1975, employed) increase the probability of producing durable packages of information. This principle is utilized by those practicing the technique of naturalistic observation. In an attempt to partially overcome or reduce observer bias, scientific investigations often make use of two or more independent observers who later come together and discard any observations on which they do not agree. Or, more commonly, a third observer is called in to resolve the disagreement. Also, the same observer may try to observe the same event many times in order to ensure that she or he has noticed all the relevant details and to rule out the possibility that the initial observation was a once-in-a-lifetime event. Thus anthropologists may visit the same primitive tribe many times and observe the tribe's activities over long periods. For the same reason another investigator may repeat a colleague's experiment, and the extent of similarity in their findings adds to the durability of their observations.

Classification/Interpretation

The final component of the field-study method involves classification of observations—their linkages, order, or pattern. This discovery or invention of pattern is the basis of science.

The development of the periodic table in chemistry represents a most fruitful use of one aspect of the field-study method—that of classification. In the nineteenth century, elements were being discovered rapidly, but as each element had different properties, no obvious sense of order or relationship could be perceived among elements. However, science doesn't just create heaps of facts; it puts facts in a framework. Attempts to classify, group, or arrange elements into some kind of order were made by several investigators, including chemists and a geologist. Mendeleev's periodic table was the most successful attempt at classification. Mendeleev believed that the properties of elements were more important than their atomic number; when arrangement by number would not work neatly, Mendeleev left holes in the table for elements still to be discovered. He even predicted the properties of some of the missing elements on the basis of his table. With knowledge of the hypothesized properties of these missing elements, their eventual discovery was stimulated. Thus classification proved valuable in the progress of a science.

The development of the system for the classification of plants and animals by Carolus Linnaeus (1707–1778), the Swedish botanist, is another famous example of the fruitfulness of taxonomy to science. Classification of organisms, both past and present, into kingdoms, phyla, classes, orders, families, genera, and species is an obvious example of an attempt to replace disorder and confusion with order. To develop such a taxonomic system, close observation of the properties of organisms had to be undertaken. Again, the technique of naturalistic observation proved invaluable.

Barker and Schoggen (1973), whose field study was briefly described earlier, attempted to produce a complete inventory and classification of the behavior settings (public places or occasions) in each community. The Midwest town was found to have considerably more public behavior settings, which in turn was reflected in the different activities of the inhabitants, ranging from public attention toward children to religious pursuits.

The construction of classification systems is very much a function of bias or point of view. In fact, classification can be seen as a primitive form of theorizing that allows for the expression of opinion or inference or speculation. With any set of data there are usually a variety of ways in which these data may be ordered or grouped, and the researchers' hunches or biases determine which particular grouping they will develop —will the researchers group people on the basis of intelligence, or skin color, or sex, or political persuasion, or aggression, or genetics, or what?

$$A = f(B \quad ? \,)$$

$$\downarrow \qquad\qquad \downarrow$$

IQ   Sex
           Skin color
           Social class

Conclusion

Just because naturalistic observation is employed to study somewhat gross behavior units and requires little in the way of elaborate equipment, don't conclude that it is no longer in vogue, has outlived its usefulness, or is a simple method that requires little training. All these inferences are wrong. There are many areas of study in which it is impossible—for ethical, moral, political, or practical reasons—for the researcher to manipulate events or to experiment. In addition, certain kinds of information can only be obtained in field or naturalistic studies. For example, if we want to investigate the phenomenon of hibernation, famine, or juvenile gangs, we must use naturalistic observation for at least some portion of our study. The work of Piaget, the famous child psychologist, was based on the technique of naturalistic observation and is the foundation for much of the current research in some areas of psychology today. Although a crude sieve, in the hands of a skilled researcher, the field study remains a valuable source of important and durable data.

One obvious advantage of this method is its superiority to casual observation and hit-or-miss recording or tabulating of events. A second advantage accrues because it does not require manipulating or controlling events; therefore many subjects normally taboo to experimental science become open to this form of study. Furthermore, the four principles of the field study (the setting, the observational task, the role of the observer, and the grouping or classification) apply, to some degree, to all the other sieves of science. Often the data gathered by the field-study method provide guidelines for later inquiry with more sophisticated sieves, as has been the case with Piaget's work. Finally, this method can be practiced by the young student scientist who has limited resources. By being analytical, passive, and accurate, the novice researcher can establish important observational checkpoints and can offer fascinating speculations.

ARCHIVAL RESEARCH

In many instances you don't have to observe behavior directly to know what has occurred; you only have to observe the marks, tracks, spoor, or deposits it leaves. One of the by-products of the revolution in communications technology is the development of information pools of oceanic proportions—data pools, rich and ready for the nets of eager scientific sailors. Newspapers, magazines, books, films, plays, songs, census statistics, radio broadcasts, suicide notes, letters, diaries, gravestones, and paintings all provide valuable information for researchers. Gribbin (1984), in the book *In Search of Schrodinger's Cat*, tells us that most mammals determine and mark their territories by leaving excretions that define the size and shape of the claimed turf. Domesticated primates, however, mark their territories by excretions of ink on paper. The analysis of these excretions, of these people-tracks or traces, is known as *archival research*. Employing this method allows the scientist to capitalize on and exploit already collected or deposited data chunks. Moving one or several steps away from direct observation, the investigator relies on the accumulated behavioral spoor and creatively analyzes, groups, combines, and juxtaposes these indirect data.

A study by Sir Francis Galton (cited in Webb, Campbell, Schwartz & Sechrest, 1966) provides an example of the creative use of archival research. Since the long life of a monarch was prayed for more frequently than was the case for less august persons, it was theorized that greater longevity should be observed for royal personages, if praying is effective. The data revealed that, in fact, royalty had shorter life spans than did the gentry. As sophisticated consumers of science you are quick to note that people of royal birth differ from gentry on a host of other variables, and Galton's study doesn't seem to have taken these other differences into account—some of them, like inbreeding, are perhaps much more relevant in affecting life span than prayer. So Galton's research on this question has only anecdotal value.

Content Analysis

Just as the principal technique of the field study is naturalistic observation, so one of the frequently employed tools of the archival researcher is *content analysis*—what Simon (1969) refers to as a method of measuring the unmeasurable. Naturalistic observation, it will be recalled, involves detailed, objective, and systematic observation of events in their typical surroundings. Similarly, content analysis requires detailed, objective, and systematic observation of verbal or symbolic communications.

Consider the following research question derived from a study by Pyke (1976). "To what extent do children's books depict traditional sex roles?" Assume that two researchers collect a representative sample of books. They then undertake an analysis of the prose and picture (verbal and symbolic) content of these books. Two coding categories are established: (1) a female figure is performing a traditional female sex-role function (mother squirrel is dusting the nest with her tail); (2) a male figure is performing a traditional male sex-role activity (a fireman is holding the net for the lady in the burning building). For comparison purposes the researchers include two more categories which are the converse of those examples: male or female figures engaged in cross-sex activities (a male cooking; a female operating a backhoe). Each researcher takes half the books and proceeds with the analysis—identifying for each figure depicted in both illustrations and text whether the figure portrayed is performing traditional sex-role functions or functions of the opposite sex role. One hundred books are analyzed; the researchers meet and share their findings.

"Why did you categorize Mary as performing a cross-sex function when she was climbing a tree? Girls climb trees," argues Researcher A.

Researcher B similarly questions A's judgments, "You've got the Daddy coded here as a traditional sex-role item, but surely shopping is a traditional female activity so he should be coded as cross-sex."

"Yes, but it's a hardware store," rebuts A.

"OK, but what do we do if we don't know what kind of store it is?" responds Researcher B.

Although these researchers have coded their observations in a detailed and systematic fashion, they have failed to satisfy the basic criterion of objectivity—independent and consistent labeling. Their understanding of what constituted a traditional sex-role activity was subjective or pragmatic. They were including a great deal of speculation (o) but had assumed they were at the observational or objective level (O), involving a large amount of solid information.

The problem was resolved by simply coding the activity or occupation (reading, sewing, driving, fighting) and by determining whether this activity or occupation was being performed by a male or female figure. With this more objective coding scheme, the two researchers achieved a high level of agreement in their individual assignment of codes. Their observational checkpoints had reduced areas of argument or speculation surrounding their coding; they moved from (o) to (O) .

Many researchers lack the luxury of readily identifiable (objective) coding categories for their content analysis of archival material. Jacobs (1979), for example, reports a phenomenological study of 112 suicide notes, one of which is reproduced below.

> It is hard to say why you don't want to live. I have only one real reason. The three people I have in the world which I love don't want me.
>
> Tom, I love you so dearly but you have told me you don't want me and don't love me. I never thought you would let me go this far, but I am now at the end which is the best thing for you. You have so many problems and I am sorry I added to them.
>
> Daddy, I hurt you so much and I guess I really hurt myself. You only wanted the very best for me and you must believe this is it.
>
> Mommy, you tried so hard to make me happy and to make things right for all of us. I love you too so very much. You did not fail, I did.
>
> I had no place to go so I am back where I always seem to find peace. I have failed in everything I have done and I hope I do not fail in this.
>
> I love you all dearly and am sorry this is the way I have to say goodbye.
>
> Please forgive me and be happy.
>
> Your wife and your daughter.[4]

How would you tackle the analysis of this material, distilling key variables? Jacobs, relying heavily on a theoretical model developed by Durkheim, indicated that 35 of the 112 notes (including the one above) fit the pattern described by Durkheim in reflecting the following themes: (1) others created the problem; (2) long history of problems; (3) recent escalation of problems; (4) death seen as necessary; (5) begging indulgence; and (6) awareness of the act. Try to identify which elements of the note exemplify these themes. Are there components not covered? Would a different classification system serve as well? Although the note allows access to the phenomenological world of the suicide, the analysis

---

[4]Reprinted by permission of the Society for the Study of Social Problems.

provides the researcher with ample opportunity to stretch or shrink or otherwise misinterpret this world.

Content analysis brings with it a host of concerns. The quality of the information derived from this technique depends on the adequacy of source sampling (was the sample of children's books or suicide notes a representative sample?), the appropriateness and relevance of the coding units, and the reliability of the coding—that is, its independence and consistency.

Spoor Analysis

Although the term *archival* suggests some form of document (from a music score to sales records), archival research encompasses a broader band of materials, including physical evidence, such as garbage, ancient pottery shards, dust, and other remnants from the past. For example, an architect consulted a psychologist, asking where sidewalks should be built on a new campus to accommodate traffic flows. The architect said, "You're an expert on human behavior, tell me where people will walk." The psychologist, having an empirical bent, visited several established campuses and carried out naturalistic observations of traffic flows. He noted that, in addition to the sidewalks, a variety of paths had been worn across the lawns. He consulted the head groundskeeper, who maintained that once a path was established, it was well nigh impossible to discourage its continued use. The psychologist advised the architect to design his sidewalks so they covered the shortest distance between any two entrances; he also advised the architect to save part of his budget to be spent a year later to put in additional sidewalks where the paths indicated natural, but unpredictable, traffic flows existed.

People leave traces indicating behavioral flows everywhere: worn linoleum, dog-eared library books, picnic sites. Analyzing garbage, not only of famous people but also of different socioeconomic classes, provides measures of certain aspects of their behavior. Furthermore, a longitudinal study of people's ashtrays can provide crude indices of patterns of stress; such a study could also provide a relatively objective index of the efficacy of New Year's resolutions to give up smoking or the impact of antismoking campaigns.

Let's consider another example of the use of physical evidence as a source of research data. Suppose, as the owner of a car rental agency, you wonder about the value of the radio advertising you've commissioned. Do many people actually hear your creative jingle on station OHM? An archival approach might involve maintaining a record of the radio dial position on all cars returned after rental. This provides a measure of the popularity of the various stations, and so you can use the most popular station (ERG) to carry your advertising (adapted from Webb et al., 1966). A moment's reflection, though, raises a question. Don't you want to reach the *potential* car renters rather than, or in addition to, those who actually use your agency? Perhaps the former group listens predominantly to station WATT rather than ERG.

Webb and colleagues (1966) provide many examples of the analysis of physical traces, including measuring the food consumption of institutionalized patients by weighing the trucks bringing in food supplies and the trucks carting garbage out; estimating the differential activity level of children by comparing the degree of wear on their shoes; determining the height of individuals in the Middle Ages by measuring the height of suits of armor; and judging the popularity of library texts by measuring the degree of wear and tear on the pages.

Strengths and Weaknesses

Archival research is perhaps one of the least exploited research methods, even though its unobtrusive quality offers some protection against a prime villain, reactivity (the on-stage effect). It is hard to imagine that a student might deliberately deface a text so that the next archival researcher who comes along will judge it to have been well or frequently read. Equally difficult to swallow is the image of a tombstone carver gleefully altering birth dates so as to mislead future generations of scientists. The man whose height is being estimated from his suit of armor can't throw our measurement off by standing on his tiptoes. Nor will the rental car clients fake their radio-listening behavior, because they don't know it is being researched. Thus archival research involves the use of unobtrusive or nonreactive measures. Researchers using this method usually need not be concerned that their observations are distorted by subjects' awareness that they are objects of study.

The value of conclusions derived from spoor analysis depends, of course, on how much of the original deposit remains available for analysis. The Nixon tapes offer a classic example of a mammoth attempt to provide a relatively complete verbal record of his office behavior, not all of which record was retained, including the infamous 18-minute erasure. Such records can be incomplete by design or by accident; they can be edited by the crude hand of sloth and decay or by the fine hand of deceit. In either case, running or episodic records provide ingenious social scientists with further fixes on human behavior—with views that go beyond the sheltered laboratory.

While deceit and sloth can affect the amount of information available in written and taped documents, so too can systematic changes in recordkeeping procedures. For example, records of crime show that rates shift in some cases as a result of improved recordkeeping, in other cases because of increased detection. In order to differentiate between these two influences, social scientists relying on archival records must be no less sophisticated than when working in the laboratory. They must be *record-wise*. For example, rates of alcoholism in a given region are frequently based on liver cirrhosis death rates. However, such estimates are frequently low because of the stigma surrounding that cause of death appearing on the certificate. Unless investigators become familiar with the practices surrounding the production of archival records, they can be badly misled.

Given the revolution in data storage and retrieval systems arising from the development and spread of computer facilities, the prognosis for archival research is excellent. How much money did consumers invest in children's toys last December? What's the unemployment rate for university graduates? How many non-nationals are currently employed in the country? Is there a sex difference in the incidence of mental disorders? How much income tax did people in the $80,000-a-year bracket pay last year? Questions such as these may soon be answered with a press of a button—data literally at our fingertips. If you think this is an idle fancy or a futuristic view, listen to a major league baseball broadcast. Every imaginable statistic is available for the pressing.

Although data may be more readily accessible, assessment of the quality of these data is still of concern. We referred earlier to the use by computer programmers of an acronym GIGO (garbage in, garbage out), which captures the notion that the computer record or memory is only as accurate and detailed as the information that is fed into it. Problems of lost and distorted data still apply. The many film plots depicting the mad, irresponsible, or criminal computer genius who erases information, plants misinformation, or otherwise deliberately distorts the computer record for his or her own ends suggest we must adopt a critical stance. Add to deliberate deception the inaccuracies deriving from carelessness and human error, and the problem is compounded. Yet the seductive computer carries with it an aura of precision and accuracy. At first glance it seems the answer to a researcher's prayer, but let the user beware.

For the imaginative and record-wise researcher, archival records—whether they be laundry lists or Supreme Court rulings, classified advertisements or death certificates—provide rich opportunities to enlarge the validity of our observations. In many instances, they also provide auxiliary information about the adequacy of such data in terms of biases affecting what was recorded and what was retained.

Perhaps the optimum use of archival research arises when it is employed in combination with other methods. Indeed, to the extent that an observational checkpoint is revealed by more than one of science's methods, our confidence in the validity of the observation is enhanced; it has picked up more "empirical robustness." In this sense all research methods are supplementary. The multimethod bracketing of hypotheses by imaginative and tenacious researchers warrants massive encouragement. A case in point is one student's attempt to study the effects of frustration on eating behavior, in which he extended his laboratory observations of rats to checking the records of the hometown fans' consumption of hot dogs when attending losing, as opposed to winning, football games.

SUMMARY

The two research methods described in this chapter—field studies and archival research—have distinct advantages over the casual observations and unsupported inferences that are an integral feature of everyday life. Although lacking the precision of the control-group model, they allow systematic exploration and enhance understanding of topics outside the reach of laboratory methods. The field-study method contributes sophisticated observational strategies and identification of patterns and classes among carefully recorded, detailed observations. All scientific methods rely on these basic tools in mapping multilayered nature. Archival research involves an analysis of behavioral remnants—the traces of tracks of past behavior. A major strength of this method is its nonreactive or unobtrusive character, but it is prey to whatever biases existed in the original deposit conditions, to the subsequent effects of time, and to whatever biases the researcher imposes.

EXAMPLE

This example was adapted from a report produced by two students. The excerpt describes the use of the archival method as it was employed in the context of a larger study investigating media representations of the desirable or ideal role for women.

MEDIA REPRESENTATIONS OF WOMEN'S ROLES

Introduction

On the basis of Betty Friedan's thesis (1963), as described in *The Feminine Mystique*, it was predicted that women's magazines in the 1950s and early 1960s would portray a relatively traditional view of the nature and role of the female. As a function of the rebirth of the feminist movement, a more liberal orientation was expected to appear in the late 1960s; however, this shift was anticipated to be minimal for two reasons. First, the magazine selected for study caters to married housewives with families. For the magazine to denigrate the traditional role would be risking some loss of readership. Second, much of the advertising in the magazine is devoted to products oriented toward the home. Producers of these products may well prefer that women maintain a traditional role model, and any attempt by the magazine to encourage alternative role structures might result in a loss of advertising revenue.

Method

Materials. Magazine X was chosen for study because it is a wide-circulation monthly magazine aimed at the middle-class housewife. Randomly selected issues from 1951 to 1957 were compared with similarly selected issues published in the period 1966-1972.

Procedure. Two issues of the magazine were randomly picked from the 12 issues published annually in 1951, 1953, 1955, 1957, 1966, 1968, 1970, and 1972. Each investigator examined one issue from each of the eight years surveyed. A total of 16 issues were reviewed—8 by each investigator. Data for the September 1955 issue were mislaid and so are not included in the results. All but two issues of 1953 were missing from the archives, so a random selection was not possible for this year.

A cursory scan of two issues selected from 1952 and 1967 revealed that the following themes were evident in the articles: home and family (marriage, love, childcare, divorce, home decorating, sewing, recipes); personal health (exercise, diet), beauty and fashion; human interest; political; travel; general interest (includes any other articles). Each article in the issues selected for study was categorized in terms of these themes.

Results

The percentage of articles of each category type for each time period is presented in Table 8–1.

TABLE 8–1   Percentage of Articles by Category

Category	*1951–1957*	*1966–1972*
Home & Family	52	35
Personal Health	6	0
Beauty & Fashion	17	20
Human Interest	16	17
Political	9	18
Travel	0	2
General Interest	0	8

Discussion

Home and family concerns as well as physical attractiveness are key components of the traditional sex-role model for women. Clearly these issues were central in Magazine X over the period from 1951 to 1957. Of all articles published, 75 percent focused on these themes over the eight-year span. The magazine thus projected a consistently traditional view of the female and her role. The articles revealed a concern with marriage as a stable and sacred institution—with advice on how to keep a marriage intact. Other articles followed the "efficient homemaker" motif—budgeting, do-it-yourself, and helpful cleaning hints.

In contrast, only 55 percent of the articles focused on these traditional themes in the late 1960s and early 1970s. A considerably broader coverage of topics is reflected in these more recent issues. Political and social awareness articles doubled in frequency, and items of more general interest began to appear regularly. Thus our prediction that the magazine would reflect a traditional view of women in the 1950s and a more liberal view in the 1960s was supported. Indeed, the change was rather larger than we had anticipated.

One event confounding the interpretation of these results was the replacement of the magazine's editor in 1961. Possibly the new editor was more liberal in her views, and the changes in the magazine were due to her direct influence rather than to a general liberalization of attitudes regarding women's role in society. Some slight evidence supporting the former interpretation exists in terms of the content and tone of her editorials. Still it may be that this person was hired specifically because her attitudes approximated those becoming prevalent in the society.

References

Freidan, B. 1963. *The feminine mystique*. New York: Dell.

Instructor's Comments

To what extent have you effectively ruled out alternative explanations for your results? Or to what extent have you tried to increase your confidence that the results you obtained do in fact accurately represent the changing orientation of this magazine?

Knowing the publication date of the article being coded, combined with your expectation that more recent articles will be more liberal, leaves you open to the possibility that your coding was shaped by your expectation (elastic ruler). This possible source of error could have been reduced or eliminated through the introduction of blind coding.

Your decision to randomly select issues may have introduced a bias. Suppose, for example, that the issues reviewed for the earlier period included (by chance) four December issues, while for the later period no December issues were selected? What implications might this have in terms of the frequency of appearance of the various themes?

The most serious obstacle to confidence in these findings is your failure to demonstrate the objectivity of the category assignment. We have no evidence that the judgments you made were not idiosyncratic. A sample of articles should have been categorized independently by both investigators, and the degree of concordance ascertained. To some extent you have avoided a systematic bias in that each investigator coded an equal number of issues from each time period. Nevertheless, it is possible that the articles categorized by one investigator as political, for example, might be interpreted by the other coder as general interest.

One of the strengths of your study is your use of a pilot run—that is, reviewing two issues not included in your sample in order to establish valid coding categories. Another admirable feature is your awareness of the change in editors (in-the-gap suspect) and your attempt to examine this factor in terms of its implications for your results and conclusions.

REVIEW QUIZ

True or False?

1. Most quantitative research methods impose an *a priori* structure on the research participants.

2. Positivism, objectivity, and replicability form the philosophical underpinnings of qualitative methodology.

3. In general, use of quantitative methods enhances external validity.

4. Qualitative researchers assume that the background and contextual situation in which phenomena occur are important influences on the nature of the data obtained.

5. Ethnographic research requires careful manipulation of experimental variables in the field.

6. The field-study approach was the research method employed by Charles Darwin.

7. The field-study method is a useful strategy for determining cause-and-effect relationships.

8. Any event that is observed is not experienced "in the raw" but is altered by past learning.

9. In the field-study model, the subject's awareness of the researcher's presence can lead to maturational (time-tied) effects.

10. Observers in field-study research must ensure that they never participate in the events they are observing.

11. The periodic table in chemistry represents a fruitful use of one aspect of the field-study method—classification.

12. The principal research technique for the archival researcher is context analysis.

13. Archival research offers some protection against reactivity (on-stage) effects.

14. Social scientists using archival research must be sensitive to variation in the production and maintenance of records.

❦ 9 ❦
Qualitative Methods:
Survey Research

─────── **Chapter Goal** ───────

Continuing our exploration of qualitative methods, this chapter describes variations of a common and familiar qualitative research strategy: survey approaches.

Like other qualitative approaches, survey methods achieve enhanced external validity at the price of reduced internal validity. Survey researchers are one step removed from both naturally occurring situations and laboratory environments. Instead of venturing into the field and observing actual behavior in its natural context, or instead of pulling subjects into an experiment and observing the effect of manipulated antecedent conditions, they utilize an ingenious shortcut. They ask people how they would (or did) behave in a variety of situations. The asking may be done via some simple, straightforward paper-and-pencil questionnaire, or through in-depth interviewing, administered face to face, on the phone, or through the mail. This efficient strategy opens doors for researchers into the worlds of values, attitudes, beliefs, preferences, aspirations, stereotypes, past experiences, and future plans, as well as into the worlds of lies, false hopes, exaggerations, selective and distorted recall, and self-delusions.

Probably you have participated in a survey research project of one type or another. If you haven't been approached by the market researcher in the local shopping plaza on a Saturday afternoon, or received a "To the Householder" questionnaire in the mail, or succumbed to the pleas of graduate student surveyors for volunteers from your class, then you may have participated in the national census.

If not familiar with this type of research from a subject's perspective, then perhaps you've conducted some informal surveys of your own. In planning what courses to take this semester, did you ask some students who had already participated in these classes what they thought of the courses? Did you inquire about the type of assignments each professor gave and how leniently these were graded or how interesting his or her lectures were? If so you were employing a rudimentary form of the survey research method. The flexibility of the survey (its multipurpose features) and its deceptively simple technology make it a popular choice for the novice researcher.

Key components of survey research include (1) the data collection instrument (the questionnaire or interview schedule), (2) the administration procedure (whether the respondent will self-administer the instrument or whether an interviewer will record responses), and (3) the sample selection (who is to be surveyed).[1]

DATA COLLECTION INSTRUMENT

Survey instruments vary enormously, not only in content, but also in format. The degree of constraint imposed on the surveyed subject's freedom of response may range from the relatively unfettered style of the semi-structured interview or open-ended questionnaire (in which respondents are permitted to share their stream of consciousness on a question or issue) to the forced choices or scaled response alternatives typical of many questionnaires. Although the former model provides a rich and fecund data pool and allows researchers the opportunity to seek clarification and to probe, there is wide latitude for researcher bias in the subjective categorization or pattern interpretation of responses. Hence, many investigators prefer the more restricted format of forced choice or scaled responses, which enable more objective scoring and enhance internal validity in exchange for less external validity. A common format for this more objective form of questionnaire is the *Likert-type* scale illustrated in items 2, 3, 6, and 8 of the example questionnaire on page 192; this particular questionnaire is designed to assess attitudes and practices regarding erotic contact between family members.

Questionnaire

Even though we have indicated to respondents that their replies are anonymous (to encourage truthful reporting and to help maintain confidentiality), because of the sensitive issues explored in the questionnaire, we may be justifiably suspicious about the veracity of the responses. Biased responding, a problem all survey researchers must face, may be particularly problematic with this questionnaire.

---

[1]Jackson (1988) provides a comprehensive and detailed analysis of all aspects of the survey research method.

Questionnaire: Erotic Contact with Blood Relatives

Please answer the following questions as honestly and truthfully as you can. Note that this questionnaire is to be completely anonymous. Do not put your name on the form. For the purposes of this questionnaire, please understand erotic contact to mean any behavior intended to arouse or satisfy sexual desire.

Age: _____   Marital Status: _____   Sex: _____

1. Do you have any children related to you by blood?

   Yes _____   No _____

2. Erotic contact between parents and their biological children is harmful.

   _____   _____   _____   _____   _____
   Strongly   Agree   No   Disagree   Strongly
   agree   somewhat   opinion   somewhat   disagree

3. Have you ever engaged in erotic contact with one of your biological parents (excluding sexual intercourse)?

   _____   _____   _____   _____
   Never   Rarely   Occasionally   Frequently   Very frequently

4. If yes, which parent? Mother _____ Father _____ Both _____

5. Who initiated this erotic contact?
   You _____ Parent _____ Not sure _____

6. Have you ever had sexual intercourse with one of your biological parents?

   _____   _____   _____   _____   _____
   Never   Rarely   Occasionally   Frequently   Very frequently

7. If yes, which parent?
   Mother _____ Father _____ Both _____

8. Have you ever engaged in erotic contact with any other relative (excluding parents) related by blood?

   _____   _____   _____   _____   _____
   Never   Rarely   Occasionally   Frequently   Very frequently

9. If you have engaged in erotic contact with another blood relative (excluding parents), please identify the kinship relationship.

   _____ Brother   _____ Sister

   _____ Aunt   _____ Uncle

   _____ Grandfather   _____ Grandmother

   _____ Nephew   _____ Niece

   _____ Female cousin   _____ Male cousin

   _____ Daughter   _____ Son

Biased responding   A common form of response bias that occurs in questionnaires, personality tests, attitude measures, and interviews is the *social desirability* bias. Most people want to present themselves in the best possible light, and often this means pretending to conform to cultural ideals—that is, respondents can often determine which option of the alternatives presented is the socially desirable one—the response blessed by society's prescriptions. This option may be selected even though it does not reflect personal views or behavior.

Incestuous relationships are not socially sanctioned, and we might suspect that at least some respondents who selected the first alternative on Item 2 were responding in the social endorsed direction instead of providing us with their "true" opinion. Indeed, almost every question on our instrument is prey to the operation of this bias.

Surveyors sensitive to this potential source of error sometimes include a scale (a few questions) in their questionnaire packet which is especially designed to measure the extent to which a subject consistently opts for the socially desirable response. Data deriving from high scorers on these particular questions are then discarded on the grounds that the subjects' propensity to endorse socially desirable alternatives may be disguising their "real" views.

"*Faking bad*," the opposite of the social desirability bias, may occur if there is some advantage for the respondent to appear markedly deviant. Brain-injured victims of car accidents, engaged in litigation for damages, may be motivated to fake bad—to exaggerate the seriousness of their disabilities. Likewise, a respondent, irritated with the invasion of privacy, might be motivated to scuttle the research by faking bad on our questionnaire; what is more likely is that he or she might simply refuse to provide the information. Corporal Klinger (Jamie Farr), who appears as a transvestite soldier in the television show *M*A*S*H**, provides a dramatic and humorous example of this form of bias. Again, some personality tests include a special set of items designed to assess the strength of the faking bad bias.

Another form of bias, "*nay-saying*," is identified when the respondent tends to respond consistently to items in a negative direction regardless of their content. "*Yea-saying*" is the exact opposite form of response bias—agreeing with items regardless of the nature of the items.

Some individuals display a *response extremity* bias—that is, they commonly select the most extreme alternative. On Items 6 and 8 of our questionnaire, consistent choices of "Never" or "Very frequently" might be suggestive of such a bias, although we would require more items with this response format (and items which are less likely to be responded to with extreme choices) in order to be certain. Items employing dichotomous response alternatives ("Yes" or "No") avoid this problem. Conversely, the tendency to consistently check the middle or neutral category on items providing a range of choices similar to Items 2, 6, and 8 might be termed the "*cop-out*" bias.

Inconsistent responding constitutes a form of response bias as well. If respondents are not motivated to complete the questionnaire in a conscientious fashion, their careless, even capricious, responding may be revealed by contradictory responses. For example, if one of our research participants indicates that he or she has engaged in erotic practices with a son or daughter (Item 9) and also reports that he or she does not have any children (Item 1), we might legitimately be skeptical about the validity of this person's responses.

Other issues   In addition to these more or less standard forms of response bias (sometimes called *response sets*), surveyors must guard against the creation of idiosyncratic biases. The manner in which questions are worded can play a big role in shaping the respondent's replies. Suppose, for example, the third question on our questionnaire had been worded as follows: "Have you ever been sexually assaulted by one of your biological parents?" This form of the question has a heavier emotional charge, and some subjects might be loath to label their experience in this way. Thus they may select the "Never" alternative when in fact the more accurate response might be "Rarely." Questions of the "When did you stop beating your wife?" variety are similarly avoided. Questionnaire designers attempt to employ terminology which is objective and clear, which permits only one interpretation, and which is as emotionally neutral (nonevaluative) as possible—an ideal continuously sought and rarely, if ever, achieved.

Miller's (1991) guide to questionnaire construction includes advice such as keep the questions short; start with easy, interesting questions (not the biographical items as in the example questionnaire); keep open-ended questions to a minimum and place them at the end of the questionnaire (assuming this does not destroy the logical progression of the questions); pretest the instrument with individuals representative of your ultimate sample to ensure that the questions are appropriate, understandable, and answerable.

Telephone Interview

One of the weaknesses of the mailed questionnaire as a data collection technique is the relatively low return rate (about 48 percent) of completed forms. Telephone interviews have been gaining in popularity as an alternative approach. Much higher return rates are achieved, and costs are still significantly less than face-to-face personal interviews. Miller (1991) provides an excellent set of instructions for investigators contemplating employing this research strategy.

Personal Interview

If exchanging a few pleasantries with a stranger on an elevator is analogous to administering a questionnaire, then an in-depth personal interview is akin to a long weekend camping trip. Perhaps the best way to explore the differences is to describe an actual interview study. Belenky, Clinchy, Goldberger, and Tarule (1986), in a study designed to assess women's experiences as learners and knowers as well as their concepts of self and relationships, conducted intensive interviews with a nonrandom, heterogeneous sample of 135 women solicited from a variety of educational institutions and family service agencies. Interviews ranged from two to five hours in duration and the transcripts generated more than 5000 pages of text that subsequently were subjected to content analysis.

Using coding categories derived from models in the literature, appropriate portions of the interview (e.g., examining women's assumptions about the nature of truth, knowledge, and authority) were initially coded independently by blind coders who were unaware of certain biographical information (interviewee age, social class, etc.). This exercise revealed that these existing classification schemes were unsatisfactory; they could not easily accommodate the data. The authors then embarked on a contextual analysis of the interview protocols, rereading the interviews many times and developing a new coding scheme. Quotes illustrating the categories were then extracted. Moving back and forth from the excerpts to the whole interview allowed the abstracted material to be viewed as an exemplar of the code, as well as within the context of the whole life story of the interviewees. This hermeneutic approach diverges markedly from the impersonal, acontextual research mode characterizing most questionnaire strategies and capitalizes on the great strength of qualitative approaches, with enhanced external validity deriving in part from the relative absence of subject constraints and in part from the efforts of the researchers to consider the responses as embedded in a complex matrix of life conditions.

Belenky and colleagues (1986) conclude that women's ways of knowing fall into five major epistemological categories. The first, termed silence, constitutes a position of mindlessness, of subjection to the whims of authorities. Received knowledge represents a position of reliance on the knowledge of external experts. Subjective knowledge illustrates a focus on personal perspectives—gut feelings. The fourth category procedural knowing, involves the application of objective rules and procedures for the acquisition and communication of knowledge. Finally, constructed knowledge, viewed as the integration of the subjective and objective voices, carries a sense that all knowledge is both created and contextual, and not independent of the knower.

An interview strategy permits investigation of a huge problem space, brings the researcher much closer to the reality to be explored, allows analysis of an issue in a context, and generates a massive, complex, and fantastically rich data pool. But, as sophisticated science consumers, we have some questions. Are the interviewee reports accurate and complete representations of the experiences sampled by the interviewers? Would other interviewers using the same interview schedule with the same set of interviewees have elicited similar responses? Would other analysts generate a similar coding scheme from the interview transcripts? If so, would individual responses be similarly classified? And would the research participants themselves agree with the Belenky and associates' assignment of them to one or the other of the epistemological categories? Are these findings generalizable to all women? Some women? Which women?

Focus Groups

Interviews can be conducted with groups as well as individuals. To supplement information obtained by individual interviews, or surveys, some researchers conduct a kind of group interview or "focus group." Particularly popular with market researchers, customers are asked to comment on, and discuss their feelings about, a product, or planned product, or what they like and don't like about a particular company. Once they get warmed up, focus groups generate spontaneous interactions and novel ideas that are less likely to emerge in more controlled individual and survey-type contexts. But because they are less controlled they are also open to very large elastic-ruler effects; that is, we are not sure whether the final analysis and report mainly reflects the ideas of the group or of the researcher. Nevertheless, this method provides an excellent way to generate creative hypotheses which can then be investigated more systematically by other methods.

Q Methodology

Imposing a structure on qualitative data, on the pages and pages of free-flowing prose transcribed from interview protocols or open-ended questionnaires, is a daunting task—all the more so because of the infinite opportunities for researcher variables to shape perceived patterns. To achieve a measure of objectivity, researchers will define coding categories, develop procedures of their recognition or identification, train others in the application of these coding strategies, and determine the extent to which various coders agree in the assignment of categories. However, such codes or categories belong to the researcher, not the subjects, and reliable coders may be those who successfully grasp or intuit the researcher's biases. A recently resurrected qualitative approach that helps to address these difficulties (but does not totally eliminate them) is the Q methodology.[2]

The essence of the Q-technique or Q-sort (Stephenson, 1935), as it is sometimes called, involves the presentation of a set of statements (or objects or pictures) to one or more research participants who then sort the items into piles according to some system of categorization (i.e., "most like me" to "least like me"). It is then possible (using objective factor analytic techniques rather than researcher-generated categories) to identify clusters of individuals with similar rankings. Celia Kitzinger (1986, 1987; Kitzinger & Rogers, 1985) for example, utilized the Q methodology in her explorations of the nature of lesbian identities. How do homosexual women understand or interpret the development/origin of their sexual preference? Do lesbians view themselves as sick or deviant, or do they see themselves as challenging this socially constructed conception? A somewhat similar procedure, designed to eliminate or minimize the researcher's influence on the subject's responses, has been used in studies of cognitive complexity (Linville, 1985).

Selection of the items to be sorted is, of course, a key issue. If the researcher creates/invents the item pool, then this technique approaches a Likert-type questionnaire situation, with its attendant constraints on tapping the subjective realities of the respondents. However, the Q researcher attempts to span the domain so that the item pool covers or does justice to both the breadth and diversity of the phenomena to be studied. Kitzinger derived her items directly from interviews of a sample of lesbians to help ensure their validity and to make them user friendly by using verbatim comments. Her interview sample was non random because the objective was to achieve representativeness (i.e., to obtain the broadest possible spectrum of views); in any case, because the parameters of the lesbian population are unknown, a random selection is not possible. Use of the Q methodology, unlike more traditional approaches, does not require the testing of large numbers of randomly selected respondents. In the interviews, Kitzinger attempted to capture personal meanings of lesbian identity—the idiosyncratic subjective conceptualizations of individual lesbians.

Interviewee comments about their views of their own lesbianism were transferred to cards (e.g., "My relationship with my father helps to explain why I am a lesbian;" "I believe I was born lesbian;" "I feel good about being different"). At this step in the research process, we perceive an opportunity for researcher edits (which of the myriad interviewee statements will find their way to the Q cards and which will be discarded?). These cards are then subsequently sorted by the interviewees

---

[2]Brown (1980) describes numerous examples of the use of this technique from a political science perspective.

themselves (which provides a useful check on the researcher's selection) or others (or both) into a quasi-normal distribution using 11 categories ranging from +5 ("most agree that the statement applies to me") to −5 ("most disagree that the statement applies to me"). If the deck of items consisted of 80 cards, the distribution might be as follows:

Scale:	−5	−4	−3	−2	−1	0	+1	+2	+3	+4	+5
Items:	5	6	7	8	9	10	9	8	7	6	5

Completed Q sorts are then subjected to a statistical procedure (factor analysis) that essentially assesses the extent to which different individual sortings are intercorrelated. In effect, the analysis distinguishes subgroups of individuals who rank-ordered the items similarly. Kitzinger's data analysis yielded seven different patterns of lesbian identity. Unlike content analysis techniques or the interpretation of unstructured interviews, which oblige the researcher to create coding or scoring categories and thus allow ample room for the biases of the researcher to influence the results, analysis of the Q sort is objective in the sense that the commonalities are determined statistically. However, an element of researcher bias may still seep in with the interpretation of these patterns, so they are presented to the research participants as a validity check. Articulating the distinctiveness and advantages of this research strategy, Kitzinger and Rogers comment, "Unlike normative methodologies, the use of Q sorts does not impose a structure in advance; and unlike the 'qualitative' methodologies (such as participant observation, in-depth interviewing, etc.), the use of Q sorts does not require the investigator to impose a structure *after* the data have been gathered (through content analysis, for example): respondents in the process of sorting the items create their own structure" (1985; p. 170).

SAMPLE SELECTION

Every scientist, whether in the lab or in the field, struggles with decisions about sample selection. If researchers could have their druthers, all their subject samples would be representative of the total population of *Homo sapiens*. Ah, what a dream of glory—to be able to generalize our findings to every single human being on (and off) the planet! But if wishes were horses, beggars would ride. The study based on such a sample has yet to be done, although computers may soon provide the technology to transform this daydream into nightmarish reality.

Meanwhile researchers must compromise by limiting or curtailing the parent population from which they draw their samples. For obvious reasons one of the most popular populations from which samples are selected and studied is the undergraduate university population.[3] However, survey researchers frequently pose questions which necessitate selection from larger, more diverse populations. How will the country vote in the next election? Polling the voting preferences of a sample of university students will not help us predict, with any degree of confidence, which party will capture the majority of seats in the Congress. Thus pollsters and other investigators interested in predicting or identifying national trends adopt more sophisticated (and more expensive) sampling techniques. First, the total population (all members of the population over voting age) is categorized in terms of certain characteristics believed to be relevant to voting preference (for example, minority group affiliation, religion, age, geographic area, socioeconomic status). Subjects are then selected so that they reflect the proportion of these characteristics in the total population. For example, if 49 percent of the population are male and 51 percent female, then this sex ratio will be maintained in the sample. Similarly, if 10 percent of the total population as defined is unemployed, then 10 percent of the sample will consist of unemployed respondents. This procedure, known as *quota sampling*, is popular with pollsters.

Many other strategies for sample selection have been devised. None are perfect in that none of them can guarantee that the sample is an exact miniature replica of the population. Studies will differ, however, in the extent to which they approximate the population. Before we buy the most recent statistic on the percentage of the population favoring capital punishment, or the number of dentists recommending toothpaste Y, or the degree of opposition to gun control legislation, we would be well advised to assess the quality of the product. Perhaps the statistic was based on responses to a telephone poll conducted on a 1-hour TV talk show last Saturday. Such haphazard sampling is totally inadequate, and we reject the findings out of hand. Maybe the *area-sampling* approach was employed with dwellings within each precinct in Des Moines being randomly sampled. We may accept the accuracy of the statistic for those Des Moines residents who were at home when the researcher called. We may be willing to go even further and generalize the findings to those who were not at home. Some of us might even include people living in comparably sized Midwest cities, but most of us would be justifiably reluctant to apply the statistic to natives of New York City.

The *panel technique*, defined as interviewing the same group of people on two or more occasions, has become an important sampling strategy. This approach is most appropriate for studying behavior, attitudes, or opinion consistency and fluctuations. Mortality (sample attri-

[3]For example, in articles published by major psychological journals, Schultz (1969) reports that psychologists rarely, if ever, use subjects taken from the general adult population.

tion) and the effects of repeat interviewing are potential problems (see Chapter 7).

Next time someone tries to hustle you with a survey statistic, finger it, stretch it, prod it, and sniff it. How was the sample selected, and does this selection procedure offer reasonable assurance that the sample is representative of the target population? Ask three simple questions: (1) Who was left out? (2) What percentage of the population does this omission represent? (3) How do nonrespondents compare with respondents?

ADMINISTRATION

The most carefully constructed questionnaire or interview schedule, combined with the most sophisticated sampling strategy, may still fail to produce accurate results if the administrative procedures are faulty. Obviously surveys based on interviews are more influenced by interviewer techniques, but the return rate of mailed-out questionnaires can also be affected by the content, and tone, of subject instructions.

Response rates to mailed questionnaires vary enormously, but, on average, 48 percent of those who receive a single mailing return the form. Follow-up mailings yield, on average, an additional 20, 12, and 10 percent return rate in response to second, third, and fourth contacts. So, although at first glance the mailed questionnaire seems to be a cheap means to gather huge amounts of data, the need to implement follow-up procedures enhances research costs considerably. Personal interviews produce the best response rates.

Research examining the effects of interviewer characteristics on subject responses has established that the interviewer's sex, social class, age, and race may affect interviewee answers. Further, just as the hypotheses of the experimenter may shape the data he or she collects in the lab, so too may the expectations and attitudes of the interviewer channel the replies obtained from interviewees. Interviewers may unknowing reinforce the expression of opinions that fit well with their own views—with a nod, a smile, an uh-huh, or, in the extreme, with a spontaneous comment like, "You're absolutely right. I couldn't agree more!" Interview responses obtained by naive interviewers often tell us more about the investigator than they do about the respondent.

Various techniques may be employed to reduce the impact of interviewer characteristics on the data. An infrequently utilized tactic is to match interviewers with their interviewees on certain demographic characteristics such as age, sex, social class, and race. An alternative strategy (equally rare) requires heterogeneity of interviewers on these variables—that is, equal numbers of male and female interviewers, black and white interviewers, and so on are sent out to the field. Then even though the harvest reaped by each interviewer is biased, we have avoided a systematic bias; we hope to average out our biases.

Careful training of interviewers may help to overcome the problem of the intrusion of the interviewer's personality, expectations, and attitudes into the interview protocol. Training is aimed at standardization. Ideally we would like to rule out the interviewer as a rogue suspect, and so we attempt to train each interviewer to follow a specific uniform procedure. Each interview is to begin with the same introductory comments; the questions are to be asked in a designated order; the wording of each question must be followed exactly; probing techniques are to be specified and instructions provided as to when to probe. Additionally, interviewers may be taught how to establish and maintain a pleasant relationship with the interviewee—how to develop good rapport. The assumption is that if the respondents feel comfortable and relatively relaxed in the interview they will be more responsive, more open, more cooperative.

The next time you watch an interview on television, try to identify the interviewer's techniques. Try to assess whether this interviewer is likely to elicit accurate responses. Does the interviewer victimize the respondent by employing a brusque, aggressive, nonaccepting stance? Whose views do you learn more about—the interviewer's or the guest's?

STRENGTHS AND WEAKNESSES

Survey methods have the advantage of getting the responses of large samples of people, even of large random samples, at relatively low cost. But notice that the responses are "lightweight" ones. Your research subjects are "telling you" what they would do—and you know that more often than not there is a world of difference between what people say they would do (or did) in a given situation and what they actually do (or did). In 1949 some 920 Denver residents were asked whether they had made contributions to a charity organization. Of those who replied in the affirmative, 34 percent had not actually done so (Parry & Crossley, cited in Oskamp, 1977).[4] Most of us recognize this inconsistency in ourselves —for example, the parent admonishes little Janey, "Do what I say, not what I do." Nevertheless, our critics, little or big, rarely miss an opportunity to point out this deficit—"I can't hear what you're saying 'cause I'm watching what you're doing." Notice that on a questionnaire we have only to move the pencil a few inches to shift our scores from being a bigot to being a humanitarian. We don't have to move our heavyweight (actual) behavior at all. Hanson (1980) has recently reviewed the research investigating the association between attitudes and behavior. Almost half of the studies he examined (20 out of 46) failed to demonstrate a positive relationship between attitudes and behavior.

---

[4]Note that this study provides evidence of the operation of the social desirability response bias.

Thus, predicting behavior, even a small, brief behavioral burst, from questionnaires or interviews is tricky. Consider the 1980 presidential election. Almost to the eve of voting day, pollsters predicted a close race, yet Reagan won by a landslide. Although this was a heavyweight decision for the country, each individual voter's contribution was a brief bit of lightweight behavior—an X on a ballot. Polling research failed to predict accurately even this tiny behavioral unit until the eleventh hour.

Lack of correspondence between questionnaire responses and behavior may reflect a lack of *internal validity*—our survey procedures were inadequate, and so we did not obtain an accurate picture of the respondent's attitudes. Or the discrepancy between the verbal and behavioral domains may suggest an *external validity* problem in that, like the control group model discussed in Chapter 5, survey research data may not generalize to life outside the survey. Still another interpretation is that humans are well able to tolerate such incongruency. One of our colleagues who was accused of behaving inconsistently replied, quite unabashed, "What's so great about consistency? Who said I have to be consistent?" A fourth possibility is that, in fact, attitudes and behavior agree but are almost continually in a state of flux. At 10:00 A.M., on Monday, November 2, Mr. Jones responds to the interviewer firmly, sincerely, and without a moment's hesitation, "Oh, I intend to vote for President Bush." If the election had taken place before November 6, Mr. Jones would indeed have voted as he indicated; but perhaps his verbal, lightweight response changed after that, and his X on the ballot followed suit.

The use of simple physical evidence can markedly extend the validity of laboratory and questionnaire data. For example, following a campaign to encourage drivers to wear seat belts, a questionnaire study indicated a large increase in the number of drivers reporting that they had begun to wear belts. Two students supplemented this data by interviewing gas station attendants and by doing spot-checks at stoplights and at service stations. Gas station attendants reported little or no shift in the percentage of customers wearing belts before and after the campaign, and observational spot-checks revealed a much lower percentage of drivers wearing belts than the questionnaire data estimated.

Questionnaire and interview techniques permit us to extend scientific horizons—to go back in time, to go forward into the future, to explore new terrain, to expand our data pool. In so doing they take us out of the lab and into a corner or two of the "real world." As is the case with all the other sieves of science, naive use of the survey approach will allow much that is valid to sift through the mesh and much that is nonsense to remain trapped—looking for all the world like fact, not fancy.

SUMMARY

Survey research, like other qualitative methods, offers promise as a strategy to enhance external validity by forcing us out of the hothouse laboratory—by leading us out to "where it's at." As usual though, there is a "kicker"—the elastic ruler comes back to haunt us. Verbal responses can be ephemeral—distorted by bias, blown away by memory loss, twisted by deceit, capriciously fluttering and gently turned upside down by environmental breezes. Much of the elasticity may be removed through careful and sophisticated instrument design, sample selection, and administration. Although qualitative methods allow considerable latitude for researchers to impose their personal views on subjects' realities, a variety of techniques, such as the Q methodology, may help to reduce the researcher's edits of the respondent's world.

EXAMPLE

The following in an abbreviated version of an interview study conducted by three undergraduate students.

POLICE OFFICIALS AND PROSTITUTES

Introduction

The purpose of this study is to determine whether police officials accurately perceive the behavior and attitudes of prostitutes and to investigate the nature of the interactions between prostitutes and police.

Method

Subjects. Thirteen subjects were interviewed: eight prostitutes and five police officers. At the time of the interview, the prostitutes, who ranged in age from 18 to 50, were all incarcerated for offenses connected with prostitution. The police officers were all connected with morality work and included two constables, two sergeants, and an inspector. All police subjects were male, and their ages ranged from 30 to 55. Permission to interview a random sample of police officers in the city was sought but not obtained.

Materials. An interview form containing nine questions was designed to provide specific information concerning the behavior and opinions of prostitutes and the nature of their interactions with the police. Similar questions, but appropriately reworded, were administered to the police to determine their perceptions of prostitutes. A copy of the interview form follows.

Interview. We are students working on a project dealing with the relationship between prostitutes and the police. We would like to ask you some questions if you don't mind. If there are any questions you would prefer not to answer, that's fine. We would appreciate any information you would like to give, but be assured that you will remain anonymous and your answers will be kept strictly confidential.

   1.   Do you tend to work a regular area?
        a. Yes
        b. No

2. How do you get your tricks?
   a. Street contacts
   b. Bars
   c. Pimps
   d. Bar or hotel employees
   e. Regular customers
   f. Police
   g. Taxi drivers
   h. Telephone
3. Do you get the same amount of money for each trick or does it vary?
   a. Same
   b. Varies
4. Are you friends with other prostitutes?
   a. Yes
   b. No
5. What is your relationship with the police?
   a. Occasionally have a drink with police?
   b. Call certain officers by their first name?
   c. Discuss personal matters with them?
   d. Ask for advice from them?
   e. Are sarcastic and/or unfriendly to them?
   f. Avoid speaking to them?
6. Do you ever make deals or bargains with the police?
   a. Inform the police about criminal acts (pushers, thieves) in return for easy or lenient treatment?
   b. Cooperate with the police to get rid of your competition?
   c. Turn a trick with a police officer to avoid getting busted?
7. Do you always keep your part of the deal or bargain?
   a. Yes
   b. No
8. Do you think the police treat you fairly?
   a. Yes
   b. No
9. Do you think the laws on prostitution should be changed?
   a. Made clearer
   b. Male prostitution should be illegal
   c. Prostitution should be legalized
   d. Rehabilitation should be offered instead of fines and jail sentences

Procedure. The three researchers conducted the interviews together, with one researcher directing the questions and the other two recording the responses. The interviews were approximately one hour in duration. Two of the police interviews were conducted in the home of one of the researchers, and the others were held in the office of the interviewees. All the prostitutes were interviewed in a small room in the jail provided for visiting purposes. At the conclusion of the interview, all subjects were thanked for their time and cooperation:

In an effort to establish rapport before commencing the interview proper, the researchers described the course under which auspices we were conducting the research. We also explored with interviewees some personal history and shared cigarettes.

Results

The percentage of prostitutes and police providing each response alternative is presented in Table 9-1. The greater the disparity between the two percentages, the greater the misperception on the part of the police.

TABLE 9-1   Accuracy of Police Perceptions of Prostitutes

Question	% Prostitutes	% Police	Question	% Prostitutes	% Police
1. a)	88	80	5. a)^a	25	0
b)	13	20	b)	13	0
2. a)^a	25	20	c)	0	0
b)	75	80	d)	0	0
c)	13	20	e)	38	100
d)	13	40	f)	50	0
e)	0	0	6. a)	0	20
f)	0	0	b)	0	20
g)	13	20	c)	0	0
h)	0	20	7. a)	—	20
3. a)	88	80	b)	—	20
b)	13	20	8. a)	13	40
4. a)	100	100	b)	88	60
b)	0	0	9. a)^a	0	20
			b)	13	20
			c)	100	20
			d)	50	40

^{a}Percentages total more than 100 because several response alternatives were provided by the interviewees on these questions.

Discussion

To illustrate the experiences and lifestyle of the prostitutes, a typical case is described. At the time of the interview, this prostitute had so many convictions on her record that she could not remember the exact number. She had been "busted" (arrested) seven times within the last 11 months by the same detective. She had been released from jail the previous week but was apprehended again three days later. She reported that she had had the assurance of a job which was to start in three weeks. Given this information the police advised her to plead guilty in the hope of a remand for two weeks. However, she received a sentence of two months. Unable to qualify for legal aid and not able to afford a lawyer, she had little chance of escaping conviction. When she is released, she will have no job and no money and will be forced to return to prostitution in order to support herself. Thus she must risk yet another conviction. In a sense the predictable and repeated chain of events is analogous to being caught in a revolving door.

The results obtained from the interviews suggest that the perceptions of the police with respect to the behavior of prostitutes is reasonably accurate on many points. The most obvious discrepancies occurred in responses about the nature of interactions between the prostitutes and the police. Prostitutes report more friendly or intimate contacts than the police do.

The major weakness of this research is the small size of the samples. As indicated earlier it was not possible to obtain permission to randomly sample police officials. In the case of the prostitutes, permission had been obtained to solicit interviewees in one jail. At the time the interviews were conducted, a total of 14 prostitutes were inmates in the jail, but 4 refused to participate, one was released before she could be interviewed, and one woman who stated that she was a prostitute but had never been arrested for this offense was excluded.

Instructor's Comments

You are to be congratulated for attempting to tackle a significant issue—one that requires the collection of data from groups that are under-researched due to the difficulties in obtaining sufficiently large samples. You made a valiant (albeit unsuccessful) effort to follow "good" research practices with respect to sample selection. Your interview form has several strengths—particularly evident is your attempt to use the vernacular of your interviewees and the effective use of probes. Your sensitivity to the need for good rapport is also noteworthy. How successful do you feel you were in establishing rapport? One concern, which you did not express, relates to the accuracy (truthfulness) of the responses obtained. Apparently you probed for some demographic information (such as number of convictions); perhaps you might have been able to check this information against official records to provide a crude indication of response "slippage." It would have been of interest to have recorded and reported the demographic data.

The use of three interviewers is puzzling. Perhaps you felt intimidated by your interviewees and wanted the moral support of a colleague. Having one person conduct the interview while another records the responses is also a good strategy. However, an interviewee might well be more circumspect in the presence of *three* interviewers. Since two people were recording, you had an opportunity to assess the reliability of the recording process, yet you do not appear to have compared recorders' responses.

Given the small sample it is inappropriate to generalize beyond your specific samples. While the five police officers may have been reasonably accurate in their perceptions of the eight prostitutes, we cannot assume that this degree of congruence would hold with more representative samples.

REVIEW QUIZ

True or False?

1. Survey researchers observe the effects of manipulated antecedent conditions.
2. Scaled questionnaire responses, as opposed to open-ended items, enhance external validity.
3. A common format for scaled responses is the Likert-type questionnaire scale.
4. A common form of response bias that occurs in questionnaire and attitude measures is the social desirability bias.
5. Corporal Klinger (actor Jamie Farr), who appeared as a transvestite soldier in the television show "*M*A*S*H**," provided a humorous example of the response extremity bias.
6. Questionnaires should be constructed so that open-ended questions are presented first.
7. Interview data collection procedures provide researchers with the opportunity to consider responses in a context.
8. Analysis of interview protocols through content analysis provides considerable latitude for the operation of researcher bias.
9. Q methodology provides an objective technique for identifying clusters of individuals with similar rankings of items.
10. Q methodology, in keeping with more traditional approaches, requires the testing of large numbers of randomly selected respondents.
11. Undergraduate university students are the most popular subject group in psychological research.
12. Quota sampling is a popular subject selection strategy with pollsters.
13. The panel technique refers to the use of a set of judges to evaluate the validity of a questionnaire.
14. The return rate of questionnaires after an initial mailing averages out at about 70%.
15. Matching interviewers with their interviewees on relevant variables is a frequently used tactic designed to reduce the impact of interviewer characteristics on the data.
16. There is a very high level of concordance between what people say they would do in a given situation and their actual behavior in that situation.

❧ 10 ❧
The Number Game

Chapter Goal

---

*To show how numbers can serve as powerful
short-hand ways to describe our experience,
on the one hand, or to mislead us,
on the other.*

INTRODUCTION

The degree of sadness is 1 per minute on the Kleenex scale.
The average American family has one and a half children.

Numbers can help us describe nature, or carve it up into unnatural parts. "Adults have 8 sexual fantasies a day"; "10% of the Japanese, and only 2% of Americans have IQs above 130"; "the average length of intercourse for humans is 2 minutes, whereas for chimpanzees, it is 7 seconds." We know that science and numbers go together, but are there no rules for this number game? In science we aim to make our observations (*O*'s) and suspects' (*X*'s) clear, to make our dependent and independent variables open to public inspection. Science and measurement go together. To understand science you must understand the simple rules of measurement.

In Chapter 2, we noted that language consists of a set of symbols, sounds, or written squiggles and a set of rules for combining them. In English, the symbols are words and the rules are our grammar.

Measurement is a language, too; its symbols are numerals. In this section we talk about tying numerals to objects and events to help us describe and order our world. Numbers condense or package data into memorable chunks.

Not only do we use numbers to label the sweaters of football players and to count poker chips but we also use them to tell how we measure up in height, school grades, and income. We use numbers to describe things we can't see, like temperature, anxiety, and the national debt. Furthermore, we use numbers to help us move from small bits or samples of information to generalizations, such as predicting the number of cases of cancer in the whole population on the basis of the number we find in a sample of the population.

In the following chapters we describe the major rules of the number game and show how breaking the rules—wittingly or unwittingly—fouls the game.

Almost everyone knows that measurement and numbers belong together. In fact, *measurement can be defined as tying numbers to objects and events according to certain rules*, in the same sense that words are tied to objects and events.

In the case of measurement, instead of tying *word* labels to shareable objects or events, we tie *number* labels to them. Measurement also involves logical rules for combining numbers, which are translated into concrete operations. For example, the logical symbol + (plus) can be concretely expressed by pouring water from one beaker and *adding* it to the whisky in another beaker.

BLACK MAGIC?

Measurement, we have said, can be defined as tying numbers to objects and events according to certain rules. Although not able to explain the rules in detail, most of us recognize when a rule has been broken, particularly when a child breaks the rules, as in the following dialogue:

> *You:*   How old are you, Kim?
>
> *Kim:*   I am five years old, and I am seven years old.

While you may not know the name of the rule, you know that Kim has broken some rule about tying numbers to objects. After some discussion you convince Kim that one age number is enough for anyone, and she finally agrees that she is five years old and that her brother is seven years old. You then continue your discussion:

> *You:*   Who is older, Kim, you or your brother? Which age number is bigger?
>
> *Kim:*   I am older; my number is bigger.

Once again, even though you may not know the name of the rule, you know that Kim has broken it. Five doesn't come after seven; five goes before seven—anybody knows that—well, anybody who's learned the rule.

On Being Number-Numb

We laugh when children break rules in tying number words to objects and events. When researchers do it, it is not so obvious, and it can be disastrous.

Have you noticed how otherwise very competent people are number-numb? A faculty member is a case in point. He speaks of numbers as "those ugly little squiggles that are the constituents of a black art." When the abolition of child labor in mines and factories freed children from punishing physical work, he claims the evil powers rushed in with arithmetic, algebra, trigonometry, and statistics as new forms of child torture.

MEASUREMENT SCALES AND RULES

Those of you who major in psychology or become social scientists will encounter different types of measurement scales ranging from crude to precise. An appropriate measurement scale will help you locate an important phenomenon, or discover a subtle change in behavior, that a crude or inappropriate scale will miss. Since the scientific method rests on systematic observation, and since measurement is the fundamental tool of observation, you need to know how to select and evaluate (perhaps even construct) these vital observational tools.

The four major types of scale encountered in social science are: (1) nominal, (2) ordinal, (3) interval, and (4) ratio scales. To understand the construction and application of these scales and to appreciate their relative power to detect differences in human behavior, you should know the different rules upon which each one rests.

At this point we could list and describe some of the logical rules for combining number symbols, such as the nominal rule, the ordinal rule, and the interval rule. An alternative procedure is to attempt to discover the logical operations by examining a concrete example of their application.

We have noted that *measurement* can be defined as rules for tying numbers to objects and events. At the concrete level a measuring instrument is a good example of tying numbers to an object according to certain rules. Therefore let's examine a common measuring tool to discover some of the rules that went into its construction. An ordinary 1-foot ruler provides an excellent example.

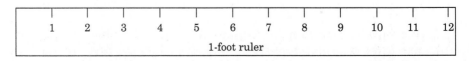

1-foot ruler

In the case of the ruler, someone has assigned numbers to this flat piece of wood. What rules were followed? Examine the ruler for a moment; notice the symbols; observe how they are placed. If you examine another school ruler, even one made by a different manufacturer, you will find many similarities. While the color of the wood or the paint or the plastic may differ, the two rulers will have several characteristics in common—the placement of the numerals in both cases has followed the same rules.

Nominal Rule

Notice first that different symbols are used to label different points on the piece of wood. If this were not the case we could be faced with a ruler of the following type:

The nominal rule—the naming or labeling rule—demands that you apply different, agreed-on labels (names, numbers, symbols) to different objects or events.

This first rule—the nominal rule—is considered by some not to be a form of measurement. They point out that it is merely a labeling operation, useful for identification purposes, but in no way does it tell us anything about "more than" or "less than" relationships. Nevertheless, since counting is a form of measurement and since it is based on the assumption that we have met the requirements of the nominal rule, it is important to include this rule as one of the rules of measurement. In other words, since the nominal rule is fundamental to all other measuring rules, it should be included. There are many examples, like that facing the psychiatrist attempting to make a diagnosis, in which we fail to meet the conditions of the nominal rule. Nevertheless, we go merrily along counting objects and reporting the results in numbers when the results are, at worst, meaningless and, at best, highly perishable or personal.

When different investigators end up with different counts, what are we to assume? Since counting itself is fairly simple, the safest assumption is that the nominal rule has been broken—that is, there is no agreed-upon way of assigning labels to the members of the various populations being counted, and so the counting operation itself becomes a counting of ghosts. Since all other rules of measurement assume that the nominal rule has been met and since there is ample evidence that the nominal rule is often ignored, we conclude that this important rule must be included among the rules of measurement.

We once assumed that individuals who were assigned to the same category were the same, that is, they all had a long list of characteristics in common (e.g., birds all fly, sing, eat worms, build nests in trees, etc.).

But penguins and ostriches are birds and do none of these things. We now realize that useful categories are fuzzier than we once thought and are used to accommodate strange bedfellows, and so we've changed procedures for assigning categories. To be a member of a category you don't have to have a long list of characteristics in common with other members, but only a few, maybe only one.

For example, officially a diagnosis of depression is acceptable if someone with a dysphoric mood shows any five of a set of nine symptoms almost daily over a period of at least 2 weeks. Notice then that two patients may be both categorized as depressed and share only a single one of the nine symptoms. If you are planning to do graduate work, keep an eye on nominal scaling and category theory, which offer rich opportunities for conceptual and empirical breakthroughs.

Ordinal Rule

Not only are different numbers assigned to different objects and events, but the numbers have a reserved place in the number series— this is the ordinal rule. If it were otherwise, we would encounter such rulers as the following, where different rulers have their numbers in different orders.

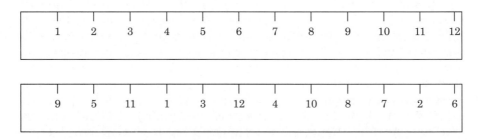

An object measured by the first ruler might be assigned the number 2, but when measured by the second ruler, it would be assigned the number 5. If numbers on a ruler, or in the number series generally, were permitted to play musical chairs, we couldn't use the numbers to talk about order or to indicate where in the series a given object or event occurs. Think of the problems involved in a simple example:

    You: How did Sally make out in the 100-meter freestyle?

    Paul: She came in second.

  George: She came in fifth.

In an effort to resolve the conflicting answers, you ask Ringo. He replies, "Sally came in *B*." Ringo doesn't like numbers and will use them only when no alternative method is available. The three foregoing systems for describing order are outlined as follows:

Paul: 1, 2, 3, 4, 5, 6, 7, etc.
George: 9, 5, 11, 1, 3, 12, 4, etc.
Ringo: A, B, C, D, E, F, G, etc.

It is important to remember that the symbols we use and the position they're assigned in the series are mere customs. As long as Paul, George, and Ringo use the same rules consistently, they are playing the game. Paul's number series has the advantage of being in common use (large-group rules); it is blessed by custom. Notice, however, that when George's number series (individual rules) is put next to Paul's, there is no contradiction in their replies to our question. In both instances Sally was assigned the position right after the beginning position—that is, Position *B* in Ringo's terms. If George wants to persist in having his own individual ordinal scale and he uses it consistently, we can learn to translate it into our own terms. He plays by the shareable rules of language, and anyone who wants to learn his system can do so. If, however, the positions of the numbers change, if George haphazardly changes them from day to day, then this would be an unstable system, and George would be breaking the "reserved-place" ordinal rule.

It should be noted that in these examples the nominal rule is also violated. You will recall that we stated that, in the case of the nominal rule, different agreed-on labels are assigned to different objects or events. In our examples, although different labels are applied to differing objects or events, they are not agreed upon—that is, there does not appear to be consensus as to the label for second place. In one case it's 2, in another 5, and in Ringo's system it is *B*. Each of the rules builds on preceding ones, so that in order to develop an ordinal scale, you must first satisfy the assumptions of the nominal rule.

So far we have considered two rules of the number system: Rule 1—by custom, different objects and events are assigned different symbols or numerals; Rule 2—by custom, the symbols or numerals are assigned a reserved position in the series of numerals. Notice that the alphabet, as well as the whole number system, fulfills these two rules. Thus if you want to label events or simply talk about their order, the alphabet will do as well as the number system, providing you don't have to talk about more than 26 objects or events. While the alphabet is a useful system for labeling events and describing their order, and while it can be used to describe relations such as "earlier than" and "bigger than," is it really of much use if we want to talk about "how much bigger" one object is than another?

The Interval Rule

Returning to our standard 12-inch ruler, notice that the symbols are placed equal distances apart. A ruler is divided into a series of equal-sized units. But how far apart are the letters of the alphabet? One alph? You see that the order rule makes no assumptions about how far apart the symbols are. All of the following scales meet the ordinal rule:

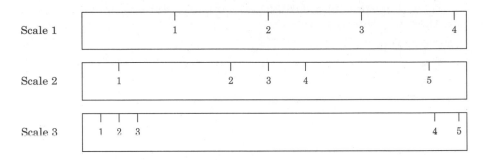

> *You:*   How did our team make out in the 100-meter free style?
> *Reply:* We placed first, second, and third.

Does that mean by Scale 1, Scale 2, or Scale 3? Usually when we ask such a question, we are not concerned about how big an interval separates the swimmers but only about the order they came in, regardless of interval. If we want to know the swimmers' times or the distances separating the best jumps of three pole-vaulters, however, can we handle the problem with only an ordinal scale? Suppose Elvis vaulted 13'9", Blane vaulted 14'0", and Turk vaulted 14'6". How do we communicate this information with only an ordinal scale? We could say Blane beat Elvis by a bit and Turk beat Blane by more than that. So we have communicated more than just "order" information.

Elvis	Blane	Turk

A bit

We have communicated some distance or interval information as well. How did we do it? By selecting a standard that we call "a bit" (the distance separating Elvis and Blane) and comparing it to the distance separating Turk and Blane, we decided that the latter distance was bigger than "a bit."

The important point, of course, is that to talk about "more than" and "less than," we need to know what a "than" is; if we want to talk about "more than a bit" and "less than a bit," we need to know what a "bit" is.

Selecting a standard, or a basic unit, is an arbitrary decision. When faced with this problem, you look around for a readily available standard and make that your "bit." People's feet were usually readily available, and so "one foot" became an early unit for measuring distance. Using people's real feet for measuring distances must have led to certain inequalities as well as inconveniences. When good old Dad's farm was divided, the son with the biggest "foot" did better.

Eventually someone with small feet recommended that they should have one special foot to avoid arguments; everyone agreed, and, of course, they decided to use the king's foot. Now a king doesn't go traipsing all over the countryside just to measure things with his foot, so they had to cut off one of his feet, to be sent around for measuring. This left the king with only one foot, hence the origin of the term *1-foot-ruler*.[1]

The point is that if we want to talk about how much more than or less than one object is in relation to another, we need a unit—a standard interval that is easy to apply. It often takes years to develop such a unit and to sell others on using our particular interval, whether it is a second, a bushel, a micromercury, a megaton, an ounce, a degree of temperature, a unit of anxiety, intelligence, depression, or a foot.

In summary, if all we want to do is to label or identify objects or packages of data by using numbers, we follow the nominal rule (different objects get different numbers). We can do this as long as we can tell the objects or the qualities of objects apart. If we also want to describe order relationships among objects by using numbers, we must include the ordinal rule. We can do this as long as we can order the objects (from earliest to latest, or smallest to biggest); then we assign the first number, 1, in the number series to the first object in the ordered series and the second number, 2, to the second object in the ordered series, and so on. If, in addition to labeling and ordering, we want to describe with numbers the interval separating objects, then we must use the interval rule and select or develop a measuring instrument that is divided into equal units.

There is one more characteristic about our one-foot ruler that deserves comment. Notice that it has a zero point. This is so obvious that its importance is often overlooked.

The Ratio Rule

Unless a measuring instrument has a zero point, it is impossible to say anything about how many times bigger or smaller one object or quantity is than another. Without assuming that there is such a thing as zero age, we would not be able to say that Harry is twice as old as Mary. Consider an example. In a test of knowledge of French nouns, we have the following results:

---

[1]There may be the odd scholar who has some reservations about the complete historical authenticity of this interpretation.

Vladimir knew none of the words.

Hamish knew 5.

George knew 10.

Gloria knew 15.

We can portray the results in the following way:

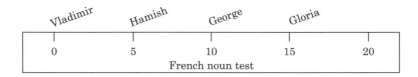

Thus our test of French nouns is a measuring instrument that appears to have all the characteristics of an ordinary ruler—that is, it appears to meet the nominal, ordinal, interval, and absolute-zero rules. If this is so, then we can say that George knows twice as many French nouns as Hamish knows, and that Gloria knows three times as many as Hamish knows. We can do so only if we are able to agree on where zero belongs on the scale. As you can guess, certain very simple French nouns weren't included on the test the teacher gave—words like *l'amour* and *la bouche*. Therefore it is quite likely that there are at least five French nouns that even Vladimir knows that, if included on the test, everyone would get correct. This would involve moving the zero point on our scale five points to the left. Now look at the old scale alongside the new, and see how this affects what we can say about how many more nouns Gloria knows than Hamish or Vladimir knows. In the case of the first scale, we had concluded that George knew twice as many French nouns as Hamish knew, but with the new zero point, this is no longer the case. Similarly, on the original scale Gloria knew three times as many French nouns as Hamish knew, whereas on the new scale, she knows only twice as many.

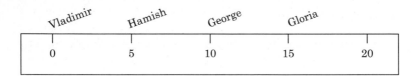

It is apparent, then, that if we want to talk about how many times greater or smaller one object is in relation to another, we must have a way of deciding where absolute zero is on the scale. In many cases, such as most test scores (arithmetic, French, intelligence, anxiety, beauty, musical talent), we use an arbitrary zero. In those cases where we are not sure where zero lies, we should not (1) attempt to say how many times bigger or smaller one score is than another or (2) attempt to use any statistical procedures that involve multiplying or dividing the scores. These rules are ignored by many social science researchers.

Arbitrary Zero

You may say that one way around the problem is simply to report that, in the case of our original French test, George knew twice as many of the words as Hamish did on *that particular test*. In this way you are making no claim about whether George knows twice as many of all French nouns but only twice as many of the ones on that particular test. And, of course, you would be perfectly right in doing so. However, most tests are designed to estimate amount of knowledge in a given field, with the test questions representing only a small sample of all possible questions in that area. Thus while it is relatively easy to say whether someone gets a score of zero on the particular sample of the questions selected, it is extremely difficult to decide whether that person would get zero if all possible questions dealing with the topic had been asked.

Most students who succeed in getting poor marks on tests know what we are talking about. When they say the test was unfair, they are saying that it was a bad sample of questions, and by poor luck the teacher just happened to select the only questions the student didn't know. Thus in your friend's eyes, your score of 80 and his score of 10 certainly does not indicate that you know eight times more about the field than he does. In fact, by the time he finishes complaining, he implies that he could answer hundreds of questions about the topic, whereas you were able to answer only the eight particular questions the teacher selected. So he goes away mumbling and concluding that he knows more about the field than you do but that the educational people seem almost diabolical in their ability to select those few questions for which he has no answers.

Actually this is a critical problem facing educators, particularly with the present knowledge explosion. No longer can we expect professors of physics to know everything about physics or professors of psychology to know everything about psychology. The professors solve this dilemma by becoming more and more specialized, by carving out smaller and smaller areas or data pools within their own discipline within which they attempt to become very knowledgeable, and then they dump all that knowledge in the student's lap. How is the student to face the dilemma of information overload at exam time? The naive student attempts to learn all the material that the professor presents, as well as to cover the outside readings. Wise students know how to study strategically. They have learned to spend more time on some parts of the course material than on others. They have learned to identify the professor's preferences. The students do this on the basis of how much time the professor spends on different topics, by noting what topics appear to excite the professor, by seeing what sorts of questions the professor traditionally asks, by looking over the professor's exam papers for the past years, and by talking to former students. This strategic approach to learning may appear to be unscholarly. Certainly some students carry it to the extreme, devoting almost all their time to attempting to predict the few questions that will be asked, and then applying their very limited remaining time and energy to studying these few questions. This is, of course, a self-defeating approach to learning. Nevertheless, serious students, facing the impossible task of preparing for all possible questions, rely not only on their own particular interests but also on the biases of the professor in guiding them on what aspects of the topic require more concentrated work than others.

This discussion is not merely a diversionary bit of advice on the strategy of getting through university. The scientific way to estimate a student's knowledge of a given area would be to have all competent professors in that area write out a list of all conceivable questions. These questions would then be put into huge drums grouped into classes from most important to least important. On a given examination a sample of 10, 15, or 100 questions would be drawn out of each drum and would constitute the exam—the number of questions to be drawn depending on the amount of time available for the examination. Such a list of questions would constitute a random sample of hard, average, and easy questions. Under the present circumstances in which a given professor decides which questions to ask, we have a biased sample of questions covering the field. If a student repeatedly does well on the series of exams based on the random sample procedure, we would conclude that the student knows the topic well. When a student does well for a given professor, we are not sure whether he or she knows the topic well or *knows the professor well*.

Similarly, when you read the results of a poll concerning who will be the next president of the United States or concerning premarital sexual relations, are you getting the answers from a cross-section of the population in the country, or are you getting the answers from the friends and colleagues of the person who carried out the poll? In other words, are you learning about the topic, or are you learning more about the biases of the person who conducted the poll? *Absolute-zero scales* refer to topics and total populations. *Arbitrary-zero scales* refer to samples and biased groups of one kind or another.

In the example of our test of French nouns, we were not talking about how many of all (population) French nouns the student knew but only about how many of those selected for the test (sample). Thus we were using an arbitrary zero, so it is impossible to talk about whether Gloria knows 2 times or 20 times as many French nouns as Hamish does. If we wanted to be able to make such statements with confidence, we would have to test the students on all French nouns. If we wanted to make an approximation, we could test them on several samples of French nouns picked at random from a data pool of all French nouns. Arbitrary-zero scales are typically interval scales masquerading as ratio scales.

Before discussing how science and measurement go together, we shall summarize measurement rules. Nominal scales are used when we compare objects or data clusters and can decide which ones are the same and which ones are different. After this we can count how many objects fall into each category. Ordinal scales enable us to talk about relations such as "more than" or "less than," or "earlier than" or "later than." As long as independent observers can rank-order objects or events on some less-to-more dimension, they have an ordinal scale.

In some cases we want to know more than who came first and second. We also want to know by how much one swimmer beat the other. In instances where we want to describe by how much objects or events differ, we use an interval scale. Finally, absolute-zero scales are used when we want to compare one event, not merely with another person or sample, but with an absolute-zero or population value (knowledge of *all* French nouns). Each of the four scales, then, has a different purpose, but each succeeding scale assumes that the rules of the preceding scales have been met. If an ordinal scale is to be used, it is assumed that the nominal rule has been met. If an interval scale is to be used, it is assumed that, in addition to the interval rule, the nominal and ordinal rules have also been met.

In primitive disciplines like social and medical sciences, remember that nominal and ordinal scales can be of invaluable assistance in describing or packaging data. For example, even before we had thermometers how might you "measure" someone's temperature using a crude ordinal scale? *Hint*: The way every parent does. By putting your hand on the person's forehead and seeing if it feels hot. Hotter than what? Hotter than your hand. This works well, providing your temperature is "normal," and they have a high fever. Just as a crude thermometer is better than no thermometer, so initially are crude measures of anxiety, or management ability, or patient improvement better than no measure, better than casual observation. Furthermore, what may start out to be crude measures are, with experience, gradually refined and transformed into more sensitive measures that can detect smaller and smaller differences and changes.

In the section to follow, we will have an opportunity to examine some of the challenges involved in constructing simple nominal and ordinal data-packaging methods.

SCIENCE AND MEASUREMENT
GO TOGETHER

Everyone knows that science and measurement go together, but not everyone appreciates the importance of the relationship. You now have some familiarity with the sieves of science:

field study   natural experiments
after-the-fact   field experiments
archival research   simulation methods
survey research   unobtrusive measures
before-and-after   developmental and longitudinal
control-group method   methods
                                    interrupted time series
                                    treatment reversal (cross-over)
                                        designs

and you are also familiar with the measurement scales:

nominal

ordinal

interval

ratio (absolute zero)

used to clearly describe suspects (X's) and observations (O's). Scientists technically refer to suspects as *independent* variables and to observations as *dependent* variables. They are variables in the sense that they can take different values, and the changes in the dependent variable are assumed to *depend* on changes in the independent variable.

Just as moving from the after-the-fact sieve to the control group sieve increases confidence in your findings, so too moving up from nominal scales to ordinal, interval, and ratio scales increases the precision of your measurement and reduces regions of uncertainty.

Recall the control-group study in Chapter 5 of treating depressed patients with a new drug. This study can be conducted at different levels of precision, depending on the precision used in manipulating the independent variable (the drug) and the degree of precision used in measuring the dependent variable (the degree of depression). At the crudest level we could manipulate the independent variable on a nominal scale (Drug A versus Drug B) and measure the dependent variable also at a crude nominal scale level (depressed versus nondepressed).[2] The following figure displays the research design as well as the results of the study:

	(O_1)	(X)	(O_2)
Group 1	10 depressed	Drug A	8 depressed
($N = 10$)	0 not depressed		2 not depressed
Group 2	10 depressed	Drug B	9 depressed
($N = 10$)	0 not depressed		1 not depressed

Not very encouraging results. But is it that the drugs have similar effects or that the scale is too crude to detect the differences? Note that the dependent variable can only take two values—depressed versus nondepressed. There is no provision for shifts in degree of depression; it may well be that Drug A helps relieve the depression of significantly more patients than does Drug B, but this result cannot show up in this study since, for example, there is no category for mild depression.

Now look what happens to our results when we increase the degree of precision by using a four-category ordinal scale instead of a two-unit nominal scale for assessing depression:

	(O_1)	(X)	(O_2)
Group 1	10 severe	Drug A	2 severe
($N = 20$)	10 marked		6 marked
	0 moderate		7 moderate
	0 mild		5 mild
Group 2	10 severe	Drug B	7 severe
($N = 20$)	10 marked		12 marked
	0 moderate		1 moderate
	0 mild		0 mild

Following treatment with Drug A, 12 out of 20 patients are well enough to go home, having shifted down to mild or moderate depression, whereas only one patient was well enough to go home following Drug B treatment.

Had Drug A been a miracle drug, a drug capable of shifting most patients from a seriously depressed state to a state of *no* depression, then we could detect its effect with a crude two-category nominal scale.

[2]You can think of this as a two-point ordinal scale rather than the two-category nominal scale, if you prefer.

However, although not a miracle drug, it is significantly better than Drug *B*, being capable of shifting severely depressed patients to a state of only moderate or mild depression. With a four-point ordinal scale, we detect this important new information; with only a crude two-point nominal scale, we missed it.

Therefore, remember that the cruder the measuring scale used to detect shifts in your dependent variable, the stronger must be the effects of your independent variable.

Notice we still don't know anything about the effects of different amounts of our independent variable (Drug *A*), since previously we used only one dosage level. In certain amounts it may prove to be a miracle drug. To find out about the effects of different amounts, we conduct a study in which we manipulate the independent variable on a milligram scale (a ratio scale with an absolute zero and equal units). The results of this study follow:

	O_1	X		O_2
Group 1 (N = 20)	10 severe 10 marked 0 moderate 0 mild	Drug *A*	150 milligrams	1 severe 3 marked 8 moderate 8 mild
Group 2 (N = 20)	10 severe 10 marked 0 moderate 0 mild	Drug *A*	100 milligrams	2 severe 6 marked 7 moderate 5 mild
Group 3 (N = 20)	10 severe 10 marked 0 moderate 0 mild	Drug *A*	50 milligrams	4 severe 8 marked 5 moderate 3 mild

Notice as the dosage becomes larger, the number of patients helped also increases. Also notice that we don't know what a larger dosage than we have tried would do; it might be even more effective, or it might start causing negative side effects—obvious ones like hives and drowsiness that can be detected by casual observation involving crude nominal and ordinal scales, or subtle ones like subsequent difficulties in carrying a baby to full term, which may take years to link to the drug.

By combining the control-group method with increased precision in the measuring scales used both to measure our dependent variables and to manipulate our independent variables, we are able to get a clearer picture of nature's rhythms. For example, Agnew and Ernest (1971), using human subjects, compared the effects over time of three dosage levels of a sedative drug and three levels of a stimulant drug with a placebo on a variety of measurement scales. The results obtained from one of the self-rating mood scales used are given in Figure 10-1.

In this large study the effects of all three independent variables (type of drug, dosage, and time since drug taken) all show up clearly on a variety of rating scales but not on certain perceptual and cognitive tests. Thus not only is it appropriate to have sufficient degrees of precision in your measuring scales, it is also important to select scales that measure relevant aspects of the behavior under study. This selection is influenced both by past experience and by theoretical hunch. In this particular study, notice that self-reports were more accurate in detecting drug type and dosages than were "objective" tests.

It is clear that science and measurement go hand in hand. If you believe your independent variable has a strong effect on your dependent variable, you can probably detect such an effect with a crude nominal or interval scale. If, however, you suspect only a mild or moderate effect, you should use a more precise measuring scale—one with small units able to detect small differences. If you are not sure what aspect of behavior will be affected, you had better use several different scales.

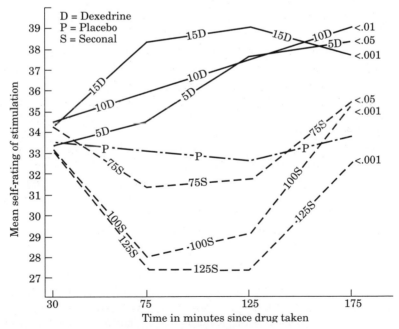

FIGURE 10-1   The Influence of a Sedative and of a Stimulant on Mood

Most wise researchers carry out naturalistic observations or conduct pilot studies to get a "feel" for the strength and rhythm of the relationship between the dependent and independent variable before launching into elaborate research projects. You would probably be wise to do the same. One wonders what kind of effort was made to check the nominal scale labeling (semantics) of "sexual fantasies," or the "interval scale" reliability of group IQ tests, or the "comparability" of the Japanese and American samples mentioned in Chapter 1?

What to Look for in Pilot Studies

A pilot study familiarizes you with some of the characteristics of your independent and dependent variables. What appeared under casual observation to be clear suspects and observations, on closer examination turned out to be fuzzy categories—the drug changes color from day to day and the patients' degrees of depression are highly variable.

Indeed, as well as giving some crude estimates of the potency of your independent variable, a pilot study helps you decide how you should scale your independent and dependent variables. Whether you need few or many categories for each and whether those categories lend themselves to nominal, ordinal, interval, or ratio scaling becomes more obvious. Whether or not observations lend themselves to one scale or another can be determined by asking certain key questions—for example, we need to know how many categories we would require to describe the independent variable and its range of impact upon the dependent variable. If we use too few categories, we lose valuable information—as was the case when we used only two nominal categories to detect the effect of our drug on depression in the previously discussed drug study. On the other hand, if we use too many categories, we raise the cost of our study and probably overtax the ability of our observers to make fine discriminations.

Many factors affect our decisions, including theoretical assumptions, past experience (our own and that described in the literature), and the availability of resources and measuring instruments.

For example, once you have satisfied yourself, on the basis of a pilot study, that you are working with an ordinal scale, the next key question is how many categories you need. Too few categories in an ordinal scale can cause trouble, but so can too many. Consider the case of a therapist who is interested in evaluating the effectiveness of a new treatment for neurosis. She sets up a five-point ordinal scale as follows:

Markedly worse	Moderately worse	No change	Moderately improved	Markedly improved
1	2	3	4	5

Improvement scale

Category 3 is to be assigned to patients who demonstrate no change; Category 4 is to be assigned to those showing moderate improvement; Category 5 to those showing marked improvement; Category 2 to those who seem to be moderately worse following treatment; and Category 1 to those who seem to be markedly worse after treatment.

Our researcher has a therapist examine the patients before and following treatment and assigns each to one of the five categories. She has another therapist independently follow the same procedure. You will recall from our discussion of nominal scales that one of the ways of determining whether you have clear categories (i.e., that the categories can be consistently applied, and your measure is reliable) is to see if different observers can *independently* label the objects or events the same way. We are essentially following the same procedure here with ordinal scales.

The worst that can happen with the ratings of our two observers is almost no agreement between them in assigning patients to categories— that is, had the patients been assigned their categories by drawing the numbers out of two hats rather than having them assigned by therapists, the results would have been similar. Or perhaps there may be large disagreements between the two—that is, therapist B has assigned some patients to Category 5, and therapist A has assigned some of the same patients to Category 1, and vice versa. Under either of the preceding conditions, it is apparent that (1) the scale is inadequate and (2) at least one of the therapists has a very personal or pragmatic view of improvement. However, if the differences occur around scale points 2, 3, and 4, the researcher will recognize that Categories 2 and 4 are fuzzy, that they contain large areas of uncertainty, and so she collapses them into one category by combining them with Category 3:

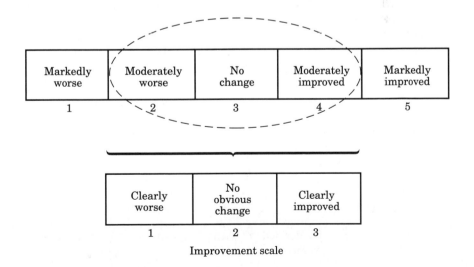

Improvement scale

If this is the case, she has an ordinal scale that will detect the results of treatments that have a large effect—that shift a significant number of patients into new Category 3. Even a crude scale like this is preferable to no scale at all or, in other words, to individual bias.

But she may decide she wants to develop a scale that will be sensitive not only to strong treatments but also to moderate treatments. If so, she devotes time to attempting to clarify the distinction between Category 3 (no appreciable change) and Category 4 (moderate improvement) of her original five-point scale. She can attempt to make these categories more distinctive by giving examples of what she considers to be moderate improvement: "patient may still have severe nightmares but not as frequently"; "patient still experiences strong anxiety in presenting class paper but is attending class more regularly." After attempting to clarify distinctions between the middle categories, she tests this scale again to see if she is now getting more agreement among independent judges in the use of the middle categories. If so, she has reduced the region of uncertainty in her original Category 4, and she has increased the sensitivity of her scale in detecting moderate, as well as marked, changes.

SUMMARY

Using a common 1-foot ruler as an example, we described four types of measurement scales: (1) nominal; (2) ordinal; (3) interval; and (4) ratio, or absolute zero. Naturalistic observations and pilot studies can help you get a feel for how you might measure your dependent variable. You also get some idea of the "power" of your independent variable. If it generates a big effect then you can get by with a crude nominal or ordinal scale, whereas if its effect is weak you require a more precise interval or ratio scale. Or perhaps you should look for a more powerful independent variable, one that more obviously pushes your dependent variable up or down.

The results you report depend not only on the type and precision of your measurement scales but also on the kind of analysis you perform. Statistics play a large role in shaping the results of science. Among other valuable functions, statistics serve to summarize the results of applying your measurement scales. The next chapter describes some of the vital descriptive functions that statistics perform in the service of science.

REVIEW QUIZ

True or False?

1. Measurement can be defined as tying numbers to objects and events according to certain rules.

2. The four main types of scales encountered in social science are (1) nominal, (2) ordinal, (3) interval, (4) multiple.

3. The nominal rule requires the application of different, agreed-on labels (e.g., names, numbers, and symbols) to different objects or events.

4. All scientists accept that the nominal rule is the most primitive form of measurement.

5. The determination and application of a psychiatric diagnosis to a patient is a good example of the use of the nominal rule.

6. The scale that tells us about "more than" or "less than" relationships is known as a nominal scale where numbers have a reserved place in the number series and we can tell where in a series a given object or event occurs.

7. To develop an ordinal scale, you must first satisfy the assumptions of the nominal rule.

8. The alphabet fulfills the rules underlying nominal and ordinal scales.

9. If we want to know the distances separating the best jumps of three pole vaulters (i.e., how much objects or events differ), we can handle this problem with an interval scale.

10. A ratio scale allows us to say how many times bigger or smaller one object or quantity is than another.

11. To say that Harry is twice as old as Mary we must assume there is such a thing as zero age. This reflects a rule of the interval scale.

12. If an arbitrary zero is used in constructing a scale then it is not legitimate to use any statistical procedure that involves multiplying or dividing the scores.

13. Absolute-zero scales are those based on samples and biased groups of items of one kind or another, whereas arbitrary-zero scales cover whole topics and total populations.

14. A typical test of a grade 9 student's knowledge of French nouns is illustrative of an arbitrary-zero scale.

15. The cruder the measuring scale used to detect shifts in the dependent variable, the stronger must be the effects of the independent variable.

16. A pilot study is a complex elaboration of the control-group method.

❧ 11 ❧
Statistical Foundations I: Packaging Information

─────────── **Chapter Goal** ───────────

*To introduce you to descriptive statistics,
which help you describe a particular set of
observations in an economical way—e.g., the
average length of intercourse for
chimpanzees is 7 seconds.*

INTRODUCTION

One death is a tragedy; one million deaths are a statistic.

This chilling statement illustrates that statistics not only condense information but in so doing also deprive us of some meaning. You are already familiar with the use of statistics to package or summarize information. The "average" American earns \$868.54 per week, comes from a family of 2.3 members, has completed 12.3 years of education, and before dying at the age of 73.6 has consumed 5387.5 hamburgers and 618.4 Alka-Seltzers.

Statistics help you simplify piles of data in two ways. In this chapter we discuss *descriptive statistics*, which help you describe a particular set of observations in an economical way of reducing a set of observations into one or two numbers. In the next chapter we focus on *inferential statistics*, which help you make educated predictions on the basis of small samples of observations.

Like any summary, descriptive statistics tell you something about everyone in general and nothing about anyone in particular. Nevertheless, such numerical summaries simplify communication when large quantities of information must be transferred. For example, listen in on the following dialogue between two professors:

Professor Blender: You have a large introductory psychology class this year—over 400 students, I believe.

Professor Makan: It's a pain teaching such a mob. What can they learn?

Blender:	How did they do on their exam?
Makan:	Sit down and I'll tell you. Aaron got 97.1, Abbott got 73.5, Agnew got 34.2, . . .
Blender:	I don't want to know what each individual student got. Don't you know the class average?
Makan:	Of course; it was 78. But what does that tell you?
Blender:	It tells me that your class average is higher than anyone else's. You must have smart students.
Makan:	From the average you can tell that? How do you know I'm not just an easy marker? One student got 97, but I've got some real dummies, too. Another student only got 18.

From this brief dialogue you appreciate that an average doesn't really tell you a lot by itself. Even when you also know that the scores ranged from 18 to 97, you still don't know whether most students scored below the class average of 78, with a few very smart ones scoring high enough to pull the average up, or whether approximately half scored above and half scored below. It is the purpose of descriptive statistics not only to summarize data but to do so with a minimum loss of important information.

There are two major types of descriptive statistics. One deals with descriptions of central values like *averages*, and the second deals with descriptions of variability like *ranges*.

Central Values

There are three main ways of describing the center of gravity of a data pile or distribution:

The mean This is the average score obtained by adding all the scores and dividing by the number of scores. For the scores in Column A of Table 11–1,

$$\bar{X} = \text{Mean} = \frac{\Sigma X}{N} = \frac{300}{15} = 20$$

This mean represents the arithmetic center of gravity in interval and ratio-scale distributions.

The median This is the middle score, on either side of which lie the low half of the scores and the high half of the scores. For the scores in Column A of Table 11–1,

Median = 19

There are seven scores higher than 19 and seven scores lower than 19. This is the *middle* score, rather than the average score, and is a particularly useful description of central position when dealing with ordinal scale data.

   The mode   This is the most common or most frequently occurring score or category. For the scores in Column A of Table 11–1,

   Mode = 17

TABLE 11–1   Descriptive Statistics

PATIENT		ANXIETY SCORE X	DEVIATION FROM MEAN $X-X$	SQUARED DEVIATION x^2
Hamish		27	+7	49
Irv		25	+5	25
Vera		25	+5	25
Bob		24	+4	16
Jane		23	+3	9
Norm	Mean $\{$	20	0	0
Joan		20	0	0
Laura	Median	19	−1	1
Dave		18	−2	4
Igor		18	−2	4
Anne		17	−3	9
Lucy	Mode	17	−3	9
Mary		17	−3	9
Charlie		16	−4	16
Neil		14	−6	36
		300	0	212
		Col. A	Col. B	Col. C

Three students obtained the score of 17. The mode doesn't tell you how well they did relative to other students; it merely identifies the score that the largest number of students achieved. The mode is generally useful for describing concentrations of people or events in nominal categories.

   Each of these measures alone tells us something about the center of gravity of a set of scores. The mean describes the arithmetic balance point; the median describes the frequency or middle balance point; and the mode describes the frequency concentration point or heaviest category. Taken individually none of these measures tells us anything about the shape of the distribution of scores, but taken together they give us some hints. For example, we have a balanced or symmetrical distribution if all three of these indices lie on the same score.

   Although knowing all three measures of central tendency for a given distribution tells you more than knowing only one, you still know relatively little about the *differences* between the scores in the set. To describe such score differences—that is, to tell you how spread out the scores are around the mean—three further descriptive statistics are used: the range, the variance, and the standard deviation.

Measures of Variability

The range   This statistic describes the difference between the highest and the lowest scores. In Column A of Table 11–1, the range equals 13. The range tells you what range of possible scores your particular distribution covers. For example, in Professor Makan's psychology quiz we discussed earlier, the mean was 78 and the range was 18 to 97, indicating large differences among individual students. While the range indicates the extremes of the distribution of scores, it is based on only two scores and may therefore give a false impression of variability. For example, the student scoring 18 may have been the only failure in the class, and without him the range may have been 58 to 97. Therefore although the range adds to your information about individual differences in performance, it is not a very representative measure because it is based on only two scores. The next statistic is much more representative because it is based on *every* score.

The variance (σ^2)   This important statistic, applicable to measures on interval and ratio scales, is the average of the squared deviations from the mean. For example, in Column B of Table 11–1, we listed how much each individual score deviates from the mean—a plus sign indicating how much a given score is above the mean and a minus sign how much a given score is below the mean. To get rid of these signs, we squared these deviations (as in Column C) and added them to get a so-called sum of squares.

$$\Sigma x^2 = 212$$

To determine the variance, we divide the sum of squares by N—that is, by the number of scores:

$$\text{Variance} = \sigma^2 = \frac{\Sigma x^2}{N} = \frac{212}{15} = 14.13$$

But squaring the deviation scores to get rid of the signs leaves us with an average of *squared* deviations, which gives a misleadingly large number. We need an average of deviations regardless of signs. The next statistic does just that.

The standard deviation (σ)   This most widely used measure of variability is merely the square root of the variance:

$$\text{Standard Deviation} = \sigma = \sqrt{\frac{\Sigma x^2}{N}} = \sqrt{\frac{212}{15}} = 3.8$$

Now we have a measure of variability that (1) is based on the deviation of *all* scores from the mean; (2) treats negative and positive deviations the same; (3) is expressed in the same units of measurement as those from which it was derived, rather than on their squares.

We claim that measures of variability help describe individual differences in a group. The standard deviation is of particular value in that it provides a standard unit for such comparisons—one that can be used on any interval or ratio scale. Suppose your class takes two tests—one in psychology and one in physics—and that you score 78 in psychology and 68 in physics. In which test did you do better? In psychology? Maybe, but that assumes it is as easy to get one grade point in psychology as it is in physics. Maybe each grade point in psychology is easier to get than a grade point in physics. We can then ask, "How well did you do relative to the rest of your group?" The group's average in physics was 53, and in psychology it was 63. This suggests that it may be easier to get a point in psychology than in physics, even though you are 15 marks above the group average in each. Does *that* mean you did equally well in both? Well, that depends on how much the marks vary around the mean—and that's why we use the standard deviation. We note that the psychology scores are much more variable than are the scores in physics. Notice that, although you are 15 points from the mean in both distributions, you were much closer to the top of the distribution in physics with a score of 68 than in psychology with a score of 78. In fact, when we calculate the standard deviations (σ) for each distribution, we find that you are 2.6 standard deviation units above the mean in physics and only 1.2 standard deviations above the mean in psychology. Thus relative to your classmates, you did better in physics than you did in psychology.

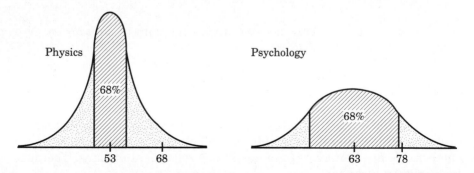

In addition to helping describe and compare individual differences in performance, the standard deviation helps us describe and analyze different data piles or distributions. Although it isn't particularly useful in describing misshapen or skewed distributions like the following skewed curve, the standard deviation is very useful in describing symmetrical distributions called normal or bell curves.

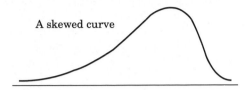

A skewed curve

The Normal Curve

The normal curve has approximately 34 percent of its area lying between the mean and +1 standard deviation, 14 percent of its area between +1 and +2 standard deviations, and 2 percent lying between +2 and +3 standard deviation units. Notice, too, that since the normal curve is symmetrical, the mean, median, and mode all lie at the same point.

A useful statistic is one that summarizes data with a minimum loss of information. The standard deviation in combination with the normal curve is such a statistic. Notice how little information I acquire from merely knowing that your score on a given test is 72. I have no idea whether you did relatively well or very poorly. Notice, however, how much more I learn about your performance if I am informed that in a normal distribution you scored 2 standard deviation units below the mean. Now I know that only 2 percent of the class obtained lower scores than you did. If, in addition, I am told that your actual score is 72 and that the standard deviation is equal to 4, I can estimate the mean to be 80 (your score of 72 plus 2 standard deviations). I can estimate the highest score to be 92 (your score plus 5 standard deviations).

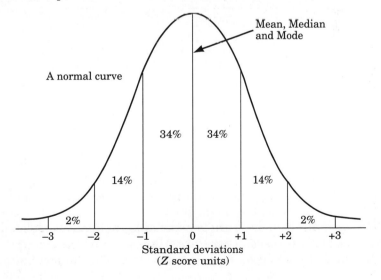

Mean, Median and Mode

A normal curve

34%   34%

14%   14%

2%   2%

−3   −2   −1   0   +1   +2   +3

Standard deviations
(Z score units)

You can see that the standard deviation (or *Z score*, as it is frequently called) combined with the normal curve becomes a powerful descriptive statistic. Knowing where your score lies in Z score units tells where your score lies in relation to all other scores in that distribution. Furthermore, because the Z score describes your relative position in a set of scores, it can be used to *compare* your relative position in two or more score sets. For example, if I say you scored 21 in Anxiety and 104 in ESP, I tell you very little. But if I say your Z score in Anxiety was +2 and your Z score in ESP was zero, you know you scored relatively high in Anxiety and only average (at the mean) in ESP. Furthermore, if I tell you that your Z score for time spent in the pub is +3 and your Z score in math is −3, it reveals that you lead your group in pub time and trail your group in math grades; some people might even wonder if the two Z scores are tied together in some way.

CORRELATION

To say that two variables are *related* indicates they are somehow tied together—like pub time and math grades. For example, two variables may be negatively related; as one score goes up, the other score goes down:

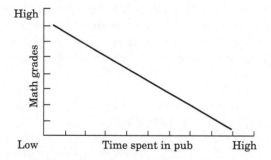

Or the two variables may be positively related; as one score goes up, so too does the other one. If hours of study and math grades were *perfectly* correlated, we would expect that each pair of scores would occupy the same relative position on their respective distributions—that your hours-of-study score and your math score would each lie the same distance, in Z score units, from their respective means. If, for your group, your study-time score was +2 Z scores above the group mean, then we would expect your math grade to also lie +2 Z scores above the group mean in math, as indicated in Figure 11–1. Notice that in the case of a perfect correlation, when you plot score pairs for each individual in the group, the plots lie along a straight line.

However, rarely, if ever, are two variables perfectly correlated, particularly human variables. There are always a few people who study very little and still get good math grades, and other unfortunates who

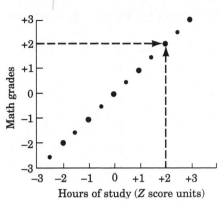

FIGURE 11-1 Perfect Positive Correlation

study a great deal and persist in getting low grades. Thus when we plot score pairs for two human characteristics, we don't expect to see them lie neatly on the straight line of a perfect correlation; rather we expect to see them marching fairly closely around such an imaginary line, as in Figure 11-2, or, in the case of unrelated variables, to be scattered all over the place, as in Figure 11-3.

By an "eyeball" analysis of these figures, you can *see* different degrees of correlation: perfect correlation in Figure 11-1, strong positive correlation in Figure 11-2, and no obvious correlation in Figure 11-3. One way for you to determine degree of correlation is to plot the score pairs—in raw, or in Z score units—and see to what degree the plots cluster around a positive or negative diagonal. This *scattergram* provides an excellent way to get a feel for your data, for its variability, and we strongly recommend you make such plots.

If you require a more precise and shorthand measure of the degree of relationship, you can calculate a *correlation coefficient*. This is noth-

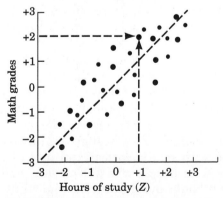

FIGURE 11-2 Strong Positive Correlation

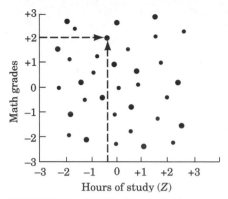

FIGURE 11-3   No Correlation

ing more than a statistical means of describing the differences between pairs of Z scores. In brief, if a pair of scores have similar positions (in Z score units) in their respective distributions, their correlation approaches 1.0, or a perfect positive relationship. However, if any given pair of scores occupy very different or unpredictable relative positions (have very different Z scores), then their correlation approaches zero. Notice that if you calculate a correlation coefficient greater than 1.0 you have made an error—numerically, 1.0 is as high as correlations go. Notice also if you discover a correlation higher than 0.90 when using human variables, check your calculations and increase your sample size—such a correlation is suspiciously high. Using a small sample of the data from Figure 11-2, we show in Table 11-2 how to calculate a Pearson product-moment correlation which is represented by the symbol γ which you can think of as meaning "degree of relationship."

In the case of the relationship between hours of study and math grades just discussed (Figure 11-2), how much confidence do you have in the very high correlation (0.94) that we reported? First notice that we used a very small sample of subjects, or observational checkpoints—only six. There is no magic sample size, but we recommend at least 100 subjects to estimate degree of correlation.

Nevertheless, apart from sample size, on the basis of your own experience how much confidence would you place on such a high correlation? What other variable, or characteristic, probably influences math grades besides hours of study? Mathematical aptitude and background are obvious additional suspects. Therefore you might anticipate a curved relationship between hours of study and math grades—the highest grade coming from people with mathematical aptitude who study a medium amount, low grades from people who don't study, and medium and low grades from people without math aptitude who study a lot, but to little avail. Perhaps the relationship might resemble that mapped in Figure 11-4.

TABLE 11-2　Pearson Correlation Coefficient

| | RAW DATA | | | | | | |
Ss	HOURS OF STUDY X	MATH GRADES Y	DEVIATIONS FROM MEANS x	y	xy	x^2	y^2
A.B.	27	88	11	28	308	121	784
B.J.	23	78	7	18	126	49	324
C.W.	22	69	6	9	54	36	81
D.N.	10	50	-6	-10	60	36	100
E.R.	8	30	-8	-30	240	64	900
F.G.	6	45	-10	-15	150	100	225

Sum: $\Sigma X = 96$　$\Sigma Y = 360$　　　　$\Sigma xy = 938$　$\Sigma x^2 = 406$　$\Sigma y^2 = 2414$

Mean: $\overline{X} = 16$　$\overline{Y} = 60$

Standard Deviations (σ):

$$\sigma x = \frac{\Sigma x^2}{N} = \frac{406}{6} = 8.22$$

$$\sigma y = \frac{\Sigma y^2}{N} = \frac{2414}{6} = 20.06$$

Correlation (γ):

$$r = \frac{\Sigma xy}{N\sigma x \sigma y} = \frac{938}{6(8.23)(20.06)} = \frac{938}{6(165.09)} = \frac{938}{990.54}$$

$r = 0.947$

Note: if you have a large number of subjects, you can calculate correlations using *raw* score data on a small computer or desk calculator—consult the machine handbook for the simple procedure:
i.e.,

$$r = \frac{\Sigma XY - \dfrac{(\Sigma X)(\Sigma Y)}{N}}{\left[\Sigma X^2 - \dfrac{\Sigma x^2}{N}\right]\left[\Sigma Y^2 - \dfrac{\Sigma y^2}{N}\right]}$$

　　The Pearson product-moment correlation is designed to measure straight-line relations (linear), not curvilinear ones, as shown in Figure 11-4. You can do thought experiments by proposing variables, which, on

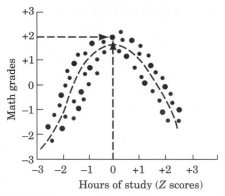

FIGURE 11-4   Curvilinear Correlation

the basis of casual observation, should be highly correlated (for example, having the same subjects repeat an intelligence test one week later) or by proposing other variables that are probably not correlated at all (people's heights and their score in mathematics exams). Great arguments ensue, and some even lead to worthy research speculations.

What Does a Correlation Tell You?

Although it is simple to calculate a correlation coefficient, it is not so simple to decide what to conclude from a high coefficient.

While a high correlation tells you that score pairs occupy similar relative positions on the two distributions, it does not tell you if they are tied together intimately like Siamese twins—when one moves, the other must move—or only related casually like two strangers on a subway—when the subway moves, they both move, but they don't necessarily move together for, unlike Siamese twins, one can move to another car without the other, and furthermore one can leave the train or the "relationship" without the other. It is each one's relation to the subway, a third variable, that is the key relationship, not their relationship to each other.

Don't leap to the conclusion that, because one variable appears to be moving with another, the first one "causes" the other. Many supposed relationships turn out to be pseudorelationships, like the young lady traveling by train from New York to San Francisco who reported to the conductor that a strange man was following her. Indeed he was; his seat was two seats behind hers! But it was the train to which he was related, not the young lady—except in her imagination. There are many instances where two variables appear to be related, but are really only incidentally related to each other through a third variable (the train, in this instance). For example, there is a strong positive correlation between the purchase of bathing suits and the sale of ice cream, but you don't conclude that buying bathing suits makes you eat ice cream; rather you say a third variable, temperature, is the independent variable to which ice cream consumption and bathing suit purchases are related.

Whenever you are tempted to conclude that a variable is dependent upon, or moves with, another, stop and think, "Does it make sense on the basis of logic and experience?" Moreover, always look for a third variable to which the two may be tied—as in the preceding cases of temperature and trains.

Beware of Correlations

You probably wouldn't be surprised to learn of a negative correlation between being a Boy Scout and getting into trouble with the law— that is, relatively few Boy Scouts end up formally charged and convicted of crimes. Also, it would not surprise you to learn about a positive correlation between university education and above-average income.

It is, however, quite possible that both of these relationships "ride" on a third *hidden* variable—namely, socioeconomic status. Notice that most Boy Scouts *happen* to be middle- and upper-class kids, and middle-class kids rarely get booked or convicted, even if they are caught doing something wrong—whether they are Boy Scouts or not. Similarly, if you took a sample of middle- and upper-class people who hadn't graduated from a university, you would probably find their subsequent incomes to be comparable to those of university graduates—the implication being that it is not so much the university education that is related to subsequent income as it is middle- and upper-class contacts and opportunities—the "old boy" network, if you will.

You may disagree with these speculations. Good! Such disagreements stimulate further research. How would you go about testing either of these hypotheses linking criminal conviction negatively and income positively to socioeconomic status of parents?

Correlation, Regression, and Prediction

Before moving to the next chapter, which focuses on prediction, we must point out that some of the statistics discussed in this chapter can also be used for prediction. For example, if you want to guess or predict the IQ of a given individual and you know the average (mean) IQ score of his or her group, you can use the group mean as a rough guess. If you also know the variance of IQs around the mean for that group you gain some notion of how much confidence you can have in making that guess. That is, if the variability around the mean is very large you know your guess could be way off, whereas if the variability is small you have high confidence that your guess will be pretty accurate. Correlation provides a more interesting example.

Suppose you have collected data on study time and math grades from 50 students and plotted the results, as in Figure 11–2. You can use this plot to predict the math scores of additional students just on the basis of their study score alone. If, for example, you know George's study score is +1 Z score units, you can follow the line up from +1 on the Hours of Study scale to the diagonal line representing the correlation: you can then use that as your best-bet prediction of his math grade (e.g., a Z score of approximately +1.3) by drawing a horizontal line from the intercept over to the Math Grade scale. However, you will not be surprised if you find that his actual math grade is a bit higher or lower than the one you predicted because you already know from the scatter-gram you plotted that people with the same Hours of Study Z score can get math scores a bit above and below the predicted point on the correlation or linear regression line. This straight line is calculated to best represent or "best fit" all the points on your plot, so it is a kind of average of the points scattered on either side of it. Standard statistics texts include detailed discussions and formulae covering regression and errors of estimate in making predictions. Here, we merely want to relate predictions to correlations.

How far above and below the correlation line the scores scatter can be seen by visual inspection, and depends on the degree of relationship between the two variables. A more precise method of estimating the kind of error of prediction you might make is called the *standard error of estimate*. How might that be determined? As you can guess, it is based on the differences between, in our example, the math scores you predict on the basis of hours of study, and the actual math scores obtained. Such an estimate will be expressed as an "average" of those differences. For strong correlations (low scatter around the line), the error of estimate will be small, whereas for low or weak correlations (large scatter around the line), the error of estimate will, of course, be large.

Correlations and Factor Analysis

In examining college grades for a variety of students, you notice that some students seem to do well in almost all their subjects, ranging from psychology to computer science (their Z scores, regardless of course of study, are high), whereas another group of students seems to get average grades in most of their courses (their Z scores, regardless of course of study, are in the middle), whereas yet another group gets low grades in almost all of their courses. In addition, there are, of course, a fair number of students whose grades range from high to low (their Z scores are all over the board).

Given this large data base—comprising perhaps several hundred students and 20 grades for each—how do you make sense of it; how do you reduce it to mind size? One way is to reduce the search space by focusing on those students who are more or less consistent in their performance: the highs, the average, and the lows. Can you reduce all that data to a simpler form, to one or two antecedents? With a little thought you conclude that you can explain the data on the bases of two variables: intelligence and work habits. You're not sure how they combine, or which is most important in given subjects or individuals. Nevertheless, you have radically reduced the data base to your own satisfaction, even though you have no measure of intelligence or work habits to use as an observational checkpoint. For example, do your students with consistently high grades score high on both intelligence and work habits, and your students with consistently low grades score lower on intelligence and work habits? If you wanted to address the same question and be more precise in your conclusions and more objective in your analysis, you might use one or another form of factor analysis.

Factor analysis is a formal way of reducing a large set of variables or measures to a much smaller number called a factor. More importantly, it describes how those small numbers (factors) are related to each other and to the original set of measures. So, what we did intuitively in reducing a large set of measures to a small one, factor analysis can help you do formally, and in a way that is more replicable and less subjective. More importantly, it specifies which of the reduced number of variables (factors) are most important in explaining and predicting certain relationships in the original data set. If we apply factor analysis to the data we used in our preceding example, it is hoped we will address our theoretical bias or hunch by including measures of intelligence and work habits in the data base.

Of course, the quality of the factors you extract, and the explanatory and predictive power of their structure, depends on the quality of the data you input—garbage in, garbage out, no matter how powerful the computer or sophisticated the software. Cross-validation (replication) of factor analytic studies has not been common because of the time and effort it takes to accumulate the new data base. Therefore, the external validity of the factors and their structure, extracted in a given study, is often unknown. Standard statistical texts explain and provide examples of various forms of factor analysis, and with the advent of the computer and selected software, factor analysis becomes much more feasible than it once was.

SUMMARY

Descriptive statistics help package information in mind-sized bits in which one number is used to describe a set of observations. Some of these statistics describe the centers of gravity of a distribution (mean, median, and mode), whereas others describe the variability or dispersion of scores (range, variance, and standard deviation). The normal curve is a mathematical invention that helps summarize a great deal of information about bell-shaped distributions. (This invention can even help determine the score you receive on an exam. How so?)

High correlations tell you that score pairs (e.g., IQ and math grades) occupy similar relative positions on the two distributions of scores—people who scored high on one tended to score high on the other, and people who scored low on one tended to score low on the other. But, beware of correlations; the relationships they describe could result from a variety of reasons, from a hidden third influence that you overlook.

REVIEW QUIZ

True or False?

1. Inferential statistics help researchers to make educated predictions on the basis of a small sample of observations.
2. The average score of any distribution of scores is calculated such that half of the scores are below it and half of the scores are higher.
3. A particularly useful description of central position when dealing with ordinal scale data is the mode.
4. If the mean, median, and mode of a set of scores are all the same, then the shape of the distribution of scores is symmetrical.
5. Measures of central tendency describe the spread of a set of scores in a distribution (i.e., the differences between the scores in the set).
6. The standard deviation, the most widely used measure of the variability in a distribution of scores, is merely the square root of the variance.
7. The standard deviation is particularly useful in describing misshapen or skewed distributions, and less useful in describing normal or bell curves.
8. The normal curve has approximately 34 percent of its area lying between the mean and +1 standard deviation.
9. If you scored 2 standard deviation units above the mean in a normal distribution, then 2 percent of the class got a higher score than you did.
10. A Z score describes someone's relative position in a set of scores.
11. If A and B are perfectly correlated, then your A and B scores would each lie the same distance in Z-score units from their respective means.
12. A correlation coefficient is a statistic that has a range from +3 to −3.
13. To provide a reasonably solid estimate of the degree of correlation between two variables, at least 100 paired scores (from 100 research participants) is recommended.
14. The Pearson product-moment correlation is designed to measure curvilinear rather than straight-line (linear) relations.
15. If A and B are highly correlated, then A causes B.
16. Factor analysis provides a statistical means of reducing a large set of variables or measures to a much smaller number by identifying which among the large set of variables is related or correlated.

❧ 12 ❧

Statistical Foundations II: Prediction

─────── **Chapter Goal** ───────

*To help you understand how researchers
make educated predictions on the basis of a
small sample of observations. You do it
intuitively every day, often effectively even if
you don't consciously know the statistical
rules that may guide you.*

INTRODUCTION

*He tossed 10 heads in a row! Then get a new coin or a new tosser.
Half the patients got better. Is that good?*

Just as the hand of lady luck helps determine whether the coin comes
up heads or tails, so too she helps determine whether your depressed
patient "comes up" improved or not improved. In the case of the coin we
have a 50–50 rule that helps us decide what to expect from chance, or
random, influences alone over a long series of tosses. If the results deviate "too far" from the rule (50 percent heads and 50 percent tails) then
we conclude that nonrandom influences are operating on the coin.

In the case of human behavior, various statistical rules help us
decide whether our results are due merely to good luck, or to good treatment—to nonrandom influences in the treatment. For example, our
control group on the "sugar pill" provide a way of estimating the effects
of random or rogue influences on our depressed patients. The control
group provides an estimate of how many patients we can expect to
"come up" improved without treatment—say, 75 percent improve just
from the effects of random in-the-gap and time-tied suspects. Therefore,
if our treatment is to look good it has to significantly beat the 75–25 rule
we derived from our control group. Notice, if we ran several control
groups we would get somewhat different rules (e.g., 78–22, 72–28, 74–26,
etc.) so remember that the rule provided by any one control group is only
an estimate of the influence of chance factors. Statistical tests help us

decide by how much our treatment must beat the particular control group generated rule before we decide the results are worth taking seriously.

What if after our "magic pill" treatment we find 78 percent improved and 22 percent unimproved? Or 80–20? How much must our treatment results surpass the control-group results before we decide that, in addition to lady luck and the rogues, our treatment is having a systematic effect? Statistical tests help us make those decisions in a disciplined, standardized, way. But always remember, the best means of determining whether your positive results were due to lady luck, on the one hand, or your treatment, on the other, is to repeat the study.

INFERENTIAL STATISTICS

Most social science experiments compare differences among two or more means or averages. For example, suppose we study the effects of two methods of teaching mathematics—one employing a text using programmed instruction à la B. F. Skinner and another based on the same material but written in a traditional manner. We divide our class at random into two groups:

Group 1 X_1 O_1
Group 2 X_2 O_2

One group studies from the programmed text (X_1), and the other studies from the traditional text (X_2). Then both groups write the same exam, and we calculate the means:

$$O_1 = 80$$
$$O_2 = 75$$

We obtained a difference. So what? Even if we had used the same text with both groups, we probably would have obtained "a difference." Groups rarely yield precisely the same means even when treated identically, because we never control the operation of all chance factors. The question is not, "Did we get a difference?" but rather, "Did we get a difference worth talking about?" In statistical language we want to know whether we got a *significant difference*.

At least four common factors produce a significant difference:

1. The operation of chance. By luck we ended up with more bright students in Group 1 than in Group 2, even though we drew the names out of a hat.

2. The operation of the chosen independent variable. The programmed text was a more effective teaching aid, and so Group 1 students did better on the exam.

3. The operation of error. A mistake was made in scoring the tests or in adding the scores that favored Group 1.

4. The operation of fraud. The researcher fraudulently manipulated the data in favor of Group 1 to accommodate the professor's bias.

Therefore while statistical tests help you decide whether you obtained a reliable or significant difference between your two group means, such tests do not tell you whether such differences arise from the operation of your independent variable, from errors in calculation, or from fraud. Such tests don't even completely rule out the possibility of chance, but such tests do *help you identify inferences that do not occur frequently by chance alone.*

So when you conduct a statistical test on your data and obtain a significant result, you have some confidence that such a large difference is not likely due to chance—although such large differences may occur five times in a hundred due to chance alone. However, you choose to decide that, rather than an unusual chance event, the difference was "caused" by something else. Having done your statistical test to control for the operation of obvious chance factors and having found a significant difference, you then puzzle over the alternatives of whether the significant difference results from the impact of your independent variable, or error, or even fraud.

Parenthetically, notice that while fraud appears as a viable alternative in fringe research areas like ESP, it is rarely so listed in traditional research areas or in research design courses—perhaps because researchers are less fraudulently inclined than are other segments of the population, or perhaps because fraud represents an alternative too threatening to the research enterprise to be contemplated openly. (A discussion of instances of possible fraud perpetrated by a famous psychologist appears at the end of Chapter 13.)

Maps of Chance

To determine whether our differences arise from chance factors, we compare our results with what we would expect by chance; we compare our results with maps or models of chance. You already know about such maps. If I flip a coin producing 10 heads in a row, you say, "Hey, wait a minute." Why? Because my results deviate significantly from your map of chance—my results were surprising. Your map of chance for tossing coins is 50-50. The further my results deviate from a 50–50 distribution of heads and tails, the more willingly you entertain the possibility of the operation of "something" in addition to chance. Like what? Like an independent variable: like a biased coin or a biased tosser— *something* more than chance.

If you keep this example in mind, you need have no fear of inferential statistics, for such statistics are merely maps of chance against which you can compare your findings and decide whether your results (your experimental tosses) have gone beyond the limits of what you willingly accept as mere chance happenings. Inferential statistics provide a model against which to compare your results. If nothing else but chance is influencing our results, inferential statistics provide you with the distribution of differences you should expect. When you get a difference that occurs rarely by chance, you have two choices open: you can either decide you obtained one of those rare, large, but unreliable differences delivered by chance, or you can decide to credit the difference, not to capricious chance, but to the operation of your independent or treatment variable.

By using inferential statistics you never rule out the operation of chance, but you do make it a less likely explanation. Ten heads in a row *could* happen by chance, but not ruddy likely!

Sampling Theory

Inferential statistics rest on sampling theory, and you already have a solid background in this theory, even though you may not know it. Sampling theory deals with the relationship between "samples" of experience and "total" experience.

For example, that sample of 10 heads in a row went against your total experience of coin tossing; that sample didn't belong to your population of coin-tossing experience. It was a sample that seemed to belong to another population of experience—to experiences characteristic of fraud and trickery.

Similarly, a host of samples make up your total experience (population of experience) concerning friendship. When a friend acts unfriendly once or twice, you take it in your stride as part of the chance ups and downs of friendship. But if the unfriendliness continues, the time arrives when you say, "No, this is too far out from friendship." These samples of behavior come from another population of experiences—an unfriendly population. That person is no longer classed as "cranky friend" but is now classed as "new enemy."

Sampling theory is a statistical means of deciding to which population a given sample belongs when such a sample may be found in both populations; unfriendly samples or bits of behavior emerge from cranky friends as well as from enemies. Similarly, friendly samples of behavior emerge from friends and also from con artists. To which population does the person producing this particular sample belong? Five heads in a row can result from tossing a legal coin and also from tossing a biased coin; from which population does this particular coin come? Ordinarily you decide such questions by getting more samples—by continuing to toss the coin or by continuing to closely observe your "friend." If in the *long run* heads or unfriendliness continue, you conclude these are not normal chance variations but rather reflect a coin that is biased toward heads and a person who is biased toward unfriendliness.

But often we must make such judgments without the benefit of long-run experience. We must make judgments on the basis of short-run experience, on the basis of *samples*. Inferential statistics and sampling theory provide help in comparing short-term sample results with the results to be expected by chance in the long run.

Sampling Error Theory

We have just indicated how the information contained in short-run samples of experience can differ from the information contained in long-run populations of experience. Research in the social sciences involves sampling; it involves conducting observations on a few individuals—on a sample—to provide estimates about the total group or population that sample represents. When we observe the impact of a new drug on a sample of depressed patients or the impact of a new teaching technique on a sample of students, we don't merely want to know how it affected that small sample of people (descriptive statistics); we want to estimate, from the sample results, what the impact of our independent variable will be on depressed patients in general or on students in general.

But because the members of a population differ from one another— some very depressed, some less depressed—and because chance factors invariably play a part in determining which individuals end up in a given sample—the patients in our treatment group may be less depressed than most—the mean or standard deviation obtained from a sample is sure to differ from the mean or standard deviation obtained from observing *all* members of the population—all depressed patients. *Therefore sample "facts" remain crude estimates of population "facts."*

How reliable are such estimates? This is the question sampling theory addresses. To appreciate the simple logic involved, consider the following example. Suppose you wish to know the mean height of American females. Measuring the height of millions of females is prohibitive, so you take a sample. Your sample consists of the first 10 females who enter the lobby of a large hotel. You determine their average height to be 5 feet 2 inches. How good an estimate is this of the average height of all American females? You decide two estimates are better than one. Just as you are about to take a second sample, much to your surprise you see some Japanese women entering the hotel. What luck! Now you can compare the height of American women and Japanese women. You measure and average the heights of the cooperative Oriental ladies and find it to be 5 feet 8 inches. What's going on? Japanese are supposed to be shorter than Americans, not taller.

After a little inquiry you discover that the hotel is housing athletes attending an international athletic event. *By chance* you measured 10 members of the American women's gymnastic team and 10 members of the Japanese women's basketball team—hardly typical or representative samples of their respective populations in either case.

From this example we learn three points about the reliability of estimates of population values based on sample values. These three points can be framed into questions you should ask about any sample:

1.　How representative is the sample of the population I want to talk about? Was it a *random* sample—that is, did every member of the population have an equal chance of getting into the sample? To the extent that this is so, you have increased the likelihood that your sample fact will provide a reliable estimate of your population fact.

2.　Does this sample "feel" representative? Before you get too far into your study, try to decide on the basis of your previous experience whether you have drawn a typical sample. For example, in your sample of American females, you may have noticed that they all smoke, or that most of them are young, or that they all carry basketballs. Your past experience can frequently guide you in assessing the representativeness, and so the reliability, of your sample data.

3.　Have you a large enough sample to obtain a reliable estimate? Intuitively you are familiar with this question. Intuitively you know that large samples of experience give more reliable estimates than small samples, whether we are estimating friendship or height. In estimating the height of American women, the means of several small samples will vary more (will prove less reliable) than the means of several large samples. The *sampling error*, or variability, of the means of small samples is larger than the sampling error of the means of large samples. As a brilliant friend observed: "The *n* justifies the means."

It is this third point in particular that inferential statistics address—the issue of how much confidence we can afford to have in comparing the mean of the experimental group with that of the control group when we know that small sample means are unreliable. The haunting question remains: "Is the difference we find between the two means due to our treatment or merely due to the fact that small sample means bounce around even without treatment?" We remain caught on the horns of a dilemma: on the one hand we can't afford to measure very large numbers of subjects in order to determine the *population* mean accurately; yet on the other hand we know the means of small samples provide unreliable estimates of the populations they are supposed to represent.

We need some rational way of helping us decide when sample means are reasonably accurate estimates of their respective population means—methods of deciding when sample "facts" are reliable estimates of population "facts." The rational solution we rely upon is called *sampling theory*. A detailed examination of this topic lies beyond the scope of our discussion; nevertheless if you keep the following principles in mind, you are less likely to be hoodwinked by chance playing tricks with sample means:

1. Sample means become an increasingly accurate estimate of their population means as you increase the size of your samples. We recommend that you use sample sizes of 30 or more per group when you want to compare an experimental sample with a control sample.

2. When deciding whether you have obtained a significant difference between your experimental and control groups, you must take into account:

    a. The size of the difference between their means, *and*
    b. The variability (i.e., standard deviation) of the two samples—the size of the variability in each sample and the similarity of the variability in each sample, *and*
    c. How much the two samples overlap each other.

Particularly when you're getting started on social science research, it is wise to obtain this information by plotting your results. Notice in the following three figures how the two means remain the same, but the variability and the degree of overlap differ; particularly notice how such differences suggest very different conclusions.

The three figures present three different versions of an experiment to test whether students using a program instruction text (Group 1) perform better on a math exam than students using a standard instruction manual (Group 2). As noted in all three examples, the experimental group scores five points higher than does the control group on the math exam. But notice in Figure 12–1 how the samples show wide variability

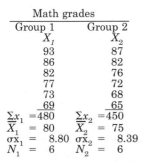

Math grades	
Group 1	Group 2
X_1	X_2
93	87
86	82
82	76
77	72
73	68
69	65

$\Sigma x_1 = 480$ $\Sigma x_2 = 450$
$\overline{X}_1 = 80$ $\overline{X}_2 = 75$
$\sigma x_1 = 8.80$ $\sigma x_2 = 8.39$
$N_1 = 6$ $N_2 = 6$

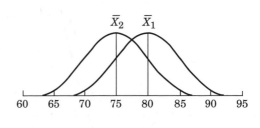

FIGURE 12–1   Large Overlap in Group 1 and Group 2 Scores

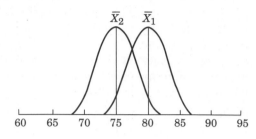

Math grades		
Group 1	Group 2	
X_1	X_2	
86	81	
82	78	
81	76	
80	73	
77	72	
74	70	
$\Sigma x_1 = 480$	$\Sigma x_2 = 450$	
$\overline{X}_1 = 80$	$\overline{X}_2 = 75$	
$\sigma x_1 = 4.14$	$\sigma x_2 = 4.09$	
$N_1 = 6$	$N_2 = 6$	

FIGURE 12–2   Some Overlap in Scores

and large overlap—such differences as this between samples occur frequently by chance. Therefore we conclude since such differences occur relatively frequently in random sampling we can have little or no confidence that the program text is responsible—that is, we can frequently expect such differences even in two samples receiving identical treatments—e.g., both groups using the same text.

In Figure 12–2 the difference between the means remains the same (5), but the sample variability is less and so is the degree of overlap. Although such differences between samples occur by chance more frequently than 5 times in 100 sample pairs, the result is promising and warrants increasing the sample sizes to see if the differences hold.

In the third case we can be relatively certain we have a difference "worth talking about"—the sample variance and overlap is relatively small, while the difference between the means remains at 5.

While eyeball examination increases our confidence in the results presented in Figure 12–3 over those in Figures 12–1 and 12–2, we can gain additional confidence by performing a statistical test (a t test). This test is designed to measure the "significance" of a difference between independent samples by comparing the difference you obtained with the difference chance alone can deal an experimenter. The procedure out-

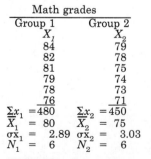
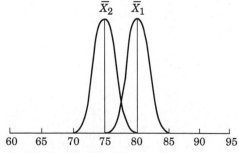

Math grades		
Group 1	Group 2	
X_1	X_2	
84	79	
82	78	
81	75	
79	74	
78	73	
76	71	
$\Sigma x_1 = 480$	$\Sigma x_2 = 450$	
$\overline{X}_1 = 80$	$\overline{X}_2 = 75$	
$\sigma x_1 = 2.89$	$\sigma x_2 = 3.03$	
$N_1 = 6$	$N_2 = 6$	

FIGURE 12–3   Almost No Overlap in Scores

TABLE 12–1   Test for Small Independent Samples

MATH GRADES

| GROUP 1[a] | GROUP 2[b] | DEVIATIONS | | | |
X_1	X_2	x_1	x_2	$x_1{}^2$	$x_2{}^2$
84	79	4	4	16	16
82	78	2	3	4	9
81	75	1	0	1	0
79	74	−1	−1	1	1
78	73	−2	−2	4	4
76	71	−4	−4	16	16

$$\Sigma X_1 = 480 \quad \Sigma X_2 = 450 \qquad\qquad \Sigma x_1{}^2 = 42 \quad \Sigma x_2{}^2 = 46$$
$$\overline{X}_1 = 80 \quad \overline{X}_2 = 75$$
$$N_1 = 6 \quad N_2 = 6$$

$$t = \frac{\overline{X}_1 - \overline{X}_2}{\sqrt{\dfrac{\Sigma x_1^2 + \Sigma x_2^2}{N_1 + N_2 - 2}\left(\dfrac{N_1 + N_2}{N_1 \cdot N_2}\right)}}$$

$$t = \frac{80 - 75}{\sqrt{\dfrac{42 + 46}{6 + 6 - 2}\left(\dfrac{6 + 6}{6 \cdot 6}\right)}} = \frac{5}{\sqrt{\dfrac{88}{10}\left(\dfrac{12}{36}\right)}}$$

$$t = \frac{5}{\sqrt{2.93}} = 2.92$$

For $df = 10$, $p < 0.05$[c]

---

[a]Group 1 studied from programmed text (Experimental).

[b]Group 2 studied from standard text (Control).

[c]For degrees of freedom = 10 ($N_1 + N_2 - 2$) probability (p) of obtaining $t = 2.92$ by chance is less than 5 in 100.

lined on page 251 in Table 12–1 uses data reflecting the differences we observed in Figure 12–3.

If we go to an appropriate map of chance (t table), we discover that for samples of this size, this particular t value would occur rarely by chance alone—that is, if 100 such comparisons were made between *control* groups of this size, we would expect such a large t value to occur less than 5 times in 100 trials. So we can decide either that we have stumbled on one of these rare tricks of chance, or that it was not the work of chance but the influence of our treatment (the programmed text) that "pushed" the samples apart.

Samples of raw data for the other two cases are listed in the figures, so for those who wish to examine the likelihood of obtaining these sample differences by chance alone, one can compare the resulting t values with those provided in the t tables of any standard statistical text (for degrees of freedom = 10, or $N^1 + N^2 - 2$).

ANALYSIS OF VARIANCE (ANOVA)

Just as a t test can help you decide whether your experimental and control groups differ by more than the hand of chance usually arranges, an F test, ANOVA, helps you decide whether your experimental group and several comparison groups are separated by differences greater than you would expect by chance alone.

One-Way Analysis of Variance (One Independent Variable)

For example, you may be studying the effects of alcohol (independent variable) on coordination (dependent variable) using a control group, group 1 (12 ounces of Coke); and three experimental groups: group 2 (12 ounces of Coke plus 1 ounce of alcohol); group 3 (12 ounces of Coke plus 2 ounces of alcohol); group 4 (12 ounces of Coke plus 3 ounces of alcohol). You speculate that as alcohol consumption increases, so too will errors in coordination, but when you plot your results (Figure 12–4), it doesn't look that way—group 3 has the lowest, not the second highest, error rate, as was predicted.

The question is whether these are more than chance differences. An analysis of variance (F test) helps you decide whether two or more of these groups differ by more than chance expectancy. An F test is based on the differences between the means, in relation to the variability and the size of the groups. A significant F test, in this alcohol experiment, tells us that two or more of the groups differ by more than expected by the usual tricks of chance.

Having obtained a significant F we can now use eyeball analysis and t tests to decide which particular pairs of groups differ. We find that group 4 differs significantly from all of the groups; that groups 1 and 2 did not differ, nor did groups 1 and 3, but that groups 2 and 3 did. On the basis of *this* study and this sample we conclude that 3 ounces of

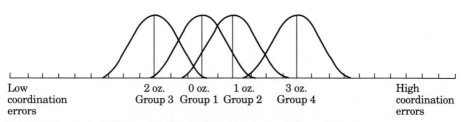

Low   2 oz.   0 oz.   1 oz.   3 oz.   High
coordination   Group 3 Group 1 Group 2 Group 4   coordination
errors   errors

FIGURE 12–4   Effect of Alcohol on Errors of Coordination

alcohol disrupts coordination, and tentatively decide that 2 ounces *may* facilitate coordination.

You are probably wondering why bother doing an analysis of variance at all since you end up doing *t* tests anyway. There are two reasons. First, if you fail to get a significant *F* test, this tells you the differences you observe are likely due to chance, and so you stop the analysis right there, saving yourself the bother of doing a series of *t* tests (six in our example). Second, when comparing several groups, an initial *F* test provides more protection against flukes of chance than you get by starting with a series of *t* tests.

But ANOVA has another great advantage: it enables researchers to measure the combined effects of two or more treatment variables; it enables us to measure what are called *interaction* effects.

Two-Way Analysis of Variance (Two Independent Variables)

In the foregoing example we studied the effect on coordination of *one* treatment variable (alcohol—a one-way analysis of variance). But suppose we wanted to add another treatment variable, such as drinking history. We now have two independent or treatment variables. This involves a *two-way* analysis of variance, the columns representing the one treatment variable (four levels of alcohol) and the rows representing the other treatment variable (two levels of drinking history).

Alcohol

	0 OZ.	1 OZ.	2 OZ.	3 OZ.
Novice drinkers	Group 1	Group 2	Group 3	Group 4
Practiced drinkers	Group 5	Group 6	Group 7	Group 8

The *F* tests in 2-by-4 analysis of variance can measure quantitatively what we observe in Figure 12–5 on the following page.

From these observed results (Figure 12–5) we can't say that more alcohol leads to significantly more errors in coordination—you *can't* make any across-the-board generalization about the effects of alcohol in this study. In addition, you can't, for example, say that being a novice drinker leads to significantly fewer errors—you *can't* make any across-the-board generalizations about drinking history. However, you *can* say "It all depends"; it depends on special combinations of amounts of alcohol *and* of drinking history—that's an interaction effect.

We usually hope for straightforward simple effects like those in Figure 12–5a. In this tidy speculation, errors of coordination increase with amount of alcohol consumed. They increase for both novice and for practiced drinkers, but more so for novice drinkers. Now these are results that make sense, results that are simple enough to remember.

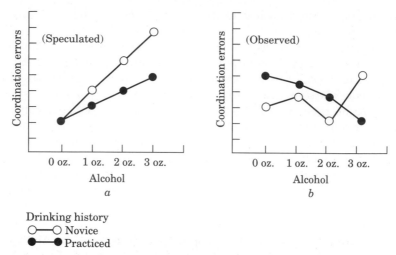

FIGURE 12–5   Effects of Alcohol and Drinking History on Errors of Coordination

Instead of such simple results, however, we frequently obtain results like those plotted in Figure 12–5b; we obtain effects where factors combine in "funny" ways (novice drinkers show fewest errors on 2 ounces of alcohol and the greatest number of errors on 3 ounces of alcohol, while practiced drinkers show fewest number of errors at 3 ounces of alcohol). Analyses of variance enable researchers to measure the statistical significance of complex effects of various treatment combinations using two-way, three-way, or four-way ANOVA designs.

When examining social science research, look for interaction effects, and expect some treatments and some people to combine in surprising ways. Look for interaction effects in the graphs, in the statistical analyses, and in the discussion. How does alcohol affect coordination? It all depends on amount of alcohol, *and* on drinking history, *and* on ?

Summarizing, we now have the scattergram to help us decide *visually* how closely two measures (taken on the same individuals) are related, and the correlation coefficient to help us decide *quantitatively* the degree of relationship. We can also map sample distributions to help us decide *visually* how two or more samples compare in terms of their means, variability, and overlap, and we have the *t* test to help us decide *quantitatively* the statistical significance of the differences between two groups, and analysis of variance to help us decide quantitatively the statistical significance of the difference between more than two groups.

META-ANALYSIS

The first, or at least an early, phase of any project involves an assessment of the current empiricism or knowledge about the particular topic of interest. Typically students, researchers, and theorists will review the scientific literature applying an after-the-fact method by going back in time and selecting from the hundreds, perhaps thousands of relevant studies, a few that pique their interest, and are easy to access from the close-at-hand journals and texts, and have been identified as classic, highly trusted studies of the topic, rightly or wrongly. Suppose you are required to do a review of the research on psychotherapeutic outcome: Does psychotherapy really help people? After reading your selective (nonrandom) sample of studies you write up your review, indicating which studies reported positive results and which reported negative results, along with your conclusions. Since this is an after-the-fact study, your conclusions will reflect your "theory frame" applied to the articles in your limited "time frame" sample of studies. So we would predict that if you believe in the efficacy of psychotherapy, you will conclude that it works if applied properly. If you don't believe in psychotherapy, if it doesn't "fit into your theory frame," you'll probably conclude it doesn't work. Even in those few studies where it seemed to work, you can conclude that there were certain weaknesses in the research methods (e.g., the four rogues were not controlled, therapist bias entered into the evaluation of the results, the investigator didn't use double-blind procedures, etc.).

A critical literature review of this traditional type has been referred to as the narrative approach (Matlin, 1992) and forms the introductory chapter of most graduate student theses. Maccoby and Jacklin (1974), whose review of gender differences is described in Chapter 14, employed a "box score" approach tabulating the number of statistically significant gender differences on a host of independent variables such as mathematical ability and aggressiveness. Their data base was a pool of 1600 studies. From their review we know how many of those investigating male and female differences in mathematical ability, for example, revealed statistically significant findings and how many showed no sex differences. Although this information is of great interest, it would be even more useful to know which of these statistically significant differences are of conceptual or practical significance. In other words are they statistical differences that made a social difference?

What alternative methods are available for obtaining more systematic and "objective" evaluations of a large body of literature? Enter meta-analysis.

Meta-analysis provides a quantitative method for drawing conclusions about the overall results of different studies that use a variety of dependent variables, but all of which presumably study the same type of independent variable (e.g., psychotherapy). In fact, Smith and Glass (1977) did such a study of nearly 400 control-group studies of psychotherapy. Even though Smith and Glass would have to rely on their theory frame, as well as a time frame, to determine which studies were selected and which excluded, nevertheless 400 studies is a much larger and more representative "sample" than the typical review article covers.[1]

Although there are a number of ways to compare studies, these authors, for each study, subtracted the mean of the control-group outcome from that of the treatment group and divided the difference by the standard deviation of the control group. In effect, they were transforming the differences into Z scores which, as you will recall from earlier discussions in this chapter, allow you to make comparisons of relative position on different measures (e.g., psychology and physics grades). In any case, Smith and Glass concluded that, in terms of relative position, the average treated patient was superior to 75 percent of the control-group patients. Although, like any method, this is not a foolproof procedure, and although researchers with a different theory frame will find much to criticize, meta-analysis techniques provide a more powerful and more objective method of drawing conclusions, or testing speculations, than do traditional after-the-fact methods.

More recent examples of meta-analysis involve the use of the d statistic. A d value provides an index of the overall size of the effect of the treatment variable on the dependent variable of interest. This approach has the advantage over other literature review strategies because it allows for an interpretation of the practical significance of a statistical difference. To illustrate, anything less than a d value of .20 is not worth getting excited about, that is, the variable in question (e.g., a new drug) has only a minimal impact on the dependent variable (e.g., depression). A moderate difference, worthy of a raised eyebrow or two, would be represented by d values of .50, and a d greater than .80 is the theorist's or researcher's dream—an effect worth shouting about.

CHI SQUARE

Another popular and useful statistical tool—the chi square test—helps us decide whether the distribution, particularly of nominal scale data, deviates significantly from chance. For example, one student proposed the provocative hypothesis that women are both more softhearted and soft-headed than are men. He also speculated that, since Republicans are more hardheaded and practical than are Democrats, women would tend to support the Democratic party.

To test his hypothesis he drew two samples at random of 60 women and 60 men from a large introductory psychology class. He then had each individual indicate his or her political preference for one of the two main parties. He got usable data from 50 males and 50 females (that is,

---

[1]For an interesting project, do a Psych-Lit. search of Smith and Glass to see critical evaluations of their classic study.

the number remaining within the sample, after refusals and after eliminating those choosing other parties—for example, Ross Perot).

He reported the following results:

	Female	Male
REPUBLICANS	10	30
DEMOCRATS	40	20

Based on visual inspection he concluded his hypothesis was supported. On being challenged to provide evidence that such a difference
was not merely due to chance (to sampling error), he performed a chi
square test—very simply as outlined in Table 12–2.

Notice that in Table 12–2 the expected cell frequencies appear in
the small boxes within each cell. If you have a complex table, consult a
standard statistics text for help in computing these expected frequencies. In our table we simply went to the row totals and assumed an
expected frequency of 50–50—half women, half men.

For 2-by-2 tables, a raw score formula allows you to avoid calculating expected frequencies by merely using the observed frequencies in
each cell (*A, B, C, D*) as seen below.[2]

A	*B*
C	*D*

	Female		Male		
Republican	*A*	10	*B*	30	40
Democrat	*C*	40	*D*	20	60
		50		50	100 (*N*)

$$\chi^2 = \frac{N(AD - BC)^2}{(A + B)(C + D)(A + C)(B + D)}$$

$$\chi^2 = \frac{100(10 \times 20 - 30 \times 40)^2}{(10 + 30)(40 + 20)(10 + 40)(30 + 20)} = 16.6$$

$$d.f. = 1 \qquad p < 0.001$$

Having demonstrated that such a combination of cell frequencies is
likely to occur less than one time in 1000 by chance, the student expresses

---

[2] χ^2 for raw score formula will closely approximate that found by calculating differences between observed and expected frequencies.

TABLE 12–2

Chi Square Test

---

1.   General Chi Square (χ^2) Formula:

$$\chi^2 = \sum_{r=1}^{r} \sum_{c=1}^{c} \frac{(fo - fe)^2}{fe}$$

where: fo = Observed frequency in a given cell
$\quad\quad\quad fe$ = Expected frequency in that cell

The Chi Square is obtained by adding the differences between fo and fe (according to the formula) over all cells—the cells in the rows (r), and columns (c) of the table.

2.   Example of Chi Square for 2 by 2 contingency table:

	WOMEN		MEN		
	$fe=$ 20		20		
Republican	$fo=$10		30		40
		30		30	
Democrat	40		20		60
	50		50		100

$$\chi^2 = \frac{(10 - 20)^2}{20} + \frac{(30 - 20)^2}{20} + \frac{(40 - 30)^2}{30} + \frac{(20 - 30)^2}{30}$$

$$= 5 + 5 + 3.3 + 3.3$$

$$= 16.6. \quad df = 1, \quad p < 0.001^a$$

---

[a]For degrees of freedom = 1 (number of rows − 1) (number of columns − 1), probability of χ^2=16.6 less than one chance in 1000.

Experts disagree over the need for a Yates' correction for small cell frequencies and for all tables with degrees of freedom less than 2. Our practice is to use the correction if a cell frequency is less than 10, or if the chi square level of significance is borderline around the 0.05 level. We follow Guilford (1956, p. 237): "The correction is particularly important when chi square turns out to be near a point of division between critical regions." With the correction, the chi square formula becomes:

$$\chi^2 = \sum_{r=1}^{r} \sum_{c=1}^{c} \frac{[(fo - fe] - 0.5)^2}{fe}$$

greater confidence in his hypothesis. An unconvinced student repeats the study, and she obtains less dramatic but still significant results:

	Women	Men
REPUBLICANS	18	28
DEMOCRATS	32	22

$\chi^2 = 4.03$ $p < 0.05$

The student decides that there is some evidence that women do indeed tend to support the Democrats, not because they are softhearted and softheaded, but rather because "intelligent" people tend to support the Democratic party, whereas simple-minded people support the Republicans. She then did a study showing that Democrats have higher grade-point averages than Republicans do:

Academic Performance

	ABOVE MEDIAN	BELOW MEDIAN	
REPUBLICAN	19 [23]	27 [23]	46
DEMOCRAT	31 [27]	23 [27]	54
	50	50	100

$\chi^2 = 2.58,$ $d.f. = 1$ $p < 0.20$

In this study the researcher drew a random sample of 100 students from another introductory psychology class and obtained the results tabulated in the preceding contingency table. It turned out, by chance, that there were 46 Republicans in her sample, and so if there was no relationship between political affiliation and academic performance, you would expect, by chance, a 50–50 split—expected frequencies (*fe*) of 23 above the whole group median and 23 below. Similarly, for the Democrats a 50–50 split would lead to expected frequencies of 27 above and 27 below the median academic performance.

On the basis of eyeball analysis the researcher is pleased with the results—more Democrats than Republicans scored above the academic median, quite a few more. Of course there were more Democrats in the sample, so that is why it is important to figure out the expected frequencies for each cell; that is why it is important to do an appropriate statistical test—like a chi square. The researcher finds, to her disappointment, that a chi square of 2.58 (*d.f.* = 1) can occur by chance close to 20 times in 100 random trials. Therefore she hasn't obtained a *statistically* significant result—which by custom is set at less than 5 times in 100 random trials.

Nevertheless, it is an *emotionally* significant result, and she argues that her findings represent a strong trend supporting her hypothesis—she will increase her sample size and prove her hypothesis next semester. Others who disagree with her hypothesis (quite a few Republicans, for example) accuse her of trying to read her own bias into the results, rather than accepting the quantitative judgment of her own statistical test.

As you can imagine, the argument continues and will continue. The chi square provides a simple and useful tool to help wage this kind of war *quantitatively* and provides a simple map of chance against which to compare your research results.

But notice when you establish chi square categories or cells (a contingency table), you provide opportunities to test how fuzzy the categories are—to test how large a region of uncertainty they contain $(\tilde{O})$.

For example, arguments about whether someone belongs to the male or female category rarely arise, apart from the female Olympics. However, whether to categorize someone as a Republican or a Democrat can become tricky. Do you accept as reliable evidence the fact that they put a pencil mark after Republican or after Democrat on one question on a questionnaire? Or do you ask for evidence of party membership? Or do you ask for evidence of active party support for at least three years? Until such issues are resolved, the various categories or cells of our first chi-square table should perhaps be drawn as follows:

	Female	*Male*	*?*
REPUBLICAN	(10)	(30)	(40)
DEMOCRAT	(40)	(20)	(60)
	50	50	100

Therefore keep a weather eye open for the fuzziness of the categories of all scales, but particularly with nominal scale data of the type used in the cells of chi-square contingency tables. When you find such fuzziness—independent observers can't agree on who goes into which cell—take the results with a grain of salt.

WHICH STATISTICAL TEST?

Consumers as well as practitioners of science must learn to "read" graphic and quantitative descriptions of the degree of relationship between observational samples (scattergrams and correlations) and the differences between observational samples (distribution plots, contingency tables, *t* tests, analysis of variance, chi squares).

You will encounter a host of statistical tools. Some, called *parametric statistics*, are based on the assumption that your samples have been drawn from populations that are *normally* distributed and have the *same variability*. Other statistical tests, called *nonparametric*, do not assume normalcy, or variance equivalence (homogeneity) in populations, and so can be applied to a wide range of observations. Arguments among experts continue over when to use a given statistical test—some preferring to use nonparametric statistics when sample data suggest the parent populations are nonnormal (skewed) and/or the experimental and control populations have markedly different variances. Other experts believe that, since parametric tests are more powerful—that is, they can detect finer differences—and are not all that sensitive to violations of the normalcy and variance assumptions, the parametric test should ordinarily be used. Our bias is to examine the data from several angles: plot it and examine it visually; do parametric tests where possible; do nonparametric tests when in doubt or when parametric tests aren't available.

The following brief list of nonparametric and parametric statistical tests are more or less matched in terms of the kind of relationships, or differences, they are designed to measure:

NONPARAMETRIC	PARAMETRIC
Spearman rank-order correlation	Pearson product-moment correlation
Sign test Wilcoxon test	—*t* test for related samples (e.g., two measures on the same subjects)
Mann-Whitney U test Median test	—*t* test for independent samples
Kruskal Wallis one-way link test Median test	One-way analysis of variance
Freedman two-way ranks test	One-way analysis of variance with repeat measures
Chi square test	No comparable parametric test

The detailed procedure for doing these tests can be found not only in statistical texts but also increasingly in the instruction manuals for desk calculators and computers.

However, if in doubt, plot your data or a random sample of it. If you are a consumer, keep a weather eye out for information that lets you do rough plots in your mind's eye of sample sizes, variances, and overlap, and also watch for fuzzy categories or scales as well.

The preceding lists represent different statistical ways of helping you to quantitatively describe your observations—nominal scale observations, ordinal scale observations, or interval and ratio scale observations. Each method lends itself to certain scales, and each method also provides a suitable map of chance so you can determine how often the differences, or changes, you observed would likely occur by chance alone— would occur between a series of two groups receiving no treatment or between a series of groups receiving the same treatment.

Statistical tests help to identify which of the many observations you make are worth talking about—worth talking about in the sense that they are statistically improbable. By *custom* social scientists consider differences that occur less than 5 times in 100 by chance alone as *statistically improbable*. So when you read, "A finding is significant at the 0.05 level of confidence," or "*p* is less than 0.05," it simply means that the researcher is reporting that such a difference between the experimental and control groups would probably occur less than 5 times in 100 if they had been drawn from the same population—that is, if both groups were given the same treatment.

But if the 0.05 level (5 times in 100 trials) is merely set by custom as the arbitrary boundary line of statistically improbable events, wouldn't it be safer to set an even more stringent boundary line? For example, why not define a statistically improbable event as one that occurs only once in 100 trials or once in 1000 trials? Then if you turned up such a rare event in your experiment, you could be almost certain it wasn't due to chance playing a trick on you. Well, the reason is that by reducing the risk of being hoodwinked by chance you increase the risk of throwing the baby out with the bathwater. By reducing the risk of one kind of error, you increase the risk of another.

Type I and Type II Errors

As noted, maps of chance provide no ironclad protection against error—particularly against two types of error. For example, in deciding whether a coin is biased, if you're "trigger happy" you can accuse the tosser of using a biased coin too soon, after perhaps five heads in a row. By rejecting the possible role of chance, you commit a *Type I error*.

On the other hand, you can be too cautious and not decide to accuse the tosser of using a biased coin until 12 or 15 heads in a row have been tossed. By rejecting the possible influence of bias you commit a *Type II error*.

Technically we are talking about accepting or rejecting the *null hypothesis*. The null hypothesis states that there is no real difference between the pretest and posttest or between the experimental and control group. It presumes that whatever differences do exist are due to random chance fluctuations.

A Type I error occurs when you erroneously reject the null hypothesis—when you mistake a chance difference for a treatment difference, when you mistake a chance grimace for a hostile look, when you mistake a useless drug for a curative one, when you mistake a true coin for a biased one.

But just as you can be too trigger happy—seeing real differences where only chance differences exist—you can also be overly cautious— refusing to recognize "real" differences. When you go on betting tails after the tosser has thrown 15 heads in a row, well, you're making a mistake, and that kind of mistake is called a *Type II error*.

Someone who cries, "Wolf," when a spring breeze rustles the leaves commits a Type I error, whereas someone who says, "Nice puppy," as the wolf snaps at his hand commits a Type II error.

The likelihood of committing one or the other of these types of errors may be related to personality characteristics—like the tendency to take or avoid risks. However, another way of thinking about the likelihood of making a Type I error is in terms of the maps of chance you use to decide whether you've got a difference worth talking about. If you wish to reduce the risk of Type I errors, you only accept differences, or results, that occur very rarely by chance—that is, once in 100 trials or once in 1000 trials. On the other hand, if you wish to reduce the risk of making Type II errors, you move in the other direction by accepting experimental results that could occur by chance 5 times, 10 times, or even 20 times out of 100 random trials.

As you can see, reducing the risk of one kind of error increases the risk of making the other. Therefore it is not merely a question of trying to avoid making an error; it becomes a question of avoiding a high-cost error. If you're betting pennies on whether a given coin is biased or not, the cost of making a Type I or a Type II error is probably no more than 25¢—so who cares? But if you're betting your life on a new surgical treatment for your brain tumor, you care; your family and friends care; the surgeons care.

In such a situation you look at the results to date: of 10 patients with your kind of tumor who have had the new surgery, 3 are dead and 7 are living and somewhat improved. Is it really a 7 out of 10—70 percent chance of success? Or is it really 50–50 or 30–70? Only more trials will decide! Should you wait for the results of more "experiments" or accept surgery now? You can decide that the surgery works (has more than a 50-50 success rate), elect to undergo surgery, risk a Type I error, and maybe die under the knife. Or you can decide to wait for more data, risk a Type II error, and die from an enlarged, inoperable tumor.

Therefore Type I and Type II errors represent more than esoteric statistical phrases; rather, they represent a rational approach to analyzing the risks involved in making decisions under uncertain and sometimes critical conditions.

Fortunately most decisions don't present us with such pressing, high-risk situations. Under more mundane circumstances how should you, a consumer of science, respond to a statistically improbable research result—one that in your opinion balances the risks of Type I and Type II errors? What questions might an informed consumer of science ask? You might consider the following:

1. "Yes, I understand your finding is statistically improbable, but it could still be due to chance. Therefore before I assign it a high level of personal confidence, I would like to see some independent researcher repeat the study and obtain similar results."

2. "Granted, you obtained a statistically improbable result, but it could be due, not to your treatment, but to some other shaping influence:
    a.   To an unusual trick of chance
    b.   To error in data recording or calculating
    c.   To (I hesitate to say it) fraud
    Therefore before I assign it a high level of personal confidence, I'd like to see some independent researcher repeat the study and obtain similar results with larger samples of people than you used."

Independent and consistent labeling is the hallmark of objective language, as we discussed in a previous chapter. Independent and consistent replication of observations is the hallmark of objective science. Statistically significant results from one-shot experiments are no substitute for independent and consistent replication of experiments. While statistical tools are helpful, they remain just that—tools. In skilled hands, they help us explore a multilayered reality. In unskilled or irresponsible hands, they help foul the media and the scientific literature with false claims and numerical noise.

N-OF-1 RESEARCH (STUDYING ONE CASE)

Just as Rodney Dangerfield "don't get no respect," so, too, is single-case research ill-respected. There are at least two reasons for this: first, *n*-of-1 research is frequently associated with the error-prone after-the-fact or case method approach; second, widely accepted statistical tests that would give us added confidence in whatever changes we see between baseline and treatment observations are lacking.

However, the ultimate criteria we apply in judging the reliability of any finding is replication, not statistical significance. Therefore, if we can replicate a reliable difference between the baseline and treatment conditions, we have met the standards of good research. Appropriately, then, *n*-of-1 studies typically take the form of a series of baseline-treatment trials on the same subject, and are typically described as *ABA*, or *ABAB* treatment reversal designs, where *A* stands for baseline observa-

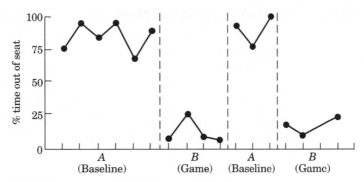

FIGURE 12–6   *ABAB* Reversal Design

tions and *B* for treatment observations. For example, Figure 12–6 maps the percentage of time a young student spent out of his seat under two conditions of teaching—*A*, a lecture method (baseline), and *B*, a game method of teaching (treatment). Notice the second *AB* series serves as a replication and produces, in this case, a reliable result. We can analyze such results in this kind of study, as in other interrupted time series designs, in a variety of disciplined ways without relying on statistics. For example, we can compare the means; the slopes as you move from one block of observations to the next; abrupt shifts in performance from block to block; a similar pattern of changes as the treatment is introduced and withdrawn, etc. (Kazdin, 1989).

A student used a series of *n*-of-1 cases to map studying behavior in average and above-average university students. Different students kept diaries for 16 weeks in which they coded their daily behavior into various categories (e.g., studying, recreation, transportations, etc.). The researcher extracted a time series for each student that mapped the rise and fall of studying behavior. We see these as *n*-of-1 studies, rather than a small group study, because different students encountered different in-the-gap, on-stage, maturational, and elastic-ruler rogues, and because our primary focus was the individual. If similarities between them appeared the researcher could use them as hypotheses for larger generalizations via group studies.

Following a baseline period each student participated in a 6-week time-management program, after which they continued their diaries over a follow-up period. Although time spent studying rose for some students during the time-management program, performance later gravitated back toward baseline. However, for all students, regardless of the operation of different rogues, one powerful factor was associated with increased study time, and that, of course, was exam and essay deadlines. All subjects showed the procrastination and cramming pattern associated with deadlines, although above-average students maintained a modestly higher baseline rate of studying.

Interviews with the students suggested that they were programmed to work to weekly deadlines in high school, and without that regular structure they fell behind in those university courses with long periods between deadlines. Setting personal deadlines and drawing up study schedules did not lead to significantly increased study time for most students. Deadlines, to be effective motivators, have to be strict.

Finally, not only do n-of-1 studies provide researchers with a more in-depth look at human behavior and the subsequent generation of interesting hypotheses, but such investigations provide individuals with an opportunity to study their own behavior. Is there a more fascinating topic than that?

There is a solid tradition within science (e.g., biology) and outside science for relying on n-of-1 data for drawing important conclusions. As you can guess, it becomes particularly powerful when you are familiar with the individual or animal being observed. In other words, you have good intuitive sense of the baseline and the degree of variability over long time frames. Thus, it is a powerful method of detecting reliable changes in certain hands; for example, most mothers, and old-time general practitioners, represent skilled investigators using the $n = 1$ design.

Statistical methods are increasingly available which can be used to supplement disciplined visual inspection rather than to replace it. The statistical principles are the same for group or individual analysis, the main difference being the kind of generalizations you want to make. In the n-of-1 study, the population of behavior you want to generalize to is that of an individual rather than a group. However, when making comparisons between two samples of an individual's behavior, as in Figure 12–6, you keep the same points in mind as when making comparisons between two groups—namely, (1) the size of the differences between the means of each block of observations; (2) the size of the variability within each block; and (3) the degree of overlap of the observations between blocks. In the case of Figure 12–6, it is clear that the means of the baseline and game blocks differ markedly; the within-block variability is low; and there is no overlap between the observations—that is, none of the observations in the treatment blocks are as high as any of the observations in the baseline blocks.

Once you have established a reliable difference between baseline and treatment conditions for the single subject, you can then work toward generalizing your results. You can test a larger time and/or a different dependent variable for that subject. In the case of our example, does the game method of teaching keep working, or does the child start reverting back to his old habits? In addition to spending more time in his seat, are there other changes as well (e.g., improvement in grades, or in relations with other students and parents, etc.)? Also, you can check to see if the method works with other, similarly restless students. Now you are starting to see if your results might generalize to a larger population, to the behavior not just of one child, but of a particular, defined group of children.

Finally, if your results are not as clear-cut as those in Figure 12–6 —if the means are closer together, or if the within-block variability is higher so that there is some overlap in the observations from block to block—then, as noted earlier, there are statistical tests available to help you draw conclusions from such fuzzy data (see Barlow & Hersen, 1984). Nevertheless, we strongly recommend that you plot your data first, so that you get a good feel for the variability, and thus for the degree of overlap, between observations in the treatment blocks and those in the baseline blocks.

If you're interested in n-of-1 studies, start by using yourself as a subject. The example at the end of Chapter 4 might give you some ideas.

SUMMARY

In the toolbox of social science, statistical devices abound. Descriptive statistics help package observations into mind-sized bites. Inferential statistics help us defend ourselves from being perpetually hoodwinked by capricious chance.

But remember that *statistically significant* findings represent a beginning, not a research climax. A statistically significant finding encourages further investigation but does not bestow a label of truth on your results. After having obtained an "improbable" research finding, you write up your research project (as outlined in Chapter 14) and submit it to a journal. Your manuscript is then critically examined by several reviewers familiar with your research area, and they decide whether your experimental procedure, your maps of chance, and your calculations seem appropriate and also whether your conclusions appear reasonable. Only if you pass all these tests is your manuscript then published. Then, other investigators can check your findings on new samples of people, perhaps controlling more carefully against the rogues, taking longer baseline measurements, or using larger samples.

In brief, although statistical tests (like t tests and chi squares) help you decide whether you have obtained a statistically significant result, it still requires experience, critical judgment, and continued research to determine whether you have obtained a result of scientific import or social consequence. Research requires not only tenacity but also courage. The researchers' code might well be taken from the famous poem "Invictus," by W. E. Henley:

Under the bludgeonings of chance my head is bloody, but unbowed.

REVIEW QUIZ

True or False?

1. Statistical tests rule out the possibility of chance, fraud, and error and ensure that observed differences are due to the operation of the independent variable.

2. Inferential statistics and sampling theory provide help in comparing short-term sample results with the results to be expected by chance in the long run.

3. The means and standard deviation statistics derived from samples provide exact estimates of the comparable population statistics.

4. Sampling theory addresses the issue of the reliability of the estimates of population parameters obtained from samples.

5. The sampling error, or variability, of the means of small samples is larger than the sampling error of the means of large samples.

6. A *t* test is designed to measure the significance of a difference between two samples by comparing the observed difference with the difference expected from chance effects alone.

7. An *F* test, or ANOVA, may be used if there are several comparison groups (i.e., more than two) or several independent variables.

8. Although an *F* test may reveal no statistically significant difference among the several experimental conditions, it is appropriate to conduct a series of *t* tests comparing the groups two at a time.

9. The particular advantage of an *F* test is that it enables us to measure interaction effects.

10. A meta-analysis is a technique for integrating the results obtained in many different studies and provides an index of the practical significance of the variable of interest.

11. A chi-square test may not be used in the statistical analysis of nominal scale or frequency data.

12. Parametric statistics are based on the assumption that the samples have been drawn from populations that are normally distributed and have the same variability.

13. A Type II error occurs when you erroneously reject the null hypothesis—when you mistake a change difference for a treatment difference.

14. *n*-of-1 studies typically take the form of a series of baseline-treatment trials on the same subject.

☙ 13 ❧

Ethics

———— **Chapter Goal** ————

*To expose you to the complexities of ethical
issues vis-à-vis research, including the extent
to which the specific content and adherence
to ethical codes are influenced by bias,
stereotypes, politics, and self-interest.*

How would you describe a scientist? What traits or characteristics come
to mind when you think about scientists in general? Although each of us
might generate a unique total list, at least some of us would no doubt
agree on certain adjectives—including, perhaps, intelligent, creative, well-
educated, absent-minded, analytical, objective, rational, honest, impartial,
fair, and trustworthy. The last four descriptors speak to the ethicality/moral-
ity of the scientist. Certainly, science is based on the assumption that the
ethical integrity of its disciples is of the highest order. Were we not to make
this assumption, the game of science would be a farce, a scam, an endeavor
suitable only for fools, dilettantes, and con artists.

Suppose this were the case and some researchers "diddled their
data"—made it do what they wanted it to. Scientific literature would
then be filled with contradictory findings. To illustrate, some investigators would have clear documentation that democratic leadership style is
the most productive; another dissenting clutch of scientists would present equally clear data that autocratic forms of leadership reign supreme;
still others would espouse a laissez-faire model; and perhaps a smaller
group would present evidence that leadership style has no relationship
to productivity. Thus replicability, a key concept in scientific research,
becomes meaningless if data are invented and observations are not public and shareable. Obviously the utility of research findings becomes
minimal under such conditions.

This assumption of ethicality is so crucial to the practice of science that
it may be seen as the pivotal point on which the science seesaw teeters. Social
science practitioners today are increasingly sensitive to questions of ethics,

morality, humanism, and civil rights. Over the last decade increased time and energy have gravitated around ethical issues; ethics committees abound within disciplines, within universities, and within research organizations. Indeed, some current effort is being directed toward the establishment of an international code of ethics for human research (Medical Research Council of Canada, 1988). Nevertheless, the view of the inherently high level of moral judgment and ethicality of scientists has served to impede the development of formal ethics codes. For example, it was not until 1966 that the American Psychological Association recognized the need for the establishment of a set of ethical standards in psychological research (American Psychological Association, 1982).

RELATIVITY OF ETHICS

Rules of ethics reflect the value substrata of a culture. Just as values and other cultural components (technology) vary from society to society, so too will ethical standards. For example, while the Navahos, in common with our own and many other cultures, have prohibitions against lying, stealing, cheating, murder, and rape, the most serious crimes are those of incest and witchcraft (Kluckhohn & Leighton, 1949). Among the Saulteaux of the Berens River, violence of any form (including verbal aggression) is strenuously avoided (Hallowell, 1940); yet, among the Hopi, who also eschew physical aggression, verbal warfare is an ever-present feature of communal life (Eggan, 1943). Both cultures regard competition as being in extremely bad taste and both revere cooperation, in contrast to our own society, in which merit is selectively attached to both traits. Ethical concerns related to the expression of sexuality show great cross-cultural variability. For the Keraki males in New Guinea, a period of passive, then active, homosexuality is regarded as a necessary prerequisite to normal heterosexual developments (Benedict, 1938).

In addition to cross-cultural variation, ethical standards change over time. As one moves from one historical period to another, rather dramatic alterations in costume fashions are accompanied by (albeit mostly unrelated to) equally astonishing modifications in laws and ethical concerns. Throughout much of recorded history, women were regarded as chattels or inferior beings, a view reflected in the "rule of thumb" of nineteenth-century English common law, which legalized a husband's right to chastise his wife with a rod not thicker than his thumb. Such practices created no ethical conflict or burden for the perpetrators of this code of ethics. Only recently are women gradually acquiring the same rights, privileges, and responsibilities as those of the opposite sex (Brown & Seitz, 1970). As Faludi (1991) notes, the struggle for equality is an uneven process—advances interspersed with episodic periods of backlash.

Even within a single culture and given time period, considerable variance in the ethical principles accepted and practiced by various subgroups may be observed. Attitudes among members of the Pentagon toward the ethicality and legality of a particular military policy are likely to be incongruent with the attitudes of their wives (Ellsberg, 1973). And certainly the ethical stance of some Nazi researchers who used Jewish prisoners as experimental subjects was divergent from that of the German "man-in-the-street."

Stereotypes may also exert a powerful influence on ethical decision-making processes. Consider, for example, the stereotype that women are more emotional, immature, and in need of more protection than men are. That stereotype seems to influence a woman's "right to die" (or more formally, the "right to refuse life-sustaining treatment"). Miles and August (1990) examined the legal courts' decisions in "right to die" cases. One of the questions they asked involved the wishes of patients who were on life-sustaining treatment and unable to communicate with anyone. Did the physician try to determine the patient's own preferences for either continuing or terminating life support, based on previous conversations? Or did the courts leave the decision to someone else, such as a family member or hospital policy? In 75 percent of the cases in which the patient was male—but in only 14 percent of the cases in which the patient was female—did the physician try to figure out what the individual wanted. So the message is this: If a man is in an irreversible coma, a conversation from 3 years ago can be used as evidence of his wishes either to die or to be sustained; if a woman is in a similar condition, her husband will probably be asked to make the decision about her fate (Matlin, 1993, p. 402).

The relationship between science and ethics has been fraught with minor spats, hurt silences, martyred expressions, and vicious, acrimonious disputes. At times scientific investigations were severely hindered by ethical concerns stemming from theological teachings. Consider, for example, how progress in medicine was retarded by the religious strictures against mutilation of the dead body. White (1955) has provided us with an inventory of illustrations that highlight the uneasy association of science and religion.

During a brief halcyon period in the history of science, the primary injunction to scientists was to search for the truth "no matter what." Admonitions to seek knowledge for its own sake were the norm; if unscrupulous minds used such knowledge in an unethical fashion, this was in no way the responsibility of the scientist. If research on methods to reduce prejudice uncovers effective techniques for producing attitude change which then are subsequently employed to manipulate prisoners of war as part of a brainwashing program, it's not the scientist's fault. The more contemporary view, however, recognizes that "the double-edged potentiality of scientific knowledge poses ethical problems for all scientists" (American Psychological Association, 1982, p. 16)—that is, that scientists have some responsibility for monsters they spawn. This modern stance, combined with a general evolution in standards of humanitarianism and respect for the human condition, has forced the scientist out of the ivory tower and into the more philosophical, religious, and political arenas where ethical issues are debated.

The moral of the story (to make a bad pun) is that principles of ethics and moral precepts are neither self-evident nor absolute. Being culture-bound and time-tied, ethics can only be understood in the context of the culture that espouses them. Our amazement at the atrocities of Genghis Khan, at the horrors of the Crusades, at the child abuse during the Industrial Revolution, at the tortures of the Spanish inquisitors, and at the heartless behavior of GIs in Vietnam reflects only our own provincial natures and our inability to divest ourselves of our own cultural trappings and, chameleonlike, take on the coloration of another. In the same way, future generations may well register disgust over many of our current "ethical" practices.

Ethics and the Social Scientist

As social scientists whose subject matter is (1) animate, (2) reactive, and (3) often human, we are perhaps more sensitized to ethical concerns than is the physicist measuring the aurora borealis from photographs, or the geologist mapping rock types on the basis of drill core, or the chemist analyzing the molecular structure of a complex protein. The onion root tip does not object to nor change its appearance because it is being examined under a microscope; yet how would we react to detailed scrutiny of our behavior in the intimacy of our own homes? Investigations related to altruism, child-rearing patterns, lynch mob behavior, leadership, authority, incest, fiscal policy, population growth, cancer, cloning, the treatment of schizophrenia, penal reform—all cry out for attention to ethical principles. A code of ethics, after all, is really meant to guide our behavior so as to protect (not contravene) the rights, privileges, and general expectations of others.

Why Have a Code of Ethics?

A key reason for designing and encouraging the adoption of a code of ethics is to inflict or impose our current sense of values on our colleagues. Secondly, the more-or-less uniform acceptance of rules of conduct helps to establish the "old boy's club"—to guarantee some sense of familiarity and comfort in interacting with other members of one's discipline. Thus some concerns dressed in ethical costume reflect protectionism or elitism or isolationism, rather than any general worry about the public weal. To police the science; identify and weed out the incompetent, the insincere, or the unworthy; and thus maintain the purity of the profession are yet other functions of a common code of ethics. Such a code helps protect the public from charlatans (those lacking the training specified for membership in the discipline) and from deviants (those adequately trained but practicing in unethical ways).

To protect the individual practitioner from pangs of conscience, gnawing doubts, and perhaps even financial ruin through legal suits is another, but less publicized, value of an ethics code. How can scientists be faulted if their research project seems to lead to negative outcomes for their subjects, especially when they scrupulously followed the rites and rituals (including ethical prohibitions) accepted by their discipline? In some sense a code of ethics serves somewhat the same function in a science as do quality control procedures in a factory.

ETHICS QUIZ

Before commencing an in-depth examination of specific statements of ethics, it may be useful to sensitize yourself to some of the issues by completing the following quiz.[1] In each case decide if the key figure has behaved ethically or not.

1. Professor V. S. decided to vote against admitting Jane Doe into the graduate program because she had lodged an official complaint, charging one of his male colleagues with sexual harassment.

   Ethical _____ Unethical _____

2. As part of her efforts to prepare a strong case for her promotion, Assistant Professor M. S. asked her graduate students for testimonials concerning the quality of her teaching and supervision.

   Ethical _____ Unethical _____

3. Researcher A. D. has published the results of a large study on the attitudes of medical personnel to euthanasia. She subsequently received a request for her data from the American Medical Association who wish to verify her conclusions through a reanalysis of her data. A. D. has refused the request.

   Ethical _____ Unethical _____

4. Professor C. S., as part of his responsibilities as a faculty member at Fly-By-Night U, acts as a supervisor of the research work for a number of graduate students. Typically, this involves several discussions prior to the beginning of the study (perhaps five hours total), some discussion concerning the analysis of obtained results, and the review of one or two thesis drafts.

---

[1]Items for this quiz are based on principles selected from the *Ethical Principles of Psychologists* (American Psychological Association, 1992) and the *Ethical Principles in the Conduct of Research with Human Participants* (American Psychological Association, 1982).

Professor C. S. and his students almost always jointly publish these studies, and C. S. is invariably senior author.

Ethical _____ Unethical _____

5. One of the assignments in a fourth-year sociology course on research methods requires that students maintain a personal journal or diary on family interactions to which a structural analysis (network approach) is subsequently applied. One of the students expresses reluctance (on personal grounds) about carrying out this assignment. The course director, convinced that the research procedures are acceptable and sensitive to the pedagogical benefits of the assignment, urges the student to conduct the study.

Ethical _____ Unethical _____

6. P. T., a professor of physical education, designed a study on the "second wind" phenomenon that required research participants to engage in grueling and arduous feats of muscular stamina and strength. The proposed project, after compulsory review by the university's Research Ethics Committee, is given a clean bill of health. P. T., much relieved at obtaining ethical clearance, proceeds to conduct the research without further independent assessment of the ethical issues involved.

Ethical _____ Unethical _____

7. Deception was employed in a study assessing the relationship between gender-role orientation and self-esteem. Research subjects, prior to participation, were informed of the requirements and purpose of the experiment to the extent possible given the deception component. Freedom to withdraw from the study, at any time, was emphasized. Following an assessment of gender-role orientation, all female subjects, irrespective of their actual performance, were told their scores revealed a masculine orientation, and male subjects were informed their scores reflected a feminine orientation. Measures of self-esteem were then administered. Immediately on completion, subjects were thanked for their participation and promised a detailed report of the study. Two months later subjects received the report, which fully described the deception.

Ethical _____ Unethical _____

8. Neuropsychologist Dr. Rabid is conducting research on the cortical changes in dogs that accompany or result from repeated severe physical pain as induced by whipping.

Ethical _____ Unethical _____

9. Social psychologist F. A. is researching the organizational structure of certain voluntary groups. Inasmuch as there is a

friendly rivalry among these groups, F. A. is frequently asked by a club how they compare with other groups under study. F. A. does not reveal any budgetary information but is willing to describe organizational hierarchy and style.

Ethical _____ Unethical _____

10. Researcher A. B. has been extremely fortunate in obtaining financial and other support for his research endeavors. He has consistently obtained large grants from the Firm Foundation, and his employing organization is heavily committed to his research in terms of purchase of equipment, administrative support, and so forth. A. B. has been scrupulous in his publications to acknowledge the support of Firm Foundation, since their financial contributions made the implementation of the research program possible.

Ethical _____ Unethical _____

11. The associate director of a research unit is aware that one of the scientists in the agency is behaving in a seriously unethical fashion. Although he has brought this individual to task several times for his violation of ethical standards, the behavior persists. The associate director takes no further action.

Ethical _____ Unethical _____

12. Part of the course requirement for an introductory psychology course is participation as a subject in an experiment. Professor W. J. is using some of the students for her research on the effects of high arousal (induced by applying shocks to the fingers) on memory. One student, when informed of the nature of the research, was reluctant to serve as a subject. The experimenter waved aside objections by reminding the student that participation was a course requirement.

Ethical _____ Unethical _____

13. A team of researchers obtained measures of achievement motivation, creativity, and liking for teacher from children selected from several private nursery schools. The directors of some of these schools requested copies of all the test scores for each child. Since the researchers felt dependent on the good will of the school administrators for subjects, they provided the information requested.

Ethical _____ Unethical _____

14. Researcher R. P. has employed a graduate student to run the subjects through his experiment on sensory deprivation. Subjects were obtained through an advertisement in the college paper, which stated that $25 would be paid to individuals who wanted to participate in some research on "peace and quiet."

No further information was provided by the graduate student when the subject came to the lab.

Ethical _____ Unethical _____

15. As co-investigators for a large grant-supported study concerned with the cultural adjustment problems of new immigrants, X. Y. and X. X. employed a number of assistants to conduct structured interviews with a representative sample of immigrants. Prior to contacting any research participant, these assistants were given extensive instructions by X. X. concerning ethical issues relevant to the research. Nevertheless, it comes to their attention that one of the assistants has implied to interviewees that their participation in the research will reflect favorably on their applications for work permits. Who bears responsibility for this breach of ethics?

    a. X. Y.

    b. The assistant

    c. X. X.

    d. The assistant, X. X., and X. Y. are all fully responsible

While the list of such quiz items could go on and on, the 15 items provided are probably sufficient to illuminate the complexity and breadth of ethical concerns. According to principles accepted by the American Psychological Association, *all* of the foregoing are unethical. Therefore to score the quiz, give yourself one point for each scenario in which you decided the key figure had behaved or was behaving unethically. The correct answer for item 15 is alternative *d*. Those readers who obtained the maximum score of 15 are highly sensitized to ethical issues.

For those of us who achieved a less than perfect score, the following explains the relevant principle breached in each vignette (American Psychological Association, 1982; 1992).[2]

1. Individuals should not be denied academic admittance, advancement, employment, tenure or promotion, based solely on their having made charges of sexual harassment (Principle 1.11[b]).

2. Testimonials should not be solicited from persons who because of their particular circumstances (e.g., graduate student status) are vulnerable to undue influence (Principle 3.05).

3. Once research results are published, the data should not be withheld from other competent professionals as long as the confidentiality of the research participants can be protected (Principle 6.25).

---

[2]Principles from the 1992 publication are identified by a number, whereas those from the 1982 report are labeled with letters.

4. Publication credit should reflect the relative contributions of the individuals involved. In the example, it would appear that Professor C. S. did not play as major a role in the research as the graduate student. Further, "a student is usually listed as principal author on any multiple-authored article that is substantially based on the student's dissertation or thesis" (p. 1609) (Principle 6.23).

5. Ethical concerns regarding the decision about whether to conduct a particular research study are covered by Principles A, B, and C. The explication of these principles indicates that professor-researchers should respect a moral reluctance on the part of their students "to carry out a research procedure" and "should not pressure them to perform the procedure" (1982, p. 30).

6. An investigator must carefully evaluate the ethical acceptability of a planned study. Given the nature of the study in this example, the investigator has a "serious obligation to seek ethical advice" (Principle A, p. 26). The approval of a review committee does not absolve the researcher from soliciting other independent assessments of the ethical issues involved (1982, p. 29). The study may also be a breach of Principle G, which requires that the researcher protect subjects from physical discomfort.

7. Although the investigator was sensitive to certain ethical issues, the study as described illustrates contravention of Principles H and I. There was no attempt on the part of the investigator to detect and remove any damaging consequences for the individual participants which may have occurred as a result of the deception. Anger or resentment of subjects on discovery of the deception was not monitored. (See also Principle 6.15.)

8. The procedures employed by Dr. Rabid contravene principles related to the humane treatment of research animals (Principle 6.20).

9. F. A. has contravened the obligation to safeguard the confidentiality of information obtained about these organizations in the course of this research (Principle J).

10. In this example the support of the host institution has not been properly acknowledged in the publications (Principle 6.23[b]).

11. The associate director failed to bring these unethical activities to the attention of the appropriate committees on ethical standards and practices for the discipline (Principle 8.05).

12. "The investigator respects the individual's freedom to decline to participate in or to withdraw from research at any time" (p. 42, Principle F). The investigator should have provided the student with a choice of alternative activities (Principle 6.11 [d]).

13. This form of reporting is unethical, since there is no indication of any limitations on the information in terms of reliability or validity nor was there an attempt to ensure that the information would not be misused (Principle 2.02).

14. R. P. did not adequately disclose aspects of the research which might have influenced the subject's willingness to participate. Also, R. P.'s assistant similarly did not explain the nature of the research and R. P. is responsible for ensuring the ethical treatment of subjects by his employee (Principles 6.07 and 6.11 and Principles C and D).

15. In instances where several investigators and research assistants are working on a project, all parties involved are fully responsible for protecting the well-being of the participants (Principle C). Further, this example illustrates the unethical use of coercion to participate in the research (Principle F).

ILLUSTRATIVE CASE STUDIES

In order to probe the intricacies of ethical concerns in more depth, three studies conducted by psychologists will be explored here in detail. The first study, reported by Milgram (1963), involved deception. A paid volunteer subject was told that the purpose of the experiment was to evaluate the effectiveness of punishment on learning. Through a further deception, the volunteer subject was to function as "teacher," and another subject (actually a stooge in the employ of the experimenter) was to act as "learner." Each time the learner made a mistake in the designated task, the teacher was to administer an electric shock, increasing the intensity of the shock with each failure. The final deception was that the stooge, communicating by intercom with the teacher, complained of a heart condition, warned that he couldn't continue, and emitted sounds of pain when shocks were applied. Subjects expressing concern about the condition of the learner were instructed by the experimenter to continue the experiment. The crucial question was the extent to which subjects would obey this directive in the face of the learner's rather dramatic pleas to desist. At the conclusion of the experiment, subjects were debriefed—that is, the deception was explained, and they were reassured that the learner was in the best of health and had not, in fact, been subjected to any shocks. Milgram states, "A friendly reconciliation was arranged between the subject and the victim, and an effort was made to reduce any tensions that arose as a result of the experiment" (Milgram, 1963, p. 374).

Was this an ethical study? Baumrind (1964) questions the ethicality of Milgram's research on several grounds. First, the conditions of the experiment contravene the subjects' expectations to be treated with respect and not be embarrassed or humiliated. Second, subjects have the right to assume that their security, self-esteem, and dignity will be protected. In Baumrind's view, the experience could well act to alter a subject's self-image. The very fact that subjects believed the deception makes them fools and thus damages their self-image. Further, they realize what they have done and that they are the type of person who could deliberately inflict considerable pain on a stranger. What harm this knowledge does to self-perceptions is unknown, but clearly the potential is there. Debriefing does not alleviate these harmful effects, since the subjects know that they would have shocked the learner had the current been turned on. Finally, involvement in a study of this type could reduce a participant's ability to trust authority in the future. Milgram (1965) disagrees, of course, with Baumrind's analysis, and the interested reader should refer to his rebuttal.

Field experiments, using covert observers, have become increasingly popular as researchers struggle to enhance the external validity of their research while at the same time sidestepping the conflict between the ethics requirement for informed consent and an experimental requirement for deception. Piliavin and Piliavin (1972) provide us with a typical example of this type of research. In their study the experimenter's confederate, walking with the aid of a cane, collapses in a subway car. What appears to be blood trickles from his mouth. If someone offers assistance, the confederate allows himself to be helped to his feet. If no one intervenes before the train slows to a stop, the experimenter, posing as a passenger, helps the stooge, and they both leave the train.

Over 45 percent of a sample of randomly selected subjects regarded this particular study as unethical (Wilson & Donnerstein, 1976). More general concerns about this genre of research have been expressed by other authors (cited in Wilson & Donnerstein, 1976, and Wiesenthal, 1974) and include the following: (1) There is no informed consent on the part of subjects who participate, (2) there is no attempt at debriefing, (3) invasion of privacy is an issue if the individuals in field settings do not normally expect to be observed, and (4) awareness of the prevalence of such research could lead to a reactive subject pool in public situations.

Another investigator, A. R. Jensen (1969a), aroused the vigilance and vitriol of the scientific community with his thesis that black–white IQ differences reflected genetic differences. On the basis of a series of studies conducted by other researchers, he reported that white children seemed to be better at associative and rote learning. Jensen noted that the IQ difference persisted even when socioeconomic status was controlled and, further, that the gap between whites and American Indians (despite poor schooling) was less pronounced than that between whites and blacks. One additional piece of supporting documentation was the failure of remedial education programs. Essentially Jensen's conclusion was that, while environmental factors are relevant, genetic factors may

be the principal causative agent underlying the alleged lower educational potential of blacks.

The Council for the Society for the Psychological Study of Social
Issues (SPSSI) was quick to respond to this heresy (1969) in what has
been labeled "a dogmatic and emotional" fashion (Hebb, 1970). The
SPSSI verbally spanked Jensen for espousing a socially dangerous view,
presented some legitimate criticism of his article, and publicly washed
its hands, in Pontius Pilate style, of any sympathy for his position. Their
principal ethical concern was as follows:

> We are concerned with establishing high standards of scientific inquiry
> and of scientific responsibility. Included in these standards must be care-
> ful interpretation of research findings, with rigorous attention to alterna-
> tive explanations. In no area of science are these principles more important
> than in the study of human behavior, where a variety of social factors may
> have large and far-reaching effects. When research has a bearing on social
> issues and public policy, the scientist must examine the competing expla-
> nations for his findings and must exercise the greatest care in his inter-
> pretation (pp. 1039–1040).

Jensen, of course, argues (1969b) that he has, in fact, maintained high
standards of scientific inquiry and scientific responsibility and suggests
that his critics have not. He refers to their rebuttal as "sheer propaganda."

Recently this debate resurfaced as an aftermath of Philippe Rushton's (1989) presentation of a paper to the American Association for the
Advancement of Science. Rushton hypothesized that Orientals were the
most intelligent, most sexually restrained, and the least criminal race.
Next in the evolutionary hierarchy were whites, followed by blacks. Evolutionary forces were assumed to operate in such a way that an expanding brain was associated with shrinking genitals. Rushton, like Jensen
before him, relied primarily on an analysis of the research done by others. Among the more questionable of these secondary sources was an
anonymously authored, quasi-pornographic book published in limited
edition in Paris in 1896. Contained in the text are detailed descriptions
of the genitalia and sexual practices of exotic and "primitive" peoples. A
storm of controversy currently rages in the media, the halls of academe,
and the scientific community over the battlegrounds of academic freedom, social responsibility, the scientific merits of Rushton's work, and
the effectiveness of peer and ethics review processes that permit the funding and publication of allegedly shoddy research (Ziegler, Wiesenthal,
Wiener, & Weizmann, 1989).

What can we conclude from these case studies? Clearly, in addition to the characteristics described earlier, we lack uniformity, except
in extreme cases, in our judgment of what constitutes a breach of
ethics. Agreement on general principles can be obtained, but when we
attempt to apply the principles to the concrete instance, we encounter

acrimonious dispute, and any decision is a subjective call. Why should this be so? Because questions of ethics resemble the Gordian knot; they are inextricably interwoven with personal, subgroup, and cultural values, attitudes, and beliefs. They are, in fact, the antithesis of the first rule of science—objectivity. Currently, controversy rages over the ethicality and morality of abortion, mercy killing, sterilization of the retarded, and the like. Even the most casual review of these debates reveals the heavy value-ridden, emotionally laden tone of the arguments both pro and con.

THE ANIMAL CONTROVERSY

Nonhuman animals comprise important subject populations for many types of research. In 1986, for example, 2,015,222 animals of 18 species were used by investigators at Canadian university, government, and commercial laboratories for the purposes of research, testing, and teaching (Canadians for Health Research, 1992). Most (90 percent) were rats, mice, fish, and fowl expressly bred for research purposes.

Among the more volatile and acrimonious debates ripping through the scientific world today is one involving animal lovers versus animal researchers. Yet, concern for the care and use of animals in research is not a recent or unique phenomenon in the scientific community. As noted by Dewsbury (1990), the arguments of the antivivisectionists in the Victorian period were not fundamentally different from those of contemporary animal rights activists. The American Society for the Prevention of Cruelty to Animals was founded in 1866, coincident with the passage of laws in various States banning or limiting vivisection. More recently, the Animal Welfare Act, first enacted in 1966 and amended by Congress in 1976, regulates the transportation, housing, and care of laboratory animals. Granting agencies, such as the National Institutes of Health, have adopted guidelines governing the use of research animals, which must be adhered to by grant recipients. Many scientific organizations have similarly tackled the issue of ensuring appropriate use of animals in research. The American Psychological Association, for example, first established a committee to address the ethics of animal experimentation in 1925. Current guidelines, approved in 1979, specify the following: that the researcher comply with all government laws and regulations; that a scientist trained and experienced in the use of laboratory animals should supervise and be responsible for their humane treatment; that researchers must minimize discomfort, illness, and pain to the animals; that pain, stress, or privation may only be used if alternative procedures are not possible and if the research is justified by its prospective value; that researchers should consult with the committee; that the principles should be posted in every facility where animals are used; that apparent violations of the principles should be reported to the supervisor and, if unresolved, should be referred to the committee.

Such efforts, however laudatory, have not silenced those concerned about animal rights. Most vociferous among the critics is the Mobilization for Animals Coalition, an international network of hundreds of animal-protectionist organizations (King, 1984). This group has accused experimental psychologists of subjecting animals to such things as repeated, inescapable, painful electric shocks; starvation and dehydration; mutilation; crushing forces which smash bones and rupture organs; and pain and stress designed to make healthy animals psychotic (Coile & Miller, 1984; King, 1984). Nor are all members of the scientific community convinced that all animal research meets appropriate ethical standards (Bowd, cited in Carroll, Schneider & Wesley, 1985).

New, more stringent regulations, recently proposed by the U.S. Department of Agriculture, and related to the promotion of the psychological well-being of nonhuman primates and dogs, have been received with some dismay by researchers (Landers, 1989). The requirements, designed to enrich the environments of captive animals, include the provision of regular exercise in special pens or the housing the animals in substantially larger cages, as well as modifications in feeding regimens to simulate foraging conditions. Among the other concerns of animal researchers are the limits on the number of operations that may be performed on a single animal, the degree of authority granted to veterinarians, and the increased administrative load involved in meeting the requirements. Implementation of these new proposals could have a significant impact on the costs of operating a laboratory and could lead to curtailment of some research programs.

Indeed, several recent surveys suggest that just such a curtailment is occurring, at least in university psychology departments. Gallop and Eddy (1990) note that one out of seven graduate departments that used to maintain animals no longer do so. The second most common reason for closure "was the prohibitive costs of compliance with existing codes and regulations" (p. 400). Similarly, Benedict and Stoloff (1991) discovered in their survey of 137 of "America's Best Colleges" that 21 percent of the 93 schools that at one time maintained animal facilities had ceased to operate animal laboratories. Finally, Thomas and Blackman (1992), reporting on events in the United Kingdom, point to a dramatic decline (25 percent) in the number of psychology departments with animal facilities, a decline in the number of animals used (70 percent), a decline in animal research (35 percent), and a decline in the number of graduate students conducting animal studies. This substantial decrease in animal work is attributed to an increasing reluctance of students to participate in projects involving animals out of concern for animal welfare.

FROM PRINCIPLE TO PRACTICE

To what extent do the mechanisms created by scientific organizations ensure that research practices are ethical? Somewhat reassuring is the report by Coile and Miller (1984) that none of the allegations of the Mobilization for Animals group were found to be true in a survey of 608 published articles involving research with animals. Less reassuring is Bowd's observation that a significant proportion of the published research involving painful animal experimentation was unnecessary in that the research did not contribute new knowledge (cited in Carroll, Schneider & Wesley, 1985). However, the American Psychological Association committee charged with responsibility for adjudicating complaints of ethical malpractice reported only one case of a failure to ensure the welfare of animal research subjects in a three-year period from 1981 to 1983 (Hall & Hare-Mustin, 1983; Mills, 1984). The most frequent type of ethical complaint concerned authorship controversies.

Adair, Dushenko, and Lindsay (1985) have examined the extent to which the development of ethical codes and practices has influenced the conduct of published social psychological research. Their survey of 284 empirical studies indicates that researchers rarely state that informed consent was obtained from their subjects or that subjects were aware of their right or freedom to withdraw from the experiment. Although the research as actually conducted may have attended to these ethical issues, the failure to report them leaves the question open.

The principle of informed consent implies that research participants must not be misled about the experiment. Nevertheless, deception is permitted under certain special conditions. Given the concern about deception, the finding of Adair and colleagues that experiments involving deception are increasing is surprising although there is more reporting of the use of debriefing procedures. Baumrind (1985) similarly reports that the ethical standards implemented by the American Psychological Association in 1973 have not decreased the incidence or magnitude of the use of deception in social psychological research and she suggests employment of alternative research strategies.

Adair and associates also highlight a number of methodological problems created by stringent application of current ethical standards. For example, it appears that when conditions of informed consent are instituted, fewer subjects agree to participate. Those who do agree constitute a biased sample. The debriefing procedure required in cases of deception may contaminate subsequent results obtained with later subjects because research participants sworn to secrecy have been found to disclose the nature of the experiment to others.

Maintaining an appropriate balance between the benefits of research and the costs to participants, while at the same time ensuring methodological purity, will tax the creativity and ingenuity of the researcher for some time to come.

Cost-Benefit Ratio

By and large the legal profession accepts the principle that it is better to let 100 guilty go free than to convict one innocent person. The costs (damages or harm) attendant on erroneous convictions are deemed to be greater than the benefits of utilizing more stringent procedures that would ensure a higher conviction rate of the guilty but would also entrap some innocent persons. Similarly, many issues in science reflect various mixes of costs and benefits. Some unpleasant and even dangerous subjects would not be pursued except that the possible gain to society is great. Milgram's (1963) study[3] is a case in point. Did it alert us to a potential social danger that ought to cause us some concern? What about the cost–benefit ratio of brain study? Although some benefits of understanding the operation of the brain are obvious, what about the dangers of a little knowledge, as sensationalized by Michael Crichton in the book *The Terminal Man?* Implanting devices to help someone see or hear is surely beneficial, but what if the appliance ultimately fosters even more serious deterioration in the nervous system? Investigations of the physical and psychological effects of starvation are meritorious, important, and useful, but how much should one try to persuade a volunteer to stay with such a study after nine months when the subject shows an inclination to drop out (Keyes, Brozek, Henschel, Mickelsen & Taylor, 1950)? How does one balance the costs to monkeys against the benefits derived from the oral Sabin vaccine for polio?

Increasingly, the needs of society influence the nature of the questions attacked by science. Each society has a need to defend itself, so we have research on the development of more deadly (more efficient) weaponry and ever more virulent strains of bacteria. Each society has a need to feed itself, so we have research on undersea farms and new frost-resistant varieties of wheat going hand-in-hand with the development of safer and more effective population control techniques, including abortion. Society has a need for more energy, so researchers strive to locate and discover new sources of energy and to use existing sources more efficiently, even though this may result in oil spills and other forms of pollution that conservationists deplore.

Are the disadvantages (costs) of such research outweighed by the advantages—the greater good for the greater number? Calculation of the total cost–benefit ratio for any of the preceding is a complex, subjective, and incomplete process—never definitive, only suggestive—and the resultant ratio figure may well differ from one calculator to another.

[3]The authors are indebted to Dr. J. Jenkins for his contributions to the analysis of this issue.

Consensus of judgments as to the ethicality of a particular piece of research is understandably hard to achieve.

SCIENCE, GOVERNMENT, AND LAW

As participants in one of society's most powerful, prestigious institutions, as creators of truth and practitioners of objectivity, scientific disciples understandably appropriated the development, application, and enforcement of ethical standards in research to themselves. Preferring to regulate their disciplines internally, scientists assumed responsibility for the maintenance of high standards and handled contraventions of ethical codes in-house. Current trends suggest that these functions may be usurped by government and the courts.

Confronted with essentially unresolvable disputes, social scientists appear to be stepping smartly along in the footprints of the physicians as they search for clarification, not of the moral or ethical bases of their research, but of its legal ramifications and possible liability threats (Nash, 1975; Silverman, 1975). Increasing consumer sophistication regarding the limits of scientific methods and the relativity of the truth product, combined with a clearer articulation and emphasis on human rights, has generated a less gullible, less deferent, less tolerant public. So, there is greater readiness to bring the scientist to task (through litigation) for infringement of civil liberties, for damages resulting from negligence and the like.

The escalating costs of scientific research, much of it funded from taxpayer coffers, legitimize government's demand for more public accountability while the tentacles of legal and governmental systems scoop up more and more of the ethical issues heretofore residing in the private domain (invasion of privacy; breach of confidentiality; information access; animal care). The erosion of public confidence in scientific ideals, as well as public attitudes of skepticism or cynicism as a consequence of exposure to science's seamy side—its dirty laundry—accelerates these trends.

Erroneous scientific findings stemming from chance factors are to be expected; those resulting from the practice of poor science (based on ignorance of proper methodology) may be forgiven. More heinous, however, are the sins of misconduct (cutting corners and misrepresentation) and fraud (fabricating results with the intent to deceive).

Trust in the honesty of research colleagues remains a cornerstone of science. To be tricked by capricious chance is frustrating enough; to be tricked by a sneaky colleague is intolerable.

Recently, evidence has surfaced suggesting that a famous British psychologist, Sir Cyril Burt, fabricated data linking IQ to heredity (Eysenck, 1979; Kamin, 1981). Burt, on whose work Jensen relied heavily, estimated that intelligence level was determined 80 percent by heredity and only 20 percent by environment.

The evidence of fraud is indicated on two counts. First, Burt reported data from sources that now appear to be imaginary or nonexistent—nonexistent theses and research reports. Second, Burt reported identical correlations for supposedly different pieces of research. Since identical results rarely arise from different samples, it would appear that Burt didn't bother calculating new correlation coefficients on the basis of new data but merely used correlations computed on earlier data.

Currently, the debate rages hot and heavy as to whether the evidence proves fraud or is merely an indication of sloppiness and aging on Burt's part. Regardless of the debate's eventual outcome, it raises at least two important issues for us. In the first place, the intensity of the debate provides a current example of how sensitive scientists are to charges of fraud against one of their own number, of how such charges threaten the integrity of science. In the second place, this debate also provides an example of how scientists, in protecting themselves against chance, also defend themselves against fraud. You will recall that the best way to increase confidence that your findings are reliable is to use large samples and to publish your procedures and findings so that others can check your results.

Fortunately, the hypothesis that intelligence has a large genetic component does not rest on Burt's work alone. A variety of studies by other investigators also support the hypothesis that IQ and inheritance are significantly related (Rimland & Munsinger, 1977). Had such independently arrived-at data not been available, the current debate would be even more acrimonious.

Although we would like to believe that fraud and data "diddling" are rare, Dr. Jerome Jacobstein suspects that as much as 25 percent of published work may be based on fudged data (cited in Stewart, 1989); Walter Stewart, the self-proclaimed vigilante of the science world, reports receipt of about 100 allegations of misconduct a year (Stewart, 1989); an Australian researcher "estimates that for every formal accusation of fraud, there are up to 1000 cases that go undiscovered or are ignored" (Birenbaum, 1992, p. 8).

Although Nobel Laureate John Polanyi (1989) places his confidence in the peer review process as science's quality control mechanism, Stewart remains unconvinced of the effectiveness of peer adjudication in protecting science from the offenses of misconduct and fraud. As a case in point, he cites John Darsee's work published in the prestigious *New England Journal of Medicine*. A genealogy was presented in the paper in which a 17-year-old was listed as having four children, one an 8-year-old daughter! Stewart's painstaking investigation of the work of Darsee and colleagues revealed that 35 of Darsee's 47 co-authors had engaged in unacceptable scientific practices. Or, consider the case of the American historian Jayme Aaron Skolow who plagiarized assorted books, articles, and theses on European and American history (Birenbaum, 1992).

Similar examples can be found in the *Casebook on Ethical Principles of Psychologists* (American Psychological Association, 1987). Two of the many cases which, upon investigation, revealed evidence of unethical behavior, are presented below. In each instance, the Ethics Committee ruled in favor of the complainant, and the maximum sanction of expulsion from the Association was imposed.

> Several faculty members at a foreign university reviewed a colleague's publications in connection with his promotion review, and found that a number of the papers he had published in their native language appeared to be nearly verbatim plagiarisms of articles and book chapters published elsewhere in English. (p. 7)
> The chair of a university-sponsored research committee became suspicious of a lengthy vita presented by a psychologist in connection with her application for a sabbatical travel grant. Upon investigation, the chair found that more than half of the nearly 80 articles listed in the vita had never been published and filed a complaint against the psychologist with the Ethics Committee. (p.8)

Material presented in this chapter not only underscores the need for ethical standards, but also reveals great variability in adherence and/or effectiveness of enforcement. Although dismissal from one's collegial network (as represented by learned society affiliation) is unpleasant and may have deleterious effects of some magnitude on career prospects, the justice system brandishes significantly more potent sanctions. In what is perhaps the first case of criminal charges springing from the falsification of research results, psychologist Stephen Breuning (who falsified medical research involving the effects of behavioral-control drugs on the severely retarded) pleaded guilty to two counts of fraud. This plea carries a maximum penalty of 10 years in prison and $20,000 in fines (Bales, 1988). Government agencies are also biting off a chunk of the action with the recent creation of two offices to prevent and investigate scientific fraud and misconduct (Adler, 1989). So, increasingly, the policing of scientific research leaks out of the hands of the scientists to be sucked up by government and the legal system.

SUMMARY

What is considered to be ethical behavior varies from culture to culture and from time to time, as does compliance with whatever codes are in vogue. Although a given group may be able to agree on a set of ethical principles, it is much more difficult to agree on whether a given principle has been breached in a particular case. Increasingly, government regulations and formal legal criteria and processes are supplementing the self-imposed standards of conduct and enforcement procedures adopted by scientists.

EXAMPLE

THE FREEMAN AFFAIR

An article, published in 1990 in the *Canadian Journal of Physics* (CJP), authored by Dr. Gordon Freeman entitled, "Kinetics of Nonhomogeneous Processes in Human Society: Unethical Behaviour and Societal Chaos," has aroused considerable consternation in the science community (e.g., Crease, 1992; Lees, cited in Freeman, 1991; Stark-Adamac, 1993; Zimmerman, 1993) and elsewhere (Strauss, 1991; Wolfe, 1991, 1992). In his provocative treatise, Dr. Freeman, a university chemistry professor, argues that mothers who participate in the paid labor force are responsible for most social ills—from murder, mayhem, and corrupt politics to drug taking and student cheating. The methodology employed in this purportedly sociological study is essentially unsystematic casual observation (see Chapter 1). Guinan (1992), noting that Freeman has failed to provide precise data in support of this thesis, comments,

> The author explains that the study involves "about 1,300 students" and "people outside the university" and 2,500 "student controls." The methods for determining sample size, enrolling subjects, or collecting and analyzing data are not described. No data are given on either the number of subjects with mothers who did or did not work or the number of subjects who cheated on exams. It is impossible to determine whether data was [*sic*] collected systematically or whether the analysis is sound, since no data or analysis are presented. Significantly, no criteria are given for determining cheaters and noncheaters. (p. 113)

Ironically, given that Freeman is concerned about the ubiquitousness of unethical behavior among university students, there appears to be a serious breach of ethics in his own work. Objecting to the artificiality of experiments and surveys, Freeman reports that he collected information unobtrusively. This raises the question of whether Dr. Freeman informed his subjects that they were in fact participating in a research study.

Despite the lack of supporting data or citation of corroborating research in the social science literature, Dr. Freeman proposes dramatic social actions based on the presumed confirmation of his thesis. For example, he advocates substantial tax credits for families in which one parent does not work outside the home, a reduction in tax credits for day care expenses in the case of dual-career families, and discouragement of the creation of on-site day care centers by businesses.

How did this article which is not physics, indeed, not science, come to appear in CJP? Dr. Freeman was the guest editor for this particular issue of the journal that was to contain the proceedings of the first International Conference on Kinetics of Nonhomogeneous Processes. Was the Freeman paper presented at the conference? No, it was not. Did this work pass the scrutiny of any ethics review committee? Apparently not. Had the CJP editorial advisory board been consulted concerning publication of this controversial article? No, again, although the regular editor of the journal, Dr. Ralph Nicholls, claims that the paper was subjected to peer review and a favorable evaluation received. However, he refuses to provide a copy of the assessment (even with identifying information deleted) to the journal's editorial advisory board. Does this article meet the criteria for scientific publication? Again, we must, in agreement with Zimmerman (1993), conclude no. It does not constitute a significant contribution to the discipline; it is not based on sound methodological or conceptual foundations; it does not use careful and appropriate data analysis procedures to support conclusions.

Following publication, letters expressing reactions to the Freeman article descended on the author, the journal editor (Dr. Nicholls), members of the editorial advisory board, and the editor-in-chief of the National Research Council (NRC) Journals (B. P. Dancik). As a consequence of detailed critical analysis and widespread disapprobation, the editor-in-chief, Bruce Dancik, published the following retraction: "This article does not comprise science and has no place in a scientific journal. The National Research Council Research Journals and the Editor of the *Canadian Journal of Physics* regret that this article was published." Still unexplained are the procedural irregularities surrounding the publication. Nor was there assurance that steps would be implemented to reduce further harm (e.g., citation of the article as if it were a scholarly piece of research) or to ensure that such an embarrassment would not be repeated. Hence, protests such as the following resolution passed by the Royal Society of Canada continued unabated.

> The Royal Society of Canada, which is strongly committed to the advancement of women in scholarship, hereby expresses its censure of the *Canadian Journal of Physics*. In publishing the article by Gordon R. Freeman, "Kinetics of nonhomogeneous processes in human society: Unethical behaviour and societal chaos," (*Canadian Journal of Physics*, 68: 794–798 (1990)), it displayed a lapse of editorial and scientific responsibility. The article is devoid of scientific content and the title is inappropriate and misleading. The *Canadian Journal of Physics* failed to publish a timely and adequate retraction. The Royal Society of Canada deplores both the insult to working mothers and the denigration of their children implicit in the published article.

Subsequent responses of NRC constituted more fulsome efforts to redress the damage—i.e., publication of a supplement issue to CJP containing commentary solicited from the social science community; organization of a symposium on ethical issues associated with publication practices; greater efforts to ensure representation of women in editorial posts; initiation of a number of formal publication policies; and review of current procedures involved in the publication process for the NRC Research Journals.

The issue here is not whether Professor Freeman's views are accurate, nor is there any quarrel with his right to share his perceptions. It is his abuse of his editorial and professional privileges and obligations that constitutes ethical contravention. Personal bias and prejudice must not be paraded under the guise of legitimate social science research.

REVIEW QUIZ

True or False?

1. Interest in ethical issues vis-à-vis science has waned in recent times.
2. There is a remarkable homogeneity or uniformity cross-culturally in ethical standards.
3. A key reason for designing and encouraging adoption of a code of ethics is to inflict or impose our current sense of values on our colleagues.
4. As a research assistant in a large research project, Psychometrist T. Y. is employed by the inner-city elementary school system to administer intelligence tests to pupils who are not performing at an acceptable level. T. Y. reports back to each tested student's teacher the following information: the child's IQ score, items on which the child did poorly, items or subtests completed at a satisfactory level, and the child's demeanor in the test situation. T. Y.'s behavior is unethical.
5. The approval of a research project by an ethics review committee does not absolve the researcher from soliciting other independent assessments of the ethical issues involved.
6. In the Milgram (1963) study involving administration of shocks by a "teacher" subject to a "learner" stooge, the subject debriefing procedure would effectively alleviate any potentially harmful effects resulting from participation in the research.
7. Informed consent is generally obtained from subjects participating in field experiments.
8. Except in extreme cases, we lack uniformity of judgment as to whether an individual study contains a breach of ethics.
9. Most animals used in research are expressly bred for this purpose.
10. Concern about animal rights and their abrogation in research is a relatively new phenomenon.
11. One survey has revealed that one out of seven graduate psychology departments that used to maintain animal facilities have abandoned animal work.
12. A decline in the number of faculty and students engaged in animal work has been observed in the United Kingdom.
13. Experiments involving deception appear to be decreasing.
14. When conditions of informed consent are instituted, fewer individuals agree to participate in the research.
15. Sir Cyril Burt apparently cited data from sources that do not exist.
16. One researcher, Dr. Jerome Jacobstein, estimates that as much as 75 percent of published work may be based on fudged data.
17. Although the Freeman study meets the criteria for scientific publication, given its sociological orientation, it was inappropriately published in the *Canadian Journal of Physics*.

❧ 14 ❧
Research Report Writing

─────── **Chapter Goal** ───────

To provide you with a standard organizational plan for the structuring of research reports.

One should always gear one's writing to fit the audience. Dr. Figmund Sreud's article in *Psychology Today* is very different from the paper he published in the *Journal of Experimental Psychology*, because the former is intended for a lay audience, while the latter is designed to inform and impress fellow researchers. The rules for popular writing about the social sciences are probably not unlike the rules for accurate journalism, and indeed most of the interpretations of scientific data for the public are relegated by default to the nonscientist. Taken in the aggregate, scientists are appallingly bad writers—technically unimpeachable but about as interesting as watching paint dry. A typical scientist has an unerring ability to take the most fascinating discovery and milk the intrigue and wonder out of it, leaving an empty husk. Notable exceptions exist, of course, such as Isaac Asimov, B. F. Skinner, J. B. Watson, Margaret Mead and a few others. Caution, pedantry, and the demands for objectivity, once ingrained, are difficult to shed.

The following report form is based in part on the specifications laid down in 1983 by the American Psychological Association (APA) for papers submitted to its journals.[1] Although originally designed by and for psychologists, the APA model has been adopted by a number of social science disciplines (e.g., anthropology, sociology, nursing, and criminology) and is increasingly becoming an accepted standard format for articles, papers, reports, and texts. This comprehensive document covers

───────

[1]Other sources which the novice report writer may find useful include: Alsip and Chezik (1974), Anderson (1966), Becker (1986), and Lester (1976).

virtually all aspects of manuscript preparation from size of margins to appropriate abbreviations. Additional materials available from the association intended to assist in mastering the APA style include an *Instructor's Resource Guide* (Gelfand & Walker, 1990a) and a training guide and workbook for students (Gelfand & Walker, 1990b). These detailed format specifications may appear compulsive and arbitrary—and they are. Their nuisance value, however, is undoubtedly outweighed by the advantages accruing from uniformity. It is much easier to extract information from a report whose organization follows a set pattern; such organization, moreover, expedites evaluation of the reports by an editor or professor. Furthermore, in a literature search one can determine the relevance of a piece of research to one's particular interest much more rapidly and locate desired information more quickly in papers that are organized the same way and written in a similar style.

LANGUAGE AND STYLE

A crude autopsy performed on the corpus—research report—reveals that the cause of death is style, not structure; so let us deal with that agent first. The main characteristics of scientific writing style are precision, terseness, and impersonality—all of which combine to produce unambiguous prose. A statement is precise if its implications are eminently clear—if it says one thing and no other. To report that the subjects in the study were relatives of the experimenter is not only bad methodology but is also vague. Are they siblings, parents, cousins, great-aunts, or what? Many statements that pass by unnoticed in the course of normal conversation would be unacceptable in a scientific paper because they are open to a variety of interpretations. Consider your responses and those of a sample of your friends to the following statements and related questions:

"Uncle Fred is a moderate smoker." How many cigarettes does he smoke in a day?

"Senator Fogbound won his seat in the recent election by an overwhelming majority." What percentage of the vote did he get?

"Ms. Simon is a middle-aged woman." How old is she?

"Aryn read several books last summer." How many books did Aryn read?

"Kyra bought an inexpensive outfit." How much did it cost?

It is apparent that the words *moderate, overwhelming, middle-aged, several*, and *inexpensive* mean different things to different people. Researchers try to avoid ambiguity in their report writing; otherwise their research is not public and shareable, and the scientists find themselves operating at the pragmatic level of language.

A statement is terse if it is economical, if it does not waste words. The aim is to be pithy, to maximize the amount of information per word, and to avoid the kind of redundancy exemplified in this sentence. Since scientists do not have to entertain, but aim only to educate or inform, the need for flowery descriptions is reduced; it is compensated for, to some extent, by the demands of caution. Rarely can researchers make a definitive statement in unequivocal terms about the implications of their findings. The world is filled with reasonable alternative explanations for the same set of data, and even with the admonition to be brief, some of those alternatives must be presented for the reader's consideration.

Researchers are increasingly being exhorted to avoid the use of sexist and ethnically biased language. Employment of unbiased, nonsexist language leads to greater precision (more semantics, less pragmatics) and avoids inadvertent implicit evaluation. To illustrate the latter, consider the phrase "culturally deprived." Use of this term to describe one group of subjects (without supporting data) suggests that there is a universally accepted cultural standard against which others are judged. Similarly, reference to a society as "primitive" is not only imprecise but also carries a negative connotation.

The most common form of sexist language is found in the inappropriate use of generic nouns and pronouns (e.g., use of "man" to mean humans or persons or males and females, "mailman" instead of letter carrier, "he" to mean he and she, etc.). Generic forms are frequently inaccurate and create ambiguity with regard to the referent. APA recommends the use of plural forms or "he or she." Other variants of the sexist use of language occur with nonparallel constructions (e.g., man and wife, instead of husband and wife) and stereotypic depictions (e.g., an aggressive business man and a pushy business woman). Several additional examples of sexist language are presented in Chapter 15.

STRUCTURE

In addition to stylistic qualities there are structural features shared by most scientific writing. In psychology the typical research paper consists of the following sections appearing in the order listed: title, author's name and institutional affiliation, *abstract, introduction, method, results, discussion, references*, and when appropriate, an *appendix*. Each of the main content sections is described in more detail below. Other disciplines may employ a slightly different format, which can be revealed by a quick look through a few recent periodicals.

Abstract

The abstract is written mainly for the benefit of the researcher who is scanning the literature in search of information germane to the researcher's own work, and it is most helpful, therefore, if the abstract is brief and summarizes the study accurately. Resemblance of the abstract to the main text is essential, not coincidental; the abstract is a faithful summary of the report, so it should not include any new material.

The abstract should describe the hypothesis, together with a brief description of the variables under investigation. The apparatus or measurement devices should be alluded to, and the procedure should be described in general terms. The results and their evaluation should be summarized briefly, while the conclusions based upon them should be listed in more detail.

Introduction

The introduction should outline the purpose of the research and describe in general terms the nature of the problem under study. A few closely related previous experiments should be cited, and any findings directly pertinent to the study should be described. Any expectations or biases (predictions) you have about how the study will turn out (derived from past research, a theory, or a personal hunch) should be specified and a rationale (theoretical background) provided.

Method

The method portion of a research paper is typically subdivided into three units: (1) subjects, (2) apparatus and materials, and (3) procedure. This section is analogous to recipe instructions and clearly describes what was done and how it was done. It is the empirical cornerstone of your work.

Subjects   This label does not refer to the issues covered by your study, but rather to the people or animals or organizations who participated—who provided you with the information to answer (it is hoped) your initial question. To bake this research cake, the following ingredients in varying amounts are required:

1. How many subjects are in your sample?
2. What are the characteristics of your sample on relevant variables (sex, age, socioeconomic class, diagnosis, education)?
3. How did you obtain your sample (by asking for volunteers, conscripting friends, or what?)?
4. If you divided your subjects into groups, on what basis was this done (at random, by age, or how?)?
5. How many subjects are in each group?
6. How many potential subjects were contacted in total?
7. How many refused to participate?

It is also important to note adherence to ethical principles in the treatment of the subjects (see Chapter 13).

Apparatus and/or materials　A brief description of each piece of apparatus employed should be presented; but if the apparatus has been described in the literature, a reference to this description will suffice. If you have specially constructed apparatus, use a labeled diagram or photograph. Include a brief description of each kind of material employed (questionnaires, tests, inventories, tasks, drawings, photographs). The identification of those tests or tasks constitutes the operational definition of the dependent measure. If you are measuring the anxiety level of your subjects, you may operationalize the concept *anxiety* by employing a commonly used test such as the Taylor Manifest Anxiety Scale (Taylor, 1953). For certain kinds of reports (theses, but not manuscripts), a copy or example of each type of material should be presented in an appendix. To continue the cookbook analogy, this section refers to the designated oven heat, kind of cake pan, and so on.

Procedure　In this unit of the report, instructions are provided for the treatment of the ingredients (fold in the egg whites; boil the syrup mixture till it forms a hard ball; mix at medium speed for two minutes with a portable mixer). Describe what you did with your subjects in sufficient detail so that your study could be duplicated exactly by someone unfamiliar with the research area. One approach is to describe what happened chronologically as the typical subjects performed in the study.

Everything that was done that might *reasonably* have had a bearing on the outcome of a study should be mentioned. While it is probably unnecessary to inform the reader of the experimenter's items of apparel, other unprogrammed events may be quite relevant. Consider, for example, the following project. A study was being conducted to determine the effects of arousal (administration of shock) on speed of recognition of unfamiliar words. In order to ensure that the subjects were actually aroused, heart rate was continuously monitored. To obtain heart rate recordings, electrodes were strapped to each leg. As the male subjects entered the laboratory, they were instructed by a glamorous female experimenter to "Please roll up your pants and pull down your socks," so as to ready the legs for electrode placement. After about 150 repetitions of these instructions, the experimenter flubbed thoughtlessly by saying, "Roll up your socks and pull down your pants, please." Experimenter and subjects alike were of little research value for the next few minutes. This event could well have influenced the performance of this particular group of subjects. Subject instructions should be paraphrased in the procedure and quoted verbatim in an appendix, if an appendix is allowed.

Results

Describe how you scored or coded and analyzed your data. Present the results of your significant analyses in clearly labeled tables or figures. Describe each result verbally, but do not repeat information that is already provided in tables or graphs. Analyses that do not yield statistically significant results should be mentioned, but tables illustrating such nonsignificant findings are typically omitted or placed in an appendix.

Discussion

Here the results are interpreted in relation to the problem under investigation. Some reference should be made to their reliability, and their limitations should be explained. Aspects of the procedure that might profitably be changed if the study were repeated should be mentioned. Uncontrolled and/or confounded variables should be identified if possible, and ways of avoiding them on subsequent occasions should be suggested. Something should be said about the extent to which the results jibe with expectations or predictions and about their agreement or disagreement with the results of previous similar experiments, as well as about their integration with relevant theory. Finally, indicate what conclusions you can draw on the basis of your study and what the practical implications of your results are.

References

In order to report your references correctly, you need to be a trifle compulsive because the rules and rituals associated with this component of scientific writing tend to be "nit-picky." References are listed alphabetically according to the author's surname. The year of publication (in brackets), and the title of the article, chapter, or book follows the author's or authors' names; then the source of the item (periodical name and volume number) is provided. For the appropriate detailed format in listing references, refer to the *Publication Manual* of the American Psychological Association (1983). References cited in the body of the report require only author identification and year of publication at the point in the text where the reference is made. To illustrate, "Anderson (1990) found that . . . ," or, "It was found that . . . (Anderson, 1990)."

Appendix

As a crude rule of thumb, include in an appendix any materials which, while important, are not crucial to a general understanding of the study and which, if included in the main body of the report, would be distracting to the reader. Students conducting a research project to fulfill thesis requirements are typically encouraged to err on the side of overinclusion and to provide copies of all tests, questionnaires, exercises, and the like, as well as tables of mean scores for every measure; in extreme cases a supervisor may even request the incorporation of raw data. Manuscripts prepared for publication in a journal, on the other hand, rarely include an appendix.

PUBLICATION POLLUTION

Like the spread of the dandelions, the social science literature proliferates at an alarming rate. The pressure to publish, as a means of attaining job security, status, or even a form of immortality, plagues us all. To cope with the burgeoning mass of articles, new journals are spawned, and into their hungry maws pour tons of tasty manuscripts. To illustrate the point: almost 1000 journals publishing material related to psychology are reviewed by *Psychological Abstracts*. As a conservative estimate perhaps another 500 periodicals exist that also contain articles of psychological content. If each journal contains about 35 articles per volume, over 50,000 psychology articles are published annually. And we haven't even mentioned the book or thesis markets. (See Miller (1991) for a guide to major journals in the social sciences.)

Under such conditions quality control becomes a critical problem. Journal editors, far from infallible, are ill equipped to deal with the multitude of papers that flood in daily. Most sophisticated researchers are aware that a negative judgment about publication from one journal needn't mean automatic rejection from others. A rejected manuscript is typically shipped off, often without revision, to the next most prestigious periodical, until the goal of publication is attained.

From the point of view of the reader, this cancerous body of literature is overwhelming. What a puerile hope to keep abreast of new developments in the field! What an idyllic fancy to assume that key studies, the classic papers, will be easy to identify! Naturally mechanisms to assist the harassed researcher have emerged. Special journals provide summaries of articles (*Psychological Abstracts, Dissertation Abstracts*), reviews of current research (*Annual Review of Psychology*), reviews of recent texts (*Contemporary Psychology*), theme articles that review the literature on a given topic (*Psychological Review, Psychological Bulletin*). In addition, computer programs now permit extremely rapid search of selected literature for specific content areas and spew out abstracts of all articles caught in the scan. As a function of the information overload, scientists must rely increasingly on summaries of research and on secondary sources.

How are we to manage this information overload? Perhaps we should propose a kind of eugenics program urging voluntary sterilization (no publication) on 50 percent of the social science labor force— selected at random, of course. Or maybe a technological device would be more effective—every second article self-destructs after five years. Or only a random sample of submitted acceptable manuscripts would be published. More realistically, but smacking of censorship, a central clearinghouse coordinating all publication vehicles might prevent the shopping around for acceptance by the repeatedly rejected manuscripts described earlier. But under such a radical scheme, we might have missed the contributions of Einstein and Skinner. In the absence of any of these radical procedures, you might pause and consider before adding your personal building blocks to the tower of Babel and then add only your "best" blocks.

SUMMARY

Like a recipe, a research report rests on clarity of procedure and reliability of results. The cornerstone of the research report is the *Method* section where the researcher describes, in unambiguous terms, the subjects, apparatus or materials, and procedure.

The acid test becomes: "Are my instructions so clear that another investigator can duplicate my procedure?"

Did you ask a "significant" question? Did you obtain "important" results? Only time will tell.

EXAMPLE

We provide here a sample of student report writing to illustrate the procedures outlined in this chapter.

ESP ABILITY AMONG BELIEVERS AND NONBELIEVERS

Abstract

Using Zener cards extrasensory ability was compared between five couples who believed they possessed extrasensory powers and five couples who did not. While there was no clear difference between believers and nonbelievers, there was a trend favoring believers, some of which was due to cheating.

Introduction

This pilot study was designed to explore the hypothesis that people who believe they possess extrasensory perception (ESP) obtain a higher number of "hits" in a standard ESP test situation than do nonbelievers.

Rhine and Pratt (1957) report some evidence that believers (sheep) perform better than nonbelievers (goats). However, there are major problems with much of the evidence supporting the reality of ESP.

First, much of the evidence is anecdotal and based on "after-the-fact" information and so is open to the usual criticism aimed at this primitive research method. For example, a person will hear that a relative died and then recall that they had dreamed about that person the night before. Such evidence is open to serious question because believers are probably more likely to report such incidents than nonbelievers and perhaps may even be inclined, unwittingly, to create or modify memories designed to support the cause for ESP. Also such after-the-fact data fail to include the "false-positives"—that is, the number of occasions when you dreamed a relative was ill and in fact was not.

Finally, much of the evidence or data is vague enough to be interpreted several ways. For example, if you dream there is "something wrong" with a relative and then check to see if he or she is having trouble, you can usually find that he or she is, because everybody always has some trouble.

In view of the many difficulties involved in interpreting after-the-fact data about ESP, this study uses the more powerful control-group model to compare ESP performance among believers and nonbelievers.

Method

Subjects. The subjects of this study were volunteers from an introductory psychology class, 10 of whom claimed to be believers in ESP because of personal experience with it and 10 of whom claimed to be nonbelievers with no personal ESP experience. The members of each group were organized into pairs, one member of each pair designated at random as the sender and the other as the receiver.

Materials. The test materials were standard Zener cards used at Duke University specifically for ESP research. Each card has one of five geometric figures printed on it; the deck consists of 25 cards, with each figure appearing five times in random order.

Procedure. Each pair of believers and each pair of nonbelievers completed 50 ESP trials. Believer and nonbeliever pairs were tested alternately so that the four rogue suspects (Agnew & Pyke, 1991) would not favor one group over another. The procedure for each pair of subjects was as follows:

1. The sender was seated in one room and the receiver in an adjoining room with an experimenter present in each room.

2. The experimenter in the sender room shuffled the deck of Zener cards and without looking at it handed the top card to the sender, who concentrated on the geometric figure appearing on it for 15 seconds. The end of this period was signaled by a bell.

3. At the sound of the bell, the receiver indicated on the report sheet which of the five symbols he or she believed was being sent. The card was returned to the experimenter who recorded it on the record sheet, then reinserted it into the deck and reshuffled the deck. This procedure was repeated until 50 such trials had been completed, after which the number of hits was calculated, the subjects informed of the results, and all were thanked for their cooperation. During the trials there was no visual contact between the sender and the receiver; experimenters were on the lookout for any sound signal codes the sender might be using. The sender was instructed not to speak during the trials.

Results

Table 14–1 represents the number of hits out of the 50 trials obtained by each pair of believers and by each pair of nonbelievers.

Since each receiver has a one-fifth chance of being right on any given guess by chance alone, we would expect the average receiver, without ESP ability, to make approximately 10 hits. According to Guilford (1965), 16 or more hits would rarely occur by lucky guessing—would occur only 5 times in 100 tests like ours. As can be seen, only Pair 3 among the believers reached this significant level of performance; they achieved 19 hits. Pair 5 among the nonbelievers approached this significant level with 14 hits.

TABLE 14–1   Number of Hits Out of 50 Trials for Believing and Nonbelieving Pairs in an ESP Study

Subject Pairs	Believers	Nonbelievers
Pair 1	11	8
Pair 2	9	10
Pair 3	19	7
Pair 4	12	11
Pair 5	11	14
TOTAL	62	50

Overall, the believers achieved more hits than the nonbelievers did.

Discussion

While this pilot study provided no conclusive evidence in support of the hypothesis that believers possess more ESP ability than do nonbelievers, it *appeared* to provide a bit of encouraging evidence. One pair of believers did perform significantly better than we would have expected by chance alone, and the overall trend favored the believers.

In ESP studies questions concerning unwitting sensory signaling arise, as do questions of cheating. During the experiment no evidence of either was detected.

However, after the experiment was completed, it was disclosed that the high-scoring pair of subjects had, in fact, cheated, with the help of one of the instructors. The cheating pair used a disarmingly simple plan based on the sender arriving at the experiment coughing and blowing his nose. Therefore the experimenters were not suspicious when he coughed and blew his nose periodically during the experiment. By prior agreement when a particular geometric figure appeared, he would merely cough, thus signaling to the receiver that the figure was before him. Consequently, the receiver got all appearances of that card correct, plus another 9 hits by lucky guessing, giving him an unusually large and significant score. While this deception led to some bitterness, it served to underline the care that must be taken in interpreting experimental results, particularly when the experimenters themselves are believers.

References

Agnew, N. McK., & Pyke, S. W. (1991). *The science game: An introduction to research in the behavioral sciences* (4th ed.) Englewood Cliffs, NJ: Prentice Hall.

Guilford, J. P. (1965). *Fundamental statistics in psychology and education*. New York: McGraw-Hill.

Rhine, J. G., & Pratt, J. G. (1957). *Para-psychology*. Springfield, IL: Charles C. Thomas.

Instructor's Comments

This is an interesting pilot study in which you introduced yourselves to the topic of ESP and gained a feel for some of the problems and possibilities involved in testing for ESP effects.

Some of the terms used in the introduction require more detailed elaboration. For example, what is the definition of a "hit" and why are believers called "sheep" and nonbelievers, "goats"? There seems to be an assumption in the introduction that there is no question about the existence of ESP. You should have indicated that this is still an open question and you should have cited additional references.

Your experimental procedures suggest that ESP can be turned on and off like a tap in 15-second spurts. Is that how you conceive it? Was it significant that the experimenter did not know which symbol was being sent? Why?

Learn not to waste data-gathering opportunities. You could have had sender and receiver reverse roles for another 50 trials without appreciably increasing your experimental workload but resulting in doubling your data base and also allowing individual differences among senders and receivers to express themselves.

Your bitterness over "cheating" by two of your subjects is understandable. Deception of subjects by experimenters is commonplace, and we can probably expect increasing incidents of counterdeception by subjects. Either way deception raises important methodological and ethical issues, as you have discovered first-hand. The cheating subjects should have been replaced, and their data omitted from your table and only mentioned in a footnote.

REVIEW QUIZ

True or False?

1. Scientific journal articles tend to follow a more or less consistent organizational pattern.
2. The APA has developed a comprehensive standardized set of rules for the preparation of manuscripts.
3. Scientific writing style is characterized by a significant degree of ambiguous prose.

4. Approximations of quantity (e.g., several, moderate, overwhelming) are helpful descriptors of empirical data in scientific reports.

5. Use of plural forms is recommended to replace the use of generic pronouns.

6. An abstract summarizes a report but may also include new material.

7. Predictions or hypotheses are typically presented in the "Method" section of a report.

8. A literature review typically appears in the "Results" section of a research report.

9. Typically researchers provide information about the time of day testing occurred, temperature in the laboratory, and details concerning the appearance of the experimenter in the "Procedure" section of their reports.

10. All analyses, both statistically significant and nonsignificant, must be presented in the "Results" section of the report.

11. In the "Discussion" section of a report, the results of the study are interpreted in relation to the problem under investigation.

12. Scientists increasingly rely on secondary sources.

❦ 15 ❧
Sex and Science

────────── **Chapter Goal** ──────────

*To alert the reader to the many ways in
which preconceptions, bias, or stereotypes
may exert powerful influences on the methods, data, and theories of science.*

To newborn infants the world probably appears as a buzzing confusion. With experience they discover order, manufacture it, or impose it upon multilayered nature. Similarly, adults, when confronted with new situations, experience a buzzing confusion—a lack of pattern. They, too, in time discover order or impose it on the unfamiliar city, the foreign language, the strange customs, or the complicated equipment. Gradually we develop simple maps inside our heads. The more complex the situation, the more we must rely on these oversimplified maps or theories of what leads to what. Such theories must be oversimplified because we can't begin to attend to or remember the multifaceted world and its myriad of shifting parts.

Not only are theories or models useful means of summarizing and bringing order into what has happened or what is happening, but they also help us make predictions that allow us to walk into the future with some degree of confidence, however ill-founded that confidence may be.

While we saunter into the unknown, however, we would do well to remember that nature doesn't come prepackaged in neat and tidy bundles. The structures, taxonomies, classifications, and processes identified and labeled by science are the artificial creations of thought, designed to make sense of our imperfectly perceived experience. Don't confuse such created or imposed packaging of the universe with the universe itself (Bleier, 1984).

In this final section we discuss how citizens and scientists wend their zigzag way through multilayered reality, with the aid of necessarily simple theories, maps, and models. An example of an organizing principle or oversimplified map familiar to most of us is a stereotype—widely shared beliefs about the characteristics of a particular group. In this chapter we describe how stereotypes about females, emerging from a patriarchal ideology (another oversimplified map), have shaped the course of science. A conception of theory as an artificial creation, as one of many possible constructions of reality, is presented in the next chapter, along with a discussion of future methodological and conceptual trends.

SCIENCE AND SYMBOLISM

At first blush, science seems to be one of the few human enterprises relatively devoid of sexual connotations. After all, science is touted as the objective search for truth (with a capital T). Scientists, as neutral, dispassionate observers, have no truck with the ardor, passion, romanticism, and political polemics permeating other less lofty human pursuits. Yet from another perspective, scientists do not so much discover truth as they construct it. Constructed truths are manufactured from the values and ideologies of the host society. And, given that our society has been guided by a patriarchal ideology for the past 6000 years, perhaps we should not be too surprised to learn that the influence of sex on science has been more ubiquitous and invidious than anyone would have supposed.

Science studies nature—physical nature, human nature—and there has always been a sexual dimension in human thought about nature. In conventional mythology, nature is typically identified as female (Merchant, 1980). Remember the margarine advertisement—"It's not nice to fool mother nature." Beyond the simple sex label, science eroticizes nature by conceptualizing her as being hidden, enclosed, and having secrets. The role of science, then, is to denude nature, to rip away her veils, to disclose her secrets. In this sense, science appears both voyeuristic and exploitative.

Linnaeus's (1707–1778) classification scheme for plants reflects the eroticization of nature in science. Of the myriad characteristics of plants that might be employed to develop a taxonomy, which did Linnaeus choose?—the stamens and pistils, the sexual parts of plants. Lascivious descriptions of Linnaeus's system appeared in the scientific literature of the day—a pansy described as a loose woman with petals gaping wantonly and pollen as titillating dust. Some scientists even attributed deviant sexual desires to women who were interested in botany.

In addition to science's erotic symbolism of nature, science also seeks to control her for she is unpredictable, wild, tumultuous, and potentially destructive. The parallel with the patriarchal view of the need to control females is obvious.

SCIENCE AND OBJECTIVITY

Just as the examples of symbolism in science reflect a prevailing cultural value (patriarchy), so too does that cherished hallmark of science—objectivity. The scientific method and its various refinements attempt to free us from the bugaboos of irrationality, emotionality, and subjectivity. Patriarchal values assert that male minds are uniquely capable of the logical, rational, objective thought required for scientific pursuits. Above all, emotional detachment is the quintessential element in scientific pursuits, and, therefore, the stereotype of women as emotionally labile fosters their exclusion from the center stage of science.

The ideology of objectivity requires the notion of a distinction between subject (the scientist) and object (that which is studied—nature). The investigator is an active agent, whereas the object is passive. Here again we pick up the scent of science as a masculine endeavor.

Finally, the objectivity principle implies an immunity and/or protection from the social/political/economic influences of society. The scientist—by virtue of natural inclinations or talents (rational mind), training (in habits of thought, critical analysis, and so forth), and appropriate use of scientific methods, techniques, and strategies— presumably can produce research free from the distorting influence of cultural values, mores, stereotypes, and similar factors. Such research should yield "pure" or absolute truth: truth uncontaminated by the cultural biases of the scientist or the scientist's society. However, Fee (1976, 1981) argues that society generates the type of scientific knowledge that best fulfills its social, economic, and political needs. Kuhn (1970) similarly suggests that our values and biases shape our knowledge of nature more than our objective observations or our rationality. Shields (1975), in a scathing indictment, contends that scientific empiricism does little more than provide a justification for prevailing social values. In a similar vein, Pyke (1982) implies that prevailing ideologies produce supporting empiricism. Bleier (1984) summarizes this position:

> Science is *not* the neutral, dispassionate, value-free pursuit of Truth . . . scientists are not objective, disinterested, or culturally disengaged from the questions they ask of nature or the methods they use to frame their answers. It is, furthermore, impossible for science or scientists to be otherwise, since science is a social activity and a cultural product created by persons who live in the world of science as well as in the societies that bred them. (Bleier, 1984, p. 193)

Can it be that a society gets the kind of science it deserves, the kind it can tolerate?

WOMEN'S ROLE IN SCIENCE

If the reader is prepared to accept (or even entertain) the assertions above that (1) the common form of social structure for humans in modern history is patriarchy; (2) ideologies vis-à-vis women and men in patriarchal social systems postulate a subordinate position for women; and (3) the processes and products of science are heavily influenced by these ideologies, then the fringe participation of women in science is easily understood.

Until recently, females have not been welcomed into science, into what was seen as an appropriately male activity. Consequently, relatively few great women appear in mainstream science. However, women are clearly visible on the periphery. For example, women frequently served as helpmates to scientist husbands, or fathers, or brothers. Carl Linnaeus's wife, Prudence, played an essential role in furthering his career by editing his work and handling his voluminous correspondence. Women also served on the fringes of science as popularizers (that is, writing science books for children) and as illustrators. Many women were active amateur scientists, particularly in the fields of botany, geology, and astronomy. Some women practiced medicine both as midwives and as local experts with specialized knowledge of the medicinal properties of plants.

Historically, however, women were excluded from institutionalized science. As science professionalized itself (through the use of Latin and the demand for particular education credentials), it became increasingly difficult for women to gain a foothold in this prestigious occupation. It was not until after World War II that the Royal Society was prepared to admit female members. White (1975) offers a more contemporary perspective, suggesting that variables such as the decreased likelihood of sponsorship, lack of role models, atypical (interrupted) career paths, and exclusion from the "old boys' network" all operate to dissuade women from careers in science. Transcending such obstacles is still no guarantee of acceptance and success. Important scientific contributions of women continue to be unrecognized or uncredited. Consider the fairly recent case of the discovery of the double helical structure of DNA. James Watson, along with Crick and Wilkins, won the Nobel prize for this work in 1962. Rosalind Franklin's unpublished crystallographic images of DNA, pirated from her locked desk without her knowledge and used by Watson and colleagues, had direct and major relevance to untangling the mysteries of DNA, yet her key contribution was never acknowledged (Sayre, 1975).

SEX BIAS IN SCIENCE

Social scientists are trained to develop certain habits of mind (critical analysis skills) and are equipped with research technologies designed to enhance the probability that social science research will reflect the principles of objectivity and impartiality. However, certain ingrained beliefs, ideas, orientations, attitudes, and habits serve as "hidden hands" molding the researcher's work. This unwitting shaping of research is certainly true of issues related to sex and gender. Indeed, the vast bulk of research and theory in social science rests on the implicit patriarchal ideology that: (1) females are different from males on most variables, (2) these differences have a biological origin, and (3) the position males hold on a variable is superior (Pyke, 1982). This androcentric bias has had an enormous impact on the production of scientific truth.

Historical Examples

Sir Francis Galton (1822–1911), considered the father of the modern study of sex differences, was firmly wedded to the view that females were inferior to (not just different from) males, not only in terms of physical traits such as strength, but also in terms of their powers of discrimination. Because he believed that sensory discriminatory ability was a valid indicator of intelligence, females were judged to be deficient in mental capacity (Buss, 1976). Galton did not confine himself to passing judgment on alleged sex differences in the physical, sensory, and ability realms; he also made some pungent remarks about personality differences. He regarded women as coy, capricious, and less straightforward than men, subject to petty deceits and allied weaknesses. As might be expected, Galton was a member of the British Anti-Suffrage Society.

Stephanie Shields (1975) provided another example of how the scientific establishment was influenced by the accepted doctrine of female inferiority. Sex differences in the localization of functions in the brain seemed a promising avenue of research. Initially, the frontal lobes were believed to be the seat of the higher functions (for example, abstract reasoning), and it was "discovered" that males had larger frontal areas whereas in females it was the parietal areas that were larger. Later, when the parietal region was thought to play a significant role in the higher functions, science reversed itself. It was then "discovered" that males had larger parietal areas whereas females had larger frontal areas. Here we have an instance of empirical findings tracking dominant social values.

More contemporary examples exist illustrating the evolution of evidence (i.e., its modification over time). Although females had long been thought to have superior verbal skills, Hyde and Linn (cited in Matlin, 1993) conducted a meta-analysis on gender differences in verbal ability and found virtually no overall difference between the sexes (an average d value of 0.11). However, they discovered that studies conducted before 1974 yielded larger gender differences than the more recent research. Have males improved their verbal competencies, or have females lost some of their edge, or both? Or, is this another instance of cultural mores influencing empiricism?

Content

Bias may also be reflected in the questions asked or research topics studied. Doherty (1973) commented on the relative dearth of empirical work on nurturance, and until quite recently, relatively little research existed on achievement motivation in women. Denmark (cited in Grady, 1981) reports that topics such as maternity, pregnancy, and sexuality are underresearched. These topics, because they pertain especially to women, are not regarded as important as are topics relevant to men. Until very recently, the subjects of sex and gender roles were ignored by most social scientists (Gray, 1977; Woolsey, 1977). Percival (1984), however, reported that the most frequently used introductory psychology texts in Canadian universities in 1981 were relatively free of sex bias.

Subject Selection

Preference for male subjects in social science research has been well documented (Carlson, 1971; Carlson & Carlson, 1960; Greenglass & Stewart, 1973; Pyke, Ricks, Stewart & Neely, 1975).

This neglect of female research participants means that we are relatively ignorant about how females would perform under these various research conditions. However, the problem is even more serious because, as Greenglass and Stewart (1973) have demonstrated, studies employing all male samples are more likely to generalize to the opposite sex than those utilizing all female subjects. Thus the scientific literature not only lacks information about women but actually perpetrates erroneous information based on the overgeneralizations from research involving men.

Theory Bias

Observations heaped on a huge table—like a bargain-basement sale—don't make a science. We rely on theories to help us select observations from the heap, link them into a pattern, and explain them. In one sense, then, a theory functions like a bias. To illustrate the biasing effects of the sorting and interpreting screens of theories, let's examine a provocative new theory—sociobiology.

Although sociobiology had many precursors—among them, Tiger's *Men in Groups* (1969), Morris's *The Naked Ape* (1967), and Ardrey's *The Social Contract* (1970)—it was E. O. Wilson who, in 1975, established sociobiology as a comprehensive and coherent theoretical position that attracted both admiration and admonition in the scientific community. In creating sociobiology—which is defined as "the systematic study of the biological basis of all forms of social behavior" (Wilson, 1975, p. 4)—

Wilson claimed that this new science subsumed or cannibalized many of the social sciences (for instance, psychology, ethology, sociology, anthropology). Parenthetically, it should be noted that Wilson, by this means, addresses the problem of the arbitrary boundaries between disciplines.

Essentially, "the basic premise of Sociobiology is that human behaviors and certain aspects of social organization have evolved, like our bodies, through adaptations based on Darwinian natural selection" (Bleier, 1984, p. 16). According to evolutionary doctrine, organisms are basically in the business of reproduction. Those organisms that survive to leave the maximum number of offspring (or other genetically related kin) are the most fit in the sense that their genetic packages remain (are well represented) in the population gene pool. These gene packages are adaptive because they are associated with maximum fitness (that is, reproductive success). *Natural selection* refers to the process whereby certain genes are progressively eliminated from the gene pool because their hosts are less fit (leave fewer progeny who carry the gene). Conversely, the representation of other genes in subsequent generations is gradually increased as a function of the reproductive success of their carriers.

From this evolutionary hub, Wilson and his colleagues extrude streamers of theoretical propositions offering genetically based explanations for (1) male sexual promiscuity, (2) altruism, (3) incest taboos, (4) warfare and aggression, (5) homosexuality, (6) ethics and morality, (7) cooperative behavior, (8) hypergamy (female tendency to marry males of higher status), (9) female infanticide, (10) smiling, (11) phobias, (12) the human sense of free will, (13) the disappearance of slavery, (14) the sexual division of labor, (15) female subordination, (16) selected religious practices, (17) private property, (18) patriarchy, (19) the family as a social structure, (20) the disappearance of the estrous cycle in females, and so forth. The handling of altruism is especially intriguing since self-sacrifice genes should have disappeared long ago from the gene pool, assuming that "self-sacrifice results in fewer descendants" (Wilson, 1978, p. 152). Wilson, observing the altruistic behavior in ants, bees, wasps, and termites, notes that the self-sacrifice evident among these social insects has the effect of protecting the other genetically related members of the colony. Hence, the genes (including those relevant to altruism) of the suicidal stinging bee are preserved in its relatives. Thus "natural selection has been broadened to include kin selection" (Wilson, 1978, p. 153).

For consumers of science, sociobiology has a seductive quality. Its comprehensiveness; its relative simplicity in terms of the reduction of complex, mystifying forms of social behavior into a fistful of basic propositions; and the personal immediacy or relevance of the phenomena under consideration combine to produce a scientific best-seller. Yet for every reader of Wilson's two volumes (1975, 1978) or Dawkins's *The*

Selfish Gene (1976), how many have read the scathing but somewhat pedantic and tedious critiques offered in Montagu (1980)? How many enthusiastic consumers have been exposed to alternate interpretations of the same evidence? Is Wilson's main appeal simplicity, buttressed with catchy anecdotal sketches of the behavior of subhuman species, or does he provide a valid and powerful insight into complex human behavior?

To dramatize the potent influence of a theoretical orientation on the selection and interpretation of observations, consider the following two excerpts from Wilson (1978) and Mackie (1983), respectively. They are both discussing the work of Money and Ehrhardt (1972). These latter authors studied 25 genetic females (XX) who were exposed prenatally to heavy doses of androgen (masculinizing hormones), which resulted in a hermaphroditic (adrenogenital syndrome) condition. Corrective genital surgery was performed and the infants were raised as females. Money and Ehrhardt compared this clinical group with a matched control group. Wilson describes this research:

> Did the girls show behavioral changes connected with their hormonal anatomical masculinization? As John Money and Anke Ehrhardt discovered, the changes were both quite marked and correlated with the physical changes. Compared with unaffected girls of otherwise similar social backgrounds, the hormonally altered girls were more commonly regarded as tomboys while they were growing up. They had a greater interest in athletic skills, were readier to play with boys, preferred slacks to dresses and toy guns to dolls. The group with the adrenogenital syndrome was more likely to show dissatisfaction with being assigned to a female role. . . .
>
> So at birth the twig is already bent a little bit—what are we to make of that? It suggests that the universal existence of sexual division of labor is not entirely an accident of cultural evolution. (Wilson, 1978, p. 132)

Mackie (1983), in summarizing the same research, reports:

> The researchers found that the fetally androgenized females were more interested in masculine clothing, games and toys. Although they regarded themselves as female, they were considered by their mothers and themselves to be tomboys. In comparison with the control group, these subjects were less interested in baby-sitting and future marriage as opposed to careers. Interestingly, no greater incidence of physical aggression was reported. Money and Ehrhardt concluded that the male sex hormone had had a masculinizing effect. However, critics point out that their behavior is within the normal range for females in our society and further, that female gender identity is not seriously disrupted by the presence of prenatal androgens. (Mackie, 1983, pp. 78–79)

In the first account of this research the meager empirical observations with their fuzzy surrounding region of doubt or area of uncertainty (see Chapter 1) are linked into an interpretive pattern supporting a genetic biological determinist position. Mackie weaves the same empirical bits into a cultural determinist tapestry. Who's right? Probably both—as a colleague remarked, "Much can be said for both sides." The point we are making is that most subsets of empirical checkpoints, given their scarcity and ambiguity, can be successfully employed to support even diametrically opposed theoretical models. Thus reliance on secondary sources is risky business indeed because the empirical data are painted (or tainted) with hues from the theoretical spectrum.

Studies reporting sex differences trigger a bias toward interpreting such differences as biological in origin (the sociobiological position) rather than as environmentally determined. Sex, after all, is a biological variable and therefore (as the reasoning goes) any observed difference between the sexes must have a biological base. Again, this bias appears in nonhuman primate studies where the tendency to ignore habitat influences on social structure and social behavior is even more pronounced (Lancaster, 1976).

Another characteristic of the androcentric bias in theory involves utilization of the male condition as the prototype. The position of males is the norm, or the natural estate, or the right condition, with women fitted into the theory later as a footnote (Leonard & Collins, 1979). As Weyant (1979) notes, behavioral scientists have often seemed incapable of viewing women except in relation to a male model.

Evaluation

To keep intact an overall frame of reference of male superiority, as dictated by patriarchal ideology, it is necessary to assume that sex or gender differences exist on many dimensions, that males outperform females on most dimensions, and that those areas where females obtain higher scores or show higher levels of functioning are of lesser importance (i.e., the skills are devalued). In essence, whatever males are better at is better than what females are better at (the evaluation bias). Evidence is rapidly accumulating that the first assumption lacks support—women and men are very similar in their cognitive abilities and where reliable differences occur, they are so small as to be of no practical significance. However, Favreau (1977) provides us with a somewhat dated example of the operation of a bias in evaluation, taken from the work of Broverman, Klaiber, Kobayashi, and Vogel (1968). These authors developed a theory that led them to predict that females should excel only on simple tasks. How can they accommodate this view to the fact that women are superior linguistically? They argue that because verbal skills require extensive prior practice, only minimal involvement of the higher cognitive processes is necessary. Hence, language, perhaps the most distinctive accomplishment of human evolution, is alleged to require only minimal cognitive involvement, in order to maintain the patriarchal ideology that females are inferior (Favreau, 1977; Pyke, 1982).

Implicit differential evaluations may also be reflected in our choice of concept labels. For example, the psychological concept of field independence/dependence refers to an individual's propensity to perceive figures embedded in a surrounding field versus perception of the overall pattern (rather than the abstraction of embedded segments). Guess which sex tends to respond to the field, rather than the figure? (Answer: females.) Equally appropriate descriptors, but with reverse evaluative connotations, are communicated by the concept labels of context awareness versus context insensitivity or blindness (Eichler, 1988).

Inference Bias

Bias may enter in when researchers interpret and generalize their research findings from the experimental situation to the real world. Garai and Scheinfield (cited in Favreau, 1977) report that females excel in perception of detail in tasks that require frequent shifts of attention, and females also show greater verbal fluency. Generalizing from these findings, the investigators note that these facilities make females better equipped than males for almost all secretarial skills. They fail to mention other occupations, such as law, writing, teaching, and broadcasting, for which women should be equally well suited on the basis of these two skills (Favreau, 1977).

Language Bias

One of the earliest targets, and perhaps the most successful of feminist critiques of science, was the attack on sexist language (Eichler, 1988; Favreau, 1977).

Consider the form of the following pairs of statements:

A. Color blindness occurs more frequently in males than in females.
vs.
B. Girls are more passive than boys.

A. Learning disabilities are more frequent among males than among females.
vs.
B. Girls are more dependent than boys.

A. Hyperactivity occurs more frequently in boys than in girls.
vs.
B. Girls are more verbally facile than boys.

Obviously the paired statements are not linguistically parallel forms. If we were to rephrase the first A statement above to a form analogous to its partner, we would say: "Males have poorer color vision than females." Similarly, the second A statement would be reworded as, "Males do not learn as well as females."

There is an inherent inaccuracy in the *B* statements because they seem to suggest that *all* females are more whatever than *all* males. This implication is not evident in the *A* constructions. Of particular interest is that the inaccurate *B*-type assertions are typically applied only to one sex—females.

Other forms of language bias abound in the scientific literature. Lionel Tiger provides a blatant type of labeling bias. Describing a pattern of bonding among male baboons, Tiger cites the work of DeVore and Hall, who indicate that bonded males ". . . tended to support each other in aggressive interaction with other males" (Tiger, 1969, p. 27). On the very next page, in describing comparable aggression in female baboons, Tiger says, "Two or more females commonly 'gang-up' to threaten or attack another female." (Tiger, 1969, p. 28). Thus if males exhibit this behavior, it's "cooperative bonding" and if females do it, it's "ganging-up."

Another form of labeling bias occurs when a generic form is used in contexts where it would be more accurate or precise to be sex-specific. For example, since about 95 percent of the cases of spousal abuse involve wife-battering as opposed to husband-battering, the term "spousal abuse" disguises the sex-specific nature of the phenomenon (Eichler, 1988).

Recently, some social scientists have studied the connotations of allegedly generically neutral terms such as *he, his, man*. Such terms, if the context is appropriate, are presumed to apply to both sexes. Moulton, Robinson, and Elias (1978) demonstrated that even in a neutral context such terms are typically interpreted as gender-specific—that is, as referring to males only. Silveira's (1980) review of 14 empirical studies investigating this issue supports the conclusions reached by Moulton and associates. Thus, many journal editors and text publishers have adopted a policy of using the forms *he/she* or *her/his* or plurals to indicate clearly that the statement is meant to include both sexes.

Selection and Distortion of Evidence

Many people have read or heard or believe that the following statements are scientifically validated facts:

1. Girls are more social than boys.
2. Girls are more suggestible than boys.
3. Girls have lower self-esteem than boys.
4. Boys are more analytic than girls.
5. Girls lack achievement motivation.

On the basis of a review of 1600 studies on sex differences published between 1966 and 1973, Maccoby and Jacklin (1974) concluded that these statements were unfounded. The accumulated available research evidence does not, in fact, support them, yet such conclusions continue to appear in the scientific literature and elsewhere.

Just as scientists selectively recycle subsamples of unfounded research findings that support cultural stereotypes, so, too, do they recylce *hypotheses* based on conventional wisdom (otherwise known as stereotypes). The Jensen/Rushton race research discussed in Chapter 13 is one such example; another derives from the literature on coping. One of the early taxonomies employed in the study of coping techniques involved the distinction between problem-focused coping (thought to be the preferred strategy of males) and emotionally focused coping (believed to be more common among females). Folkman and Lazarus (1980) tested this sex difference hypothesis and concluded that, contrary to stereotypic beliefs, women and men coped quite similarly and that, moreover, both forms of coping occurred in virtually every stress encounter. Although familiar with the work of Folkman and Lazarus, a number of other investigators continue to test, with limited success, the unsupported hypothesis that males and females differ in their coping strategies along the lines dictated by traditional conceptions of the sexes (Billings & Moos, 1981; Marotz-Baden & Colvin, 1986; Stone & Neale, 1984).

In some instances actual distortion of evidence may exist. Favreau (1977) cites an article by Hutt in which Hutt reports that three studies support the claim of male superiority on a particular task. However, one of these three studies does not support Hutt's position.

Statistical Bias

Many scientists use statistical techniques to help decide if their observations are worth getting excited about, or worth sharing with their colleagues. Suppose a scientist compares the performance of females and males on a perceptual restructuring task, such as identifying a simple figure hidden in a more complex pattern. The scientist's pet theory about the relationship between sex and cognitive/perceptual abilities leads him or her to suspect that the males will be superior on this task. Males obtain an average score of 15, whereas the average for females is 10. To help determine whether this difference is a "true" difference—one worth shouting about, one that supports the pet theory—the researcher submits the data to a statistical test. Statistical convention requires that the scientist start off with an assumption that the two groups do not differ—the null hypothesis. Then, statistical maneuvers are applied that provide information on the probability that the difference of 5 units is a random or chance finding. A probability level of 0.01 obtains ($p < 0.01$), which means that there is one chance in 100 that this difference of 5 units is due to sampling error or some other uncontrolled or unknown factor. Our scientist then rejects the null hypothesis and concludes that a real, authentic, true, significant difference does exist between males and females on this task. Note that the scientist could be wrong because there is still that one chance in 100 that the observed difference is artifactual.

What if the investigator had found, after application of a statistical test, a probability value of 0.15? Then our investigator knows that there are 15 chances in 100 that this difference of 5 units is due to chance. Again, by convention, this probability is regarded as too high, too risky, to permit a conclusion of a real or significant difference in performance between males and females. However, by the rules of statistics, the scientist cannot confirm the null hypothesis and conclude that he or she has discovered that males and females have similar perceptual restructuring abilities. Hence, a failure to obtain a real difference (defined as a probability of 0.05 or less) equals an ambiguous result. Returning to our discussion of sex and science, the implication is that one can never statistically "prove" that the sexes are similar, that they do not differ. Our main decision aid in science fails to help us make decisions about similarities.

Favreau (1977) describes another biasing effect of the use of statistical procedures. On a test of mathematical ability, the average score for boys was 40.39; for girls, it was 35.81. This difference proved to be significant at the 0.01 probability level. The conclusion that boys have significantly superior mathematical ability is tempting and implies that all boys perform better than all girls. Yet, as illustrated in Figure 15–1, the lowest scores in the group of boys are as low as those of the lowest girls, and the scores of the best-performing girls are as high as those of the highest boys. In essence, the use of the statistical procedure disguised the extensive overlap between the sexes on this measure of mathematical ability.

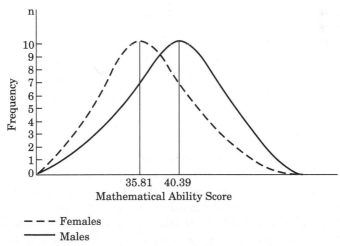

FIGURE 15–1   **Mathematical Ability Score**

Hyde (1981) provides us with another example of how ideologies, with the help of statistics, can lead us down the garden path. Maccoby and Jacklin, in the review cited earlier, identified four well-established sex differences in the psychological domain—superior verbal ability occurs more frequently in girls, whereas aggression, as well as superior visual/spatial and mathematical abilities, occur more frequently in boys. Hyde subjected the studies on which the Maccoby and Jacklin conclusions were based (excluding studies on aggression) to a meta-analysis and found that sex differences in these areas account for no more than 1 percent to 5 percent of the population variance. So, although these differences are statistically reliable and replicable, they are so small that they lack conceptual or practical significance. The bottom line with respect to the study of sex differences might well be that, "Never has so much been said by so many about so little" (Pyke, 1982).

Publication Bias

Because of the ambiguity of results that do not permit the investigator to reject the null hypothesis, many scientific journals have an explicit or implicit policy that only studies reporting statistically significant differences will be published. Consequently, many studies appear in the literature reporting "real" sex differences when, in actuality, the difference reflects that one chance in 100 that the difference is artifactual. The other 99 studies that failed to show a sex difference didn't get published. This publication bias then leads us to assume differences between the sexes where, in fact, no such differences exist (Type I error).

Journal policies may also be biased against publishing reports of sex differences that are contrary to established, accepted findings. There also seems to be an avoidance of the publication of replications—studies that try to duplicate the procedures of previously published work. Both of these factors tend to augment or exacerbate the problem of accepting as authentic those findings that are really attributable to chance. Finally, as Grady (1981) notes, journals may eschew certain research topics or content areas, regarding them as trivial or overresearched. This may be particularly the case for topics related to women's issues.

Design Sources of Bias

In a fascinating program of research, Rosenthal (1963) and his colleagues demonstrated that a researcher's knowledge of the hypotheses or predictions associated with a piece of research may actually shape results in keeping with the hypotheses. In other words, the experimenter's expectation about how the study will turn out works like a self-fulfilling prophecy. Recalling our earlier discussion about ideology producing the supporting empiricism (Pyke, 1982), Weyant (1979) has argued that experimenter expectancy effects serve to enhance the possibility of revealing a sex difference.

The demand characteristics of an experiment (Orne, 1962) are a potential source of bias for any study. Essentially, an experimenter may inadvertently structure an experiment so that the probability of obtaining certain results increases. For example, the researcher's demeanor in interacting with the research participants will obviously have an impact on the behavior of the participants.

More specifically, the particular task that the investigator assigns to the participants may bias the findings. Weyant (1979) provides an example of the operation of this type of bias in research on sex differences. A consistent sex difference cited in the psychological literature has been the greater social conformity of females as compared with males, leading to the conclusion that females were more susceptible than males to group pressure or influence. However, the tasks employed in these conformity studies were typically of the spatial/perceptual variety—a selection that favored males. When the tasks used were of roughly equal familiarity for both sexes, the sex difference in conformity disappeared. The view that women are conformists has a long history. In the fifteenth century, two Dominican priests believed that more witches were female because females were more susceptible to Satanic pressure and enticements.

Grady (1981), reviewing studies of aggression, identified a similar source of bias in both the experimental condition utilized and the type of response option available to the research participants. In studies involving female participants, aggression is typically induced by requiring the subjects to read a story presumed to arouse aggression; to measure the amount of aggression so induced, subjects complete some sort of questionnaire. When male subjects are used, aggression is more actively and directly induced through threat or hostile treatment and the effect is assessed in terms of the administration of shocks to a victim. These demand characteristics could well yield experimental findings supporting a conclusion that males are more aggressive than females.

Researcher Bias

We have already learned that characteristics of a researcher may affect the nature of the data obtained. Sex of the investigator appears to be a potential source of bias of some magnitude. Alice Eagly and Linda Carli (1981) conducted a meta-analysis of studies dealing with gender differences in conformity and influenceability. They found that women were more easily influenced than men, but the size of the difference was small, accounting for only 1 percent of the variability in influenceability. In the course of this analysis, they uncovered another source of bias— sex of researcher. Male investigators tended to find larger gender differences in influenceability than did female investigators. Intrigued by this discovery, these authors reviewed a body of research dealing with the ability to guess what emotion people are feeling (i.e., sensitivity). Here it was found that female researchers obtained the larger gender differences—revealing that women are more sensitive. As Matlin (1993) notes, "each gender finds results that are most flattering to their own gender. Male researchers find easily influenced women, who are not particularly sensitive to others' feelings. Female researchers find sensitive women, who are not particularly easily influenced" (p. 227).

RESTRUCTURING SCIENCE

Reform

There can be little doubt that normal social science is sex biased, yet it would be wrong to assume that those pointing the finger are immune to surreptitious edits of belief systems. Although the section above is slanted in terms of a selection of examples revealing forms of biases that result from adoption of a patriarchal ideology, a feminist ideology can function similarly. To illustrate, Jeanne Block (1976) has identified several sources of bias evident in the review of the sex difference literature conducted by Maccoby and Jacklin (described earlier). Perhaps one test that might be applied before accepting the validity of any phenomenon is that it be studied by adherents of different ideological persuasions. If a finding withstands scrutiny from opposing ideological/theoretical perspectives, our confidence in the "reality," "truth," or authenticity of the empiricism if even greater.

As Fee (1976) suggests, the biological determinism so prevalent in theories about sex differences during the Victorian era gradually gave way to environmental or cultural conditioning theories, in part because of the influx of women scientists. Ensuring a heterogeneous population of scientists almost guarantees that a smorgasbord of world views or ideologies will prevail; thus, our chances of locating robust effects increase, and opportunities for falling prey to an artifactual effect accordingly diminish. As McCormack (1989) notes, "If we are all white, middle-class feminists, if we replicate ourselves, feminist research will be biased even though our individual studies are beyond reproach." (p. 25).

Presumably, the heightened sensitivity (or raised consciousness) of the social science disciplines to sex bias promotes increasingly objective (less biased) research. Although insight or awareness may not necessarily produce change, the exposé tone of the feminist assault on the foundations of science has no doubt led some researchers to exert greater care in the design, analysis, and reporting of their work. And, on a variety of fronts, scientists are being exhorted by granting agencies, journal editors, and their professional associations to "clean up their act." Stark-

Adamec and Kimball (1984), for example, couple their comprehensive description of the many avenues by which sex bias may enter research with a set of guidelines to aid researchers in their efforts to generate nonsexist research. These guidelines have been adopted and endorsed by the Canadian Psychological Association.

Other researchers—feminists mainly—in attempting to counteract the neglect and distortions of women's experience in the extant scientific literature, have adopted a woman-centered approach (Belenky, Clinchy, Goldberger & Tarule, 1986; Chodorow, 1978; Gilligan, 1982). Typically, such studies employ more qualitative methods in recognition of the validity of a phenomenological approach, the relevance of personal experience, and the importance of context. Women are thus added into the existing, albeit expanded, traditional paradigm.

Restructure

Despite such laudable reform efforts to move scientific praxis closer to its advertised claims of comprehensiveness, impartiality, and objectivity, an increasing number of feminist scholars, pessimistic about the prospects of a revisionist approach and/or distrustful of the inherent masculine orientation in science, are calling for a restructuring of the social science enterprise (Bleier, 1984; Crawford & Marecek, 1989; Eichler, 1988; McCormack, 1989; Pyke, 1988). Although the outlines of a new paradigm are yet vague, there are some clear points of emphasis. The value of experiential knowledge (Rose, 1986), of a phenomenological approach (Wallston, 1981), of a transcendence of dichotomies (Pyke, 1988) are among the characteristics of a feminist perspective on science.

Bleier (1984) advocates an emphasis on contextuality, interaction, process, and change, as opposed to, or in addition to, the cause-and-effect paradigm, with its emphasis on hierarchy and control. Bleier's model implies an awareness that:

> There can be no single "correct" explanation, no simple dramatic "cause." Rather, there will be an array of factors, some more important than others, each factor having its own historical course of development and its own situation specificities, interacting with other such factors over time and eventually leading to the phenomenon under scrutiny. (Bleier, 1984, p. 203)

Edicts about the necessity to consider the researcher as a relevant variable in the research process (i.e., as an active participant rather than a disinterested observer) are also frequently cited. Particularly noteworthy is the feminist goal of promoting a benevolent society in which individual self-actualization is possible (Lott, 1985), of enhancing the status of women through social change (Kahn & Yoder, 1989).

More precise prescriptions for feminist research are provided by Judith Worell (1990), the editor of the *Psychology of Women Quarterly*.

We look for research that meets one or more of the following criteria: (a) challenges traditional or devaluing views of women; (b) uses methods of inquiry that provide alternative views of women's lives; (c) looks at women within the meaningful context of their lives; (d) engages in collaborative efforts with research participants . . . ; (e) solicits samples other than college sophomores, including diversity in age, ethnic and economic status, relational preferences, and so on; (f) considers sex and gender comparisons in context rather than simply looking for "sex differences"; (g) interprets women's response repertoires (traits, behaviors, cognitions) in ways that do not blame the victims of violence or injustice; (h) explores alternatives that empower women and minorities; (i) examines the structural and interpersonal hierarchies that render women and other minority groups less powerful; and (j) contains implications for social change toward establishing equality and social justice for all oppressed groups. (pp. 4–5)

Several texts have recently been published in which a feminist orientation(s) to research methodology in the social sciences is described (Fonow & Cook, 1991; Nielsen, 1990; Reinharz, 1992; Zalk & Gordon-Kelter, 1992). Taken in the aggregate these works provide a comprehensive compendium of feminist research methods. Ultimately, however, a restructuring of science (i.e., the creation of a truly nonsexist science) may require a restructuring of society—a move from the male-oriented model of social reality now extant to a model that conceptualizes the social universe as constructed around both women and men (Eichler, 1988).

SUMMARY

This chapter highlights the sensitivity of science to belief systems, values, and ideologies—the "taken for granted" implicit world view of the scientist. Although focusing on one particular theme—namely, the conception of females inherent in patriarchal thought—other ideological perspectives, although less ubiquitous, would have served as well. Recognition of the imperfections and vulnerabilities of the scientific enterprise remains vital for the production of better-quality science and is important for all of us if we are to be sophisticated consumers of science's products.

EXAMPLE

The following is an historical example of the impact of ideology on empiricism (Fee, 1976).

A SMALL BRAIN = SMALL MIND.

Physical anthropologists of the Victorian era eagerly embraced Darwin's theory of evolution, published in 1859. Within the patriarchal structure of Victorian society, women were regarded as inferior and subordinate to men. Applying evolutionary theory, many scientists of that period concluded that females represented an earlier stage of evolutionary development. This then explained the lower status of females—socially, economically, politically. Because they had not climbed as high up the evolutionary ladder as men, women therefore could not be expected to function as creatively, intelligently, and productively as their male counterparts.

A related part of the argument, which helped to explain why in some "primitive" cultures women held considerable power and status, was the premise that, as one proceeded up the evolutionary scale, the sexes became more and more divergent or differentiated. Hence, the great distinctions between males and females in Victorian England were justified because the Victorian upper class obviously represented the epitome of civilization—the acme of evolutionary progress.

Interest in developing a measure of intelligence led some scientists to resort to the use of brain size as a possible indicator, and so the science of craniology was born. The following predictions regarding brain size might be generated from the propositions outlined above:

1. Females would have smaller brains than males.
2. The difference between male and female brains in primitive cultures would be less than that observed in more advanced cultures.
3. Within more advanced cultures, the difference between male and female brains would be less in lower socioeconomic classes than in higher classes.

As expected, the predictions were confirmed. Women were simply not equipped, as a result of their evolutionary history, to function on a par with men. It seemed they were destined to be always subordinate to men. As George J. Romanes (1887) put it, "It must take many centuries for heredity to produce the missing five ounces of the female brain" (cited in Fee, 1976).

As science moved into the twentieth century, patriarchal ideology remained, but changing economic conditions required some adjustment to the evolution paradigm of the Victorian era. Science itself changed its complexion with the trend toward increasing precision and experimentation. At the turn of the present century, Karl Pearson, a statistician of some renown, expressed his disgust with the quality of Victorian evolutionary theorizing and set about to demonstrate the absence of any correlation linking brain size, cranial measurement, and intelligence. Pearson's assault proved fatal to the "science" of craniology, which disappeared from the scientific scene.

Somewhat reminiscent of the craniology debate is the recent controversy on brain laterality (the extent to which functions or abilities are localized in the right or left hemisphere of the brain). Many researchers assume that being lateralized is preferable to lack of lateralization, primarily because children with various learning problems exhibit ambiguous cerebral dominance. Because the incidence of learning problems in young males is higher than the frequency of these difficulties in young females, and because females are more lateralized for verbal functions than males, it has been hypothesized that males are less lateralized than females. On the other hand, females appear to be less lateralized than males because they show less impairment following damage to either brain hemisphere than do males with a comparable degree of cerebral assault. In some sense, then, females have the best of both worlds. These incongruent findings have led some researchers to conclude that the female brain specializes, that is, lateralizes, *too* early and is thus not able to "advance" further (Pyke, 1982; Unger, 1979). Thus after a hundred years, the Victorian view of female evolution is reborn, albeit in a more sophisticated and elegant guise.

REVIEW QUIZ

True or False?

1. The structures, taxonomies, classifications and processes identified and labeled by science are the artificial creations of thought, designed to make sense of our imperfectly perceived experience.

2. Some of the symbolism in science reflects the eroticization of nature.

3. The Royal Society began admitting female members in 1920, right after World War I.

4. Sir Francis Galton, the father of the study of sex differences, was a member of the British Suffrage Society.

5. Research studies on sex differences conducted before 1974 tend to show larger sex differences than more recent studies.

6. Researchers employing all female samples are more likely to generalize their findings to the opposite sex than those utilizing only male subjects.

7. Most subsets of empirical data can be successfully employed to support even diametrically opposed theoretical models.

8. Field independence and context sensitivity are more typical of males.

9. Girls are more passive than boys.

10. Even in a neutral context, generically neutral terms are typically interpreted as gender specific.

11. A failure to obtain a real difference (defined as a probability of 0.05 or less) confirms the null hypothesis.

12. One can never statistically prove that the sexes are similar, that they do not differ.

13. Journal publication policies may lead us to assume differences between the sexes where in fact no such differences exist.

14. The restructuring of science proposed by some feminists involves in part the addition of qualitative techniques to the scientist's list of legitimate research methods.

15. Many scientists in the Victorian era believed that the sexes became more and more divergent or differentiated as one proceeded up the evolutionary scale.

✾ 16 ✾

The Truth Spinners

───────── **Chapter Goal** ─────────

*We now move beyond focusing on "normal"
science—the generation and testing of specific hypotheses—to considering "big" science,
and discussing whether science discovers
or constructs its "truths."*

INTRODUCTION

> *There are more things in heaven and earth . . .
> than are dreamt of in your philosophy.*
>
> —Hamlet

Most of us think of our nervous system as a trusted messenger—like
Federal Express—that delivers unadulterated news, with the sender
and receiver clearly labeled. But if this is the case:

> How is it that you can have pain in your toes even if you're an
> amputee?
>
> How is it that one day I can be certain who is the "real me," and
> the next day certain the real me is someone else!
>
> How is it that even scientists argue among themselves: about the
> causes of cancer; about whether genetics or the environment is
> more influential in producing certain kinds of behavior; about
> whether scientific facts are discovered or constructed?

If you set aside the notion of the nervous system as a kind of
Federal Express, and if you assume, as we did in Chapter 1, that we
construct the truth out of streams of messages—incomplete, fuzzy, and
conflicting—then we would expect different people (even scientists) to
construct (discover) different truths. Furthermore, we should expect as
messages accumulate that some truths will change with time, as they do
in science over a generation, and expect other truths to change over

days, or even hours, for example, concerning the source of pain in the amputee's toes, or concerning who is the "real you."

What we have presented in the previous 15 chapters represents the authors' current truths about small-scale sciencing. In those chapters we focused on relatively small questions—for example, evaluating the effects of a given drug on a small group of depressed patients. This focus makes sense in an introductory text because small-scale sciencing is what most researchers practice. But in this last chapter we want to take a larger view of the science game; we want to introduce you to a relatively new perspective on human reasoning in general and to sciencing in particular. Here we will introduce you to some trusted messages and messengers who have helped construct this new larger perspective, this view of "big" science.

WHAT DOES THE WORLD REST ON?

The story goes that Bertrand Russell, the famous philosopher, was giving a lecture about the earth orbiting the sun. A little old lady in the front row stood up proclaiming, "That's utter nonsense . . . everyone knows the earth rests on a giant turtle!" Russell replied, "And what pray madam does the turtle rest upon?" The old lady responded; "You think you're very clever young man, but it's turtles all the way down."

A little voice in the back of your mind is saying, "But all the way down to where?" That tiny voice is asking a very profound question, one that has confounded religious leaders, philosophers, and scientists. The question, of course, is: On what foundations do our "truths" rest? Only in the last chapters can we afford to ask such disturbing questions; otherwise we fall out of our minds. We have learned that certain kinds of reasoning, like looking for the ultimate turtle, leads us into mind-eating black holes.

We suggest that avoiding cognitive black holes is a characteristic of human reasoning; our brains and our cultures have evolved to help protect us from pushing our reasoning beyond its capacity. For example, the old lady generated a mental black hole by proposing, "turtles all the way down," and young children do the same thing by trying to ask a string of "whys" that go on forever. However, young children quickly learn that they can't get away with asking more than two or three "whys" in a row because in frustration grown-ups figuratively slap their little curiosities.

First, through negative feedback, children learn to *suppress* a string of "whys," and eventually they learn to *censor* them—not to even think about asking more than one or two whys in a row (Minsky, 1983). Adults have successfully installed a censor in the child's mind, a socially and logically functional censor. These children grow up to become adults—

some of them scientists—who have all learned not to ask too many whys in a row. Otherwise they overload their reasoning capacity or that of others. According to this view, all human reasoning rests on a foundation of censorship, on turtles, located just a little way down. These core beliefs serve as "safe" foundations below which questioning or exploration is cognitively dangerous. Fortunately for the sake of our cognitive health we are usually unaware of our own trusted turtles, unaware that we are standing on unproven and unprovable beliefs or assumptions. Periodically, however, we are able to identify questions, and dig under the core assumptions of others, and if their defenses are down we cause them cognitive vertigo.

In brief, neither turtles, nor questions, can be allowed to go all the way down; rather, lack of knowledge, of reasoning capacity and of patience force us to stop and "take a stand" a little way down. What are some of the trusted, or enforced, stopping places you have encountered as you started your search down, seeking the bedrock of knowledge and the foundations of truth? Do any of these "bedrocks," or turtles, sound familiar?

- "Because I say so."
- "Because your father says so."
- "Because the Bible says so."
- "Because the Pope, priest, rabbi, or minister, says so."
- "Because the *New York Times* says so."
- "Because the president says so."
- "Because Dan Rather says so."
- "Because the doctor says so."
- "Because the teacher says so."
- "Because the textbook says so."
- "Because the *Scientific American* says so."
- "Because the *Psychological Bulletin* says so."
- "Because the Nobel Prize winner says so."
- "Because it's an axiom, because it's logical, because it's statistically significant, because it was proved by a control-group, double-blind experiment.

Enough! Enough! But to protect our ignorance, or sanity, or time, we have all stopped, at various times, and made a stand on one or more of these temporary or trusted turtles. We do so because neither citizen nor scientist can afford, socially or logically, to continue climbing down the infinite ladder of "whys." But surely some of the preceding turtles are "better" foundations to stop and stand on, and build your world on than others? Surely what the *Scientific American* says is a more solid foundation to build on, and trust, than what my father, or Dan Rather, or Jimmy Swaggert, or my teacher says?

Well, sometimes you don't have access to the *Scientific American*, and even if you did it probably doesn't address your current question, or deal with your current whys. So we must construct our answers from the available messages and messengers. We now present a few of our most trusted messengers and their messages, the trusted turtles on which we stop and construct our views of human reasoning and of big science.

THE REACH OF HUMAN REASONING

Although we don't often stop to think about it, our views about science rest on certain unspoken assumptions concerning human reasoning.

The traditional view of human reasoning stops and builds its case on the assumption (the turtle) that humans have unlimited rationality, and that given the appropriate information and time we can "solve" any problem. Some citizens and scientists still trust this message.

Various modern scholars (messengers) disagree with this classical view of human rationality and, instead, build their case on the assumption (the turtle) that human rationality is limited, and so we must rely on nonrational and semirational foundations to stand on so as to shrink to mind size the questions we ask. Human rationality, although useful, is highly fallible. We trust this message and introduce a few of its major messengers now.

Bertrand Russell, the philosopher, proposed that human reasoning invariably encounters inconsistencies—even the most disciplined human reasoning such as that employed in formal logic and mathematics. Just as all popular generalizations (e.g., men are taller than women) encounter inconsistencies (very tall women and very short men), so too do mathematical and logical generalizations (e.g., set theory) encounter inconsistencies. In brief, certainty lies beyond our rational, though not our emotional, reach.

From Russell's message we conclude that all human reasoners—including scientists—must somehow deal with inconsistencies, with messages that don't fit their theories or previous findings. How do you do it? How do scientists do it? We'll see.

Another trusted messenger, Herbert Simon (1983) lends his voice to those proclaiming the limited reach of human reason. Simon, who won a Nobel Prize for his work on human decision making, concludes that humans possess bounded rationality. Because we have restricted short-term memory and limited analytical capacity—only a limited capacity to analyze a lot of information at one time—we can't make optimal decisions. Rather most of the time we must make do with decisions based on small amounts of information and simple analysis, with relatively quick and dirty answers. If you accept this assumption, that is, if you rest your views of human reasoning on this turtle, then all conclusions, including scientific conclusions, are based on the limited analysis of partial and conflicting information. Because scientific decisions are based on the partial analysis of incomplete information those decisions remain conditional—open to argument, revision, and replacement.

We don't have enough rationality to manage big questions, so we must rely on rules of thumb, and emotional anchors to cut complex issues down to mind size. Neither home buyers, nor courting couples, nor investors, nor scientists have access to all the relevant information, and even if they did they don't have adequate memory or analytical capacity to process it, even with the aid of computers. Therefore, all decision makers must base their decisions on fallible cognitive processes and incomplete information.

Scientists, like the rest of us, do not make optimal decisions but rather make *cognitively affordable decisions*. Scientists too have limited memories and analytical capacity, must work to meet deadlines (e.g., granting agency and publication deadlines), and must process conflicting messages of indeterminate reliability.

From Simon's work we conclude that scientists, like citizens, don't have the rational capacity to deal with all the inconsistencies they encounter. Therefore, they must handle some inconsistencies by nonrational or semirational means. On what kind of turtles do they stop and make a stand. What kinds of weapons do they use to defend themselves against inconsistencies and attacks from their critics? It is hoped we use more sophisticated defenses than losing our temper, ridicule, only reading compatible material, hanging out with "right thinkers," nitpicking, and so forth. We'll see.

Building Defended Islands of Truth

A third trusted messenger, Marvin Minsky (1983), one of the fathers of Artificial Intelligence, proposes that human reasoners face the following two tasks:

1. To work to discover (construct) islands of consistency within which human reasoning is safe
2. To work to mark and defend the boundaries of such islands

We take Minsky's messages, and combine them with those of Russell and Simon, and construct a simple visual model of human reasoning, which includes scientific reasoning. As outlined in Figure 16-1 the human reasoner, possessing only bounded rationality, is immersed in a changing sea of human experience. Although handicapped by limited rational capacities—so we can't get and hold the big, moving picture— evolution has equipped us to discover, or construct, islands of consistency in that changing sea, and equipped us as well to mark and defend the boundaries of those islands, where we can safely practice our fallible reasoning. The islands may be small or large, well or poorly defended,

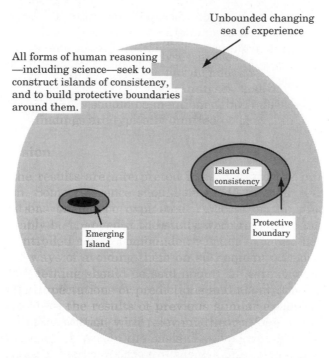

Unbounded changing
sea of experience

All forms of human reasoning
—including science—seek to
construct islands of consistency,
and to build protective boundaries
around them.

Island of
consistency

Protective
boundary

Emerging
Island

FIGURE 16–1   Constructing Functional, though
Fallible, Islands of Consistency in
a Changing Sea of Experience

temporary or apparently permanent. But constructing them and defending them is what human reasoning and the science game are all about.

An island of consistency represents a generalization, a minitheory, a mind-saving simplification and classification, a kind of stereotype. It may represent a large generalization such as "All men are . . ."; "All women are . . ."; "All blacks are . . ."; or "All those who practice unsafe sex will get AIDS." Or it may be a smaller generalization such as "Some men are . . ."; or "Some women are . . . ." Or it may be a very small generalization like, "Every Friday night Willie gets drunk." But big or small, generalizations play a vital role in human reasoning. They simplify our experience and reduce the mental burden on our limited cognitive capacity; they represent islands of consistency where we "know" what to expect. And, even more important, they are defended islands, where, as with all stereotypes, inconsistencies have trouble landing, and if they do land the *cognitive police* "take care of them" by discrediting the message or the messenger. Failing that, the *emotional police* are called out, and the offending messages are figuratively burned, or the messenger has his or her tongue cut out; no "respectable" publisher will print their dumb stuff, their faulty reasoning, their wobbly assumptions.

You can usually tell when an interloper has sneaked past the cognitive police and is threatening the center of someone's island. Like other animals, the owner gives off emotional warning signals. In the case of humans we see name calling and even threats of physical violence. For example, following the riots outside the democratic convention in Chicago, during a television "discussion," Gore Vidal called William Buckley a "crypto-fascist." Buckley replied by calling Vidal a "queer" and threatened to punch him in the face. Here we have two of the most articulate, and presumably cognitively competent, men in America defending their trusted generalizations by resorting to name calling and threats. The backlash against feminism may be another example. The point we are making is that anger and aggression frequently signal that someone feels they are in danger of being knocked off a trusted turtle.

Why can't people discuss their core assumptions dispassionately and critically examine each other's trusted turtles in a spirit of open, friendly enquiry? They can't because these foundational assumptions protect us from falling off the edge of our minds into cognitive black holes. The only turtles we can examine dispassionately are those we are not standing on, namely, those of other people.

Two famous scholars generate light, but also some heat, concerning how open to critical examination our core assumptions really are. Karl Popper (1970, p. 56), a philosopher of science, admits "that at any given moment we are prisoners caught in the framework of our theories . . . but we are prisoners in a Pickwickian sense: if we try we can break out of the framework at any time. Admittedly, we shall find ourselves again in a framework [on a trusted turtle] but it will be a better and roomier one." For Popper our core assumptions appear to be flexible working hypotheses, readily open to revision resulting from cognitive or empirical feedback.

Not so for Thomas Kuhn (1972, p. 232), the historian of science, who sees our preconceptions (trusted turtles) as robust shapers of our knowledge, well protected from negative messages, and certainly not readily open to revision. In commenting on Popper's view Kuhn says, "if frameworks are the prerequisite of research, their grip on the mind is not merely 'Pickwickian,' nor can it be quite right to say that 'if we try, we can break out of our framework at any time.' To be simultaneously essential and freely dispensable is very nearly a contradiction in terms. My critics become incoherent when they embrace it."

Here we see Kuhn rejecting Popper's message. Popper returns the favor, rejecting Kuhn and his ilk [history of science scholars] with the following comment: "I cannot conclude without pointing out that to me the idea of turning for enlightenment concerning the aims of science, and its possible progress, to sociology (or, as Pearce recommends, the history of science) is surprising and disappointing" (Popper, 1970, p. 57). Neither Popper nor Kuhn show any signs of changing turtles.

We agree with both Popper and Kuhn—with Popper in the sense that we have access to explicit premises and to a few temporarily available, conceptually close implicit assumptions—particularly when we are calm and in the presence of trusted others. Pylyshyn (1985, p. 271) acknowledges the issue when he says, "Science progresses via a delicate balance between open mindedness and prejudice." But we agree most strongly with Kuhn that the core assumptions, on which explicit premises rest, represent highly resilient cognitive structures, and as such provide robust, adaptive defenses against rational/empirical overload, against evidence not in keeping with our treasured generalizations. Next, consider a familiar and widely trusted generalization.

MALES HAVE SUPERIOR ANALYTICAL CAPACITY

Consider, for example, an island of consistency, a generalization, represented by a familiar stereotype: "Men have better analytical capacity than women." On this island believers accumulate messages that are consistent with their trusted generalization (e.g., personal examples of boys leading the class in math; published studies of males outscoring females on standard math exams; males outnumbering females in academic positions and awards related to analytical capacity, etc.).

But like every generalization this one encounters inconsistencies or negative evidence. So, as noted by Minsky, we must mark off and protect the island's boundaries. First, in the face of obvious inconsistencies (e.g., a girl leads your class in math or a study is published showing females outscoring males), you can "work" to maintain the island (the generalization) by defending its boundaries. You can use various devices such as discrediting the messages carrying the negative evidence: "the girl who led your class cheated, was lucky, or was teacher's pet"; "the author of the publicized study was a radical feminist; didn't include all the male data; used a math test of questionable validity; faulty statistics, etc.).

So whether citizen or scientist we typically protect our generalization by means of popular defenses against inconsistent or negative messages, namely: (1) if possible ignore them; (2) discredit them; (3) discredit the messenger (e.g., "crypto-fascist," "queer"); and (4) do away with the messenger (e.g., fire him; punch him in the face; figuratively cut off the head of the bearer of bad news).

In science the most common defense against messages that are inconsistent with your own position is to attempt to discredit them. As you now know no research method is foolproof, most samples are small or nonrandom, measuring scales have limited reliability and validity, the four rogues play their tricks, and so forth. Therefore, any particular study is legitimately open to challenges concerning its internal and external validity (see Chapter 6). Furthermore, even meta-analysis of many studies involves investigator judgment, and so is open to bias in deciding which studies to include and which to exclude. So, if an investigator trusts a generalization he or she can defend that island of consistency against negative evidence by raising "scientifically legitimate" questions or criticisms concerning inconsistent evidence.

Probably the most common defense of all is the bliss of ignorance concerning the number of inconsistent messages floating around in the great sea of experience. No researcher can ever cover the voluminous and growing literature in his or her field. Consequently they typically protect their limited rationality by reading journals, conversing with colleagues, sharing common generalizations, and standing on the same turtle. So emerging inconsistencies, or negative findings, don't necessarily get within hailing distance of their island.

Nevertheless, sciencing remains exciting because while one group of researchers is wittingly or unwittingly avoiding negative evidence, other investigators, perhaps long-suffering targets of the generalization, are starting to build an island of messages consistent with a conflicting generalization, such as: "there is no real difference between men and women in analytical capacity, if they are given 'equal' opportunity." Unable to penetrate the defenses of the prevailing generalization of male superiority, energetic scholars start accumulating and constructing contrary evidence (see Chapter 15). Under such conditions science, and life, becomes more interesting.

New islands of consistency, like old ones, must be constructed on layers of supporting assumptions, or turtles. Core assumptions don't usually become obvious until a generalization is attacked. Remember you can't afford to ask too many whys, or you overload your bounded rationality. If you are forced to deconstruct your generalization you uncover some of these submerged, tacit assumptions.

Recall the initial generalization, "Men have better analytical capacity than women." Where did the assumed superiority come from? The tacit assumption was that it came from their brains or genes; we encounter the turtle of "genetic determinism."

The challenging generalization, from the other island now under construction, states that any difference between men and women in analytical ability is not due to brains or genes, but rather to access to more resources, opportunities, training, old-boy networks, and so forth; here we encounter the turtle of "cultural determinism."

Sciencing becomes increasingly exciting when a new island is under construction and an old one is being deconstructed or reconstructed, and the defenders of each island are both interested in some of the same building materials. Under such circumstances the fight is occurring at several levels: first, there is the polite surface level of reviewing the literature, designing studies, gathering data, and publishing small-scale science messages that support your particular generalization; second, there will be special publications and conferences where opponents criticize each other's work—academic wrestling matches where none of the combatants ever seem to change their minds; third, and most interesting, is the gradual emergence of the core assumptions—the most trusted turtles—on which the original generalization rests. These core assumptions are typically so strongly held, and so well defended, they remain beyond the reach of rational argument or debate. The proponents don't give them up; they either remain part of the foundational beliefs of the discipline, or retire with their proponents, to be replaced by a new generation of investigators standing securely on their own trusted turtles.

In the case of gender differences in analytical capacity some members of the two opposing camps differ in their core assumptions concerning the relative contribution of environment, on the one hand, and genetics, on the other. Most of social science has been based on the critical assumption that human behavior is shaped mainly by environmental factors. It became politically incorrect to suggest otherwise—a classic example of defending a network of social science islands. At the heart of feminist generalizations in social science lies the endorsement of the environmental core assumption and a discounting of genetic contributions. At the core of the male "superiority" generalization lies the assumption of a strong genetic influence favoring males. We can expect some rousing academic slug fests arising between people advocating the extremes of these fundamental differences, but we will also see the emergence of investigators who pay more than lip service to the basic assumption that human behavior is strongly shaped by *both* environment and genetics. It is from such investigators that new theories and compatible research designs will emerge—emerging islands of consistencies plus their defenses.

But who is "really" right? Well, that depends on your turtle.

PUTTING YOUR CORE ASSUMPTIONS IN A SAFE PLACE

When early tribes stopped putting their gods on the mantle piece, where disbelievers could break them, and started putting them in a safe place like heaven, religious beliefs became secure.

A big theory—like environmental or genetic determinism—is similar to a god. This theory resides in a safe place where disbelievers can't really get at and break it.

Any large generalization that covers a lot of our experience—that covers a huge space-time domain of messages—cannot be empirically tested. Relative to the huge sea of experience that a large theory covers only an infinitesimal number of relevant messages can be collected; only a few islands can be constructed. So, on these tiny outcrops, the believers accumulate and display the positive messages on their islands, and the disbelievers accumulate and display the negative messages on theirs. Neither side readily changes his or her mind because there remains so much free, pragmatic, syntactic, semantic space in which to practice any generalization and faith.

Big scientific theories, like big religion and politics, are based on faith (on a trusted turtle), which in turn supports scattered islands of selective evidence. Big genetics theory versus big environment theory will never be tested empirically; they cover too much space and time to ever be justified with large, systematically linked, islands of evidence and critical analysis. Nevertheless, some ingenious battles will be fought over a few islands populated with messages from increasingly creative twin and adoptive studies. However, the side with the largest number of true believers will construct or collect the most favorable messages, and they will dominate the introductory texts, as the cultural determinists have for the last 50 years.

THEORY OF SCIENCE

Graduate students taking methods classes, or theory of science seminars, will be exposed to critical evaluation of both sides of the debate. In some cases these messages will be delivered by professors who have no particular loyalty to genetic or cultural determinism as they relate to gender, but rather have loyalty to another big theory—the theory of science. Like us, they will stand on a trusted turtle and construct, collect, and display messages that reflect their faith, while ignoring or discrediting contrary messages and messengers. They, too, will build islands of consistency and surround them with defensive boundaries.

Currently two factions battle to build the biggest islands of consistency concerning the theory of science. The traditional faction, the rational empiricists, stand on the turtle of "realism." They believe that (1) there is a directly knowable reality out there; (2) this reality sends clear messages; (3) these messages are ones we can detect and accurately display; and (4) use of "the scientific method" is based on the rational analysis of empirical data. This is an intuitively appealing view of science, and seems to describe mature sciences that have discovered or constructed, some familiar, well-defended, islands of consistency. We suspect that most of us have at least one foot on the realism turtle—at least some of the time—particularly when we encounter very strong messages like stubbing a bare toe, smelling a skunk, or seeing the launch of the space shuttle.

Opposing the realists are those who stand on the constructivist turtle. They believe that (1) there may be a reality out there, but we have no direct way of knowing it; (2) we receive incomplete, conflicting, fuzzy messages; (3) the clear messages we display are constructed out of fuzzy messages; and (4) we do so by using our bounded rationality, but mainly by relying on nonrational and semirational mechanisms that have evolved over millennia.

The Popper-Kuhn argument would find a place in theory of science seminars with different "professors" siding with Popper or Kuhn, depending on their realist or constructivist inclinations. Those standing on the realist turtle would favor Popper's belief that our core assumptions are readily open to modification by empirical feedback and critical analyses, and so increasingly approximates "the truth." In contrast, those planted firmly on the constructivist turtle would favor Kuhn's view that core assumptions are highly resistant to critical analyses and empirical feedback. If it were otherwise, we would overload our bounded rationality and would fall into cognitive black holes.

Although we favor a constructivist stance, we admit to a glaring weakness. If our beliefs about reality, and our decisions, are mainly based on fuzzy messages cobbled together by limited human reasoners relying heavily on nonrational mechanisms, how on earth have we survived this long? To help handle this legitimate question we must introduce several other trusted gurus or messengers.

NONRATIONAL WISDOM

Don Campbell, a psychologist, and Karl Popper, a philosopher, independently introduced a provocative message about human reasoning, and how we create and maintain knowledge. Their core assumption being that, like species, human ways of reasoning, and human beliefs, evolved through trial-and-error winnowing over millennia. That is, ways of reasoning and beliefs only survive if they fit consistencies in the physical/social environment of the times. From this perspective our evolved bounded rationality can work because it is supported by evolved nonrational and semirational mechanisms (turtles) that represent environmental consistencies and automatically give priority to, or trust, some messages over others and serve the purpose of cognitive reflex actions. Such automatic message processors reflect long-term stabilities or consistencies in the sea of experience, freeing up our limited rationality to fine-tune a few pet constructions.

Although based on the idea of the selective survival of trial-and-error gambits, the preceding proposal should not be confused with traditional evolutionary theory. The traditional view of evolution—the survival of the fittest—implies some kind of absolute superiority for survivors. Our view, conversely, can better be described as the survival of the "fittingest"—the survival of beliefs and ways of reasoning that fit the times, which may be nonsensical. For example, beliefs, and ways of reasoning, that fit the old-boy's network will survive as long as the old-boy's network is viable—even though it may be on its last legs. Similarly, beliefs and ways of reasoning that fit the emerging "old-girl's network" will survive as long as the network remains viable. As viewed through the long lens of history—a larger environment—both sets of beliefs will likely be viewed as parochial if not quaint. If you keep the distinction between "fittest" (absolutist) and "fittingest" (relativistic) in mind you will better appreciate a constructivist view of knowledge, which reflects the "turtles of the time." Turtles take the form of core assumptions (cultural versus genetic determinism or rational empiricism versus constructivism), and networks of supporters who build defended islands of evidence consistent with their core assumptions.

According to this revised evolutionary perspective, our observations and our logics, like our immune system and our evolved system of light-detecting pigments (eyes), are selected through blind trial and error to fit (represent) stable physical-social niches in the environment. Such nonrational message editors have been selected to be relevant to environmental consistencies rather than providing veridical maps of it. From this perspective many of our nonrational and semirational core assumptions, or our trusted turtles, may not just be arbitrary places to stand. Rather, some of them may be the end result of thousands of years of trial-and-error winnowing. For example, although our most common form of reasoning, induction (collecting and displaying positive evidence, and building defended islands of consistency) is fallible, it is also functional in a survival sense. Thus, ways of reasoning, and even some cross-cultural beliefs, like species, may be seen to represent functional if fallible adaptations that fit stable aspects of the physical-cultural environment.

In brief, like species, some of our beliefs about reality, and some of our social customs have been selected because they "fit" certain stabilities in the environment. Like species, the fits may be crude or temporary, but they represent hard-won trial-and-error survivals; some will be seen as wisdoms (viewed within one frame of reference), or as species threatening stupidities (viewed within another reference frame). Also, like species, some of the belief trials will fail to find a nourishing niche and will die. Others will languish in the conceptual backwaters for centuries until, like the theory of evolution, a nourishing niche emerges, and the message is finally received from Darwin's hands and widely reproduced, and then further cut and pasted to fit emerging physical-cultural consistencies.

NO CONCLUSIONS WITHOUT PREMISES

The traditional view of human reasoning is that it is based on information; the better the information, the better are the reasoning and the conclusions. In contrast, the emerging view of human reasoning is that it is based mainly on trusted assumptions and expectations. The amount of actual and potential information available for rationally making even a trivial decision, like buying a pair of socks, is cognitively overwhelming—never mind the actual, and potential, amount of information (messages) concerning important decisions like choosing a mate, career, cancer treatment, research design, theory of gender differences, and so forth. So, we cut a decision space down to mind size by relying on trusted assumptions to help us select and edit a few messages from the available flood of fuzzy, delayed, and conflicting messages available.

The traditional view of reasoning, and of science, focuses on getting good information. For small decisions this is not a bad model. But for big decisions, and big science, the emerging view focuses not on information but on *expectations*. If you want to predict what kind of conclusions people will reach about big decisions, focus on their assumptions and expectations, not on "the evidence"; for big decisions, "evidence" is used to decorate the turtle. For big decisions that cover a large space-time domain there is never enough solid information available. For big decisions, like choosing a mate or a career, or choosing between environmental versus genetic determinism, there are always more informational gaps than filled spaces. We bridge the gaps with expectations. For big decisions, locate the turtle the decision maker is standing on, and you can pretty well predict the general conclusions they will draw regardless of the "evidence." Big decisions in science, like big decisions in life, are based more on assumptions than on information; no conclusions are made without premises.

In brief, we suggest that science can be seen, not as solving the jigsaw puzzles of reality, but rather as our most sophisticated means of *constructing* crude maps from small, incomplete samples of our experience. We propose then that the goal of science is the sophisticated management of uncertainty; as Bertrand Russell said, all reasoning leads to uncertainty.

MANAGEMENT OF UNCERTAINTY

The management of uncertainty is the focus of a research domain called "decision theory"; here we encounter our most disciplined attempts to map or model the process of making decisions with incomplete information. Various scholars have engaged in this puzzle (e.g., Kahneman and Tversky, 1973; Nibett & Ross, 1980; Einhorn and Hogarth, 1978). Despite some differences in approach, a common theme prevails—namely, that we manage uncertainty, we make sense, valid or otherwise, of the flow of experience by employing "anchoring and adjustment" mechanisms. In other words, beliefs and expectations serve as "feedforward processes" which simplify and edit the flow of experience ("feedback processes"). For the purposes of this discussion, we focus on a particular anchoring and adjustment model, based on adaptive expectations theory (Agnew & Brown, 1986; 1989a), which emphasizes the powerful role played by initial belief in knowledge constructions and revisions.

Confidence in Initial Beliefs

You will recall that presuppositions about knowledge evolved from the simple supposition that knowledge was a direct reflection of reality, to suppositions that knowledge was a reflection of rational, semirational, and irrational editing mechanisms processing small samples of incomplete and transformed or distorted data (observational checkpoints surrounded by various regions of uncertainty). Although this provides a general idea of how knowledge is constructed in social science, it's still vague, and we need to make the ideas clearer by being more explicit about the syntax and about observational checkpoints. The syntax is relatively simple, so even if you've forgotten your high school algebra, you will have no trouble following the ideas. The syntax reflects the commonsense notion that the higher your confidence in your initial belief or estimate, the less impact new evidence will have in influencing your final belief or estimate. The syntax states:

$$E_f = f[C, E_i + (1-C)g(E_1, E_2, \ldots, E_j \ldots, E_n)]$$

In other words, a revised or final estimate (E_f) of, say, how intelligent you are, depends on your confidence (C) in the initial estimate of your intelligence (E_i), adjusted by distributing the remaining confidence $(1-C)$ over subsequent evidence or estimates, such as a failed exam (E_1), criticism by friends for doing something dumb (E_2), forgetting an important appointment (E_j), getting an A on a statistics exam (E_n), with the flow of that evidence being edited by some rational, semi-rational, or nonrational editing mechanisms (gs).

Now here is the most important part of the model. In this particular model of decision making, or belief revision, C can take values ranging from 0 to 1 (Kmenta, 1971). Therefore, if C is very high (for example, 1), then $(1 - C)$ is very low; in fact, it's zero, so when you multiply the subsequent evidence by zero, you get zero. So the model reflects the power of initial beliefs (or core assumptions) to act as feedforward mechanisms canceling, or reducing, the impact of subsequent information—serving to help defend the island. In contrast, when confidence in initial belief is very low, $(1 - C)$ is high, and so subsequent evidence $(E_1, \ldots, E_n)$ and the particular editing mechanisms employed (g) have a major impact on your revised or final belief. Now you can see why such models are called anchoring and adjustment, or adaptive expectation models—they permit you to describe and predict under what conditions subsequent information will influence initial beliefs. Furthermore, the model explicitly provides for the assumption that any given decision is the result of a weighting of the adjustment mechanism $[(1-C)g(E_1, \ldots, E_n)]$, relative to the weight given to the anchor or initial estimate $[C, E_i]$.

Notice that with low confidence in your initial assumption (or turtle) you become Popperian and respond to the evidence. With high confidence in your initial assumption, however, you become Kuhnian and ignore or discount subsequent evidence that challenges your assumption.

Take a minute or two now and play with the model. Notice what happens if your initial confidence is low, and if your editing mechanism (g) gives special weight to the latest news. In this case, E_n (the A grade in statistics) becomes the major influence, and your final estimate (E_f) is that you have high intelligence. But suppose the same conditions prevail, except that the operating editing mechanism (g) is not a recency bias, as above, but a primacy bias in which early news gets the greatest weighting. Then you would give the greatest weight to E_1 (a failed exam), and so your final estimate would be that you have a low IQ. If confidence in initial estimate is average (e.g., 0.4 to 0.5), your initial estimate serves as a model anchor; thus, subsequent estimates will still have some effect, but not as much as when confidence is low (e.g., 0 to 0.1).

Confidence as Keystone Concept

Recall that traditional views of science assume that our final estimates (our knowledge) are determined by empirical data and rational editing mechanisms, with initial estimates acting only as working hypotheses readily changed in the light of the evidence à la Popper. According to this traditional view, in relation to our model, scientists start with low confidence in their hypothesis (E_i), gain access to a representative and reliable sample of reality ($E_1, \ldots, E_n$), and use highly rational ways of selecting, transforming, and analyzing it. That is, the scientific method (g) produces valid maps of reality. We, on the other hand, are proposing that our knowledge depends strongly upon: (1) the confidence (C) we have in our initial hypothesis (E_i); (2) the type of rational, semirational, and nonrational editing mechanisms we employ (g_1, g_2, g_3); and (3) the sample of clear and fuzzy observational checkpoints we have access to ($E_1, \ldots, E_n$). Thus, we are proposing a much stronger role for feedforward mechanisms in knowledge construction than do traditional views. We are proposing, as well, that hypothesis generation and maintenance are as important a part of ongoing sciencing, if not more important, than is hypothesis confirmation. If we are correct, social science methods and theories should provide a much larger place for disciplined hypothesis generation and theory building than they are now accorded. In fact, some of our so-called qualitative and error-prone methods should gain a more respected place in our classrooms and research domains.

In Figure 16–2, we present a simple schematic outline of decision making under uncertainty in a multidimensional moving reality. Recall that, because of our bounded rationality, we must drastically reduce our search and choice regions; we must rely on simplifying frames of reference. Decision making involves using feedforward mechanisms to extract mind-sized general frames of reference for us to explore with our bounded,

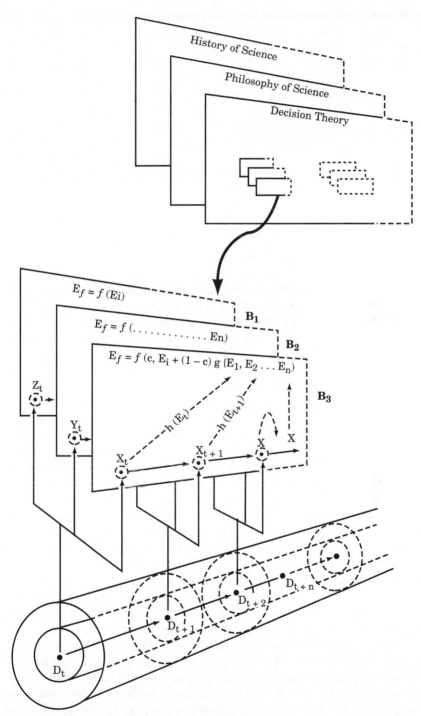

FIGURE 16–2 Constructing "Reality"

semi-rational, and rational editing mechanisms. In Figure 16–2, we have extracted three simple decision-making frames of reference. Guided by strong beliefs (high confidence), and influenced by the explicit and implicit presuppositions of their specialties, and by their subspecialty frames of reference (B_1,B_2,B_3), various theorists and researchers diligently abstract and compile various representations (X_t,Y_t,Z_t) of "observational checkpoints"—for example, averages—samples drawn from their particular personal and professional flow of experience in moving, multidimensional experience $(D_t, D_{t+1}, \ldots, D_{t+n})$.

As you can see, B_1 displays a frame in which the final estimate (E_f) is completely determined by the initial estimate (E_1). This represents a confidence level of 1 in our adaptive expectations model discussed above, and would represent the bigot, or the theorist who is "blind" to subsequent evidence. In frame B_2, we have an instance in which the final estimate is determined completely by the latest evidence (E_n), a radical recency effect, whereby you believe the last thing you heard, or the results of the last experiment you did. Although frame B_1 decision makers are inflexible, frame B_2 decision makers are at the mercy of the latest fad, theory, or method. However, notice that both B_1 and B_2 deciders employ low-cost decision strategies that are designed to reduce information processing costs or cognitive effort, and so accommodate our bounded rationality.

And now for a provocative question and answer. What percentage of the people you know rely very heavily on both B_1 and B_2 strategies? What percentage of scientists would rely heavily on them? Our answer to both questions is 100 percent! In other words, most of the time, we either avoid or ignore information relevant to most of our strong beliefs; or, if we have no strong belief, we rely on the low-cost editing mechanism of remembering or reporting the last thing we heard. In other words, we are proposing that most of our decision making and most of our knowledge is based on the low-computing-cost information processing mechanisms outlined in B_1 and B_2. We are not alone in this heresy. Both Quine and Campbell (see Agnew & Brown 1989b) suggest that, because of the cognitive cost, the vast majority of our beliefs must remain unexamined. For example, we operate with a 99:1 trust to doubt ratio at any given time—that is, we can afford to examine critically only 1 percent of our beliefs at any given time or we risk cognitive and emotional overload. An analogy would be the repair of a ship at sea—you can only afford to work on one timber at a time, while presuming that the other timbers (beliefs) are sound. Depression, paranoia, anxiety, and academic ennui can all be conceived of as states in which the individual has lost confidence in some core beliefs, and/or some low-cost information processing mechanisms, and is deviating from a viable trust:doubt ratio.

However, not all of our decision making and knowledge construction proceeds in frames B_1 and B_2. Even according to the pessimistic estimate just presented, at least 1 percent of our beliefs are open for review. We reserve a few special domains for high-cost analytic processing, such as those depicted in B_3. Notice the syntax in B_3 is the same as that in the formula (page 337) of our adaptive expectations model, a general model that enables us to address different degrees of confidence (C), different editing mechanisms (g), and different types and amounts of data or evidence $E_1, \ldots, E_n$).

We next consider the implications of such a model for theorists and researchers in social science. For example, what mix of variables in the model would presumably make productive theorists and researchers, and which mix would not?

Confidence in Hypothesis and Editing Mechanisms

If, as Simon suggests in his bounded rationality model, we are like Pooh—that is, we are bears of very little brain—then we must protect our limited cognitive resources, and ration them out carefully to a precious few hypotheses and/or editing mechanisms. In Table 16–1, we present five types of decision makers or investigators based on the degree of confidence they have in their hypothesis or belief, and we relate them to the syntax in frame B_3 of Figure 16–2.

True Believers   At the top of Table 16–1, we encounter the true believers or bigots. These are people who have very high confidence ($C = 0.9$ to 1) in a particular hypothesis so that subsequent evidence or data have little or no effect. Therefore, the final estimate (E_f) equals the initial estimate (E_i). In the scientific domain, such true believers would probably lose support, and would be unlikely to be productive theorists, unless, at least for a time, they run their own journals or own their own publishing house.

True Technicians   At the other extreme, at the bottom of the table, we encounter the decision maker with little or no confidence (0 to 0.1) in

TABLE 16–1   Styles of Decision Making

CONFIDENCE LEVEL	DESCRIPTION
$C = 0.9$ to 1	True deductive believer—rejects (-) evidence
$C = 0.7$ to 0.8	Strong deductive believer—discounts (-) evidence
$C = 0.4$ to 0.6	Reasonable person who becomes overwhelmed by information overload and conflicting evidence; unproductive because of inability to settle on a given hypothesis (E_i), or evidence-sorting ritual (g), long enough to go to press
$C = 0.2$ to 0.3	Strong inductive believer—sophisticated (g's)
$C = 0.1$ to 0	True inductive believer—dogmatic (g) rituals

the particular hypothesis. Therefore, the weight $(1 - C)$ will flow to the particular editing mechanisms they use (g) which, in turn, will strongly influence the final estimate (E_f). Such people are likely to be pure technologists, married to their particular data-processing hardware or software—sort of a "have gun, will travel" data processor, or a "have multiple regression or Liseral statistical package, will apply it to any data" investigator. Some opinion pollsters are perhaps the best example of pure (g) data processors who have no loyalty to any particular hypothesis or data. We don't view them as scientists, but rather as technicians.

Middling Believers   Next, according to the model, we should encounter the largest group of unproductive scientists—namely, those whose confidence in the hypothesis is middling (e.g., $C = 0.4$ to 0.6). Here we encounter the procrastinators who can't quite make up their mind about whether the hypothesis is worth investigating. Furthermore, if they were thinking of investigating it, they wouldn't be sure which data collection and editing method (g) to use. So they vacillate back and forth, and make false or faint-hearted attempts because they don't have enough confidence in either a particular hypothesis or in a particular method or technology. In this category, we find thousands of undergraduate and graduate students vacillating and procrastinating over research projects and thesis topics. Moreover, they continue to do so until a semi-rational decision aid, like a deadline, forces them to make a choice and go through the motions, at least. Alternatively, their professor may assign them their hypothesis (and their method), perhaps one that the professor is working on excitedly, or one that serves to meet a grant deadline. In this middling confidence category we find most Ph.D.s who never do any more research after they graduate. We find, too, a host of faculty who stop doing research because they are "too open-minded," because there is much to be said for *and* against any hypothesis, and for *and* against any research method or statistical analysis. So, according to our model, being open-minded is not an advantage for social science researchers, but a marked liability.

Strong Believers   In Table 16–1, just above the middling believers are the productive theorists or speculators who possess strong confidence $(C = 0.7$ to $0.8)$ in the hypothesis, and yet also have enough energy left $(1 - C)$ to drive functional editing mechanisms that help him or her select out from the subsequent flow of evidence reinforcing positive instances, while also discounting or rebutting negative evidence. Such strong believers have enough energy to believe and to practice what has been called the scandal of induction—a general-purpose information-processing mechanism (g) that enables believers to edit in positive evidence and edit out negative evidence. Thus, a theorist reviewing the literature about a pet hypothesis can always find flaws in any study that challenges that hypothesis, but it requires cognitive energy, which strong believers have. If they are also very bright, then their inductive editing is impressive, and critics must remain on their toes to challenge them effectively.

Unlike the bigot, then, these investigators engage in critical analysis and debate, publish their findings, and attract disciples for varying lengths of time. For example, many graduate students who are unable to make up their own minds about hypotheses or methods become protégés and research assistants. Notice, with these additional cognitive resources (temporary academic slaves?), the professor can commence doing multi-method, multi-measure research, extending the methods (g's) and the data base ($E_1, \ldots, E_n$) of his/her explorations, as well as perhaps extending the external validity. Of course, during such conditions, some students eventually find a hypothesis or method of their own to believe in and research. Or, after graduation, as noted previously, many students give up sciencing completely, or become critics, or revert back to "there's much to be said for and against any hypothesis," concentrating their confidence instead on teaching, administration, criticism, golf, or wine making.

Strong Methodologists   In Table 16–1, just below the middling believer are investigators with enough confidence ($C = 0.2$ to 0.3) in a given hypothesis to help focus their editing mechanisms and data collection, but their true commitment ($1 - C$) is to their methods and technologies. They devote their cognitive energy toward developing and applying sophisticated hardware, software, and/or statistics to a limited content domain. They are not caught in the vacillating cycle of the middling believer who procrastinates. Rather, the mild belief of strong methodologists merely serves to help focus the driving methodological energy ($1 - C$), unlike the true technician who has no content focus. These strong methodologists can be very productive doing sophisticated explorations and publications in a special research area, such as one type of perception (e.g., perception of motion), or a particular slant on personality (like some factor analysts have done).

Strong Believers and Strong Methodologists   If the chemistry is right between a strong believer and a strong methodologist, it may generate the cognitive energy and skill to drive a very powerful and productive research team. The theorist provides the conceptual richness and sophistication, whereas the methodologist provides the sophisticated data collection and editing mechanisms to link multi-method, multi-measure research to the theory. Also, if their positive chemistry persists, they will attract others, including students, theoretical and methodological specialists, and camp followers, who will find niches in an expanding critical mass of speculations and observations the research team provides.

Eventually, however, as the enterprise grows exponentially, the founders will tend to become overloaded; they will run the risk of becoming research managers and of being overwhelmed by the mass of puzzling or conflicting results, methods, grant applications, staff turnovers, and conflicts. They will have spawned a monster that gradually will overwhelm their bounded rationality, and they will seek to return to a manageable theoretical or methodological space, perhaps becoming theoretical bigots, or methodological purists, or simply depressed.

AN OVERVIEW: THE MODEL
AND THE SIEVES OF SCIENCE

If one adopts the view of traditional philosophy of science—namely, that science is in the business of solving jigsaw puzzles, of confirming hypotheses—then there are very few methods or sieves to be discussed. The logic and the methods of confirmation are highly restrictive. Under such presuppositions, you must focus on control-group methods, and on researching the restricted space-time frames they require, settling for the internal validity they may generate, the highly local conclusions they produce.

If, on the other hand, you are familiar not only with the philosophy, but also with the history of science, and so are prepared to entertain the view that knowledge is the product of strong feedforward mechanisms selectively editing incomplete, and transformed, samples of experience, as outlined in Figure 16–2, then all the sieves of science become highly relevant to the enterprise, with some focusing on the feedforward mechanisms, some of the feedback mechanisms, and some on the interactions between the two. The adaptive expectations model we presented on page 237 presents a crude map of how these two mechanisms may interact to help us manage uncertainty—to help us produce functional, if fallible, knowledge. From this perspective, social science becomes an enterprise for conducting disciplined explorations aimed at generating functional frames of reference, theories, and hypotheses, as well as attempting to confirm hypotheses in selected, and limited, space-time domains. From this viewpoint, many of the qualitative and error-prone sieves of science cease being secondhand scientific citizens, and move into the front ranks as vitally important methods of generating disciplined hypotheses, and of functionally managing uncertainty, in a way that some traditional methods, such as the control-group approach, could never do.

The logic of confirmation, on which the so-called "scientific method" is based, has nothing to say about the two issues scientists worry about most: generating promising hypotheses, rather than merely "testable hypotheses"; and generalizing results from small sample observations in highly controlled or artificial settings (e.g., the issue of external validity discussed in Chapter 6).

The traditional and simplistic linear description of science looks like this:

Test hypothesis by scientific method and report results.

This view presents science as a kind of fact machine. Elaborating on this notion, but still keeping to the idea of one step following in orderly fashion after another, is the research cycle notion (see Figure 16–3). Student training focuses, in particular, on three of these steps: research methods, data collection, and analysis of results. We probably focus on these steps because they are the easiest to teach and test, not because we believe that sciencing is that simple. If we are researchers, we know that the most important step is selecting a "worthy" hypothesis—not just a testable hypothesis. But how does one teach that concept? We also know that our discussion and conclusions determine the scientific and social significance, rather than merely the statistical significance, of our work. But how do we teach this?

We know that sciencing is not a neat linear process of one step following another, as outlined in Figure 16–3, but rather a dynamic, nonlinear interplay of activities similar to those portrayed in Figure 16–4. But how do we teach this? Such dynamics are better learned by apprenticeship than by lecturing.

Although we have not found any sure-fire way of teaching these things—hypothesis generation, generalization of results, and the dynamics of sciencing—we believe we have made some progress. Our approach involves encouraging students to use the so-called qualitative methods,

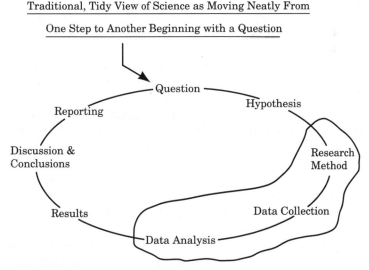

FIGURE 16–3   Science as Taught

An Open System View of Sciencing with Bounded

Rationality & Attention Shifting Unpredictably

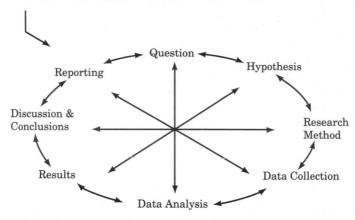

FIGURE 16–4   Science as Practiced

not merely as second-best choices (compared to control-group methods) in testing hypotheses, but as first-choice methods to facilitate the generation of a worthy hypothesis, the estimation of external validity, and the discovery and enjoyment, firsthand, of the dynamics of sciencing.

So, rather than presenting the qualitative methods as inadequate means of testing and confirming hypotheses, we present them as excellent means of exploring and generating personally and socially significant hypotheses. We attempt to demonstrate that hypothesis testing, as emphasized by confirmation theory, occupies a very small portion of the scientific decision space, as outlined in Figure 16–5. Real, live scientists implicitly rely on the qualitative methods to manage hourly most of the decision making of science, to make most important decisions, to decide which questions are worth devoting their lives to, as well as which theories are most useful.

Currently, the history of science, the sociology of science, and the psychology of science present embarrassing questions for the traditional scientific method. If such questions are covered at all in research training, they are covered in passing, rather than by using them to demonstrate that there are important tradeoffs to be made between generating nontrivial hypotheses and generating testable hypotheses. We need to point out that we are currently erring on the side of triviality and testability—establishing narrow internal validity. In meeting the conditions of the logic of confirmation, we are in danger of throwing out the baby with the bathwater. In relying so heavily on sampling theory and statistical significance, we are avoiding the tough issues of theoretical and

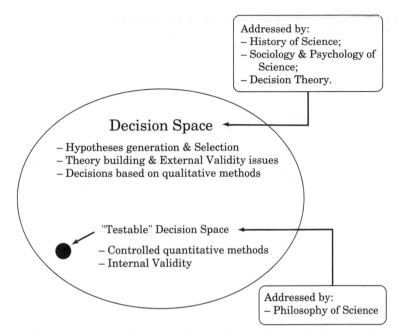

FIGURE 16–5   The Testable Decision Space Is Only a Tiny
Fraction of Scientific Decision Space

social significance; we are taking the easy way out, and are often leading our students down the path of frenetically testing trivial, off-the-
shelf hypotheses.

In Table 16–2, we list the major methods for not merely confirming
hypotheses in the narrow sense, but also for generating and evaluating
hypotheses. We need all these methods for managing the decision space
of science. We list the methods in order of "student affordability"—in
order of the ease of application—so that, through firsthand experience,
students learn to make wiser tradeoffs between the potential *relevance*
of a hypothesis, on the one hand, and its *testability*, on the other.
Through such explorations and pilot studies, students derive a better
chance of experiencing the dynamic excitement of sciencing, rather than
becoming disenchanted with, or addicted to, hypothesis-testing rituals
and the mass production of selective statistical significance (the publishing and recycling of type I errors).

CONCLUSIONS

Like Bacon, we might describe our own contemporary science—"the
method of reasoning which men now ordinarily apply to nature"—as consisting of "anticipations, rash and premature" and as "prejudices." (Popper,
1959, 278–279)

TABLE 16–2   Methods for Generating and Evaluating Hypotheses

DESIGN	TYPICAL DATA COLLECTION METHOD	RESEARCH CONTEXT
After-the-fact	Interview; archival; retrospective questionnaire	Historical time frame; may or may not be obtrusive
Before-and-after	Naturalistic and unobtrusive observations; questionnaire	Present time frame; obtrusive; on-stage
Field study	Naturalistic and/or unobtrusive observations	Usually extended space/time frame; may or may not be obtrusive
Survey	Interview; questionnaire	Past/present/future time frame; obtrusive
Natural experiment	Archival; retrospective questionnaire	Usually extended time frame into past; usually unobtrusive
Simulation	Real time observation and archival tracking; interviews; questionnaires	Contrived space/time frame; obtrusive
Longitudinal	Archival; tests; interviews; questionnaires	Extended time frame; may or may not be obtrusive
Field Experiment	Archival; tests; interviews; naturalistic or unobtrusive observations; questionnaires	Can be extended space/time frame in natural setting; usually obtrusive
Control Groups	Tests; real time observation; interviews; questionnaires	Restricted and controlled space/time frame; usually obtrusive

> The fallibility of reasoning is guaranteed both by the impossibility of generating unassailable propositions from particular facts, and by the tentative and theory-infected character of the facts themselves. Second, the principle of "no conclusions without premises" puts forever beyond reach normative statements. (Simon 1983, p. 6)

A quiet revolution is taking place in social science. Gradually, the main rule of the game is shifting from "rational/empirical confirmation of hypothesis" to the prime rule, *no conclusions without premises*. Notice how this new rule places the emphasis not on the conclusions, but rather on the premises on which the conclusions are based.

The key premise underlying rational/empirical research is unbounded rationality. But we no longer accept that premise; so, according to the new rule, we can hardly be very confident about the resulting conclusions or results of rational/empirical research. According to the bounded rationality premise, we can only practice rational/empirical research on a tiny portion of the decision-making domain of science—portions that have been radically reduced to mind-size by arbitrary, nonrational premises.

According to the bounded rationality premise, most of the decision making in science—most of our conclusions—must be based on nonrational, low-cognitive-cost information-processing mechanisms (e.g., after-the-fact methods).

If we accept as our main premise "no conclusions without premises," and if we also accept the bounded rationality premise, then the policies and practices of social science must change, and change significantly. For example, as noted earlier, we would recognize that rational/empirical methods can be applied to only an infinitesimal fraction of the puzzles we face, and then only after the time-space frame of the research domain had been radically reduced by nonrational premises; we would shift some of our rare rational resources to examining the importance of premises, shifting them from our current overcommitment to mindless data collection and analysis rituals; we would encourage the disciplined use of the qualitative sieves of science, for it is these sieves that enable us to explore large speculative spaces in search of functional premises for managing uncertainty and for making functional, if fallible, conclusions in large domains; we would select a treasured few of these well-winnowed premises for rational-empirical exploration, rather than wasting our rare resources on the uncritical selection and ritualistic investigation of hypotheses whose underlying theoretical and methodological premises have not, in most cases, been examined even casually, and if they were, would probably be unacceptable to the investigator.

In brief, we propose that social science would be better served by focusing on the disciplined use of qualitative methods for the trial-and-error winnowing of functional premises concerning human behavior; from this winnowing, a treasured (high confidence) few would be selected for focused testing by multimethod, multimeasure methods. Such a shift would involve more intense exploration of pragmatic, or speculative, space (for example, many disciplined thought experiments before real experiments), as well as a critical examination of the premises underlying (1) the prized logical and mathematical models (syntactics) and (2) the prized research methods (semantics), of the discipline or its gurus.

After rereading the foregoing, we detect a slight note of self-righteous indignation, and are nervously reminded of a quotation:

> Whoever undertakes to set himself up as a judge in the field of truth and knowledge is shipwrecked by the laughter of the Gods. (Einstein, 1972, p. 920)

REVIEW QUIZ

True or False?

1. Human brains and cultures have evolved to help protect us from pushing our reasoning beyond its capacity.
2. All human reasoning rests on a foundation of censorship.
3. The traditional view of human reasoning assumes that humans have unlimited rationality and that given the appropriate information and time humans will ultimately be able to solve any problem.
4. Herbert Simon, who won a Nobel Prize for his work on human decision making, proposed that human reasoning is highly rational.
5. All conclusions, including scientific conclusions, are based on the limited analysis of partial and conflicting information.
6. Marvin Minsky's constructed islands of consistency represent generalizations of a sort.
7. Thomas Kuhn, the historian of science, suggests that our core assumptions are flexible working hypotheses, readily open to revision as a result of cognitive or empirical feedback.
8. The assumption of cultural determinism is employed to support the generalization of superior analytical ability of males as compared with females.
9. Any large generalization that covers a lot of our experience (i.e., that covers a huge space-time domain of messages) cannot be empirically tested.
10. Naive realists believe that there is a directly knowable reality whose messages can be accurately determined using the scientific method based on the rational analysis of empirical data.
11. Karl Popper is a constructivist.
12. The goal of science is the sophisticated management of uncertainty.
13. Anchoring and adjustment models, as opposed to adaptive expectation models, allow you to describe and predict under what conditions subsequent information will influence initial beliefs.
14. In the case of someone with a very high level of confidence in a particular hypothesis (the true believer), the particular editing mechanisms used will strongly influence the final estimate.
15. Science is currently erring on the side of triviality and testability, focusing on the testability of a hypothesis rather than its relevance.
16. Most of the decision making in science (most scientific conclusions) must be based on nonrational, low-cognitive-cost information-processing mechanisms.

References and Suggested Readings

As well as citing articles referred to in the text, the following list includes a sampling of classic references concerning research design and theory construction.

ABRAHAMSEN, D. (1977). *Nixon vs Nixon: An emotional tragedy.* New York: Farrar, Straus, & Giroux.

ADAIR, G., Dushenko, T. W., & Lindsay, R. C. L. (1985). Ethical regulations and their impact on research practice. *American Psychologist, 40,* 59–72.

ADLER, T. (1989, June). HHS, Congress seeks ways to thwart fraud. *APA Monitor,* pp. 4–5.

AGNEW, N. M. (1964). The relative value of self report and objective tests in assessing the effects of amphetamine. *Journal of Psychiatric Research, 2,* 85–100.

AGNEW, N. McK., & BROWN, J. L. (1986). Bounded rationality: Fallible decisions in unbounded problem space. *Behavioral Science, 31,* 148–161.

AGNEW, N. McK., & BROWN, J. L. (1989a). Foundations for a model of knowing: I. Constructing reality. *Canadian Psychology, 30,* 152–167.

AGNEW, N. McK., & BROWN, J. L. (1989b). Foundations for a model of knowing: II. Fallible but functional knowledge. *Canadian Psychology, 30,* 152–167.

AGNEW, N. M., & ERNEST, C. H. (1971). Dose-response and biased set study of an amphetamine and a barbiturate. *Psychopharmacologia, 19,* 282–296.

AGNEW, N. M., & MILLER, G. (1975-76). An epidemiological paradigm for alcohol studies. *Drug Forum, 5,* 5–38.

AGNEW, N. McK., & PYKE, S. W. (1991). *The science game: An introduction to research in the behavioral sciences* (5th ed.). Englewood Cliffs, NJ: Prentice Hall.

AGNEW, N. McK., PYKE, S., & PYLYSHYN, W. W. (1966). Absolute judgment of distance as a function of induced muscle tension, exposure time and feedback. *Journal of Experimental Psychology, 71,* 649–654.

AJZEN, I., & FISHBEIN, M. (1980). *Understanding attitudes and predicting social behavior.* Englewood Cliffs, NJ: Prentice Hall.

AMERICAN PSYCHOLOGICAL ASSOCIATION. (1982). *Ethical principles in the conduct of research with human participants.* Washington, DC: Author.

AMERICAN PSYCHOLOGICAL ASSOCIATION. (1983). *Publications manual of the American Psychological Association* (3rd ed.). Washington, DC: Author.

AMERICAN PSYCHOLOGICAL ASSOCIATION. (1987). *Casebook on ethical principles of psychologists.* Washington, DC: Author.

AMERICAN PSYCHOLOGICAL ASSOCIATION. (1992). Ethical principles of psychologists and code of conduct. *American Psychologist, 47,* 1597–1611.

AMES, E. W., & CARTER, M. C. (1992, June). A study of Romanian orphanage children in Canada: Background, sample, and procedure. In E. W. Ames, Chair. *Development of Romanian orphanage children adopted to Canada.* Symposium presented at the Canadian Psychological Meeting, Quebec.

BAKAN, D. (1975). Speculation in psychology. *Journal of Humanistic Psychology, 15,* 17–25.

BALES, J. (1988, November). Breuning pleads guilty in scientific fraud case. *APA Monitor,* p. 12.

BARLOW, D. H., & HERSEN, M. (1984). *Single case experimental designs: Strategies for studying and changing behavior* (2nd ed.). New York: Pergamon Press.

BAUMRIND, D. (1964). Some thoughts on ethics of research: After reading Milgram's "Behavioral study of obedience." *American Psychologist, 19,* 421–423.

BAUMRIND, D. (1985). Research using intentional deception: Ethical issues revisited. *American Psychologist, 40,* 165–174.

BECKER, H. S. (1986). *Writing for social scientists: How to start and finish your thesis, book or article.* Chicago: University of Chicago Press.

BELENKY, M. F., Clinchy, B. McV., Goldberger, N. R., & Tarule, J. M. (1986). *Women's ways of knowing.* New York: Basic Books.

BEM, S. L. (1975). Sex role adaptability: One consequence of psychological androgyny. *Journal of Personality and Social Psychology, 31,* 634–643.

BENEDICT, J., & STOLOFF, M. (1991). Animal laboratory facilities at "America's Best" undergraduate colleges. *American Psychologist, 46,* 535–536.

BERKOWITZ, S. D. (1982). *An introduction to structural analysis: The network approach to social research.* Toronto: Butterworth.

BERRY, W. D., & LEWIS-BECK, M. S. (Eds.). (1986). *New tools for social scientists: Advances and applications in research methods.* Beverly Hills, CA: Sage.

BIRENBAUM, R. (1992). Establishing guidelines for research integrity. *University Affairs,* May, 6–9.

BLEIER, R. (1984). *Science and gender.* New York: Pergamon Press.

BLOCK, J. H. (1976). Debatable conclusions about sex differences. *Contemporary Psychology, 21,* 517–522.

BROWN, C., & SEITZ, J. (1970). "You've come a long way baby": Historical perspectives. In R. Morgan (Ed.), *Sisterhood is powerful.* New York: Vintage Books.

BRUNSWIK, E. (1952). The conceptual framework of psychology. In O. Neurath, R. Carnap, & C. Morris (Eds.), *International Encyclopedia of Unified Science* (Vol. 1). Chicago: University of Chicago Press.

BURNHAM, J. C. *How superstition won and science lost: Popularizing science and health in the United States.* New Brunswick, NJ: Rutgers University Press.

BUSS, A. (1976). Galton and sex differences. *Journal of the History of the Behavioral Sciences, 12,* 283–285.

CAMPBELL, D. T. (1960). Blind variation and selective retention in creative thought as in other knowledge processes. *Psychological Review, 67* 380–400.

CAMPBELL, D. T. (1969). Reforms as experiments. *American Psychologist, 24,* 409–429.

CAMPBELL, D. T. (1974a). "Downward causation" in hierarchically organized biological systems. In P. Dobzhansky & F. J. Ayala (Eds.), *Studies in the philosophy of biology.* London: Macmillan.

CAMPBELL, D. T. (1974b). Evolutionary epistemology. In P. A. Schlipp (Ed.), *The philosophy of Karl Popper: Vol. 14. The library of living philosophers.* La Salle, IL: Open Court Publishing.

CAMPBELL, D. T. (1975a). On the conflicts between biological and social evolution and between psychology and moral tradition. *American Psychologist, 30,* 1103–1126.

CAMPBELL, D. T. (1975b). Assessing the impact of planned social change. In G. M. Lyons (Ed.), *Social research in public policies*. Hanover, NH: Dartmouth College, Public Affairs Center.

CAMPBELL, D. T. (1975c). Degrees of freedom and the case study. *Comparative Political Studies, 31*, 178–193.

CAMPBELL, D. T. (1987). Selection theory and the sociology of scientific validity. In W. Callebaut & R. Pinxten (Eds.), *Evolutionary epistemology: A multiparadigm program* (pp. 130–158). Dordrecht, Holland: D. Reidel.

CAMPBELL, D. T., & ROSS, H. L. (1968). The Connecticut crackdown on speeding: Time-series data in quasi-experimental analysis. *Law and Society Review, 3*, 33–53.

CAMPBELL, D. T., & STANLEY, J. C. (1966). *Experimental and quasi-experimental design for research*. Chicago: Rand McNally.

CAMPBELL, N. R. (1928). *An account of the principles of measurement and calculation*. London: Longmans Green.

CANADIANS FOR HEALTH RESEARCH. (1992). *A true story*. Westmount, PQ: Author.

CARLSON, E. R., & CARLSON, R. (1960). Male and female subjects in personality research. *Journal of Abnormal and Social Psychology, 61*, 482–483.

CARROLL, L. (1939). *Alice's adventures in wonderland and through the looking glass*. London: William Collins & Sons.

CARROLL, M. A., Schneider, H. G., & Wesley, G. R. (1985). *Ethics in the practice of psychology*. Englewood Cliffs, NJ: Prentice Hall.

CHODOROW, N. (1978). *The reproduction of mothering*. Berkeley, CA: University of California Press.

COILE, D. C., & MILLER, N. E. (1984). How radical animal activists try to mislead humane people. *American Psychologist, 39*, 700–701.

COOK, T. D., & CAMPBELL, D. T. (1979). *Quasi-experimentation and analysis issues for field settings*. Boston: Houghton Mifflin.

CRAWFORD, M. P. (1985). Psychology, technology and professional service. *American Psychologist, 40*, 415–422.

CRAWFORD, M. & MARECEK, J. (1989). Psychology reconstructs the female 1968–1988. *Psychology of Women Quarterly, 13*, 147–165.

CREASE, R. P. (1992). Canadian chemist takes on working women. *Science, 255*, 1065–1066.

CRICHTON, M. (1972). *The terminal man*. London: J. Cape.

DAMON, A. (1965). Discrepancies between findings of longitudinal and cross-sectional studies in adult life. *Human Development, 8*, 16–22.

DANZIGER, K. (1985). The origins of the psychological experiment as a social institution. *American Psychologist, 40*, 133–140.

DARWIN, C. (1936). *The origin of species*. New York: Random House.

DAWKINS, R. (1976). *The selfish gene*. New York: Oxford University Press.

DEWSBURY, D. A. (1990). Early interactions between animal psychologists and animal activists and the founding of the APA Committee on precautions in animal experimentation. *American Psychologist, 45*, 315–327.

DOHERTY, M. A. (1973). Sexual bias in personality theory. *The Counselling Psychologist, 4*, 67–75.

EICHLER, M. (1988). The relationships between sexist, nonsexist, woman-centered, and feminist research. In A. T. McLaren (Ed.), *Gender and society* (pp. 31–61). Toronto: Copp Clark Pitman.

EINHORN, H. J., & HOGARTH, R. M. (1978). Confidence in judgement: Persistence of the illusion of validity. *Psychological Review, 5*, 395–416.

EINSTEIN, A. (1972). Aphorism for Leo. In G. Seldes (Ed.), *The great quotations* (p. 920). New York: Pocket Books.

EINSTEIN, E., & INFELD, L. (1966). *The evolution of physics*. New York: Simon & Schuster.

ELLSBERG, D. (1973). Women and war. In F. Klagsbrun (Ed.), *The first Ms. reader*. New York: Warner Paperback Library.

FALUDI, S. (1991). *Backlash*. New York: Crown.

FAVREAU, O. E. (1977). Sex bias in psychological research. *Canadian Psychological Review, 18*, 56–65.

FEE, E. (1976). Science and the woman problem: Historical perspectives. In M. S. Teitlebaum (Ed.). *Sex differences*. Garden City, NY: Anchor Books.

FEE, E. (1981). Is feminism a threat to scientific objectivity? *International Journal of Women's Studies, 4*, 378–392.

FESTINGER, L. (1946). *When prophecy fails: A social psychological study*. New York: Harper & Row.

FISCHBEIN, E. (1987). *Intuition in science and mathematics: An educational approach*. Dordrecht, The Netherlands: D. Reidel.

FOLKMAN, S., & LAZARUS, R. S. (1980). An analysis of coping in a middle-aged community sample. *Journal of Health and Social Behavior, 21*, 219–239.

FONOW, M. M., & COOK, J. A. (Eds.). (1991). *Beyond methodology: Feminist scholarship as lived research*. Bloomington: Indiana University.

FREEMAN, G. R. (1990). Kinetics of nonhomogeneous processes in human society: Unethical behaviour and societal chaos. *Canadian Journal of Physics, 68*, 794–798.

FREEMAN, G. R. (1992, January). Science of complexity. *Physics in Canada, 48*, 5–6.

FRIEDAN, B. (1963). *The feminine mystique*. New York: Dell.

GAINES, B. R. (1984). Methodology in the large: Modeling all there is. *Systems Research, 1*, 91–103.

GALLUP, G. G., JR., & EDDY, T. J. (1990). Animal facilities survey. *American Psychologist, 45*, 400–401.

GELFAND, H., & WALKER, C. J. (1990a). *Mastering APA style: Instructor's resource guide*. Washington, DC: American Psychological Association.

GELFAND, H., & WALKER, C. J. (1990b). *Mastering APA style: Student's workbook and training guide*. Washington, DC: American Psychological Association.

GELL-MANN, M. (1985, May). Omni.

GERGEN, K. J. (1976). Social psychology: Science and history. *Personality and Social Psychology Bulletin, 2*, 373–383.

GILLIGAN, C. (1982). *In a different voice*. Cambridge, MA: Harvard University Press.

GOULD, S. J. (1981). *The mismeasure of man*. New York: W. W. Norton.

GRADY, K. E. (1981). Sex bias in research design. *Psychology of Women Quarterly, 5*, 628–636.

GRAY, V. A. (1977). The image of women in psychology textbooks. *Canadian Psychological Review, 18*, 46–55.

GREENGLASS, E., & STEWART, M. (1973). The underrepresentation of women in social psychological research. *Ontario Psychologist, 5*, 21–29.

GUINAN, M. E. (1992). A vendetta against working mothers published as science in the *Canadian Journal of Physics*: The editor's role. *Journal of the American Medical Women's Association, 47*, 113–114.

HALL, J. E., & HARE-MUSTIN, R. T. (1983). Sanctions and the diversity of ethical complaints against psychologists. *American Psychologist, 38*, 714–729.

HANEY, C., BANKS, C., & ZIMBARDO, P. (1973). Interpersonal dynamics in a simulated prison. *International Journal of Criminology and Penology, 1,* 69–97.

HANSON, D. J. (1980). Relationship between methods and findings in attitude-behavior research. *Psychology, 17,* 11–13.

HARPER, T. (1985, April 17). Abortion bombers like "knights" not terrorists, lawyers tell trial. *Toronto Star,* p. A25.

HAWKING, S. W. (1988). *A brief history of time.* New York: Bantam Books.

HEBB, D. O. (1970). A return to Jensen and his social science critics. *American Psychologist, 25,* 568.

HEDGES, L. V. (1987). How hard is hard science, how soft is soft science? *American Psychologist, 42,* 443–455.

HEINSENBERG, W. (1975, March). The great tradition. *Encounter,* 52–58.

HOYENGA, K. B., & HOYENGA, K. T. (1988). *Psychobiology: The neuron and behavior.* Pacific Grove, CA: Brooks/Cole.

HYDE, J. S. (1981). How large are cognitive gender differences? A meta-analysis using w^2 and d. *American Psychologist, 36,* 892–901.

INVANCEVICH, J. M., & MATTESON, M. T. (1978). Longitudinal organizational research in field settings. *Journal of Business Research, 6,* 181–201.

JACOBS, J. (1979). A phenomenological study of suicide notes. In H. Schwartz & J. Jacobs (Eds.), *Qualitative Sociology* (pp. 156–167). New York: The Free Press.

JENSEN, A. R. (1969a). How much can we boost IQ and scholastic achievement? *Harvard Educational Review, 39,* 1–123.

JENSEN, A. R. (1969b). Criticism or propaganda? *American Psychologist, 24,* 1040–1041.

JICK, T. D. (1979). Mixing qualitative methods: Triangulation in action. *Administrative Science Quarterly, 24,* 602–611.

KAGAN, D. (1985, May). *Omni,* pp. xx.

KAMIN, L. J. (1981). Intelligence. In J. M. Darley, S. Glucksberg, L. J. Kamin, & R. A. Kinchla (Eds.), *Psychology.* Englewood Cliffs, NJ: Prentice Hall.

KAZDIN, A. E. (1989). The power to detect differences between alternative treatments in comparative psychotherapy outcome research. *Journal of Consulting and Clinical Psychology, 57,* 138–147.

KING, F. A. (1984, September). Animals in research: The case for experimentation. *Psychology Today,* 56–58.

KITZINGER, C. (1986). Introducing and developing Q as a feminist methodology: A study of accounts of lesbianism. In S. Wilkinson (Ed.), *Feminist social psychology* (pp. 151–172). Milton Keynes, UK: Open University Press.

KITZINGER, C. (1987). *The social construction of lesbianism.* London: Sage.

KITZINGER, C., & ROGERS, R. S. (1985). A Q-methodological study of lesbian identities. *European Journal of Social Psychology, 15,* 167–187.

KMENTA, J. (1971). *Elements of econometrics.* New York: Macmillan.

KOEING, K. P., & MASTERS, J. (1965). Experimental treatment of habitual smoking. *Behaviour Research and Therapy, 3,* 235–243.

KUHN, T. (1970). *The structure of scientific revolutions* (2nd ed.). Chicago: University of Chicago Press.

KUHN, T. (1972). Reflections on my critics. In Lakatos, I., & Musgrave, A. (Eds.), *Criticisms and growth of knowledge.* Cambridge, MA: Cambridge University Press.

LAKOFF, G. (1986). Cognitive models and prototype theory. In E. Neisser (Ed.), *Concepts and conceptual development: Ecological and intellectual factors in categorization.* Cambridge, MA: Cambridge University Press.

LANCASTER, J. B. (1976). Sex roles in primate societies. In M. S. Teitlebaum (Ed.), *Sex differences* (pp. 22–61). Garden City, NY: Anchor Books.

LANDERS, S. (1989, June). New animal care rules greeted with grumbles. APA *Monitor, 1,* 4–5.

LANDSBERGER, H. (1958). *Hawthorne revisited.* Ithaca, NY: Cornell University Press.

LATANE, B., & DARLEY, J. M. (1968). Group inhibition of bystander intervention in emergencies. *Journal of Personality and social Psychology, 10,* 215–221.

LATANE, B., & RODIN, J. (1969). A lady in distress: Inhibiting effects of friends and strangers on bystander intervention. *Journal of Experimental Social Psychology, 5,* 189–202.

LEONARD, M. M., & COLLINS, A. M. (1979). Women as footnote. *The Counseling Psychologist, 8,* 6–7.

LESTER, J. D. (1976). *Writing research papers: A complete guide* (2nd ed.). Agincourt, Ontario: Gage.

LINVILLE, P. (1985). Self-complexity and affective extremity. *Social Cognition, 3,* 94–120.

LUCE, D. (1988). The tools-to-theory hypothesis. *Contemporary Psychology, 33,* 582–583.

MACCOBY, E. E., & JACKLIN, C. N. (1974). *The psychology of sex differences.* Stanford, CA: Stanford Press.

MACKIE, M. (1983). *Exploring gender relations.* Toronto: Butterworths.

MAROTZ-BADEN, R., & COLVIN, P. L. (1986). Coping strategies: A rural-urban comparison. *Family Relations, 35,* 281–288.

MATLIN, M. W. (1993). *The psychology of women* (2nd ed.). Fort Worth, TX: Harcourt Brace Jovanovich.

MCCORMACK, T. (1989). Feminism and the new crisis in methodology. In W. Tomm (Ed.), *The effects of feminist approaches on research and methodologies* (pp. 13–30). Waterloo, Ontario: Wilfrid Laurier University Press.

MEDICAL RESEARCH COUNCIL OF CANADA. (1988). *Towards an international ethic for research with human beings.* Ottawa, Ontario: Minister of Supply and Services.

MERCHANT, C. (1980). *The death of nature.* San Francisco: Harper & Row.

MILGRAM, S. (1963). Behavioral study of obedience. *Journal of Abnormal and Social Psychology, 67,* 371–378.

MILGRAM, S. (1965). Issues in the study of obedience: A reply to Baumrind. *American Psychologist, 19,* 848–852.

MILGRAM, S. (1970). The experience of living in cities. *Science, 167,* 1461–1468.

MILGRAM, S., BICKMAN, L., & BERKOWITZ, L. (1969). Note on the drawing power of crowds of different size. *Journal of Personality and Social Psychology, 13,* 79–82.

MILLER, D. C. (1991). *Handbook of research design and social measurement* (5th ed.). London: Sage.

MILLS, D. H. (1984). Ethics education and adjudication within psychology. *American Psychologist, 39,* 669–675.

MINSKY, M. (1983). Jokes and the logic of the cognitive unconscious. In Groner, R., Groner, M., & Bischof, W. F. (Eds.), *Methods of heuristics* (pp. 171–193). Hillsdale, NJ: Lawrence Erlbaum.

MONEY, J., & EHRHARDT, A. A. (1972). *Man and woman, boy and girl: The differentiation and dimorphism of gender identity from conception to maturity.* Baltimore: Johns Hopkins University Press.

MONTAGU, A. (Ed.). (1980). *Sociobiology examined.* New York: Oxford University Press.

MOULTON, J., ROBINSON, F. M., & ELIAS, C. (1978). Sex bias in language use. *American Psychologist, 33*, 1032–1036.

NASH, M. M. (1975). "Non-reactive methods and the law." Additional comments on legal liability in behavior research. *American Psychologist, 30*, 777–780.

NEWTON, I. (1972). In G. Seldes (Ed.), *The great quotations* (p. 929). New York: Pocket Books.

NIELSEN, J. M. (Ed.). (1990). *Feminist research methods: Exemplary reading in the social sciences*. Boulder, CO: Westview.

ORNE, M. T. (1962). On the social psychology of the psychological experiment: With particular reference to demand characteristics and their implications. *American Psychologist, 17*, 776–783.

OSKAMP, S. (1977). Methods of studying social behavior. In L. S. Wrightsman (Ed.), *Social psychology* (2nd ed., Chap. 2). Monterey, CA: Brooks/Cole.

PARLEE, M. B. (1981). Appropriate control groups in feminist research. *Psychology of Women Quarterly, 5*, 637–644.

PERCIVAL, B. (1984). Sex bias in introductory psychology textbooks: Five years later. *Canadian Psychology, 25*, 35–42.

PILIAVIN, J. A., & PILIAVIN, I. M. (1972). Effect of blood on reaction to a victim. *Journal of Personality and Social Psychology, 23*, 353–361.

POPPER, K. (1969). *The logic of scientific discovery*. New York: Basic Books.

POPPER, K. (1972). *Objective knowledge: An evolutionary approach*. Oxford: Clarendon.

POPPER, K. (1973, April). Indeterminism is not enough. *Encounter*, 20–26.

POPPER, K. (1974). Autobiography of Karl Popper. In P. Schilipp (Ed.), *The philosophy of Karl Popper: Book I* (pp. 2–181). LaSalle, IL: Open Court.

POSAVAC, E. J., & CAREY, R. G. (1989). *Program evaluation: Methods and case studies*. Englewood Cliffs, NJ: Prentice Hall.

PREMACK, D. (1970). Mechanisms of self-control. In W. Hunt (Ed.), *Learning and mechanisms of control in smoking*. Hawthorne, NY: Aldine.

PYKE, S. W. (1976). Children's literature: Conceptions of sex roles. In W. C. Mann & L. Wheatcraft (Eds.), *Canada: A sociological profile* (3rd ed., pp. 158–171). Toronto: Copp/Clark.

PYKE, S. W. (1979). Cognitive templating: A technique for feminist (and other) counselors. *Personnel and Guidance Journal, 57*, 315–318.

PYKE, S.W. (1982). Confessions of a reluctant ideologist. *Canadian Psychology, 23*, 125–134.

PYKE, S. W. (1988). Dichotomies: An alien perspective. *Atlantis, 14* (1), 56–61.

PYKE, S. W., Agnew, N. McK., & Kopperud, J. (1966). Modification of an overlearned maladaptive response through a relearning program: A pilot study on smoking. *Behaviour Research and Therapy, 4*, 197–203.

PYKE, S. W., RICKS, F. A., STEWART, J. C., & NEELY, C. A. (1975). The sex variable in Canadian psychological journals. In M. Wright (Chair), *The status of women psychologists*. Symposium presented at the meeting of the Ontario Psychological Association, Toronto.

REINHARZ, S. (1992). *Feminist methods in social research*. New York: Oxford University.

RIMLAND, B., & MUNSINGER, H. (1977). Burt's IQ data. *Science, 195*, 248.

ROBINSON, P. W., & FOSTER, D. F. (1979). *Experimental psychology: A small-n approach*. New York: Harper & Row.

ROETHLISBERGER, F. J., & DICKSON, W. J. (1948). *Management and the worker*. Cambridge, MA: Harvard University Press.

ROSENTHAL, R. (1963). On the social psychology of the psychological experiment: The experimenter's hypothesis as an unintended determinant of experimental results. *American Scientist, 51*, 268–283.

ROTH, P. A. (1987). *Meaning and method in the social sciences: A case of methodological pluralism*. Ithaca, NY: Cornell University Press.

RUCKDESCHEL, R. A. (1985). Qualitative research as a perspective. *Social Work Research & Abstracts, 21*(2), 17–21.

RUSHTON, J. P. (1989). Evolutionary biology and heritable traits (with reference to Oriental-white-black differences). In *Evolutionary theory, economics and political science: An emerging theoretical convergence*. Symposium presented at the meeting of the American Association for the Advancement of Science, San Francisco.

SELDES, G. (1972). *The great quotations*. New York: Pocket Books.

SHIELDS, S. A. (1975). Functionalism, Darwinism, and the psychology of women: A study in social myth. *American Psychologist, 30*, 739–754.

SILVEIRA, J. (1980). Generic masculine words and thinking. *Women's Studies International Quarterly, 3*, 165–178.

SIMON, H. A. (1970). *The science of the artificial*. Cambridge, MA: Massachusetts Institute of Technology Press.

SIMON, H. A. (1979, September). Rational decision making in business organizations. *American Economic Review*, 493–515.

SIMON, H. A. (1983). *Reason in human affairs*. Stanford: Stanford University Press.

SMITH, M. S., & GLASS, A. L. (1977). Meta-analysis of psychotherapy outcome studies. *American Psychologist, 32*, 752–760.

STARK-ADAMEC, C. (In press). Social science and scientific responsibility: Invited commentary on "Unethical Behaviour and Societal Chaos." *Canadian Journal of Physics*.

STARK-ADAMEC, C., & KIMBALL, M. (1984). Science free of sexism: A psychologist's guide to the conduct of nonsexist research. *Canadian Psychology, 25*, 23–34.

STEWART, D. (1989, February). Interview Walter Stewart. *Omni, 11*, 65, 87.

STEWART, I., & PALL, D. (1977). *The foundations of mathematics*. Oxford: Oxford University Press.

STONE, A. A., & NEALE, J. M. (1984). New measure of daily coping: Development and preliminary results. *Journal of Personality and Social Psychology, 46*, 892–906.

STRAUSS, S. (1991, July 31). Journal apologizes for article. *The Globe and Mail*, p. A7.

SULLIVAN, M. A., QUEEN, S. A., & PATRICK, R. C. (1970). Participant observation as employed in the study of a military training program. In W. J. Filstead (Ed.), *Qualitative methodology: Firsthand involvement with the social world* (pp. 91–100). Chicago: Markham.

TESHER, E. (1981, April 16). Tranquilizers tested for link with cancer. *Toronto Star*, p. A2.

THOMAS, G. V., & BLACKMAN, D. (1992). The future of animal studies in psychology. *American Psychologist, 47*, 1679.

TRICE, H. M. (1970). The "outsider's" role in field study. In W. J. Filstead (Ed.), *Qualitative methodology: Firsthand involvement with the social world* (pp. 77–82). Chicago: Markham.

TVERSKY, A. (1977). Features of similarity. *Psychological Review, 84*, 327–352.

UNGER, R. K. (1979). Toward a redefinition of sex and gender. *American Psychologist, 34*, 1085–1094.

WALLSTON, B. S. (1981). What are the questions in psychology of women? A feminist approach to research. *Psychology of Women Quarterly, 5*, 597–617.

WATSON, D. L., & THARP, R. G. (1977). *Self-directed behavior: Self-modification for personal adjustment.* Monterey, CA: Brooks/Cole.

WEBB, F. J., CAMPBELL, D. T., SCHWARTZ, R. D., & SECHREST, L. (1966). *Unobtrusive measures: Nonreactive research in the social sciences.* Chicago: Rand McNally.

WEYANT, R. G. (1979). The relationship between psychology and women. *International Journal of Women's Studies, 2,* 358–385.

WHITE, M. S. (1975). Women in the professions: Psychological and social barriers to women in science. In J. Freeman (Ed.), *Women: A feminist perspective* (pp. 227–237). Palo Alto, CA: Mayfield.

WIESENTHAL, D. L. (1974). Reweaving deception's tangled web. *Canadian Psychologist, 15,* 326–336.

WILSON, D. W., & DONNERSTEIN, E. (1976). Legal and ethical aspects of nonreactive social psychological research: An excursion in the public mind. *American Psychologist, 31,* 765–773.

WILSON, E. O. (1975). *Sociobiology: The new synthesis.* Cambridge, MA: Harvard University Press.

WISPE, L. G., & THOMPSON, J. R., JR. (1976). The war between the words, biological versus social evolution and some related issues. *American Psychologist, 31,* 341–384.

WOLFE, M. (1991, July 18). Why does a scholarly journal publish prejudice passed off as science? *The Globe and Mail,* p. D1.

WOLFE, M. (1992, April 28). Morris Wolfe ponders the NRC's belated action in the Freeman affair. *The Globe and Mail,* p. C1.

WOODWARD, B., & ARMSTRONG, S. (1981). *The brethren.* New York: Avon.

WOOLSEY, L. (1977). Psychology and the reconciliation of women's double bind: To be feminine or to be fully human. *Canadian Psychological Review, 18,* 66–78.

ZALK, S. R., & GORDON-KELTER, J. (Eds.). (1992). *Revolutions in knowledge: Feminism in the social sciences.* Boulder, CO: Westview.

ZIEGLER, M., WIESENTHAL, D. L., WIENER, N. I., & WEIZMANN, F. (1989, February 3). Is science too eager to stake its claims? *The Globe and Mail,* p. A7.

ZIMBARDO, P. G. (1970, April). *Symposium on social and developmental issues in moral research.* Paper presented at the meeting of the Western Psychological Association, Los Angeles.

ZIMMERMAN, S. (1993). The National Research Council *Canadian Journal of Physics*: Publication of the Freeman article. *Canadian Society for Cellular and Molecular Biology Bulletin, 17,* 7–9.

Answers to Review Quiz Questions

Chapter 1 (p. 37–38)

1. False	6. False	11. True	16. True
2. True	7. True	12. False	17. True
3. True	8. True	13. False	18. False
4. True	9. False	14. False	
5. True	10. True	15. True	

Chapter 2 (pp. 68–69)

1. True	6. False	11. True	16. False
2. True	7. True	12. False	17. False
3. True	8. True	13. True	18. True
4. False	9. True	14. True	19. True
5. False	10. False	15. True	20. True

Chapter 3 (pp. 89–90)

1. True	4. True	7. True	10. True
2. True	5. False	8. False	11. False
3. False	6. True	9. True	12. True

Chapter 4 (pp. 108–109)

1. True	4. False	7. True	10. True
2. False	5. True	8. True	11. False
3. True	6. True	9. False	12. True

Chapter 5 (pp. 128–129)

1. False	5. True	9. True	13. True
2. True	6. True	10. True	14. True
3. False	7. False	11. True	15. True
4. False	8. False	12. True	

Chapter 6 (pp. 144–145)

1. True	5. False	9. False	13. True
2. False	6. True	10. False	14. True
3. True	7. True	11. True	
4. True	8. False	12. False	

Chapter 7 (pp. 164–165)

1. True	5. True	9. True	13. True
2. True	6. True	10. True	14. True
3. False	7. False	11. True	15. False
4. False	8. False	12. False	

Chapter 8 (p. 189)

1. True	5. False	9. False	13. True
2. False	6. True	10. False	14. True
3. False	7. False	11. True	
4. True	8. True	12. False	

Chapter 9 (p. 207)

1. False	5. False	9. True	13. False
2. False	6. False	10. False	14. False
3. True	7. True	11. True	15. False
4. True	8. True	12. True	16. False

Chapter 10 (pp. 226–227)

1. True	5. False	9. True	13. False
2. False	6. False	10. True	14. True
3. True	7. True	11. False	15. True
4. False	8. True	12. True	16. False

Chapter 11 (p. 242)

1. True	5. False	9. True	13. True
2. False	6. True	10. True	14. False
3. False	7. False	11. True	15. False
4. True	8. True	12. False	16. True

Chapter 12 (p. 268)

1. False	5. True	9. True	13. True
2. True	6. True	10. True	14. True
3. False	7. True	11. False	
4. True	8. False	12. True	

Chapter 13 (p. 290)

1. False	6. False	11. True	16. False
2. False	7. False	12. True	17. False
3. True	8. True	13. False	
4. True	9. True	14. True	
5. True	10. False	15. True	

Chapter 14 (pp. 301–302)

1. True	4. False	7. False	10. False
2. True	5. True	8. False	11. True
3. False	6. False	9. False	12. True

Chapter 15 (p. 322)

1. True	5. True	9. False	13. True
2. True	6. False	10. True	14. True
3. False	7. True	11. False	15. True
4. False	8. False	12. True	

Chapter 16 (p. 350)

1. True	5. True	9. True	13. False
2. True	6. True	10. True	14. False
3. True	7. False	11. False	15. True
4. False	8. False	12. True	16. True

Index

ABAB reversal design, 264–65
Abstract, research report, 293–94
Adair, G., 283
Adaptive expectations model, 337–38, 344
Adler, T., 287
Administrative procedures, survey, 200–201
After-the-fact method, 70–89
  benefits of, 80–81
  concept of, 71
  counselor example, 82–89
  court example, 72–75
  historian example, 75–76
  major problems in, 79–80
  physician example, 76–77
  popularity of, 79
  risk of error, reduction of, 77–79
Agnew, N. McK., 118, 223, 336, 340
Ajzen, I., 136
Alsip, J. E., 291n
Ambiguity, 292–93
American Psychological Association (APA), 270, 271, 273n, 276, 281, 283, 287, 291–93, 296
American Society for the Prevention of Cruelty to Animals, 281
Ames, E. W., 114–15
Analysis of variance (ANOVA), 251–54
Anchoring and adjustment models, 337–38
Anderson, B. F., 291n
Animal research, 281–82
Annual Review of Psychology, 297
Antecedents, 20, 29–33, 55
Apparatus unit, research report, 295
Appendix, research report, 296–97
Arbitrary-zero scales, 217–19
Archival research, 180–86
  concept of, 180
  content analysis, 181–83
  example of, 186–88
  spoor analysis, 183–84
  strengths and weaknesses of, 184–86
Ardrey, R., 308
Area sampling, 199
Asimov, Isaac, 291

Bales, J., 287
Banks, C., 123
Barker, R. G., 178, 179
Barlow, D. H., 267
Baumrind, D., 278–79, 283
Becker, H. S., 291n
Before-and-after method, 91–108

concept of, 92
elimination of stray suspects and, 98–99
example of, 100–108
misleading suspects in, 92–96
quick-acting suspects and, 97–98
stable observations and, 96–97
stages of, 91
Belenky, M. F., 195, 319
Beliefs:
  decision making style and confidence in, 337–38, 341–44
  distortion caused by, 173
  initial, confidence in, 337–38
  observation based on, 13–17
Bem, S. L., 175, 176, 178
Benedict, J., 282
Benedict, R., 270
Berkowitz, L., 123
Bias, 6–7, 76, 79
  arbitrary-zero scales, 219
  control-group method and, 120–21
  "cop-out," 194
  experimenter, 121
  "faking bad," 193
  inconsistent responding, 194
  "nay-saying," 193
  researcher, 198
  sex, 306–18
    in content, 308
    design sources of, 316–17
    in evaluation, 311–12
    historical examples of, 307–8
    inference bias, 312
    language bias, 312–13
    publication bias, 316
    researcher bias, 317–18
    selection and distortion of evidence, 313–14
    statistical bias, 314–16
    in subject selection, 308
    theory bias, 308–11
  social desirability, 193
  "yea-saying," 193
Biased dropout, 120
Biased responding, 193–94
Biased selection, 120–21, 174–75
Bickman, L., 123
Billings, A. G., 314
Birenbaum, R., 286
Blackman, D., 282
Bleier, R., 303, 305, 309, 319
Block, Jeanne, 318
Bounded rationality, 326–27, 348–49

Breuning, Stephen, 287
Broverman, D. M., 311
Brown, C., 270
Brown, J. L., 336, 340
Brown, S. R., 197n
Brozek, J., 284
Buckley, William F., 329
Burt, Cyril, 285–86
Buss, A., 307

Campbell, D. T., 92, 122, 131, 153, 180,
    334, 340
Canadian Journal of Physics (CJP), 288–89
Canadian Psychological Association, 319
Canadians for Health Research, 281
Carli, Linda, 317
Carlson, E. R., 308
Carlson, R., 308
Carroll, M. A., 282, 283
Casebook on Ethical Principles of
    Psychologists (APA), 287
Case method, 72 (See also After-the-fact
    method)
Cause and effect, 18–20
Ceiling effects, 148
Central values, 229–31
Chance, maps of, 245–46
Change, mapping of (see Time series
    studies)
Chezik, D. D., 291n
Chi square test, 256–60
Chodorow, N., 319
Classification of observations, 178–79
Clinchy, B. McV., 195, 319
Code of ethics (see Ethics)
Coding categories:
    for content analysis, 181–82
    for personal interviews, 195
Cognitively affordable decisions, 327
Cognitive template, 86–87
Cognitive theorists, 81
Coile, D. C., 282, 283
Collins, A. M., 311
Colvin, P. L., 314
Commentary, 16–17
Commonsense vs. scientific reasoning, 2–8,
    21, 22, 27–28
Concurrent validity, 136–37
Consequence, 20
Consistency, islands of, 327–33
Constructivism, 333–36
Construct validity, 137
Contemporary Psychology, 297
Content analysis, 181–83
Content of research, sex bias in, 308
Content validity, 136
Control-group method, 99, 110–28, 344
    biased selections and, 120–21
    concept of, 111, 113
    differential mortality and, 120

elaboration of, 115–21
example of, 126–28
extension of, 122–24
limitations of, 121–22
longitudinal studies and, 156–58
misleading suspects in, 111–13
selection of comparison group, 113–15,
    120–21
statistical regression and, 119–20
unobtrusive measures and, 124
Cook, J. A., 320
Cook, T.D., 153
Coordinated research, 139–40
"Cop-out" bias, 194
Correlation, 234–41
    cautions in use of, 239
    degree of, 234–38
    factor analysis and, 240–41
    interpretation of, 238–39
    Pearson product-moment, 236–38
    prediction and, 239–40
Correlation coefficient, 235–36
Cost-benefit ratio, ethics and, 284–85
Council for the Society for the
        Psychological Study of Social Issues
        (SPSSI), 280
Counselor, after-the-fact method used by,
    82–89
Courts of justice:
    after-the-fact method used in, 72–75
    labeling by, 51
Covert observers, 176
Crawford, M. P., 32, 319
Crease, R. P., 288
Crichton, Michael, 284
Crossley, H. M., 201
Cross-over design, 118
Cross-sectional studies, 149–51
Curiosity, compelling, 23–24

Damon, A., 150
Dancik, B. P., 289
Darsee, John, 286
Darwin, C., 170
Data collection instruments, 191–98
    focus groups, 196
    personal interviews, 195–96, 203–6
    Q methodology, 196–98
    questionnaires, 135, 136, 191–94, 202
    telephone interviews, 194
Data drift, 131
Data mortality, 131, 132, 200
Dawkins, R., 309–10
Decision theory, 336–44
Demand characteristics, 139
Dependent variables:
    measurement scales and, 220–26
    (See also Observations)
Descriptive statistics, 228–42
    central values, 229–31

correlation, 234–41
  cautions in use of, 239
  degree of, 234–38
  factor analysis and, 240–41
  interpretation of, 238–39
  Pearson product-moment, 236–38
  prediction and, 239–40
  defined, 228
  variability measures, 231–34
Design sources of sex bias, 316–17
Developmental studies (see Time series
  studies)
Devore, I., 313
Dewsbury, D. A., 281
Dickson, W. J., 159
Differential mortality, 120
Discussion section, research report, 296
Dissertation Abstracts, 297
Distortion:
  ethnographic research and, 173–74
  of evidence, 313–14
  (See also Bias)
Doherty, M. A., 308
Donnerstein, E., 279
Double-blind procedure, 112
d statistic, 256
Durkheim, E., 182
Dushenko, T. W., 283

Eagly, Alice, 317
Eddy, T. J., 282
Eggan, D., 270
Ehrhardt, A. A., 310
Eichler, M., 312, 319, 320
Einhorn, H. J., 336
Einstein, A., 349
Einstein, E., 48–49
Elastic-ruler suspects (see Instrument-
  decay suspects)
Elias, C., 313
Ellsberg, D., 271
Equivalence relations, 53
Ernest, C. H., 223
Errors, 3, 4
  after-the-fact method and, 75n, 77–79
  before-and-after method and, 93–96
  control group method and, 111, 117–18
  sampling, theory of, 247–51
  Type I and Type II, 262–64
Ethics, 269–89
  animal research, 281–82
  case studies, 278–81, 288–89
  government and law and, 285–87
  influence of ethical codes and practices
    on conduct of research, 283–85
  quiz on, 273–78
  relativity of, 270–73
Ethnographic research, 169–80
  classification/interpretation of observa-
    tions, 178–79

conclusions about, 179–80
  observational task, 172–75
  observer role, 176–78
  setting, 171–72
Evaluation bias, 311–12
Evaluation research, 154–59
Evidence, selection and distortion of,
    313–14
Expectations, 5
  constructivist view and, 336
  observation based on, 13–17
Experimental science, 21–22, 27
Experimentation, systematic, 21, 26–29
Experimenter bias, 121
Expert judgment, 45, 51
Explanation, 17–20
External validity:
  concept of, 132
  measurement restrictions and, 133,
    135–37
  research context restrictions and, 134,
    138–40
  sample restrictions and, 133–35
  survey research and, 202
  treatment restrictions and, 133, 137–38
Eyeball technique, 170
Eysenck, H. J., 285

Factor analysis, 240–41
"Faking bad," 193
Faludi, S., 270
Favreau, O. E., 311, 312, 314, 315
Fee, E., 305, 318, 320, 321
Festinger, L., 177
Field experiments, 123, 176
Field studies (see Ethnographic research)
Fishbein, M., 136
Focus groups, 196
Folkman, S., 314
Fonow, M. M., 320
Formal language, 52–67
  decoding scientific news with, 64–67
  life expectancy of a scientific concept,
    63–64
  linking with observational language,
    56–63
  symbol relationships in, 52–56
Franklin, Rosalind, 306
Fraud, 285–87
Freeman, G. R., 288
Freeman, Gordon, 288–89
F tests, 251–54

Gallop, G. G., Jr., 282
Galton, Sir Francis, 180–81, 307
Garai, J. E., 312
Gell-Mann, M., 48
Gender, science and (see Sex, science and)
Gibbin, J. R., 180
Gilligan, C., 319

Glass, A. L., 255–56
Goffman, E., 177
Goldberger, N. R., 195, 319
Gordon-Kelter, J., 320
Government, ethics and, 285–87
Grady, K. E., 308, 316, 317
Gray, V. A., 308
Greenglass, E., 308
Group pressure, 51
Guilford, J. P., 258
Guinan, M. E., 288

Hall, J. E., 283, 313
Haney, C., 123
Hanson, D. J., 201
Hare-Mustin, R. T., 283
Hawthorne effect, 159–60
Hebb, D. O., 280
Henley, W. E., 267
Henschel, A., 284
Hersen, M., 267
Historians, after-the-fact method used by, 75–76
Historical (in-the-gap) suspects:
  before-and-after method and, 93–94
  control-group method and, 111–12
  research context and, 138
Hogarth, R. M., 336
Hutt, N., 314
Huxley, Aldous, 7–8
Hyde, J. S., 307, 316

Impersonality, in report writing, 292, 293
Inconsistent responding, 194
Independent variables (suspects):
  before-and-after method and, 92–98
  control-group method and, 111–13
  ethnographic research and, 176, 177
  evaluation research and, 156
  external validity and, 138
  internal validity and, 132
  measurement scales and, 220–26
Infeld, L., 48–49
Inference bias, 312
Inferential statistics, 243–67
  analysis of variance (ANOVA), 251–54
  chi square test, 256–60
  defined, 228
  factors producing significant
    differences, 244–45
  maps of chance, 245–46
  meta-analysis, 254–56
  N-of-1 research, 264–67
  nonparametric tests, 261
  parametric tests, 260–61
  sampling error theory, 247–51
  sampling theory, 246–47
  statistically improbable events, 262
  t tests, 250–51
  Type I and Type II errors, 262–64

Informed consent, 283
Initial beliefs, confidence in, 337–38
In Search of Schrodinger's Cat (Gribbin), 180
Instrument-decay (elastic-ruler) suspects:
  before-and-after method and, 94, 95
  control-group method and, 112
Interaction effects, 131, 253
Internal validity:
  concept of, 131, 132
  survey research and, 202
  threats to, 132
Interpretation:
  in after-the-fact method example, 82–89
  of correlation coefficients, 238–39
  in ethnographic research, 178–79
Interrupted time series:
  concept of, 153–54
  evaluation research example, 154–59
  student project on testimonials in rela-
    tion to, 161–64
Interrupted time series control group
  design, 156
Interval scales, 213–15, 219
Interviewer characteristics, 200–201
Interviews, 202
  personal, 195–96, 203–6
  telephone, 194
In-the-gap suspects (see Historical suspects)
Introduction, research report, 294
Intuition, 29–32
Invisible observers, 176
Islands-of-truth concept, 327–33

Jacklin, C. N., 255, 313, 316, 318
Jackson, W., 191n
Jacobs, J., 182
Jacobstein, J., 286
Jenkins, J., 284n
Jensen, A. R., 279–80, 285

Kahneman, D., 336
Kamin, L. J., 285
Kazdin, A. E., 265
Kelly, G. A., 12
Keyes, A., 284
Kimball, M., 319
King, F. A., 282
Kitzinger, C., 197, 198
Klaiber, E. L., 311
Kluckhohn, C., 270
Kmenta, J., 337
Knowledge, managing uncertainty in
  construction of, 336–44
Kobayashi, Y., 311
Kuhn, Thomas, 305, 329–30, 334

Labeling:
  observational language and, 44–45
  speculative language and, 46–47, 51–52

Lancaster, J. B., 311
Landers, S., 282
Languages of science, 39–68
    formal, 52–67 (*see* Formal language)
        decoding scientific news with, 64–67
        life expectancy of a scientific concept,
            63–64
        linking with observational language,
            56–63
        symbol relationships in, 52–56
    observational, 43–46
        key rule in using, 43–44
        linking with formal language, 56–63
    in research reports, 292–93
    sexist, 292, 312–13
    speculative, 46–52
    validity and, 140–42
Law, ethics and, 285–87
Lazarus, R. S., 314
Leighton, D., 270
Leonard, M. M., 311
Lester, J. D., 291*n*
Likert-type scale, 191
Lindsay, R. C. L., 283
Linnaeus, Carolus, 179, 304
Linville, P., 197
Literature, proliferation of, 297–98
Longitudinal studies, 152–64
    Hawthorne effect, 159–60
    interrupted time series:
        concept of, 153–54
        evaluation research example, 154–59
        student project on testimonials in rela-
            tion to, 161–64
    problems with, 152

Maccoby, E. E., 255, 313, 316, 318
Mackie, M., 310–11
Majority vote, 51–52
Maps of chance, 245–46
Marecek, J., 319
Marotz-Baden, R., 314
*Mastering APA style: Instructor's resource
    guide* (Gelfand and Walker), 292
*Mastering APA Style: Student's workbook
    and training guide* (Gelfand and
    Walker), 292
Matlin, M. W., 255, 271, 307, 318
Maturational (time-tied) suspects:
    before-and-after method and, 94–95, 110
    control-group method and, 113
    research context and, 138
McCormack, T., 318, 319
Mead, Margaret, 176–77, 291
Mean:
    defined, 229, 230
    prediction and, 239
    regression toward, 119–20, 131, 160–61
Measurement, 208–26
    defined, 208

external validity and, 133, 135–37
pilot studies, 224–26
scales, 210–20
    arbitrary-zero, 217–19
    interval rule, 213–15, 219
    nominal rule, 211–12, 219–23
    ordinal rule, 212–13, 219, 221–22
    ratio rule, 215–17, 222
    science and, 220–26
Median, 229–30
Medical Research Council of Canada, 270
Mendeleev, D. I., 178–79
Men in Groups (Tiger), 308
Merchant, C., 304
Messenger model, 5–7
Meta-analysis, 254–56
Method section, research report, 294–95
Mickelsen, O., 284
Milgram, S., 123, 172, 278, 279, 284
Miller, D. C., 194, 297
Miller, N. E., 282, 283
Mills, D. H., 283
Minsky, M., 324, 327
Mobilization for Animals Coalition, 282
Mode, 230
Money, J., 310
Montagu, A., 310
Moos, R. H., 314
Morris, D., 308
Mortality, 131, 132, 200
Motivation, in scientific method, 21, 23–24
Moulton, J., 313
Multiple observers, 178
Munsinger, H., 286

Naked Ape, The (Morris), 308
Narrative approach, 255
Nash, M. M., 285
National Institutes of Health, 281
Natural experiment, 122–23
Naturalistic observation, 173, 178–81, 224
"Nay-saying," 193
Neale, J. M., 314
Neely, C. A., 308
New England Journal of Medicine, 286
News service, science as, 10–17
Nibett, R., 336
Nicholls, Ralph, 289
Nielsen, J. M., 320
N-of-1 research, 264–67
Nominal scales, 211–12, 219–23
Nonparametric tests, 261
Nonparticipant observers, 176–77
Nonrational wisdom, 334–35
Normal curve, 233–34
Novelty, effects of, 159
Null hypothesis, 262
Numbers (*see* Measurement; Statistics)

Objective information, 40–43

Objective observations, 15
Objectivity:
  content analysis and, 182
  ethnographic research and, 173–74
  ideology of, 305
Observational language, 43–46
  key rule in using, 43–44
  linking with formal language, 56–63
Observational science, 21, 22
Observational task, field study, 172–75
Observations, 12–17
  beliefs and, 13–17
  in ethnographic research (*see* Ethno-
      graphic research)
  expectations and, 13–17
  explanation and, 17–20
  levels of, 32–34
  objective, 15
  personal experience and, 12–13
  speculation combined with, 41–43, 48–50
  surface, 15–16
  systematic, 21, 24–26
  uncertainty and, 14–16
  unobtrusive, 124
Observer role, 176–78
One-way analysis of variance, 252–53
On-stage suspects (*see* Testing suspects)
Order relations, 54
Ordinal scales, 212–13, 219, 221–22
Orne, M. T., 317
Oskamp, S., 201

Panel technique, 199–200
Parametric tests, 260–61
Parry, H. J., 201
Participant observers, 177–78
Patrick, R. C., 177
Pearson, Karl, 321
Pearson product-moment correlation, 236–38
Peers, majority vote by, 51–52
Percival, B., 308
Perfect correlation, 234, 235
Periodicals, 297
Personal experience:
  distortion caused by, 172–73
  observation based on, 12–13
Personal interviews, 195–96, 203–6
Phenomenology, 40
Physical evidence, 183–84, 202
Physicians, after-the-fact method used by,
      76–77
Piaget, J., 135, 180
Piliavin, I. M., 279
Piliavin, J. A., 279
Pilot studies, 224–26
Polanyi, John, 286
Popper, Karl, 329–30, 334
Pragmatics, 46–52
Precision, in report writing, 292
Prediction:

correlation and, 239–40
inferential statistics and (*see* Inferential
      statistics)
mean and, 239
variance and, 239
Predictive validity, 137
Probabalistic thinking, 21, 29
Problem solving, scientific, 21, 22
Procedure unit, research report, 295
Professionals, 32
Programmatic research, 139–40
Psychological Abstracts, 297
Psychological Bulletin, 297
Psychological Review, 297
Publication bias, 316
Publication Manual (APA), 296
Publication proliferation, 297–98
Pyke, S. W., 118, 181, 305, 307, 308, 311,
      316, 319, 322
Pylyshyn, W. W., 118, 330

Q methodology, 196–98
Qualitative methods, 166–88, 338, 345–48
  archival research, 180–88
    concept of, 180
    content analysis, 181–83
    example of, 186–88
    spoor analysis, 183–84
    strengths and weaknesses of, 184–86
  characteristics of, 168–69
  ethnographic research, 169–80
    classification/interpretation of
        observations, 178–79
    conclusions about, 179–80
    observational task, 172–75
    observer role, 176–78
    setting, 171–72
  function of, 166
  vs. quantitative methods, 167–68
  survey research, 190–206
    administration, 200–201
    concept of, 190–91
    data collection instruments (*see* Data
        collection instruments
    sample selection, 198–200
    strengths and weaknesses of, 201–2
Quantitative methods, 167–69
Queen, S. A., 177
Questionnaires, 135, 136, 191–94, 202
Quine, W. V. O., 340
Quota sampling, 199

Random samples, 248
Rational empiricism, 326, 333, 335, 336,
      338, 344–48
Ratio scales, 215–17, 222
References, research report, 296
Regression, statistical, 119–20, 131, 160–61
Reinforcement, 140
Reinharz, S., 320

Reliability, 2
Replicability, 269
Replication:
    of experiments, independent, 131
    of observations, 264
Replications, publication of, 264
Report writing (*see* Research report writing)
Research checklist, 143–44
Research context restrictions, 134, 138–40
Researcher bias, 317–18
Researchers, 32–34
Research report writing, 291–301
    example of, 298–301
    language and style, 292–93
    publication proliferation, 297–98
    structure, 293–97
Responding, biased, 193–94
Response extremity bias, 193
Response sets, 194
Restrospective studies, 151–52
Results, research report, 296
Ricks, F. A., 308
Rimland, B., 286
Robinson, F. M., 313
Roethlisberger, F. J., 159
Rogers, R. S., 197, 198
Romanes, George J., 321
Rosenthal, R., 316
Ross, L., 336
Ruckdeschel, R. A., 168
Rushton, Philippe, 280
Russell, Bertrand, 324, 326, 336

Sample restrictions, 133–35
Sample selection, 198–200
Sampling, 2, 8
    arbitrary-zero scales, 219
    area, 199
    external validity and, 133–35
    panel technique, 199–200
    quota, 199
Sampling error theory, 247–51
Sampling theory, 246–47
Sayre, A., 306
Scales, measurement, 210–20
    arbitrary-zero, 217–19
    interval rule, 213–15, 219
    nominal rule, 211–12, 219–23
    ordinal rule, 212–13, 219, 221–22
    ratio rule, 215–17, 222
Scattergrams, 235, 236
Scheinfield, A., 312
Schneider, H. G., 282, 283
Schoggen, P., 178, 179
Schultz, D. P., 199*n*
Schwartz, R. D., 180
Science:
    discovery vs. construction of truth issue
        (*see* Truth, discovery vs. construction of)
    experimental, 21–22, 27
    measurement and, 220–26
    observational, 21, 22
    overview of, 1–37
        commonsense vs. scientific reasoning
            in general, 2–8
        levels of observation and speculation,
            32–34
        maps of human experience and behavior, 8–10
        news service analogy, 10–17
        scientific method (*see* Scientific
            method)
    sex and (*see* Sex, science and)
Scientific method, 20–32, 344, 345
    motivation, 21, 23–24
    probabalistic thinking, 21
    systematic experimentation, 21, 26–29
    systematic observation, 21, 24–26
    theory, 21, 29–32
Scientific problem solving, 21, 22
Scientist-as-safecracker analogy, 30–32
Sechrest, L., 180
Seitz, J., 270
Selection:
    biased:
        in control group method, 120–21
        in ethnographic research, 174–75
        sex bias, 308, 313–14
    of comparison group, 113–15, 120–21
    of sample, 198–200
Selfish Gene, The (Dawkins), 310
Semantics (*see* Observational language)
Setting, field study, 171–72
Sex, science and, 303–22
    erotic symbolism and, 304
    ideology of objectivity and, 305
    sex bias, 306–18
        in content, 308
        design sources of, 316–17
        in evaluation, 311–12
        historical examples of, 307–8, 320–22
        inference bias, 312
        language bias, 312–13
        publication bias, 316
        researcher bias, 317–18
        restructuring of science and, 318–20
        selection and distortion of
            evidence, 313–14
        statistical bias, 314–16
        in subject selection, 308
        theory bias, 308–11
    women's role in science, 306
Sexist language, 292, 312–13
Shields, S. A., 305, 307
Silveira, J., 313
Silverman, I., 285
Simon, Herbert, 326–27
Simon, J. L., 181
Simulation research, 123–24

Single-case reasearch, 264–67
Skinner, B. F., 140, 291
Skolow, Jayme Aaron, 286
Smith, M. S., 255–56
Social Contract, The (Ardrey), 308
Social desirability bias, 193
Sociobiology, 308–10
Speculation, 18–20
  levels of, 32–34
  observation combined with, 41–43, 48–50
Speculative language, 46–52
Spoor analysis, 183–84
Standard deviation, 231–34 (*See also*
    Z scores)
Standard error of estimate, 240
Stanley, J. C., 92, 131
Stark-Adamac, C., 288, 319–20
Statistical bias, 314–16
Statistically improbable events, 262
Statistical regression, 119–20, 131, 160–61
Statistics, 228–67
  descriptive, 228–42
    central values, 229–31
    correlation (*see* Corrleation)
    defined, 228
    variability measures, 231–34
  inferential, 243–67
    analysis of variance (ANOVA), 251–54
    chi square test, 256–60
    defined, 228
    factors producing significant
        differences, 244–45
    maps of chance, 245–46
    meta-analysis, 254–56
    N-of-1 research, 264–67
    nonparametric tests, 261
    parametric tests, 260–61
    sampling error theory, 247–51
    sampling theory, 246–47
    statistically improbable events, 262
    t tests, 250–51
    Type I and Type II errors, 262–64
  measurement (*see* Measurement)
Stephenson, W., 197
Stereotypes, 314
Stewart, J. C., 308
Stewart, M., 308
Stewart, Walter, 286
Stoloff, M., 282
Stone, A. A., 314
Strauss, S., 288
Style, research report, 292–93
Subjective information, 40–43
Subjective realities, 168–69
Subject selection, sex bias in, 308
Subjects unit, research report, 294–95
Sullivan, M. A., 177
Surface observations, 15–16
Survey research, 190–206
  administration, 200–201

concept of, 190–91
data collection instruments, 191–98
  focus groups, 196
  personal interviews, 195–96, 203–6
  Q methodology, 196–98
  questionnaires, 135, 136, 191–94, 202
  telephone interviews, 194
  sample selection, 198–200
Symbolism, erotic, 304
Syntactics (*see* Formal language)
Systematic experimentation, 21, 26–29
Systematic observation, 21, 24–26

Tarule, J. M., 195, 319
Taylor, H. L., 284
Taylor, J. A., 295
Taylor Manifest Anxiety Scale, 295
Technicians, 32
Telephone interviews, 194
Terminal Man, The (Crichton), 284
Terseness, in report writing, 292, 293
Testing (on-stage) suspects:
  before-and-after method and, 94–96
  control-group method and, 112
  ethnographic research and, 176, 177
Test validity, 136–37
Theoretical orientation, 86–87
Theorists, 32–34, 47, 81
Theory, 16–20, 21, 29–32, 52, 333–34
Theory bias, 308–11
Theory frames, 77–79
Thomas, G. V., 282
Tiger, L., 308, 313
Time frames, 77–79
Time series studies, 146–64
  cross-sectional, 149–51
  longitudinal, 152–64
    Hawthorne effect, 159–60
    interrupted time series (*see* Interrupted
        time series)
    problems with, 152
    regression toward the mean, 160–61
  rate of change, 147
  retrospective, 151–52
  upper limits of change, 148–49
Time-tied suspects (*see* Maturational
    suspects)
Treatment restrictions, 133, 137–38
Triangulation strategy, 169
Trice, H. M., 177
Truth, discovery vs. construction of,
    323–49
  bounded rationality premise, 326–27,
    348–49
  building defended islands of truth,
    327–33
  capacity for reasoning, 324–26
  constructivism, 333–36
  hypotheses:
    confidence in, 341–44

generation and evaluation of, 344–48
management of uncertainty, 336–44
nonrational wisdom, 334–35
qualitative methods and, 344–48
rational empiricism, 326, 333, 335, 336,
    338, 344–48
theory of science and, 333–34
t tests, 250–51
Tversky, A., 336
Two-way analysis of variance, 253–54
Type I and Type II errors, 262–64

Uncertainty:
    in cross-sectional studies, 150
    management of, 336–44
    regions of, in observation, 14–16
Unger, R. K., 322
Unobtrusive measures, 124
    in evaluation research, 157, 158
    in spoor analysis, 183–84

Validity, 130–43
    external:
        concept of, 132
        measurement restrictions and, 133,
            135–37
        research context restrictions and, 134,
            138–40
        sample restrictions and, 133–35
        survey research and, 202
        treatment restrictions and, 133,
            137–38
    internal:
        concept of, 131
        survey research and, 202
        threats to, 132
    languages of science and, 140–42

Variability, measures of, 231–34
Variables (*see* Dependent variables;
    Independent variables)
Variance, 239
    analysis of (ANOVA), 251–54
    defined, 231
Vidal, Gore, 329
Vogel, W., 311

Wallston, B. S., 319
Watson, J. B., 291, 306
Webb, F. J., 180, 183, 184
Weiner, M., 173
Weizmann, F., 280
Wesley, G. R., 282, 283
Weyant, R. G., 311, 316–17
White, A. D., 271
White, M. S., 306
Whyte, W. F., Jr., 177
Wiener, N. I., 280
Wiesenthal, D. L., 279, 280
Wilson, D. W., 279
Wilson, E. O., 308–10
Wolfe, M., 288
Women's role in science, 306 (*See also* Sex,
    science and)
Woolsey, L., 308
Worell, Judith, 319–20

"Yea-saying," 193

Zalk, S. R., 320
Ziegler, M., 280
Zimbardo, P. G., 123, 171–72
Zimmerman, S., 288, 289
Z scores, 234, 236, 240 (*See also* Standard
    deviation)